the
Celluloid
Closet

VITO RUSSO

REVISED EDITION

the CELLULOID CLOSET

homosexuality in the movies

HARPER & ROW, PUBLISHERS
New York, Cambridge, Philadelphia, San Francisco, Washington
London, Mexico City, São Paulo, Singapore, Sydney

Cartoon on page 269 reprinted from the book *Fun City: Gertrude's Follies Come to Town.* Copyright © 1985 by Tom Hachtman. Reprinted by permission of Arbor House Publishing Company.

THE CELLULOID CLOSET, Revised Edition. Copyright © 1987, 1981 by Vito Russo. All rights reserved. Printed in the United States of America. No part of this book may be used or reproduced in any manner whatsoever without written permission except in the case of brief quotations embodied in critical articles and reviews. For information address Harper & Row, Publishers, Inc., 10 East 53rd Street, New York, N.Y. 10022. Published simultaneously in Canada by Fitzhenry & Whiteside Limited, Toronto.

Designer: Ruth Bornschlegel

Library of Congress Cataloging-in-Publication Data
Russo, Vito.
   The celluloid closet.
   Filmography: p.
   Includes index.
   1. Homosexuality in motion pictures.   I. Title.
PN1995.9.H55R8 1987   791.43′09′09353   86-45684
ISBN 0-06-096132-5 (pbk.)

87 88 89 90 91 MPC 10 9 8 7 6 5 4 3 2 1

For Jeffrey Sevcik
Who Will Always Live in My Heart

Contents

Acknowledgments

Many people helped me to identify and locate films, still photographs and reference materials for this edition. Others granted me interviews in spite of busy schedules. My friends supported me in emotional ways during what has been a very difficult time for all of us. I would like to express my love and gratitude to Arnie Kantrowitz, Larry Mass, Jim Owles, Arthur J. Bressan, Jr., John Bovee, Lily Tomlin, Joel Levitt, Judy Peabody, Charles Silver, Stephen Harvey, Larry Kardish, Jan Oxenberg, Jed Mattes, Clovis Ruffin, Betty Bourne, Eric Meyer, Maxine Feldman, Barbara Kerr, Dorothy Allison, Robb Epstein, John Wright, Armistead Maupin, Mark Pinney, Dean Pitchford, Marcia Pally, Nancy Shaw, Alan Sawyer and Craig Zadan. For their help in making this book possible I would like to thank Bruce Yves, Liz Smith, Mark Thompson, Jerry Wheeler, Steve Badeau, Gary Steele, Stuart Byron, Ron Magliozzi, Stephen Frears, Bill Sherwood, Barry Sandler, Catherine Olim, Lois Smith, Marci Bloom, Nora Ephron, Brandon Judell, Penelope Spheeris, Tom Steele, Howard Mandelbaum, Carlos Clarens, Christopher Reeve, Helen Shaver, Bingham Ray at Samuel Goldwyn Studios, Linda Duchin at Cinecom, Paul Mowry at Orion Classics, Larry Mark at Twentieth-Century Fox, Donna Deitch, Robert Plunket, Kevin Cortland, Granger Hines, Eliott Stein, Michael Bronski, Jimmy Coco, James Kirkwood, George Hadley Garcia, Marie Kuda, Peter Lowy, Michael Lumpkin, Barbara Noda and Joe Brewer.

Introduction
on the closet mentality

It became one of the chief problems in discussing this book. Everywhere I went for more than three years, the same misconception arose with a disturbing regularity. At dinner parties, at family gatherings, at lunches in Manhattan and on picket lines in Berkeley, on the beach at Fire Island and on lecture tours in the Midwest, everyone had the same question when the subject of this book was raised in conversation. People would always ask what *The Celluloid Closet* was about, and I would always say that it was an exploration of gay characters in American film. The response seldom varied. "Oh, really?" they would ask with a leer. "Are you using people's real names?"

This is not a book about who in Hollywood is lesbian or homosexual. Nor is it a book about how gays have expressed themselves in Hollywood. Yet both approaches to the subject are valid and important. The public should in fact be aware of the sexuality of gay actors just as it is aware of the heterosexuality of the majority. I do not believe that such a discussion is nobody's business, nor do I believe that it is one of a sexual and therefore private nature. Discussing such things in a book without the knowledge or consent of the people in question is, alas, immoral and libelous. It is immoral because unless people by their own choice come out of the closet, the announcement is valueless; it is libelous because such information has been known to destroy people's lives. Some of us will change that in time.

As to the second approach, that of studying the various ways in which gays, as a group almost exclusively closeted, have expressed themselves on film, this will also be pursued, but much sooner. Openly gay writers and critics have already begun to examine the works of Jean Vigo, Dorothy Arzner, F. W. Murnau, James Whale, Edmund Goulding, Mitchell Leisen, Sergei Eisenstein and Pier Paolo Pasolini, taking into account the dynamic of their sexual personalities. Openly gay directors such as Rosa von Praunheim, Wolfgang Petersen, Richard Benner and Rainer Werner Fassbinder can and will speak for themselves.

What especially depressed me, though, listening to the initial reactions to *The Celluloid Closet*, was that they reflected the oppressive assumptions that form the basis for most screen images of lesbians and gay men. They reflected the closeted mentalities of gay people themselves. Almost all the people I spoke with reacted as though they had never considered a discussion of homosexuality as anything but potential gossip; the idea of examining some images

of gay people onscreen was a barely legitimate concept to most. To see homosexuality as a dirty secret is something we all learned as children, both gays
and straights. In Hollywood closeted gay people are among the most uptight
and uncooperative stumbling blocks in the path of positive gay projects. The
screen work of gays as well as straights has reflected the closet mentality almost
exclusively until very recently. I sought to interview almost two hundred people
for this book. Screenwriters and directors were almost always willing to talk.
Actors were terrified and remained silent. Only two or three, all heterosexual,
were willing to discuss their work.

Any type of openly gay enterprise is still highly suspect in the culture in
general. Before 1970, most gays in America mistrusted or avoided gay-owned
businesses and services. Books on gay subjects and even books on non-gay
subjects by openly gay writers have rarely been taken seriously in the straight
press—when they are noticed at all. Such oversights are occasionally of an
obviously homophobic nature. The Reverend Malcolm Boyd has written twenty
books. His last, *Take Off the Masks,* was the only one in which he openly
discussed his homosexuality; it is also the only one of the twenty not reviewed
by the *New York Times.* There is enormous pressure to keep gay people
defined solely by our sexuality, which prevents us from presenting our existence
in political terms. Gay research is often discounted or ignored. Jonathan Katz's
extraordinary volume *Gay American History* has been sadly overlooked by
scholars and critics because it places the struggle for gay liberation in a firm
historical context and, importantly, ties our existence to the American dream.

In her book on women in film, *From Reverence to Rape,* Molly Haskell
says that "the big lie" is that women are inferior. The big lie about lesbians
and gay men is that we do not exist. The story of the ways in which gayness
has been defined in American film is the story of the ways in which we have
been defined in America. In Eldridge Cleaver's *Soul on Ice,* Beverly Axelrod
says, "Our tragedy does not derive from our fantasy of what homosexuals
are but from our fantasy of what America is. We have made each other up."
As expressed on screen, America was a dream that had no room for the
existence of homosexuals. Laws were made against depicting such things onscreen. And when the fact of our existence became unavoidable, we were reflected, onscreen and off, as dirty secrets.

We have cooperated for a very long time in the maintenance of our own
invisibility. And now the party is over.

the
Celluloid
Closet

Who's a Sissy?

homosexuality
according
to Tinseltown

"Oh, it's sad, believe me, missy,
when you're born to be a sissy
without the vim and voive. . . ."

Bert Lahr as the Cowardly Lion in The Wizard of Oz
(1939). (John Kobal Stills Collection)

> **There's two things got me puzzled**
> **There's two things I just can't understand**
> **That's a mannish actin' woman**
> **And a skipping, twisting woman actin' man.**
>
> **—Bessie Smith,**
> **"Foolish Man Blues," 1927**

> **Most of our pictures have little,**
> **if any, real substance. Our fear of**
> **what the censors will do keeps us**
> **from portraying life the way it**
> **really is. We wind up with a lot of**
> **empty fairy tales that do not have**
> **much relation to anyone.**
>
> **—Samuel Goldwyn, 1938**

> **The movies didn't always get history**
> **straight. But they told the dream.**
>
> **—Charlton Heston,**
> **narrating *America on Film*, 1976**

Nobody likes a sissy. That includes dykes, faggots and feminists of both sexes. Even in a time of sexual revolution, when traditional roles are being examined and challenged every day, there is something about a man who acts like a woman that people find fundamentally distasteful. A 1979 *New York Times* feature on how some noted feminists were raising their male children revealed that most wanted their sons to grow up to be feminists—but real men, not sissies.

This chapter is concerned primarily with the genesis of the sissy and not the tomboy because homosexual behavior onscreen, as almost every other defined "type" of behavior, has been cast in male terms. Homosexuality in the movies, whether overtly sexual or not, has always been seen in terms of what is or is not masculine. The defensive phrase "*Who's* a sissy?" has been as much a part of the American lexicon as "So's your old lady." After all, it is supposed to be an insult to call a man effeminate, for it means he is like a woman and therefore not as valuable as a "real" man. The popular definition of gayness is rooted in sexism. Weakness in men rather than strength in women has consistently been seen as the connection between sex role behavior and deviant sexuality. And while sissy men have always signaled a rank betrayal of the myth of male superiority, tomboy women have seemed to reinforce that myth and have often been indulged in acting it out.

In celebrating maleness, the rendering invisible of all else has caused lesbianism to disappear behind a male vision of sex in general. The stigma of tomboy has been less than that of sissy because lesbianism is never allowed to become a threatening reality any more than female sexuality of other kinds. Queen Victoria, informed that a certain woman was a lesbian, asked what a lesbian might be. When the term had been explained, she flatly refused to believe that such creatures existed. Early laws against homosexuality referred only to acts between men. In England the penalty for male homosexual acts was reduced from death to imprisonment in 1861, but the new law made no mention of lesbianism. Nor did the target of the pioneering German gay liberation movement, Paragraph 175, which outlawed homosexual acts between men but omitted any mention of lesbians.

The German movement, begun in 1897, was eliminated by the Nazis in the early 1930s. The trial and jailing of Oscar Wilde in England had already silenced leading literary figures who had vocally supported homosexual rights, and such movements as existed had little effect in the United States. The first American gay liberation group, the Society for Human Rights, chartered in 1924 by the State of Illinois, was disbanded after less than a year when its members were arrested by Chicago police. An organized gay visibility did not re-emerge in America until after World War II. In many ways, Queen Victoria spoke for everyone. In the popular mind, no such creatures existed except in a national fear of effeminacy, a word listed in *Roget's Thesaurus* as a synonym for weakness.

A nation of immigrants recently mesmerized by the flicker of the nickelodeon seized the larger-than-life images of the silent screen to play out its own dream of itself, and there was little room for weakness in the telling. Suspicions of inadequacy, however, were rife. The predominantly masculine character of the earliest cinema reflected an America that saw itself as a recently conquered wilderness. Actually there was not much wilderness left in the early twentieth century, but the movies endlessly recreated the struggles, the heroism and the romance of our pioneer spirit. There were western movies but no easterns; our European origins were considered tame and unworthy of the growing American legend. Men of action and strength were the embodiment of our culture, and a vast mythology was created to keep the dream in constant repair. Real men were strong, silent and ostentatiously unemotional. They acted quickly and never intellectualized. In short, they did not behave like women.

Unspeakable in the culture, the true nature of homosexuality haunted only the dim recesses of our celluloid consciousness. The idea that there was such a thing as a real man made the creation of the sissy inevitable. Men who were perceived to be "like women" were simply mama's boys, reflections of an overabundance of female influence. It became the theme of scores of silent films to save the weakling youth and restore his manhood. Although at first there was no equation between sissyhood and actual homosexuality, the danger of gayness as the consequence of such behavior lurked always in the background. Tomboys (and the very idea of lesbianism) emerged as an exotic and often fascinating extension of the male myth, serving as a proving ground for its maintenance. A look at heterosexual pornography shows that lesbian eroticism in the service of male sexuality has been a consistent theme in heterosexual fantasy, appearing often as the preliminary to the "real" event, sex between men and women. True lesbianism, relationships defined by and in terms of women's needs and desires, was not contemplated. In the popular arts especially, such women were simply perceived to be "like men," and they conjured up a far more appealing androgyny than did male sissies. The tomboy image was amusingly daring and aspired to strength and authority, while the sissy image discredited those values.

The idea of homosexuality first emerged onscreen, then, as an unseen danger, a reflection of our fears about the perils of tampering with male and female roles. Characters who were less than men or more than women had their first expression in the zany farce of mistaken identity and transvestite humor inherited from our oldest theatrical traditions. Rougher and broader than their classic predecessors, male and female impersonations, informed by a breezy vaudeville legacy, were a fascination of the movies from the beginning. As early as 1903 the innovative American director Edwin S. Porter used as one of his subjects a transvestite posing before a mirror. An experimental film directed by William Dickson at the Thomas Edison Studio in 1895 shows two men dancing a waltz. It was titled *The Gay Brothers.*

Men in silent comedies often took women's roles, but total character impersonation disappeared early. The use of female garb by male comics became just another device for a one-scene joke. In *Miss Fatty's Seaside Lovers,* directed by Fatty Arbuckle in 1915, he plays the daughter of a rich man on a beach outing with the family. In *Bumping into Broadway* (1919), Gus Leonard played Ma Simpson, the vigilant landlady of a theatrical boardinghouse. When, in 1915, Harold Lloyd played a female pitcher on an all-woman baseball team in *Spit-Ball Sadie, Motion Picture News* called the scenes "repellent." The

The Gay Brothers, *an experimental sound film directed by William Dickson for Thomas Edison in 1895.* (Museum of Modern Art)

critics said the same thing about Jack Lemmon's performance in *Some Like It Hot* in 1959 because Lemmon seemed to be enjoying his role too much. It was virtually the only female impersonation sustained throughout an entire film since the teens.

Albin, the professional female impersonator in *La Cage aux Folles* (1978), was French and therefore suspect (unlike Lemmon, who was an all-American actor). The remarkable success in the United States of a film like *La Cage aux Folles* is a testament to the durability of the old-fashioned expansive femininity used to type male homosexuality. John Bunny's hilarious pomposity as a Marie Dressler-type gorgon in *The Leading Lady* (1911) has a lot in common with Michel Serrault's delightful Albin. Bunny's forays into drag and Wallace Beery's coy Swedish maid in the successful "Sweedie" series (1914–1916) were among the funniest if not the most subtle of the early impersonations. Fatty Arbuckle, who left the Keystone Studio for Paramount in 1917, made his sausage-curled bathing beauty a familiar comic characterization in film after film. *Miss Fatty's Seaside Lovers* and *Fatty in Coney Island* (1917) had him at his eye-rolling, umbrella-twirling best, forever in a heap of trouble with the local gents.

"Enchanté, monsieur!" Michel Serrault as Albin. The "mother" of the groom meets the father of the bride in La Cage aux Folles *(1978).* (United Artists)

John Bunny in drag in The Leading Lady *(1911).* (Museum of Modern Art)

Wallace Beery in the "Sweedie" series of 1914–1916. (Larry Edmund's Bookstore)

Fatty Arbuckle is wooed by Al St. John in Miss Fatty in Coney Island *(1917).*

The very idea of calling Fatty "Miss Fatty" was funny. In *La Cage aux Folles* Albin tries to imitate John Wayne with what comes out as a hilarious Mae West swagger. It is the best he can do. His lover Renato (Ugo Tognazzi) throws up his hands and cries, "That's *Miss* John Wayne!" and the scene is funny because of the sound of John Wayne's name with "miss" in front of it. Yet such characters were always irritating to masculine men in silent comedy. In *Miss Fatty's Seaside Lovers,* the penetration of Fatty's disguise leads to the conclusion that "it's the women who cause all the trouble in the world after all," which reaffirms the superiority of the male point of view while using feminine manners to draw the weaker side of human nature as comedy.

Many of the male and female impersonations of the American silent screen are stunning and of the finest comic creativity. The strident but vivacious foolishness of Fatty Arbuckle, John Bunny and Wallace Beery was the genesis of the Milton Berle school of drag humor, in which the joke lies in the very appearance of a man dressed up as a woman. But the subtlety and grace of others—like Charlie Chaplin in his Essanay film *A Woman* (1915) or the drag of Stan Laurel, whose levels of relating to Oliver Hardy were in some ways typically "feminine" in every nuance—hinted at the deeper levels of a visual language that could at times capture the possibility of pure androgyny.

Charlie Chaplin, sans mustache, in the title role of his Essanay film A Woman *(1915).*

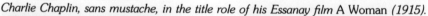

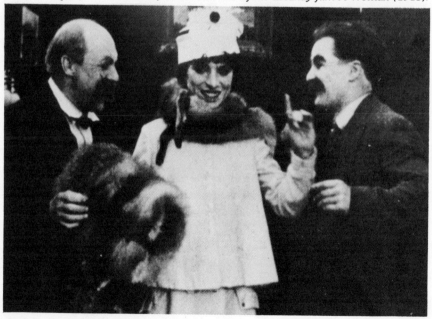

The startlingly uncanny drag of Stan Laurel in a scene from The Further Perils of Laurel and Hardy, *a 1968 compilation film from Twentieth Century-Fox.*

From the Broadway stage of 1896, where as a play it created a modest sensation, emerged the first and one of the very few films to deal with the sexual characteristics of men and women entirely through the use of farcical impersonation. Sidney Drew's adaptation of *A Florida Enchantment* (1914) was a sex reversal comedy with first class male impersonations and wry comment on the privileges of the male sex. Interviewed in the New York *Dramatic Mirror* after the opening of his play, author Archibald Gunter announced that his primary reason for "perpetrating" the farce was to show that "in a measure, men have a better time than women amid the social environment of our present civilization."

In the film version, Lillian Travers, a young northern heiress who is visiting her aunt in Florida, comes upon a hundred-year-old chest containing seeds that, if swallowed, will turn a man into a woman and vice versa. In a fit of pique over a suitor, she takes one and awakens the following morning sporting a thick black mustache, which she promptly shaves off. Pretending to be female still, but possessed of male instincts, she persistently woos other women, causing a general stir in her aunt's staid southern home. The male impersonation of Vitagraph star Edith Storey is impeccable. Visually uncanny, especially in her scenes of dapper male attire on a visit to New York, her performance throughout

(A)

A Florida Enchantment *(1914). (A) Edith Storey (center left) woos a woman at a ball. (B) Storey and her servant don male clothing for their trip to New York. (C) Sidney Drew shocks the locals in his female drag.* (Library of Congress)

(B)

(C)

is laced with an insouciance that tempers male arrogance with a secret, barely withheld sensitivity.

Desiring a valet instead of a maid, she gives one of the magic seeds to her mulatto servant and together they go out on the town, to be seen as notorious womanizers. The shock with which their actions are met, however, is tempered with fascination for their boldness. Lillian's aunt and her guests are titillated by her behavior as they would be by that of a male roué among them. Yet not until Lillian's doctor friend (played by director Sidney Drew) hears her story and takes one of the seeds himself does anyone become genuinely upset. Drew first begins to eye the men in town strangely, then decides to pursue a few of them in earnest. Unlike the restrained impersonation of Edith Storey, Drew's eye rolling is pure travesty. He also plays an aggressive woman who actively pursues men. In both cases, then, it's a male view of the sexes that dominates the impersonation. Drew's activities in town arouse the hostilities of a group of men who hastily form a posse and call out the police to deal with the "unnatural" man in their midst. Finally they form a mob and chase him through the town and off a pier into the river.

The conclusions would be interesting, but they are not drawn in *A Florida Enchantment.* Lillian awakens suddenly to discover that it was all only a horrible dream, and the sexes resume their natural order as she departs Florida with her newfound love, the suitor responsible for the mixup in the first place. Perceptible in the dream sequence, however, is a higher tolerance for women who relate emotionally, or even sexually, to other women than for men who behave similarly toward other men. Women did not merit the serious attention afforded male "unnaturalness" because they did not betray the male myth by aspiring to male behavior; they simply mimicked it and lent it credibility. In a review of the film in the New York *Dramatic Mirror,* it was pointed out that "while Edith Storey made quite an attractive man, Sidney Drew is far from a handsome woman."

The playwright's original contention that men have a better time of things in society in general is borne out finally in ways far more subtle than he probably intended. The reinforcement of the male myth is countered sharply by the female inferiority evidenced in the correspondingly degrading female impersonation chosen for the film version by Sidney Drew. The apparently higher tolerance for "mannish" women was deceptive, though. Rendering the idea of actual lesbianism all but invisible, the identification of such women in exclusively male terms served only to reinforce the idea that sexuality is the proper domain of men. Sissy men, after all, were never the objects of fascination bred in audiences by their female counterparts.

Marlene Dietrich kisses a woman on the lips in Morocco *(1930).*

The fresh-faced Huck Finn appeal of Katharine Hepburn's *Sylvia Scarlett* (1936) and the magnetic sexual power of Marlene Dietrich in *Morocco* (1930) and *Blonde Venus* (1932) put such women in a class by themselves, unsullied by innuendo. There could be all kinds of women who were considered "real" women, to be manipulated sexually for maximum fantasy appeal to men, but there could be only one kind of real man, with no deviation allowed. In *Morocco,* Dietrich's intentions are clearly heterosexual; the brief hint of lesbianism she exhibits serves only to make her more exotic, to whet Gary Cooper's appetite for her and to further challenge his maleness. In *Sylvia Scarlett,* Hepburn's young boy is obviously attractive to Cary Grant and we are meant to find her equally irresistible. "It's nippy out tonight," Grant says to the boyish Hepburn, "you'll make a proper hot water bottle tonight." Her appearance introduced the possibility of homosexual activity into the film for a covert gay audience while providing laughs for the majority.

Katharine Hepburn gets too much attention from Dennie Moore, who thinks she is a boy, in Sylvia Scarlett *(1936).*

In a scene reminiscent of the meeting between Garbo and Gilbert in *Queen Christina,* Grant tells Hepburn, "There's something that gives me a queer feeling every time I look at you." Such situations are simply nonexistent when men appear in drag. Hepburn's appeal to both Cary Grant and their female traveling companion (Dennie Moore) in *Sylvia Scarlett* gave the impression of an androgynous sexuality and at the same time raised, although in a bogus way, the issue of lesbianism and male homosexuality. The entire focus of men in drag, however, was always antisexual, to be indemnified by the outstanding virility of the hero once he emerged from his disguise.

Bothwell Browne as a femme fatale in Yankee Doodle in Berlin *(1919).* (Courtesy John Kobal Stills Collection)

In Richard Jones' *Yankee Doodle in Berlin* (1919), produced by Mack Sennett, an American aviator hero named Bob White dresses as a femme fatale, playing up to the Kaiser in order to obtain information of a secret nature. To play Bob White, Sennett hired noted theatrical female impersonator Bothwell Browne, who like Julian Eltinge was at the top of his profession, and Browne carried off his portrait equally well in and out of drag. The use of female sexuality by a male hero suggested that feminine qualities are just a tool. Devastating an entire regiment of German soldiers and securely establishing his true virility despite his female appearance, Browne saves the heroine (Marie Prevost) from the clutches of the enemy by dressing her in male clothing. As a soldier she escapes to safety, able to do for herself as a man what she could not do as a woman (intrigue and escape were clearly "a man's job"). Although both stars of *Yankee Doodle in Berlin* spend the major portion of the film in drag, the hero of the story is clearly American masculine courage. Early sissies were yardsticks for measuring the virility of the men around them. In almost all American films, from comedies to romantic dramas, working class American men are portrayed as much more valuable and certainly more virile than the rich, effete dandies of Europe, who in spite of their success with women are seen as essentially weak and helpless in a real man's world. In *Wild and Woolly* (1917), for example, Douglas Fairbanks, as the New York City son of a railroad mogul, attacks the "pansy" life of the big city and longs for the outdoor pleasures of the old American West, which he mythologizes without ever having seen. In *The Mollycoddle* (1920), Fairbanks starts out as a foppish expatriate living in Europe, far from the rugged virtues of his western ancestors. He seems to have forgotten his heritage and forsaken his male image for the sharp life of a man about town; he has grown weak and soft, and in the course of the film he is suddenly confronted with his lack of masculine status. In both films he is shown the way home in a ritualized process, through the use of cowboy hero images of early America. He finally returns, in spirit if not in fact, to his old self, the real man his forefathers had envisioned as the inheritor of the new wilderness. A title card in *The Mollycoddle* describes the word *mollycoddle* as a "body of men entirely surrounded by a super civilization," and in many films, big city life is blamed for the weakening of the male image. Indeed, in a 1951 issue of *Coronet* magazine, an "exhaustive" study listed "high tension city life" as one of the "chief causes of homosexuality" in our society.

A similar reclamation of manhood took place in the rescue of Richard Barthelmess in Henry King's *Tol'able David* (1921). Edmund Goulding's screenplay provided the classic elements of the formula by which the effeminate mama's boy is forced to prove his manhood by fighting a local band of thugs. This theme was a staple of American film, occurring naturally in various contexts. In *That Certain Woman* (1937), directed by Edmund Goulding, when Henry Fonda is presented for the first time with the son he has never seen, his first question is, "Hiya, fella. Can ya fight?" Goulding was also responsible for the screenplay of the extraordinarily successful musical *The Broadway Melody* (1929), which featured the most explicitly homosexual sissy of the pre-Code years—the unidentified "costume designer" for Zanfield's hit Broadway musical.

Webster defines *sissy* as the opposite of male, and the jump from harmless sissy characters to explicit reference to homosexuality was made well before sound arrived. The line between the effeminate and the real man was drawn routinely in every genre of American film, but comedies more often allowed the explicit leap to the homosexual possibilities inherent in such definitions. Indeed, the relationship between sissyhood and real homosexuality was born in the "anything can happen" jests of silent comedy. The outrageous nature of such films left a lot of room for nonsensical possibilities, and occasionally real sexuality of a "different" nature would intrude as one of them, though it was never taken seriously as a realistic option.

In the films of Buster Keaton, Charlie Chaplin and especially Harold Lloyd, combat with the bully and the winning of the girl were as much tributes to the spirit of America as the conquest of the land itself. And in the end, the dreams they evoked were equally transparent. All films reflected and reinforced such an impossibly pure masculine drive and image that the pressure to be a real man was absolute and unyielding. Even Carole Lombard admitted that, in bed, Clark Gable was no Clark Gable, but that didn't stop men from trying. Gable was a purveyor of the dream onscreen and off, at first refusing to cry as Rhett Butler in *Gone With the Wind* because it might tarnish his masculine screen image, and later referring to Montgomery Clift, his co-star in *The Misfits,* as "that fag."

Crucially at issue always was the connection between feminine behavior and inferiority. The conclusive message was that quiet souls could be real men—but not if they displayed qualities that properly belonged to women. And proof was always necessary. The spectre of the real, underlying fear, homosexuality, arose in several Harold Lloyd comedies, always by farcical chance. Lloyd's inveterate weakling, perennially dubbed "foureyes," was made to discover his own intrinsic value through constant trial of his manhood. Lloyd himself was extremely anti-sissy; "hard knocks," he said, "will bring out any man's mettle, if he has any."

In *Grandma's Boy* (1922), Lloyd is the "meek, modest and retiring youth" whose "boldest moment is singing out loud in church." In a scene with his rival, a bully, for the affections of the girl (Mildred Davis), the two men sit on opposite sides of her on a park bench, each thinking that he is holding her hand. When she rises unexpectedly, they discover that they have been holding each other's hands, and Lloyd is roughly beaten and thrown down a well. In *The Kid Brother* (1927), Lloyd invites a young woman home to spend the night after her medicine show has burned down. His brothers, each thinking the young woman is sleeping behind a curtain, take turns reaching through to pat her hand, making increasingly bold advances until they discover that it is the sleeping Lloyd they have been fondling, not the woman. Again Lloyd is trounced as the source of the brothers' embarrassing mistake.

Harold Lloyd faces a bully in Grandma's Boy *(1922)*. (John Kobal Stills Collection)

In one of Lloyd's earliest efforts, *Sailor Made Man* (1921), scores of sailors are dancing together on the deck of a battleship. Lloyd, ever the victimized weakling, dances with the sadistic bully of the story, who cuffs him soundly whenever the captain turns his back. Thus the effeminate man, the symbol of weakness, takes it on the chin for everyone, becoming the scapegoat for the unstated homoerotic activity of the real but insecure men around him. Using in each case male intimacy as the thing all males secretly dread, the issue is raised indirectly yet goes unmentioned. In this way, the sissy remained asexual while serving as a substitute for homosexuality.

The love that dared not speak its name in English was surprisingly fluent in German throughout the silent era. While America was using its new toy to play cowboys and Indians, recreating the fading dreams of its own mythology, European cinema was shaping the older lessons of life into a more realistic look at the battle of the sexes. In America the battle of the sexes was Marie Dressler throwing dishes at Wallace Beery; in Europe homosexuality was often just another aspect of the panorama of human relationships. This has always been true. In 1956, theatrical producers had a lot of trouble producing Robert Anderson's *Tea and Sympathy* in France. A French producer told Anderson, "So the boy thinks he is a homosexual and the wife of the headmaster gives herself to him to prove he's not—but what is the problem, please?"

The age of sexual enlightenment that flourished in prewar Berlin spawned the first gay liberation movement, led by Doctor Magnus Hirschfeld, whose Institute for Sexual Science was the focal point of the battle against the anti-gay Paragraph 175 which outlawed homosexual acts between men. It also produced the first film to discuss homosexuality openly and to contain many of the seedling issues of the gay liberation movement. Directed by Richard Oswald and starring Conrad Veidt, *Anders als die Anderen (Different from the Others),* released in 1919, openly pleaded tolerance for what it termed the Third Sex. The following are excerpts translated from the original program distributed at the showings and sent recently to a West Berlin gay liberation group by an anonymous gay man who was there.

Paul Körner, violin player	Conrad Veidt
His father	Leo Connard
His mother	Ilse v. Tasso Lind
His sister	Alexandra Willegh
Her husband	Ernst Pittschau
Kurt Sivers	Fritz Schulz
His father	Wilhelm Diegelman
His mother	Clementine Plessner
Else, his sister	Anita Berber
Franz Bolleck	Reinhold Scheunzel
Mrs. Hellborn	Helga Molander
A doctor	

Camera: Max Fassbinder

**Sacrifices are held,
neither lamb nor bull,
but human sacrifices
unheard of before.**

—Goethe

False beliefs and unjustified prejudices concerning a sector of male and female sexual behavior known as homosexuality, or love of the same sex, have been predominant up to the present and still influence a large part of our population.

These homosexual men and women who are attracted to persons of their own sex, are often regarded as wicked criminals and libertines. But scientific research has determined that homosexuality is an inborn tendency for which the individual cannot be held responsible; that in Germany as well as in many other countries, every thirtieth person has homosexual tendencies; that there are homosexuals in every class, among the educated and among the uneducated, and in the highest and lowest sectors of our population, in the great cities and the small towns, among the strict moralists and among the most easygoing; that love for one's own sex can be just as pure and noble as love for the opposite sex, the only difference being the object of desire, not the nature of one's love.

So much worse that in Paragraph 175 of the German Penal Code, homosexual men (and in Austria homosexual women) are threatened with disgraceful penalties through which they are to be exposed as outlaws and surrendered to extensive oppression, and because of which a large number of people have been driven to disgrace, despair and even insanity and suicide.

The Scientific Humane Committee, founded in 1897, and its tireless and courageous director and medical advisor, Dr. Magnus Hirschfeld, have taken on the task of bringing about the abolition of Paragraph 175 and eliminating false prejudices against homosexuals by enlightening the public.

Different from the Others avoids all sensationalism. Using an individual fate as an example, it shows us how people with such tendencies are made to suffer for no reason, how they are exploited by oppressors and how, because of society's rejection of them and because of the accursed Paragraph 175, homosexuals are driven to despair and suicide.

Magnus Hirschfeld himself introduced the first showing of the film.

The matter to be put before your eyes and soul today is one of severe importance and difficulty. Difficult, because the degree of ignorance and prejudice to be disposed of is extremely high. Important, because we must free not only these people from undeserved disgrace but also the public from a judicial error that can be compared to such atrocities in history as the persecution of witches, atheists and heretics. Besides this, the number of people who are born "different from the others" is much larger than most parents know or care to realize. I am conscious of the fact that whoever wants to use intellectual weapons to fight for human progress must overcome attacks and opposition. The first scholars who, after they had discovered the printing press, put their ideas into letters were also violently attacked. But these are side issues. The film you are about to see for the first time today will help to terminate the lack of enlightenment, and soon the day will come when science will win a victory over error, justice a victory over injustice and human love a victory over human hatred and ignorance.

Oswald's film, like others of that time dealing with abortion, incest, sex education and venereal disease, was propagandistic in treatment; Hirschfeld himself appeared as resident expert. Only one print of *Anders als die Anderen,* a fragmented copy, survives. It has never been seen in the United States. Other prints were destroyed by the Nazis in the early Thirties. Christopher Isherwood recalls that performances of the film were broken up by the Nazis. In Vienna one of them fired a revolver into the audience, wounding several patrons. In his memoir *Christopher and His Kind,* Isherwood gives a firsthand account of the film.

Three scenes remain in my memory. One is at a ball at which the dancers, all male, are standing fully clothed in what seems about to become a daisy chain. It is here

Conrad Veidt as Paul Körner, a famous violinist, embraces his homosexual blackmailer in a scene from Richard Oswald's Anders als die Anderen *(Different from the Others, 1919). (Berlin Film Archives)*

that the character played by Conrad Veidt meets the blackmailer who seduces him and then ruins him. The next scene is a vision which Veidt has of a long procession of kings, poets, scientists, philosophers and other famous victims of homophobia, moving slowly and sadly with heads bowed. Dr. Hirschfeld himself appears. I think the corpse of Veidt, who has committed suicide, is lying in the background. Hirschfeld delivers a speech (that is to say a series of titles) pleading tolerance for the Third Sex.

And so the very first gay man to be presented on film ended in the obligatory suicide that would mark the fate of screen gays for years to come. The suicide of Veidt and the images of blackmail presaged the fates of American screen characters who would suffer for their sexuality in like manner when the U.S. cinema reached a similar starting point almost fifty years later.

A convict is about to molest a fellow prisoner in Geschlecht in Fesseln *(Sex in Bondage, 1928). (Jim Steakley Collection)*

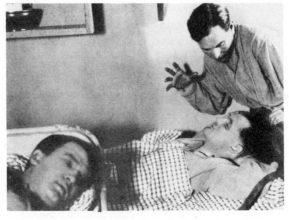

In Germany the issues of sexuality remained vital for more than a decade. Other films dealing with liberal approaches to sexuality included *Geschlecht in Fesseln (Sex in Bondage),* which was made in 1928 by William Dieterle and portrayed homosexuality as a part of prison life in an attack on the penal system. Dieterle starred as a man who, sent to prison for an accidental killing, is drawn into a homosexual relationship with a fellow prisoner. The prisoner, it turns out, is really homosexual and has a male lover waiting on the outside. When Dieterle gets out of prison, the homosexual goes to his home and confronts his wife, seeking to blackmail them but succeeding only in precipitating their double suicide.

Anders als die Anderen was remade in 1927, again by Magnus Hirschfeld and Richard Oswald, as *Gesetze der Liebe (The Laws of Love).* Of this film nothing survives; in the next decade a million homosexuals were swept into Nazi concentration camps along with Jews, Gypsies and other undesirables. In the summer of 1979, a partially restored print of *Anders als die Anderen* was discovered in the Ukraine and shown at a West Berlin gay film festival. It was the first time the sixty-year-old film had been shown outside East Germany.

The acknowledgment of the Third Sex in Europe was apparently not bound up in a definition of masculinity as it was in America. The emotional qualities of the passions aroused in human relationships rather than the sexual characteristics of such relations were the focus of the drama and intrigue. Carl Theodor Dreyer's *Mikael* (1924) is a homosexual love story in which a famous artist named Zoret (Benjamin Christiansen) falls in love with his young male model Mikael (Walter Slezak), whose nude portrait he has painted as Siegfried. Mikael, however, is an ungrateful opportunist who saps his benefactor's artistic spirit and uses his money, eventually spurning his affections for the more promising charms of a wealthy young princess. In spite of Mikael's indifference, Zoret leaves all his possessions to the youth and, on his deathbed, declares, "I can die in peace. I have known a great love."

The film, adapted from Hermann Bang's novel *Mikael,* played briefly in America in 1926 under confusing circumstances. The censors objected to its first American release title, *The Inverts,* so it ran for a short time at New York's Fifth Avenue Playhouse as *Chained: The Story of the Third Sex,* with a "scientific lecture" tacked on and without credit to Dreyer as the director. The title changes illustrate perfectly the American mentality with regard to homosexuality. The subtitle, *The Story of the Third Sex,* reveals how any story dealing, however seriously, with homosexual love is taken to be a story about homosexuality while stories dealing with heterosexual love are seen as stories

A gay café in Gesetze der Liebe (The Laws of Love, 1927).
The film does not survive. (Jim Steakley Collection)

Walter Slezak as Benjamin Christiansen's young lover in
Carl Dreyer's Mikael *(1924).* (Cinemabilia)

about the individual people they portray. This is as much a problem today for American filmmakers who cannot conceive of the presence of gay characters in a film unless the specific subject of the film is homosexuality. Lesbians and gay men are thereby classified as purely sexual creatures, people defined solely by their sexual urges.

In 1926, *New York Times* critic Mordaunt Hall identified *Chained* as *Mikael,* a Carl Dreyer film, and pointed out that the Hermann Bang story was said to be based on the life of French sculptor Auguste Rodin. Hall then took a shot at the subject matter: "German producers delight in taking an occasional fling at France, England and Russia by filming stories dealing with historical characters who were not a credit to their respective countries . . . if producers were bent on delivering such a theme to the screen, it might have been vastly more to their advantage to picturize Oscar Wilde's story *The Picture of Dorian Gray,* which, distasteful though it may be, at least possesses real dramatic value." Although Hall never mentions homosexuality in his review, he was the first in a long line of critics who were so blinded by the subject matter of homosexuality that they would review it with obvious distaste. It is apparent in Hall's choice of an alternative, *The Picture of Dorian Gray,* that Dreyer's direct and uncritical approach to such unorthodox passions had unnerved him. He asked not for something with more dramatic value but for something with a strong sense of moral judgment. The homosexualizing of Rodin he considered an insult to France. Thus the "theme" of homosexuality relegated *Mikael* to the level of sexploitation, and few Americans saw the film.

G. W. Pabst's *Pandora's Box (Die Büchse der Pandora,* 1929) featured what is probably the first explicitly drawn lesbian character on film. The adaptation of Frank Wedekind's two-part drama about Lulu, a woman "driven by insatiable lusts," starred Louise Brooks as Lulu and Belgian actress Alice Roberts as her passionate lesbian admirer, the Countess Geschwitz. Pabst explores the personality of Geschwitz with great range, manipulating the performance of Alice Roberts to achieve a believable woman with a lesbian nature. At first the countess is an angry, repressed woman whose nostrils flare in her jealousy of Lulu's affair with her own stepson, Alwa. Later, when the pain and self-destruction of Lulu and Alwa's dissolute life threaten to destroy them, Geschwitz proves her love by engaging in a heterosexual blackmail ploy to raise money for Lulu. She submits to a crude yet powerful man who beats and humiliates her for her efforts. Although the love Geschwitz feels for Lulu is officially considered "sterile" in the context of both the Wedekind drama and the film, it is a motivating force in the action and it makes the debut of Sapphic passion onscreen an exciting cinematic event.

In the creation of a powerful and convincing performance, Roberts found it necessary to improvise in order to play a lesbian realistically. In a 1974 conversation with filmmaker Richard Leacock, preserved on film at New York's Museum of Modern Art, Brooks tells of Roberts' apprehension during the filming of *Pandora's Box.*

Alice Roberts was prepared to go no further than repression in mannish suits. Her first day's work was the wedding sequence. She came on the set looking chic in her Paris evening dress and aristocratically self-possessed. Then Mr. Pabst began explaining the action of the scene in which she was to dance the tango with me. Suddenly she understood that she was to touch, to embrace, to make love to another woman. Her blue eyes bulged, and her hands trembled. Anticipating the moment of explosion, Mr. Pabst caught her arm and sped her away out of sight behind the set. A half hour later, when they returned, he was hissing soothingly in her ear in French and she was smiling like the star of the picture . . . which she *was* in all her scenes with me. In both two-shots and close-ups, she cheated her look past me to Mr. Pabst [who was] making love to her off camera.

Alice Roberts as the Countess Geschwitz glares at the man who dares to come between her and Louise Brooks in the famous waltz scene from G. W. Pabst's Pandora's Box *(1929).* (Museum of Modern Art)

Roberts' fears of playing a lesbian were not unfounded. "At the time," Brooks says, "I thought her conduct was silly. The fact that the public could believe an actress' private life to be like one in a role in a film did not come home to me until I was visited by a French student last year. Explaining why the young people in Paris loved *Lulu,* he put an uneasy thought in my head. 'But you talk as if I really were a lesbian,' I said. 'But of course,' he answered in a way that made me laugh to realize that I'd been living in cinematic perversion for thirty-five years."

American audiences were spared such scintillating discussion, for the British censors deleted the character of Geschwitz from *Pandora's Box,* and she did not appear in the initial release version of the film in the United States (the character was later restored).

One of the earliest direct references to male homosexuality in an American film came, predictably, in a comedy spoof. Stan Laurel's one-reel comedy short *The Soilers* (1923) was a takeoff on Rex Beach's popular 1914 western *The Spoilers.* Set in Alaska during the gold rush, the film offers Stan Laurel as Bob Cannister, a patsy who strikes it rich only to be fleeced by an unscrupulous local sheriff. Most of the action consists of a drawn-out fight scene between Laurel and the sheriff, who brawl the entire length of an old-time saloon. During the fight, an ordinary-looking cowboy flounces gaily onto the set, hand on hip. He bats his eyes at both men, fluffs his hair before a mirror and primps a bit before sashaying out of the room as the two men continue to fight. Laurel beats the villain, but nobody seems to care, and he ends up sitting dejectedly outside the saloon, his face buried in his hands. The gay cowboy pokes his head out of a second-floor window and extravagantly blows

A gay cowboy gazes down at his hero Stan Laurel in the last scene from The Soilers *(1923).* (UCLA Film Archive)

Laurel a kiss, mouthing the words "My Hero" (reinforced by a flowered title card). When Laurel spurns him with a disgusted wave of his hand, the miffed cowboy drops a potted petunia on his head. In the final shot, the street cleaner sweeps Laurel away with the trash.

This is one of the first examples of the use of the "harmless sissy" image to present homosexuality. The sometimes silent connection between effeminate and homosexual was unmistakably evident here because the gay cowboy looked not like a woman but like any other cowboy in the film. The difference was that he preferred men—and therefore "behaved" like a woman. The primping and fussing mannerisms of the cowboy were certainly woman-identified, even though female impersonation was not a factor. Yet this was exactly the sort of thing the censors were watching for. Ordinances already empowered censorship bodies to look at films in advance of their public showing, and although such groups had no real clout, their guidelines for morality in the movies specifically included "sex perversion" as a *don't.*

In 1915 the U.S. Supreme Court had ruled that "the exhibition of motion pictures is a business, pure and simple, originated and conducted for profit, like other spectacles, not to be regarded or intended to be regarded . . . as a part of the press of the nation or as organs of public opinion." This meant that the movies were not covered by the First Amendment guarantee of freedom of speech. Within a few years of the ruling, censorship laws were passed in New York, Florida, Massachusetts, Maryland and Virginia. The New York law, enacted in 1921, was typical; it provided that "a film should be licensed by the State unless such a film or part thereof is of such a character that its exhibition would tend to corrupt morals or incite crime." Indecency, immorality and obscenity were nowhere described or defined in the statute, and thus there was considerable latitude for interpretation.

Early efforts of the film colony to regulate itself proved clearly inadequate to moral and religious leaders. To complicate matters, there were inconsistencies as a result of local interpretations of the laws. Scores of films dealing with supposedly forbidden subject matter, including homosexuality, slipped through the censors' fingers. Comedies such as *The Soilers* were passed as harmless. Other films were clearly passed or rejected as concessions to certain attitudes and prejudices. One of the first instances of lesbians kissing onscreen was in a brief orgy scene in Cecil B. De Mille's *Manslaughter* (1922). The vision of two passionate women locked in a forbidden embrace was used by De Mille to condemn the excesses he was busy portraying so graphically. In return for his judgment on the "crime," he was consistently allowed to paint a more explicit picture of evil, especially sexual sins, than was ordinarily permitted. This was particularly true when the evil transpired in a biblical city. Quoting scripture on their title cards, De Mille's films became moral lessons rather than exploitation. They also became box office.

Censors and critics did not buy "religious convictions" when Alla Nazimova presented *Salome* in 1923 with a reputedly all-gay cast, in tribute to Oscar Wilde (though in 1921 the censors had let slip a brief lesbian scene in her version of *Camille*). *Salome* was greeted with the kind of enthusiasm that is usually reserved for Off Off Broadway plays about Puerto Rican transvestites. (In fact the last time *Salome* had a major theatrical release, in 1971, it was double-billed with *Broken Goddess,* starring Andy Warhol's Puerto Rican transvestite superstar, Holly Woodlawn.) The sets and costumes for *Salome* were taken from illustrations by Aubrey Beardsley and executed by Natasha Rambova, who was reportedly Nazimova's sometime lover and the wife of Rudolph Valentino. The credit for direction, given to Nazimova's husband Charles Bryant, also belonged to Rambova, who wrote the screenplay under the name Peter M. Winters. The film, a financial and critical failure, wiped out Nazimova's life savings and destroyed her artistic credibility for some time to come. In Ken Russell's unremarkable *Valentino* (1977), Nazimova, played by Leslie Caron, encounters a reporter as she sweeps into Valentino's funeral at the beginning of the film. "Is it true," he asks, "that Rudolph Valentino refused to be in your all-homosexual production of *Salome?*" Offended not at his presumption of her lesbianism but at his suggestion that Valentino would turn her down, she snaps, "He was not available at the time!" Russell's light, campy bantering about the sexuality of such people stands in stark contrast to the climate of the Twenties, though people are still as naive and misinformed.

By 1922 there were censorship bills before the legislatures of thirty-two states, and throughout the nation the distinct odor of moral indignation was

Leslie Caron (right) as Nazimova arrives at the funeral of Rudolph Valentino with her lover Natasha Rambova (Michelle Phillips) in Ken Russell's Valentino (1977). (United Artists)

Alla Nazimova in the title role of her own production of Salome *(1923), a tribute to Oscar Wilde.*

A naked slave is chained to a galley wall in the 1926 production of Ben-Hur. *Note how the slave is illuminated by the spotlight.* (Homer Dickens Collection)

Charles Laughton and his slave boy in Cecil B. De Mille's The Sign of the Cross *(1932). Scenes such as this precipitated stronger censorship rules.*

rising at an industry that at times seemed to embody wicked behavior of all sorts. The censors were horrified by *Salome* and ordered the elimination of several sequences, including one that made clear a homosexual relationship between two Syrian soldiers. The handwritten report of the examining censor in New York, filled out at a screening in 1923, concluded: "This picture is in no way religious in theme or interpretation. In my judgment, it is a story of depravity and immorality made worse because of its biblical background. Sacrilegious."

Nazimova, using her characters sensually and artfully as allusions to decadence and androgyny, failed to condemn them. People found this offensive
and repellent both visually and thematically. A later experimental film of a
much higher order, James Watson and Melville Webber's Lot in Sodom (1933),
depicted the judgment and destruction of the biblical city in lurid and sometimes
racist but always fascinating terms. The film was welcomed grudgingly by highbrow critics on the basis of its innovative artistic merits, but its theme, hardly
mentioned by most writers, was condemned by the few who spoke of it. According to Jack Babuscio, film critic of London's Gay News, the British critic Norman
Wilson wrote in 1934, "It must be welcomed as an attempt at experiment
even though we deplore the choice of theme and the decadent artiness of its
treatment."

Both Salome and Lot in Sodom brilliantly executed exotically artificial mi-
lieus, but the costuming, the posturing and the highly stylized exaggeration
were alien to the expectations of a broad general public unable to find a
frame of reference for the excesses in visual style that such films presented.
They were presages of Sixties camp decadence, and it is ironic that Salome's
revival should come with a similar effort by a Warhol superstar, for mainstream
audiences tried as hard to pigeonhole the meanings of Warhol as they did
Nazimova's artifice, again failing to enjoy their audacity. After exasperating
an ABC television talk show host, Geraldo Rivera, in 1976 with a series of
flip answers to his serious questions, Holly Woodlawn finally listened to his
definitive plea. "Please answer me," Rivera begged at the close of the show.
"What are you? Are you a woman trapped in a man's body? Are you a heterosexual? Are you a homosexual? A transvestite? A transsexual? What is the answer
to the question?"

Woodlawn, who could have been answering Nazimova's critics as well, took
a measured breath, looked at Rivera incredulously and dismissed his earnest
concern with, "But, darling, what difference does it make as long as you look
fabulous?"

The censors in the late Twenties and early Thirties were not interested in
what was or was not fabulous. They were under pressure from all quarters.
In 1926 a Photoplay magazine film critic decried the use of "disgusting perverts"
in Rex Ingram's Mare Nostrum, which featured a vaguely lesbian spy. The
arrival of sound brought a new element of realism to the screen, and the
watchdogs of the public morality began to bear down on the industry. But
while censorship laws were becoming more specific and explicit homosexuality
remained a forbidden subject in every statute, it was clear that cross dressing,
weakness in men and overintellectualism were sometimes direct statements

about deviant sexuality. And whether expressed directly or not, the classic definition of homosexual men as frivolous, asexual sissies was firmly established during the last of the pre-Code years.

In the late 1920s Will Hays, a former postmaster general of the United States and a Hoosier Presbyterian elder, had been drafted to head the Motion Picture Producers and Distributors of America, an organization formed mainly to provide favorable public relations for the studios and to protect the industry from the threat of outside censorship. The latter goal was achieved in 1930 with the creation of the Motion Picture Production Code, by which the industry regulated itself. The Code survived under different names until the late Sixties, often taking the name of its current administrator. Thus, at various times it was called the Johnston Office, the Hays Office and the Breen Office. When, under tremendous pressure from the Catholic Church and other civic and religious groups, the Code was strengthened in 1934, borderline gay characters fell into well-worn innuendo and reliable sissy credentials, but said the same things.

Edward Everett Horton's mild-mannered Bensinger, the poet reporter in Lewis Milestone's *The Front Page* (1931), is more explicitly a pansy ("All those New York reporters wear lipstick") than the Bensinger of Ernest Truex in Howard Hawks' 1940 version, *His Girl Friday,* but the bare bones are the same in each film. Just as the sailors who waltzed together in Harold Lloyd's *Sailor Made Man* needed Lloyd as a scapegoat for their insecurities, the tough-guy reporters of Hecht and MacArthur needed similar protection. Bensinger, clearly their yardstick sissy, is made to do all the things that intellectuals are caricatured as doing. In *His Girl Friday,* Hildy (Rosalind Russell) asks Bensinger to be a bridesmaid at her wedding. He fusses endlessly over his lousy poetry, faints at the sound of a gunshot, flies into a tizzy when someone uses his private desk and sprays the telephone receiver with disinfectant when-ever someone else has used it. He is treated no differently than Ralph Bellamy's dotty old mother, but he's funnier because he's a man. From the bespectacled, bookish Harold Lloyd to the "sensitive" student Tom Lee in *Tea and Sympathy,* a certain amount of anti-intellectualism is basic to the ingredients of the sissy stereotype. A Bensinger was needed to throw off suspicion. At the end of *The Front Page,* the male version of Hildy Johnson sloppily acknowledges his editor's friendship: "Aww, Jesus no, Walter! You make me feel like some kind of fairy or something."

The rough, no-nonsense masculine image of the film business was constantly at odds with its reputation for feyness, just as was journalism. The sissy was used onscreen and off, as both scapegoat and weapon, to expose a mistrust of brightness or wit in men who were not also pushy or aggressive. In his book *See No Evil,* censor Jack Vizzard recalls an informal chat with Columbia Pictures head Harry Cohn at which several other Hays Office representatives were present. Cohn was describing how he had planned to have his current big star, Grace Moore, sing "La Marseillaise" at the fall of the Bastille in her new film, and censor Geoffrey Shurlock interrupted with, "You can't do it, Harry. 'The Marseillaise' wasn't written until three years after the fall of the Bastille."

"Who cares?" Cohn shouted. "Who would know a thing like that but a queer like you, anyway?"

Onscreen this kind of hostility was stated hardly more delicately, but since homosexuality did not officially exist, the thrust of such basically homophobic sentiment was directed elsewhere. *Symbols* of masculinity were defended by the use of *symbols* for homosexuality. The fact that most early movie sissies were homosexual only if one chose to see them as being homosexual was simply a reflection of the fact that the existence of homosexuals in society was acknowledged only when society chose to do so. Although the presence of sissies in the Thirties and Forties did not imply that homosexuality in fact existed, it implied that homosexuals *could* exist if things were topsy-turvy, and it provided a subtextual reminder that the basic illusion of America was pretty shabby. Sissies were an outlet for unspeakable ideas.

Sissies were fun, too. They were a refuge for nonconformity. The hovering presence of little Eric Blore as Leslie Howard's dresser, Diggs, in Archie Mayo's *It's Love I'm After* (1937) is a delightful example of the sissy who, though harmless and sanitized by the Code, provides a lurking reminder of an alternative truth. Blore epitomized the elegant yet down-to-earth manservant. In filling his master's needs, he referred solicitously to "our little nap" or "our nice brandy and soda," treating his charge as a mother would. Blore's relationship with Shakespearean actor Leslie Howard is defined in old vaudeville terms even though the two of them move in elegant society. They could as easily perform the Garland-Astaire tramp number from *Easter Parade* or an old burlesque skit. Their bond of friendship is a clear comic translation of buddyhood. In a significant bedroom scene, Howard has his brief moment of homosexual panic. It is New Year's Eve, and Howard's spat with Bette Davis has them locked in separate penthouse suites, sulking. Gazing out the window, Howard murmurs, "Down there in the streets a carnival of people, and up here one man alone!"

"*I'm* here, sir," says the plaintive Diggs, close on his heels, his hands clasped before him in anxiety.

"I love you, sir." Eric Blore as Diggs with his master Leslie Howard
in It's Love I'm After *(1937).*

"Oh, Diggs, *you're* always here," Howard snorts impatiently. *"Why* does
no one love me?"

"I love you, sir," comes the timid response.

"Oh, don't confuse the issue," Howard snaps, annoyed.

The issue was masculinity, and as always, the subtextual reference was to
the possibility that male love could be considered valid in a romantic context.
Of course the film makes fun of the very idea. Such comedies contained a
lot of offhand defense of masculine values, but it was good-natured and self-
assured, and it lacked the paranoid desperation to be found in the use of
sissy characters in the Sixties and Seventies. Once the Code had been revised
in 1961 to allow the subject of homosexuality onscreen, sissies took on a
new and less charming role.

It was much more engaging when men were slightly innocent of such implications. Fred MacMurray refused to sing for a living in *Sing, You Sinners* (1938)
because "singing is okay for *those* fellows, but *I'm* a man." And because he
is such a man, presumably, and not a four-eyed, singing sissy, he is dense
enough to allow his old mother to convince him that it is all right to sing
for a living when it is only for the money and there is hardship at home.
The god of masculinity would no doubt be appeased with this excuse, and
mama herself provides it as though she were writing a note to her son's teacher.

Because they were only symbols for failed masculinity and therefore did
not represent the threat of actual homosexuals, most sissies during the reign
of the Code were not demeaned, nor were they used in cruel or offensive

ways. It was not the sissy but what he stood for that was offensive. Some actors created memorable galleries of gossipy snoops, harried professors and snippy shopkeepers who were always a little on the innocent side, even in malice. To say that Franklin Pangborn played a sissy in the Thirties would be like saying that Michael Dunn played a dwarf in *Ship of Fools.* An inventive satirist with expert timing, Pangborn seized on his brief screen moments and made them shine. An indication of his coming glory can be seen in D. W. Griffith's *Lady of the Pavements* (1929), in which Pangborn's character offered one of the first blueprints for a malleable sissy image. Hired to teach Lupe Velez how to behave like a lady in polite society, he is officially heterosexual yet abdicates his masculinity through his clear identification with female manners. He is in fact a teacher of feminine behavior. When he tries, awkwardly, to make love to Velez, she beats him mercilessly until he cowers on the floor, hiding behind the legs of a man standing nearby. A sense of proper, almost regal outrage runs through his entire portrayal, even when he is scared to death. In more than a hundred films throughout the 1930s alone, Pangborn played kaleidoscopic variations on the role and became the archetypal sissy.

In an RKO-Radio Pictures press release for *Professional Sweetheart* (1933) the studio wrote:

Call Franklin Pangborn a sissy offstage and he'll plant five hard knuckles on your proboscis. But call him a sissy on the stage or screen and he'll pat you on the back and call you "pal" . . . for Pangborn is famous for his portrayals of "sissified" characters . . . those chaps usually known as Adelbert, who go in for arched eyebrows and a mincing walk . . . and in RKO's *Professional Sweetheart,* he plays a typical role . . . that of a male dressmaker who flutters about . . . adding to the general hilarity of this uproarious satire.

The public acknowledgment that private sissyhood deserved a punch in the nose made clear the onus that society put on such real-life behavior. Yet Pangborn won hearts with it onscreen. He could turn a one-line part into a tour-de-force. As a radio gossip reporting on the rise of new star Vickie Lester in William A. Wellman's *A Star Is born* (1937), he confides in a conspiratorial whisper to an entire nation that the studio is "keeping her under wraps, but those who've peeked tell me she just *couldn't* be more divoon!" In one of his lengthier roles, that of a hat shop proprietor in Mitchell Leisen's *Easy Living* (1937), he is the quintessential busybody and definitely one of the girls at heart. Spreading the rumor that Jean Arthur is Edward Arnold's mistress, he begins a telephone conversation with, "Hello, Mary Smith? Don't breathe a word dear, *but . . .*" and ends it with a knowing, "My dear, wherever there's smoke, there must be . . . um . . . somebody smoking." Showing up at Jean

Arthur's hotel room door festooned with ladies' jewelry and hats, he exclaims, "Just pour yourself into these, my dear, and fall into a faint!"

To characterize such behavior as homosexual simply because it is stereotypical is of course a mistake. There is a difference between the Milquetoast ninny or the innocent clown and those sissies who evince a specific homosexuality. In a *New York Times* article of 1975, "Let the Boys in the Band Die," openly gay writer Arthur Bell equated the "gay" roles of Franklin Pangborn, Eric Blore and Grady Sutton with the demeaning stereotypes of black roles played by Butterfly McQueen, Hattie McDaniel and Stepin Fetchit. Actor Erik Rhodes responded in an angry letter to the *Times* a week later, defending such characterizations and the "ghosts" of Pangborn and Blore against what he considered slurs: "the roles we appeared in were not conceived along those lines and . . . Mr. Bell's campaign is his own." Attempts like this one on the part of gay writers to explore the tone of certain performances as homosexual in nature have often been met with outrage. Of course Rhodes would defend his contemporaries against what he sees as defamation of the characters they played. Yet, Bell is correct. To the public, these characters were homosexual. To gays they represented a pattern of oppression similar to the one suffered by blacks, long typified onscreen as simpletons and domestics.

Erik Rhodes played the lovable gigolo Tonetti in the Fred Astaire-Ginger Rogers musical *The Gay Divorcee* (1934). His character ("Your wife is safe with Tonetti, he prefers spaghetti"), which provides some of the high moments of the film, could be described as gay only in the original sense of the word.

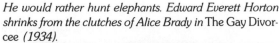

He would rather hunt elephants. Edward Everett Horton shrinks from the clutches of Alice Brady in The Gay Divorcee *(1934).*

On the other hand, the role of Egbert Fitzgerald, played to a fare-thee-well by Edward Everett Horton in one of his classic portrayals, is an obvious instance of the barely restrained Code sissy, scrubbed on the surface yet brimming with tantalizing sexual and psychological ambiguities. As Astaire's closest friend, whose "soul has always *yearned* to express itself in the dance," he is known also as Aunt Egbert or Pinky. The latter, he says, is something his father used to call him, "ever since I was a golden-haired little tot, paddling about the ancestral home in pale pink pajamas." Pinky, who plays with dolls when alone in his office, once almost married Hortense (Alice Brady) but decided to go elephant hunting instead. His whistling scene with the bellboy and his tea scene with the butler (Eric Blore), who has "an unnatural passion for rocks" are inspired pieces of comedy and innuendo. It is one of Horton's priceless renderings. If there is any complaint to be made about Erik Rhodes' Tonetti, however, it should come from the Italian-American Anti-Defamation League.

If Pangborn and the others were indeed "supposed" to be playing homosexuals, they were doing so with little consciousness of that fact. Their sissies were often the most charming and winning aspects of our films and regularly saved them from mediocrity. But conscious or not, whenever elements of sissy-hood were present, the suspicion of homosexuality emerged. Like America, American film is obsessed with sexual curiosity of every sort. Sexuality will lurk beneath the surface if it must, yet it never disappears. That there was a visual and verbal code for homosexuality in the movies is certain; powerlessness, femininity in men, decadence and sometimes anarchy were consistently colored with sexual references that became more explicit each year until the Code clamped down in 1934.

George K. Arthur's portrait of the dressmaker Madame Lucy in *Irene* (1926) is a textbook lesson in how effeminate men could intimate homosexuality while remaining essentially asexual and without threatening the status quo. Arthur's Madame Lucy, given to severely tailored suits and lace hankies, is a whimsical creature described as a man living in a woman's world. He plays the snippy queen in a drag-like performance filled with extravagant gestures and eye popping. When he takes a first look at the working class Irish immigrant girl from the slums (Colleen Moore) who is to be his new fashion model, he exclaims, "As I live and hemstitch, she's impossible! Even *I* cannot make a peach melba from a prune." Later, watching Irene's inadequate attempts to model a new creation, he throws up his hands in disgust. "You're impossible!" he cries. "You walk *almost* like a man." Miffed, finally, at his constant derision, Irene shoots back, "So do *you.*"

Jokes about men who behave like women have never ceased to be funny.

George K. Arthur walks "almost like a man" in his role as Madame Lucy in Irene *(1926).* (Homer Dickens Collection)

Like Grady Sutton fluttering hysterically atop a table at the sight of a mouse in *Movie Crazy* (1932), Arthur was "queer" because he was feminine. That the public and the critics routinely made such connections is certain. Cross dressing, for example, came to *mean* sexual perversion in some cases. In Alfred Hitchcock's *Murder* (1930), Esme Percy plays a transvestite trapeze artist who murders a young woman to keep her from revealing to his fiancé that he is a half-caste. Although Hitchcock, always interested in any form of sexual perversity, used the sexual implications of Percy's impersonation for colorful theatrical effect, the term *half-caste* referred clearly to the hero's mixed blood. Yet many critics took the liberty of interpreting this as a sudden awareness on the part of Hitchcock of dissolving ethics and moral change. On the strength of a few sequins and feathers, critic Raymond Durgnat took *half-caste* to mean "left handed which means bisexual or homosexual."

Whenever a character displayed open signs of homosexuality in a comic context, there was nary a comment on it in print. In *The Broadway Melody* (1929), the costume designer for the big Broadway musical is a thin, hawklike nervous nellie who flits around like a butterfly, his hands ever in midair. He is the object of sexual innuendo in two of his three scenes in the film.

Approaching the big-shot producer, Mr. Zanfield, with a white ermine coat draped over his arm, he presents the costume with a bill for two thousand dollars. Zanfield, surrounded by yes-men in tuxedos, shouts, "What? Two grand for a coat worn less than two minutes? I *won't* pay it."

Unperturbed, the giggling designer blurts out, "But you *said* ermine. It's a gorgeous garment, isn't it?"

Taking the coat from him and draping it over his shoulders, one of Zanfield's yes-men squeals thinly, in a mocking tone of voice, "Oh! *Isn't* it gorgeous? In fact, it's the gorgeousest thing we ever saw, you sweet little cutie."

As the offended sissy departs in a huff, one of Zanfield's drunken henchmen begins to weave after him but is forcibly restrained by another, who says, "Come back here, unconscious!"

On opening night, a group of chorus girls are having trouble getting out of their dressing room because the hats they are wearing are too large to pass through the door. The designer whirls around the room hysterically, waving his arms in protest. "Girls! Girls! My hats! Be *careful* of my hats. I *won't* allow you to ruin them."

The wardrobe mistress, a very large woman in a black dress, intervenes. Towering over him, hands on hips, she says, "Say, *listen.* I *told* you they were too high and too wide."

Drawing himself up into a sassy sissy position and imitating her hands on hips, he retorts bitchily, "*Well,* big woman, I design the costumes for the show, not the doors for the theater."

"I know that," she snaps back. "If you had, they'd have been done in lavender."

The sissy in *The Broadway Melody* was not "just" effeminate. *Lavender,* a

Costume designer confronts wardrobe mistress in The Broadway Melody *(1929).* (MGM)

popular code word for boys who were "that way," was used in several films to designate homosexuality. In George Abbott's *Why Bring That Up?* (1929), a somewhat racist musical about two "black crows," the connection is made in a backstage scene when two chorus boys are caught in mid-conversation. As the camera pans the wings of the theater on opening night, one is discovered telling the other, "And my new drapes are the most *gorgeous* shade of lavender."

Another word used either in conversation or as an epithet to signal queerness was *pansy.* The opening sequence of Samuel Goldwyn's dreadful musical *Palmy Days* (1931) featured a flaming sissy who rushes into a bakery shop and orders a cake. When the saleswoman asks, "Would you like roses on it?" he replies archly, "No. Pansies!" and disappears from the film.

Two pre-Code fantasies that dealt with role reversal, *Just Imagine* (1930) and *The Warrior's Husband* (1933), made liberal use of such terminology to refer to men in societies dominated by women. In *Just Imagine,* the society of the future is set in 1980, in part on Mars, a world of fiction within the film where the women are the thinkers and the men silly creatures who are called "queens" by visitors from Earth and who rattle their beads to ward off intruders. A better film, yet one more loaded with fag jokes, *The Warrior's Husband* takes place in 800 B.C., when the Amazon women, a title declares, "had all the rights—and pretty good lefts, too. Women who believed that a man's place was in the home." In an outrageous performance, Ernest Truex plays Sapiens, a "progressive thinker" who enters the court of the Amazon Queen Hippolyta (Marjorie Rambeau) to the tune of "Oh, You Beautiful Doll" and sits curling his beard while the women make all the important decisions on affairs of state.

Two visiting Greeks, Homer and Theseus, enter the court and are shocked. They are also shocking to the gentle men of the Amazon world; Truex calls them "hussies" and berates them for shaving their legs to be like women. When Hippolyta congratulates them for being "like women of the world," Homer says to Theseus, "By the gifts that fortune hands me, she takes you for a pansy!" Examining Truex more closely, Homer is outraged but not speechless. "What *is* this creature?" he demands of Hippolyta. "I abhor it! Why, even the Greeks have no word for it."

Actually the Greeks had several words for it, but the movies had Ernest Truex, and there are times when words are unnecessary. In a battlefield sequence, Truex lounges inside Hippolyta's tent, preening and adjusting his bracelets. A handsome Greek messenger arrives. Truex takes a long, hard look at the soldier and greets him by wiggling five fingers. The messenger takes a long, hard look and mutters, "You find them wherever you go."

Ernest Truex as Sapiens in The Warrior's Husband *(1933).*
(Twentieth Century-Fox)

The censors were finding them, too. In late 1933 the Hays Office sent out memos to several studios announcing that *pansy* was now a forbidden word. A few months later Raoul Walsh's *Sailor's Luck* opened and, in a bathhouse scene, James Dunn pointed at a lisping attendant and said to his seafaring buddies, "Hey, fellas, etgay the ansypay!" To which the ansypay replied by saying, "Hi, sailors!" and wiggling five fingers.

That such exchanges were considered patently homosexual in theme was evidenced in subsequent censoring action taken on similar sequences. A well-known scene from *Wonder Bar* (1934) in which two men dance together was cut slightly to eliminate what the censor's report called "the indecent action of Harry's lips as he leaves Al on the dance floor." Inconsistently, the two dancing men, not comic but romantically serious, were left intact, with Al Jolson exclaiming, "Woooo! Boys will be boys."

Stripping such moments of direct sexual reference was necessary in order to retain a safely comic point of view where male-male contact was concerned. By 1933 censor-proof insinuation had become an art form and the explicitly homosexual sissy flourished. During that year the existence of homosexuality was alluded to more often than at any other time in film history before the loosening of the Code in the early 1960s. In 1933, Franklin Pangborn appeared in both *International House* and *Only Yesterday*. In both films the barrier between sissy and homosexual is all but erased during moments of seemingly conscious innuendo. As the flustered manager of the International House Hotel in Wu Hu, China, Pangborn is kept in a perpetual tizzy by the antics of the Paramount roster of comic talent. When W. C. Fields, soused as usual, lands his strange flying machine on the terrace of the hotel, Pangborn is beside himself with nervous tension. Fields calls down from the cockpit of the plane, "Hey, Charlie, *where* am I?" Startled, Pangborn replies musically, "Wuuu Huuu!" Inspecting his own person, Fields spies a flower in his lapel and throws it from the plane disgustedly, telling Pangborn, "Don't let the pansy fool ya."

In 1978, Billy Wilder used the same joke in *Fedora*. Jose Ferrer, wearing a small gold earring, asks William Holden, "Why are you interested in me?" Holden says he finds him fascinating. Departing quickly, Ferrer says, "Don't let the earring fool you."

In *Only Yesterday,* Pangborn plays perhaps the most explicitly homosexual character of his long career, the society decorator of a swank New York penthouse apartment where he is about to attend a party. On their way to the affair, he and his friend Thomas (Barry Norton) are window shopping, engaged in arch conversation about decorating while the city around them reels in turmoil following a stock market crash. "I *say,* Thomas," Pangborn enunciates, stopping suddenly at a shop window. "Look! That heavenly blue against that mauve curtain. Doesn't it excite you? That kind of blue just *does* something to me." The juxtaposition of their flighty, inconsequential chatter with images of businessmen about to leap from office windows serves to place the two homosexuals in the position of women who play bridge while their husbands

Franklin Pangborn plays and Edna May Oliver listens in Only Yesterday *(1933).*

run the world. When Thomas looks around and asks what all the fuss is about, Pangborn replies, "Oh, something about that silly stock market." Thus their nonproductive, sterile lifestyle is contrasted vividly with the problems of real men who trade in power and affect the destinies of others.

Later, at the party, it is clear that Thomas is Pangborn's date; upon arriving, they join the women, leaving the men to ponder the crisis while they sing and gossip in the next room. In the same way that Pangborn and his date are contrasted with real men, they are set apart from the real world, in which they clearly cannot live. Their own world is one of artifice, a covering up of the truth to make it look better. They are archetypes, they are meant to be alienated from the normal American family-oriented lifestyle; they are barren and otherworldly, a context in which gay sissies often appeared both comically and seriously.

The Martians in *Just Imagine* and the Amazonian men in *The Warrior's Husband* were literally aliens, created from fantasy. In most other films they were found in isolation—in worlds unto themselves, like those of the theater, dance and fashion, worlds where presumably they engaged in the pursuit of the artifice that filled their empty lives. Heterosexual society has a vested interest in keeping homosexual relationships untenable and mystical because, made real, they are seen as a threat to family living. Homosexuals have always incorporated this repression into their lives and their work. Homosexual characters have often been drawn as darkly alien and monsterlike in a twilight world of horror and dread. As an outlet for unspeakable ideas, then, the sissy often became a monster or an outlaw.

The homosexual as inherently antisocial and probably anarchist is given further treatment in a Clara Bow comeback vehicle, *Call Her Savage* (1932). John Francis Dillon's film has Bow out on the town in New York with a hired gigolo who is really a wealthy capitalist wooing her in disguise. Bow asks where she is being taken for the evening, and her escort replies urbanely that since she wanted to go slumming, he picked a place "down in the Village where only wild poets and anarchists eat. It's pretty rough."

The scene shifts from the interior of their taxicab to the interior of what is obviously a gay bar of the Thirties. Or as much of a gay bar as could have existed in the Thirties, a smoky nightclub filled with cartoonish bearded revolutionaries and artists, the only people willing to tolerate the other patrons of the club, who are pairs of neatly dressed men and slightly tweedy women sitting in booths with their arms draped around each other. Tailored women in slouch hats and wide ties mix well with the berets and artist's smocks, typifying the Greenwich Village experience years before *My Sister Eileen*. In

Possibly the first representation of a gay bar in a commercial American film, the drag number from Call Her Savage *(1932). Note the two men at lower left.*

the aisles, two willowy young men in frilly white aprons and maid's caps are performing a musical number. Each carries a feather duster, a prop for the song in progress. The lyrics erase any doubt about the sexuality of characters who for years were "just sissies."

> **If a sailor in pajamas I should see**
> **I know he'll scare the life out of me**
>
> **But on a great big battleship**
> *(Together)* **We'd like to be**
> **Working as chamber maids!**

After a few moments, Clara Bow's date is recognized by a young socialist who identifies him to the crowd as the son of a wealthy industrialist. Apparently this is enough to get a person killed on the spot; the two are driven from the restaurant amidst a free-for-all in which bottles and plates fly in protest of society's intrusion into the refuge of a gay ghetto.

The ghetto was one otherworld in which gays could regularly be found onscreen both before and after the reign of the Code. The underworld life as a haven for homosexuals is a staple of music and literature, and of course this reflects the reality of most gay experience, which has been limited to expression in ghettos of one sort or another since the beginning of time. The gay ghetto has often been connected with the underworld to the extent that wherever illicit activity flourishes, organized crime moves in to control it and turn a profit. Also, unlike other minority groups, homosexuals hold criminal status in most places. A black ghetto may be crime ridden but the people who live there are not criminals for being black. In *Bessie,* his book on blues singer Bessie Smith, Chris Albertson discusses the singer's lesbian experiences, which are detailed further by historian Jonathan Katz in *Gay American History.* In an interview with Smith's niece (available on record in a blues and jazz collection of homosexually oriented songs from the Twenties and Thirties), Albertson sees homosexuality as a part of the jazz subculture. Describing a "buffet flat" of the early 1930s, Smith's niece says, "A buffet flat [was] nothing but a bunch of faggots and bull dykers—everything. Everything went on in that place. Everything that was in the life." In the life.

In 1933, Rowland Brown's gritty and atmospheric *Blood Money* created a great deal of ambiguous sexual tension in a wider underworld than that of *Call Her Savage*. In *Blood Money* the existence of homosexuality is openly acknowledged in the subculture that shelters it on the fringes of acceptable society. Sandra Shaw is featured in several sequences as a fun-loving blonde who likes men's clothes. Wearing a full-dress tuxedo and sporting a monocle as she awaits the arrival of her boyfriend at a nightclub bar, she provides a sounding board for a few in-jokes and some innuendo. Offered a cigar by the star of the film, George Bancroft, Shaw throws back her head and roars with laughter at his blasé attitude.

"Why, you big sissy!" she snorts, slapping him on the shoulder. Although it is not apparent in society in general, such feigned recognition is classic in gay surroundings, where it signals that the dress or demeanor of a person has communicated the unspeakable.

Shaw's boyfriend, meanwhile, the younger brother of the glamorous nightclub owner (Judith Anderson), is upstairs preparing for their date. Anderson warns him about the kind of women he has been running around with—she calls them "french pastry"—but he waves her fears aside. "Oh, don't worry, Sis, this one's different. Wears a tuxedo."

Anderson arches an eyebrow and shrugs in relief. "Oh. Then *you're* safe." Getting her meaning, he tells her it's not what she thinks, that the girl is just full of fun. But later in the film Shaw turns up again in double-breasted tweeds, this time not with Anderson's brother but with another woman in tow.

The placement of homosexuality or the real possibility of it in an antisocial context is quite natural. Homosexuality when it is visible *is* antisocial. The only condition under which homosexuality has ever been socially acceptable has been on the occasion of its voluntary invisibility, when homosexuals were willing to pass for heterosexuals. Obvious homosexual behavior is reflected onscreen, as in real life, only in the "twilight world" of misfit conduct. During the brief period of explicit reference to homosexuals in pre-Code films of the early 1930s, gay characters were psychologically ghettoized by their routine relegation to a fantasy world or an underworld life. In films like *Just Imagine* and *The Warrior's Husband,* they are freak products of imaginary worlds gone haywire, the result of tampering with the natural order.

Sandra Shaw accepts a cigar from George Bancroft in the bar scene from Rowland Brown's Blood Money *(1933).* (Paramount Pictures)

In addition to strengthening the Code in 1934, Will Hays reacted to criticism by inserting morals clauses in the contracts of performers and compiling a "doom book" of 117 names of those deemed "unsafe" because of their personal lives. Homosexuality was denied as assiduously offscreen as it was on, a literally unspeakable part of the culture. By 1940 even harmless sex-role farces such as Hal Roach's *Turnabout* were considered perilous in some quarters. The film, about a married couple (Carole Landis and John Hubbard) who switch roles by wishing on an Oriental statue, was described by the Catholic Legion of Decency as dealing with "subject matter which may provide references dangerous to morality, wholesome concepts of human relationships and the dignity of man."

Upholding the dignity of man in order to strike a blow for masculine pride was given various interpretations. In 1940 the censors allowed a scene in Tay Garnett's *Seven Sinners* in which a man is beaten and robbed because his address book lists a telephone number for "Bruce in Bombay."

In *The Broadway Melody, Wonder Bar* and *Why Bring That Up?* ghetto creatures are tucked away in the theatrical ghetto, where their artificial surroundings prevent them from intruding on society at large. This practice too was carried into the noncommittal Forties and Fifties. Many people think that Clifton Webb's ultimate sissy portrait was that of Waldo Lydecker in Otto Preminger's *Laura* (1944), perhaps because the character was a bitchy gossip columnist. Yet Webb's characterization of Elliott Templeton as an aging and then dying male spinster in *The Razor's Edge* (1946) is for most homosexuals his classic portrayal of a homosexual. And there is no mention of homosexuality in either film. In the original script for *Laura,* dated April 18, 1944, numerous allusions to the homosexuality of Waldo Lydecker were cut before shooting began. In an opening scene showing Lydecker's apartment, the script says "the camera pans the room. It is exquisite. Too exquisite for a man." Later, the narrating voice of Dana Andrews says, "You like your men less than one hundred percent, don't you, Mr. Lydecker?" It is widely acknowledged that director Otto Preminger had to fight to get Clifton Webb for the role because the studio brass had labeled him a homosexual.

Hollywood has always been more restrained onscreen than real life dictated at any given time. In 1968, at the height of the gay exploitation boom in the movies, Daniel Massey was playing Noel Coward like a virginal Mayfair queen in the musical biography of Gertrude Lawrence, *Star!* while down the street Noel Coward himself was busy playing the most outrageous screaming faggot in all Europe, the Witch of Capri in Joseph Losey's *Boom!*

In *Blood Money* and *Call Her Savage,* homosexuality is just another pocket of an underworld that exists outside the law. The gay presence in such subcultures was sometimes reflected in the language, especially in the use of slang, in films dealing with lawless people. In *Blood Money,* the word *fag* is used without reference to homosexuality. When George Bancroft warns a timid taxi driver not to betray his destination to the police, he threatens, "Lissen, fag"—and is rebuked by Judith Anderson for "scaring the little fellow half to death." Sexual connotations often surrounded the attitude of powerful men toward hired boys or servile companions. This remark in *Blood Money* was perhaps the first time *fag* was used onscreen in this context. Taken from its use in British boarding schools as a term for underclassmen "fagging" for upperclassmen, the word in underworld jargon denoted a subservient person or lackey, especially young men "used" for favors. Edward G. Robinson's sidekick Johnny in *Little Caesar* (1931) was such a character; when he decides to give up the rackets to be a tap dancer, Robinson cracks, "Dancin' just ain't my idea of a man's game."

Although the character of Joel Cairo (Peter Lorre) in *The Maltese Falcon* (1941) is identified by Sam Spade's secretary in Dashiell Hammett's novel as a homosexual, the film version just turns him into a perfumed fop with lace hankies. A brief, sarcastic reference by a venomous Mary Astor to "that young boy in Istanbul," the character with whom Cairo had a little trouble, is murky and unexplored. Elisha Cook, Jr., as Sidney Greenstreet's bodyguard Wilmer, however, is implicitly homosexual. He is referred to as "sonny," "boy" and "kid," and Bogart derisively calls him a "gunsel." Since about 1915, bums and prisoners had used the German word *gansel* or *gosling,* corrupted to *gunsel,* for a passive sodomite, especially a young, inexperienced boy companion. From the mid 1920s it gradually came to mean a sneaky or disreputable

"I've just gone gay—all of a sudden."
Cary Grant and May Robson in Bringing Up Baby *(1938).*

person of any kind. By the 1930s it meant petty gangster or hoodlum. That film characters like Wilmer and the taxi driver in *Blood Money* shared a feminine status is obvious. The only variation was the degree to which that equation was carried to its common underworld conclusion.

Only once during the reign of the Code, it seems, in Howard Hawks' *Bringing Up Baby* (1938), did an unscripted use of the word *gay* appear to refer to homosexuality. When Katharine Hepburn's Aunt Elizabeth (May Robson) discovers Cary Grant in a lace nightgown, she asks him if he dresses like that all the time. Grant leaps into the air and shouts hysterically, "No! I've just gone *gay* . . . all of a sudden!" This exchange appears in no version of the published script. The official first and second drafts of the sequence are the same:

> *Aunt Elizabeth:* Well, young man . . . I uh, *hope?*
> *Dexter:* I . . . I suppose you think it's odd, my wearing this. I realize it *looks* odd . . . I don't usually . . . I mean, I don't *own* one of these.

Thus what was probably an ad-lib on the day of shooting provides a rare textual reference to the word *gay* and to the concrete possibility of homosexuality in Hawks' work, which is fairly brimming over with what people used to call repressed sexual tension between men.

Once the Code had been revised in 1961, homosexuality officially became visible and the words *fag, faggot, fruit, dyke, pansy, lezzie* and sometimes even *gay* were used unequivocally as labels for lesbians and gay men, often by the same writers who had used them, denying their implications, in pre-Code times.

When the word gay *meant happy and nothing else . . .*

And just as in the briefly explicit films of the early Thirties, gay characters in the newly liberated Sixties were reflected exclusively as being alien to the culture. Visible again, this time with official sanction, such characters were once more placed in ghetto situations or created in terms of horror and fantasy.

Gays as predatory, twilight creatures were a matter of style and personal interpretation in the horror films of the 1930s. The equation of horror with the sins of the flesh is easily seen in monster movies of the period. Creatures like the Frankenstein monster and Dracula were almost always linked with the baser instincts of human beings; Frankenstein especially is a film character created outside every boundary the film calls normal.

Gays were often created as monsters. In her review of John Flynn's *The Sergeant* (1968), Pauline Kael points out that Rod Steiger's gay soldier isn't *just* homosexual—he's psychopathic—and part of that has to do with his appearing in "normal" surroundings. "Why," she asked, "are all the other soldiers so incredibly, so antiseptically straight that it really begins to look as if you *did* have to be crazy to be a homosexual? In this army situation, there is nothing in the atmosphere that links up with the Sergeant's homosexuality . . . and homosexuality is, to all appearances, unknown and without cause [so that] it does begin to seem as if only a monster could have such aberrant impulses."

Gloria Holden hypnotizes a young woman in Dracula's Daughter *(1936).*

The essence of homosexuality as a predatory weakness permeates the depiction of gay characters in horror films. In *Dracula's Daughter* (1936), Countess Alesca (Gloria Holden) has a special attraction to women, a preference that was even highlighted in some of the original ads for the film. ("Save the women of London from Dracula's Daughter!") Roger Vadim's *Blood and Roses* (1960) and Joseph Larraz' *Vampyres* (1974) both deal with lesbian vampires. Homosexual parallels in *Frankenstein* (1931) and *The Bride of Frankenstein* (1935) arose from a vision both films had of the monster as an antisocial figure in the same way that gay people were "things" that should not have happened.

The hitchhiking lesbian vampires Marianne Morris and Anulka put the bite on the nice man who picked them up in Vampyres *(1974).*

Dorothy Arzner with Joan Crawford on the set of The Bride Wore Red *(1937).*

In both films the homosexuality of director James Whale may have been a force in the vision. Director Robert Aldrich recalls that "Jimmy Whale was the first guy who was blackballed because he refused to stay in the closet. Mitchell Leisen and all those other guys played it straight, and they were onboard, but Whale said, 'fuck it, I'm a great director and I don't have to put up with this bullshit'—and he *was* a great director, not just a company director. And he was just unemployed after that—never worked again." According to Aldrich, an obviously lesbian director like Dorothy Arzner got away with her lifestyle because she was officially closeted and because "it made her one of the boys." But a man who, like Whale, openly admitted his love relationship with another man, in this case producer David Lewis, did not stand a chance. Although James Whale worked again briefly in 1943, he fell into obscurity soon after. In 1961 he was found dead at the bottom of his swimming pool, and there has never been a full investigation of the circumstances surrounding the event.

Whale's Frankenstein monster was the creation that would eventually destroy its creator, just as Whale's own "aberration" would eventually destroy his career. The monster in *Frankenstein* bears the brunt of society's reaction to his existence, and in the sequel, *The Bride of Frankenstein,* the monster himself is painfully aware of his own unnaturalness. In a graveyard scene, character actor Ernest Thesiger, a friend of Whale and a man who played the effete sissy with as much verve and wit as Franklin Pangborn or Grady Sutton, listens as the monster confesses his knowledge of his own creation. In *Frankenstein,* it is the monster who limits Henry Frankenstein's contact with the normal world. The old baron, Frankenstein's father, continually beseeches his son to "leave this madness," to come home and marry the young Elizabeth. Finally, the father, Elizabeth and Henry's best friend go to the castle and force him, for his health and sanity, to leave his creation, to be free from his "obsession." Later the monster fulfills Mary Shelley's prophecy by joining his creator on his wedding night, carrying off Elizabeth and thereby preventing the consummation of the impending marriage. The monster is then hunted by the townspeople in the same way that groups of men in silent comedies had once run effeminate men off piers and out of town. Their outrage echoes again and again in film. "What is this creature? I abhor it!"

In *The Bride of Frankenstein,* it is the odd, sissified Dr. Praetorius (Ernest Thesiger) who comes to entice Henry Frankenstein from his bridal bed in the middle of the night. Praetorius too has created life, and Henry's curiosity again overcomes his "good" instincts and proves his downfall. Praetorius proclaims himself to be in love with evil and professes to detest goodness. No accident, then, that the monster, seeing the unnaturalness and folly of his own existence, takes the evil Praetorius with him when he pulls the lever to destroy

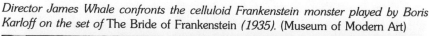

Director James Whale confronts the celluloid Frankenstein monster played by Boris Karloff on the set of The Bride of Frankenstein *(1935).* (Museum of Modern Art)

himself and his bride, crying out to Henry and Elizabeth, "Go! *You* live. We belong dead."

One may see Whale's horror films, including *The Old Dark House* (1932), in which all the characters can be read as gay, as either revisionist thinking (and therefore dangerous and false) or as crackpot theory (and therefore harmless and irrelevant). But one may no longer ignore the implications of the homosexual artist's being tied to a heterosexual dream. Of gay filmmaker F. W. Murnau, Natalie Edwards wrote for the Toronto Film Society, "His homosexuality had been cruelly subverted during his German period due to incredibly strict German laws, and it may well be that it was partly as a result of this forced restriction that his films of that period so often contained horror, dread, fantasy and perversion." Once homosexuality had become literally speakable in the early 1960s, gays dropped like flies, usually by their own hand, while continuing to perform their classically comic function in lesser and more ambiguous roles. In twenty-two of twenty-eight films dealing with gay subjects from 1962 to 1978, major gay characters onscreen ended in suicide or violent death.

Probably the "gayest" film yet made by a major studio and an excellent spoof of gay/horror conventions is *The Rocky Horror Picture Show,* a cult rock musical that Twentieth Century-Fox has never given a proper release in the United States. Since 1976 the film has been playing midnight shows in cities throughout the country. A truly subversive and anarchistic film on the subjects of sexuality, movies, sex roles and the homosexual as monster, *Rocky Horror* features two innocents (Susan Sarandon and Barry Bostwick) whose car runs out of gas not far from a haunted mansion that appears to be a parody of the creepy mansion in James Whale's *The Old Dark House*. In it they discover Dr. Frank N Furter (Tim Curry), the apotheosis of deviant sexuality, who introduces himself by singing a sizzling "I'm a Sweet Transvestite from Transsexual, Transylvania." Frank N Furter is an androgyne who comes from outer space, from a galaxy called Transsexual and a planet called Transylvania. When the timid couple arrive, he is in the process of showing off his latest creation, a hunky blond named Rocky, who is straight off the slab and wears nothing but tight gold lamé trunks. Pointing to Rocky, Frank N Furter sings a lusty "In Just Seven Days, I Can Make You a Man," then proceeds to introduce Brad and Janet to the joys of the unmentionable.

As both catalogue and spoof of old monster movies and science fiction films, *Rocky Horror* becomes almost dizzying in its references, but its most expert satire is of the age-old fear with which straight society encounters deviant sexuality. This is established at the beginning of the film (Janet says, "Brad, there's something *unhealthy* about this place") and is followed through to

Tim Curry looks over his new creation and sings "In Just Seven Days, I Can Make You a Man" in The Rocky Horror Picture Show *(1976).*

the very end, when Frank N Furter is destroyed "for the good of society," having been carried by Rocky, in the manner of King Kong, to the top of the RKO-Radio Pictures tower. Nevertheless he returns to life to perform, with the entire cast, an underwater ballet version of the film's message, "Don't Just Dream It, Be It," and the song becomes an anthem of hope for an androgynous world. Tim Curry's performance, especially in his rendition of "Sweet Transvestite," is the essence of what every parent in America fears will happen if our sexual standards are relaxed. It becomes the living horror of making deviant sexuality visible and tangible in the only kind of setting in which it could possibly work, an old dark house populated by lesbians, transvestites, acid freaks and goons who sing rock and roll as they seduce the innocent youth of America. Hollywood didn't know what to do with *The Rocky Horror Picture Show* when it had been completed, but despite its shabby treatment, it has grossed a fortune as a popular cult film, and it continues to play throughout the country to audiences made up largely of young people who dress for the showings like the characters in the film.

The incidental flaming faggots and bull dykes who passed through films in the 1960s to liven up the action were the same 1930s window dressing, but now they were nastier and ugly as sin in their newfound certainty. Roman Polanski's *The Fearless Vampire Killers* (1967) featured a gay vampire so

Ian Quarrier as Herbert the gay vampire in Roman Polanski's The Fearless Vampire Killers, Or Pardon Me But Your Teeth Are in My Neck *(1967).*

viciously stereotyped that Polanski should have called his film *Dracula's Hairdresser.* Other aberrations, including Peter Cook's two "gay" deadly sins, Vanity and Envy, in *Bedazzled* (1967), were similarly unsympathetic in their roles as sin itself. The transvestite behavior of Ray Walston's murderous cosmetician in *Caprice* (1967) is his ultimate downfall; he is pushed to his death from a balcony by the virtuous Doris Day. Walston's flaw is used in the same way as Martin Balsam's cowardice as the prissy antique dealer and thief in Sidney Lumet's *The Anderson Tapes* (1971). Both weaknesses of character betray the sexuality of the deviants to the audience. The comic elements of the Teens and Twenties were unchanged in the Sixties and Seventies; they had simply come to be used in "serious" ways, to point out the fatal flaw of difference in doomed characters. Outlaws like the vicious killer lovers Wint and Kidd in *Diamonds Are Forever* (1971) or the superfaggy Jack Cassidy character (his dog is named Faggot) in *The Eiger Sanction* (1975) shared a cartoon status and similar fates. Their homosexuality was rooted in harmless sissy behavior, but modern times had let the true nature of the aberration out of the bag, and the penalty was death.

Being illegal in society, homosexuality was always surrounded by reference to its status. In 1926, Mae West, one of the few performers of her time to acknowledge the existence of homosexuals, was jailed when her notorious play *The Drag* was closed by the New York police. In 1933, her film *She Done Him Wrong* contained two references that were typical of her style and humor. On a visit to her onetime boyfriend Chick Clark, now "up the river," West saunters past a jail cell that contains two men whose arms are wrapped around each other and, taking notice, she refers to them nonchalantly as "the Cherry Sisters." (The Cherry Sisters were a well-known vaudeville act that closed the first half of the bill and were so bad that people often threw food at them.) In a later scene, after West has attempted to seduce Cary Grant, he tells her, "I'd better be getting back to the mission now. Sally's father is waiting for me." Obviously considering the possibilities of such an encounter, she responds lewdly, "Yeah, well *that* oughta be interestin'!"

Mae West made the connection between effeminate men and homosexuals in her personal beliefs as well as in her scripts. In a *Life* magazine interview on April 18, 1969, she remarked that in 1926, when her play *The Drag* was running, she often cautioned the New York police not to beat up homosexuals because "a homosexual is a female soul in a male body. 'You're hitting a woman, I says.' " This quaintly sexist attitude was reflected in her work, which always held female impersonation to be synonymous with homosexuality.

Another play shuttered by the censors on the same evening in 1926 offered a much more serious look at lesbian love. Arthur Hornblow, Jr.'s adaptation of Bourdet's *La Prisonnière,* produced at New York's prestigious Empire Theater as *The Captive,* was the story of a French diplomat's daughter seduced by another woman and then involved in a long-term lesbian relationship. It was deemed "offensive" by the district attorney, who could, under New York's repressive Padlock Law, close any theatrical show without notice. Producer Gilbert Miller, who hoped that *The Captive* would one day become a motion picture, opted to fight the court order closing *The Captive,* but he was overruled by coproducer Adolph Zukor, who wanted the entire case dropped to avoid the unsavory publicity it would engender.

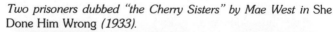

Two prisoners dubbed "the Cherry Sisters" by Mae West in She Done Him Wrong *(1933).*

In 1931, two young producers, Gifford Cochran and John Krimsky, spotted Leontine Sagan's film *Mädchen in Uniform* at a theater in Paris and promptly bought the American distribution rights. Two weeks later they were notified that the film had been screened in New York and rejected by the censors, and Krimsky sailed for New York to defend their property. *Mädchen in Uniform*, adapted from Christa Winsloe's antiauthoritarian play *Yesterday and Today*, deals with the love of a sensitive student named Manuela (Hertha Thiele) for her sympathetic teacher, Fräulein von Bernbourg (Dorothea Wieck), in a Potsdam boarding school for the daughters of poor Prussian officers. Manuela blurts out the news of her forbidden passion in a drunken moment after the school play and is forcefully ostracized by the stern headmistress, who shouts *"ein Scandale!"* and confines Manuela to the school infirmary.

In the stage version, Manuela jumps to her death from the second-floor window of the school. The headmistress, on hearing the news, murmurs serenely, "What an unfortunate accident. We must notify the police at once . . . ," and the curtain falls.

The film was shown in two versions. In most countries, *Mädchen in Uniform* ended with the rescue of Manuela by her classmates as she prepared to leap from a stairwell, a central vortex in the school building that Sagan uses virtually as a character throughout the film, cutting to it ominously from the outset. But, as Margaret Kennedy points out in *The Mechanized Muse*, "the version of *Mädchen in Uniform* shown everywhere on the continent ended with a tortured child leaping from the top of a building to lie, mangled and dead, at the feet of the fiendish headmistress."

The topic of distinctly lesbian affections was certainly present in the story. Winsloe, one of Germany's best known poets, had been the lover of journalist Dorothy Thompson; in 1944 she was murdered in Vichy, France, after a lifetime spent writing about and fighting fascism. *Mädchen in Uniform* attacked conformity and tyranny over people's minds and emotions, using lesbianism as a means of rebelling against authoritarianism just as Lillian Hellman used it in *The Children's Hour* to attack the use of powerful lies as weapons. Yet the lesbianism in *Mädchen in Uniform* is much more basic and certainly more natural than it is in Hellman's melodrama. One of the few films to have an inherently gay sensibility, it is also one of the few to be written, produced and directed by women. Thus the film shows an understanding—missing from most films that touch on lesbian feelings—of the dynamic of women relating to women on their own terms. And just as Lillian Hellman's *The Children's Hour* was first filmed by Hollywood devoid of its original story line, American

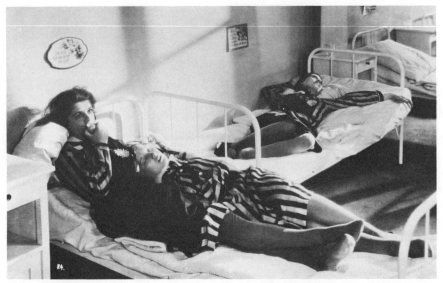

"Many intimate scenes are shown throughout the picture of boarding school life, revealing the prevalence of abnormal relationships"—from the censor's report on Mädchen in Uniform *(1931).*

censors first condemned *Mädchen in Uniform* outright, then accepted a revised version which made the lesbianism a matter of interpretation.

The first written censor's report on *Mädchen in Uniform*, dated May 24, 1932, denied the film a license because "Manuela is saved by her fellow students, most of whom have indulged in this exorbitance or are in sympathy with her repressed desires. Many intimate scenes are shown throughout the picture of boarding school life, revealing the prevalence of abnormal relationships. . . . these, together with the definite story of Manuela's affinity for her teacher, make this picture totally unsuitable for showing in any theater."

When John Krimsky arrived in New York from Paris, he met with representatives of the Hays Office and agreed to certain cuts that would obscure the sexuality of the relationship between Manuela and her teacher. The film was approved in August 1932 with these changes:

Reel four: Eliminate all views of Manuela's face as she looks at Miss von Bernbourg in the classroom.

Reel five: Eliminate line of Manuela's—"In the evening, when you say goodnight to me and go away from my bed and close the door, I must always stare at the door through the darkness and then I would like to get up and come across to you, and yet I am not allowed to. And then I think I will grow older and will have to leave school and that you will remain here and every night you will kiss other children goodnight."

Also eliminated, from a scene in reel nine in which the headmistress calls Manuela's affection a "sin," was Bernbourg's reply, "What you call sins, Principal, I call the great spirit of love, which has thousands of forms." This deletion, a political act, effectively removed any defense of such emotions and thereby perverted the intent of both Winsloe and Sagan.

The word *lesbianism* was hardly spoken in the ensuing controversy. In an interview in the New York *Herald-Tribune* in September 1932, Krimsky said, "I don't believe that there is anything of *The Captive* theme in our picture, for it deals definitely with adolescence. If you're saying it has a *Captive* angle, you're saying that in every girls' school all over the world, *The Captive* theme is present." This unthinkable possibility formed the basis for the newspaper coverage that followed, much of which echoed Krimsky's deliberately twisted view that only homosexuals would find homosexuality in *Mädchen in Uniform*.

Bland Johnson, in the New York *Mirror,* wrote, "Whisperings among the peculiar citizens of our community identified *Mädchen in Uniform* as the celluloid *Well of Loneliness*. So all the mental experimentalists were on hand to see it last night. Ah! but they were surprised. It is a simple, clean, wholesome little tale of schoolgirl crushes." Al Sherman, the motion picture editor of the New York *Telegraph,* said, "There are some who profess to see, in the picture's story, a hint of that neuroticism which forms the basis for *The Captive*. If that is true, then every adoring friendship of a youth for his elder becomes perversion while frantic crushes of adolescent schoolgirls prove no less than a Freudian descent into lesbianism." At last, the word!

But the denial of one of the film's central themes was too easy. After all, the censors, with Krimsky's help, had already eliminated from the film the substantial evidence of lesbianism. *Mädchen in Uniform* is a classic example of how American society has willfully deleted the fact of homosexual behavior from its mind, laundering things as they come along, in order to maintain a more comfortable illusion. The censors removed it; the critics said, "Well, look! It isn't there"; and anyone who still saw it was labeled a pervert. In the late 1970s, John Krimsky continued to control the rights to *Mädchen in Uniform* and would not allow it to be shown in any situation in which it would be advertised as having a lesbian theme, thereby effectively barring it from screenings at lesbian film festivals and other women's events.

There were hints of lesbianism in *Queen Christina* (1933) and distinct lesbian overtones in *Dracula's Daughter* (1936), but they were minimized, and they were noticed and condemned in the press. In the New York *World-Telegram* it was pointed out that Dracula's daughter (Gloria Holden) went around "giving the eye to sweet young girls." Specific reference to such passion, however, was carefully eliminated from films in which it appeared more explicitly. Jacques Duval's *Club des Femmes* (1938), which had a lesbian subplot, was released in America only after the Hays Office had ordered the elimination of some dialogue between Josette Day and Else Argal ("You're so pretty . . . if I were a man, I'd really love you"). Although role reversal was a popular form of comic relief, the real thing was scissored as well from Jean Cocteau's *Blood of a Poet* (1930), from both the spoken titles and the visual representation. The censor's report on *Blood of a Poet* demanded the elimination of the subtitle, "In room 23 there is held a desperate rendezvous of hermaphrodites." It also required the cutting of "the entire representation of a hermaphrodite seated on a couch. Reason: Indecent."

Once the connection between homosexuality and coded references to it was established, the fact of homosexuality had entered, however vaguely, the public consciousness. It was mainly to prevent the focusing and exploration of this awareness that the censors acted. The inspired lunacy of the professional sissies disappeared in the Forties and has never really returned. Sissy characters did not disappear, but the delightful never-never land inhabited by Franklin Pangborn, Grady Sutton, Edward Everett Horton and so many others disappeared like the movies they embellished. The word *innocence* has been used to indicate what was lost in those films.

To be sure, sissies were still used to suggest homosexuality and to serve as yardsticks for the masculinity of the men around them; but the innocence of those who played the roles and those who believed them was lost. Sissies who appeared in the films of the Forties were often victims, at times sophisticated but vaguely sinister outsiders, but no longer familiar members of an old family group. Clifton Webb and George Sanders took up a little of the slack from Pangborn and Horton, yet the entire concept of sissy had become distanced from the humorous and had become just a little deadly. For attitudes toward queerness were shifting because men were going off to war. All male behavior suddenly seemed to be strongly suspect. The fey, harmless image dropped away as people began to realize what Queen Victoria once could not allow—that such creatures did indeed exist after all.

The Way We Weren't

the invisible
years

Dewey Martin gives Kirk Douglas a loving look in Howard Hawks' The Big Sky *(1952).* (British Film Institute)

It's supposed to be about homosexuals,
and you don't even see the boys kiss
each other. What's that?

—Jean Renoir
on Alfred Hitchcock's *Rope*

As for overt homosexuality in pre-1960
films, it was not attempted and not
possible. Sonnets have fourteen lines.
You wrote sonnets then and there was
never an extra or an odd line . . . but
subtexts did occasionally insert
themselves.

—Gore Vidal
on writing for the screen

The first gay meeting which grew into
the gay liberation movement was held in
1950 in someone's apartment in Los Angeles,
and the door was locked and the blinds
were drawn and there was a lookout posted because they
thought it was illegal to talk
about homosexuality.

—Barbara Gittings,
head of the Gay Task Force of
the American Library Association

Hollywood's admittedly casual relationship with the truth protected the American dream from a host of unwanted realities and niggling intrusions. And while lesbians and gay men were often among the architects of that dream, they were never a part of it. It is said that Samuel Goldwyn once suggested filming Radclyffe Hall's notorious *The Well of Loneliness,* only to be informed by a producer that he could not because the leading character was a lesbian. "So what?" Goldwyn retorted. "We'll make her an American." Apocryphal or not, the simplicity of his solution captured the spirit of the truth. It was not as American as apple pie to be queer, and the closeted visions of countless gay screenwriters, directors, actors and technicians were submerged into the

heterosexual, all-American fantasies of the majority. Gay characters and references to the existence of homosexuality were routinely laundered off the screen
for the better part of half a century.

Goldwyn did in fact Americanize lesbianism when he brought Lillian Hellman's *The Children's Hour* to the screen as *These Three* in 1936. Directed
by William Wyler and rewritten for the cameras by Hellman herself, the story
of two teachers accused of lesbianism by a vicious child became, on the screen,
an adulterous heterosexual triangle in which one teacher is accused of being
in love with her best friend's fiancé. The substitution of a problem that Americans
could understand and accept did not violate Hellman's basic theme, that a
lie can have the power to destroy people's lives; it remained only to cover
the play's original tracks. Any mention of the fact that Wyler's *These Three*
had been based on *The Children's Hour* was forbidden by the censors, and
the prohibition was enforced by the studio with the cooperation of the press.
A *Variety* review mentioned that "it is verboten to ballyhoo the original source"
and went on to say that Goldwyn had been very clever to create an entirely
new film from Hellman's thesis. According to Arthur Marx, Goldwyn's biographer, Hellman originally prevailed on Goldwyn to approach the Hays Office
with the idea of lifting the ban on lesbianism if the subject could be treated
tastefully. The reaction, according to Marx, was, "Lesbianism on the screen?
Who ever heard of such a thing? And how could it possibly be done tastefully?"

And so the Americanization of lesbianism meant simply an unwillingness
to deal with it openly, an aping of the American cowardice about sex in general
and the American hypocrisy about sexual deviation in particular. Technically,
homosexuals were just as invisible onscreen as they were in real life. They
continued to emerge, however, as subtextual phantoms representing the very
fear of homosexuality. Serving as alien creatures who were nonetheless firmly
established as part of the culture in every walk of life, they became the darker
side of the American dream. In a society so obsessed with the maintenance
of sex roles and the glorification of all things male, sissies and tomboys served
as yardsticks for what was considered normal behavior. The discomfort that
has consistently arisen in response to "buddy" films springs from the paranoia
and fear that surrounds exclusively male relationships. American society has
always begun at square one, with the belief that men are never attracted to
each other as masculine equals (one of them is always seen as wanting to be
a woman or to act like one). Thus the denial of the existence of homosexuality
did not suppress the national fear of it but instead served to point it up continually. Nor did this denial belie for long the fact of it in history.

In 1933, less than a year before the release of *Queen Christina,* Rouben

Mamoulian's romantic fantasy starring Greta Garbo as the Swedish monarch, Elizabeth Goldsmith published *Christina of Sweden* ("A Psychological Biography"). In reviewing the book and anticipating the film by Mamoulian, Lewis Gannett wrote in the New York *Herald-Tribune,* "The one persistent love of Christina's life was for the Countess Ebba Sparre, a beautiful Swedish noblewoman who lost most of her interest in Christina when Christina ceased to rule Sweden . . . the evidence is overwhelming, but will Miss Garbo play such a Christina?"

Garbo did no such thing, of course, but the collision onscreen of her own androgynous sensibility with the fact of Christina's love for male attire and pursuits gave the film a truth of its own. Garbo, who once expressed to Katharine Cornell her desire to play in a film version of Oscar Wilde's *The Picture of Dorian Gray* with herself in the title role and Marilyn Monroe as a young girl ruined by Dorian, created a particular dynamic in *Queen Christina,* one which penetrated the fundamental deceptions of the script. Her melancholy longings to escape her destiny (marriage) and her deft rejections of a series of male suitors are interrupted in the first half of the film by her encounter with the Countess Ebba Sparre (Elizabeth Young). Their brief scene together is charged with sexuality and real affection, the *only* such display in the film between Garbo and another woman. In that scene Garbo lifts the emotional barriers that characterize her encounters with male suitors. When Ebba bursts into the queen's chamber, the two kiss passionately on the lips. Ebba suggests brightly that they go for a sleighride, but Christina tells her sadly that Parliament awaits and that they will see each other that evening. "Oh, no we won't!" Ebba pouts. "You'll be surrounded by musty old men and musty old papers, and I won't be able to get near you." The Queen caresses her face gently and promises that they will soon go away to the country together "for two whole days."

Later, when pressed by a statesman to marry and produce an heir to the throne, Christina defiantly refuses. "But, your majesty," he cries, "you cannot die an old maid!" Dressed now in men's riding clothes, she pauses at the door and replies, "I have no intention to, Chancellor. I shall die a bachelor!" and she stomps out of the room. The battle between the heroic tomboy and the tortured, doomed queen is sustained throughout the film, and her love affair with Antonio (John Gilbert) does not resolve it. Her need to escape the role assigned her by life was Christina's true driving passion; *Queen Christina* makes this abundantly clear.

Gazing out the window, Christina murmurs, "The snow is like a wild sea. One could go out and be lost on it." She flees into the snow a little later,

Garbo kisses Elizabeth Young good morning in Queen Christina *(1933).*

when she discovers that Ebba Sparre has betrayed her love. That is when she meets Antonio, the one man who seems to accept her and love her for all the things that so horrify her court. He falls in love with her, thinking at first that she is a man, and he seems quite willing to explore whatever this strange situation may bring. In an amusing scene, Antonio's servant enters the bedroom at the inn where Christina and Antonio have spent the night, to find that his master is still in bed with the young "man" with whom he had retired the night before. He takes an order for two morning chocolates and withdraws in astonishment.

When Antonio dies, Christina resolves to ride out on the open sea, to be lost to her former life, as though whatever peace she had to find was yet ahead. Richard Dyer, in *Gays in Film,* points out that gay people, reacting to their isolation from one another and from their heterosexual peers while growing up, could sometimes practice on the cinema what Claude Lévi-Strauss has termed *bricolage,* that is, playing around with the cinematic images offered us so as to bend their meaning to our own purpose. In *Queen Christina,* Garbo tells Gilbert that there is something inside her that will not allow her to rest. "It is possible," she tells him, "to feel nostalgia for a place one has never seen." Similarly, the film *Queen Christina* created in gay people a nostalgia for something they had never seen onscreen.

For the dread general public, however, the illusion remained intact. The important thing about Christina was that she had met the man she loved and had abdicated her throne for him. After *Queen Christina* opened, the

Herald-Tribune asked, "What do facts and theories matter? Christina, to all those who see Garbo's film, will always be the lovely girl who fell in love with the Spanish Ambassador in the snow, and no amount of professional research will ever change her."

Accidents such as the collision of Garbo's chemistry and Christina's stubborn maleness, the kind that produce something more than is in the script, happen rarely, though not as a rule in biographies; the lives of famous lesbians and gay men were altered significantly or were not attempted. The need for invisibility is reflected in the very character of the American experience: heroes may certainly not be homosexual. Real-life gays almost never tampered with the illusions; rather, they subscribed to them. In 1946, Cole Porter and Monty Woolley, lifelong friends but not lovers, created their own dismal myth in Warner Brothers' Technicolor musical "biography" of Porter, *Night and Day*. Porter and his wife Linda, by choosing Cary Grant and Alexis Smith for the title roles, opted for a sophisticated Ozzie and Harriet look while Monty Woolley, playing himself, chose the grand old man of letters motif—pinching the chorus girls and all the rest of the heterosexual repertoire.

The portrayals of noted persons as heterosexual without regard for their true sexuality has never been seen as a serious offense against a person's identity—not even by the person whose life is falsified. No, it is better to be straight. And gays believed that. Films such as *The Agony and the Ecstasy* (1965) and *Khartoum* (1966) reflected the care with which their sources masked or denied the homosexuality of Michelangelo and General Charles Gordon, just as uninspired confections of the Fifties such as *Valentino* (1951), *Hans Christian Andersen* (1952) and *Alexander the Great* (1956) bypassed history for the safe illusions held tightly by the majority.

America's ostentatious fascination with the difference between masculine and feminine behavior and society's absolute terror of queerness, especially in men, continued to be served by the requisite yardstick sissy. Such comedies as *The Warrior's Husband* and *Turnabout* warned of the dangers inherent in mixing the sexes, and sissies flourished in contrast to the screen's real men. Grady Sutton, Kathryn Grayson's Milquetoast suitor in *Anchors Aweigh* (1945), is easily disposed of by all-American sailor boy Gene Kelly. The difference between the sissy and the real man is underscored when Kelly teaches buddy Frank Sinatra how to pick up a girl on the street and in doing so acts out the part of the imaginary female (to the horror of a lone male passerby). The same comic routine that made Sutton famous as a movie sissy here establishes Kelly's virility. It also serves to allay any lurking fears in the minds of the audience about the nature of the relationship between Sinatra and Kelly.

Sinatra's hero worship of Kelly is played so broadly and so repeatedly through-out the film that it is clear he prefers Kelly's company at all times.

Fred MacMurray played the real male specimen to another yardstick sissy in Mitchell Leisen's *No Time for Love* (1943). MacMurray, a rugged coal miner, refers to Paul McGrath, a weak and effeminate composer engaged to Claudette Colbert, as "dollface" and takes the opportunity to show Colbert what a real man is like. The New York *World-Telegram* reported promptly that "McGrath heads the effeminate bunch that MacMurray can lick with one punch." This type of masculine intolerance and hostility toward suspected homosexuality surfaced pointedly in *Up in Arms* (1944), in which two sailors (Dana Andrews and Danny Kaye) sit with their dates on a crowded bus, obscur-ing the two women from the view of the other passengers. Their overheard conversations shock and outrage the crowd, which thinks they are making love to each other.

Open contempt for men who are perceived to be like women was not new. In John Ford's *Three Bad Men* (1926), the grizzly "Bull" (J. Farrell MacDonald) tells a fancy Dan who says he has just reached manhood, "Then you'd better reach again." Essentially the same scene occurs in the "feminist" *Adam's Rib* (1949), in which David Wayne's Kip, a yardstick sissy par excellence, functions as Katharine Hepburn's girlfriend, a high-class Ethel Mertz to her feminist

David Wayne as Kip, the man who "wouldn't have far to go" to be a woman, with Spencer Tracy and Katharine Hepburn in Adam's Rib *(1949). (MGM)*

Lucy Ricardo. Spencer Tracy is clearly uncomfortable with him in spite of Hepburn's defense ("Oh, darling. He's *so* sweet"). Leaving the room after a heated feminist debate, Wayne says to Hepburn, "Amanda, you've convinced me. I might even go out and become a woman!" When Wayne has gone, Spencer Tracy mutters to Hepburn, "Yeah, and he wouldn't have far to go, either." Hepburn's Amanda can only whisper, "Shhh! He'll *hear* you," an indication that her feminism, like that of contemporary feminists who want their sons to grow up to be "real men," goes only so far and breaks down at the thought of actually obscuring sex roles altogether.

The rigid belief in the male role and the intolerance that belief engendered was almost always played on a comic level and seldom emerged in the kind of dead serious hostility shown by the crowd on the bus in *Up in Arms,* who were reacting to the possibility of real homosexuality between two sailors. More often that possibility was denied. In the wartime musical *Star Spangled Rhythm* (1942), Bob Hope, the master of ceremonies of an all-star Navy show, introduces an extended sissy joke. "You know, in these war times, women are taking the place of men in every occupation. In this next scene we're gonna show you how men are replacing women in the home, and we've got four of our manliest men to give you a rough idea." The comedy skit that follows, "If Men Played Cards as Women Do," stars Fred MacMurray, Franchot Tone, Lynne Overman and Ray Milland in a stereotypical ladies' bridge club routine. They gossip, check the host's living room for dust, forget what has been bid and trade recipes until Milland spots a mouse and they all jump onto the table screaming. The scene, a replica of the Grady Sutton tabletop scene in *Movie Crazy,* was almost hysterically defensive about the wartime fate of the masculine image. The homosexual panic, to be repeated endlessly in similar scenes, was on.

Yet there was real danger here. War had brought men together in the buddy system, closer than they had ever been before. The all-male environment of the armed services forced to the surface a confusion about the inherent sexuality between men who preferred each other's company but always chose women to prove their masculinity. The fear that these chaste male relationships might in any way be labeled odd or queer was very real, and the movies assured that no hint of perversion would be introduced into such bonding.

There might have been even less suspicion of homosexuality had the level of paranoia surrounding its mention not been so very high. In 1946, Richard Brooks' novel *The Brick Foxhole* dealt with obsessive masculinity in the military. In it, a homosexual decorator is murdered by a soldier he brings home to his apartment for a drink. Edward Dmytryk's film adaptation, *Crossfire* (1947),

Grady Sutton jumps on top of a table at the sight of a mouse in Movie Crazy *(1932).* (Adam Reilly)

Fred MacMurray, Lynne Overman, Ray Milland and Franchot Tone at the climax of "If Men Played Cards as Women Do," from Star Spangled Rhythm *(1942).* (John Kobal Stills Collection)

made the victim a Jew and thus became an example of Hollywood's maturity in dealing with antisemitism. The *New York Times* noted the change in a review but said only that the motivation for the murder had been changed from that in the novel, "to good advantage." The novel's crucial discussion of men's striking out at what they fear in themselves was omitted. It has yet to be raised onscreen with any real awareness of the magnitude of the problem.

Whenever all-male situations were the subject of the movies, whether they involved cowboys, athletes or soldiers, the dream of the free, perpetually adolescent male in pure and unsullied comradeship fought with the ever present cultural taboo against male intimacy. Peter Pan, after all, was a fairy tale; grown men had real responsibilities that necessarily included growing up and settling down to marriage with a woman. Yet the opening title of Herbert Brenon's *Beau Geste* (1926) spoke of the dream.

> **Love of man for woman waxes and wanes.**
> **Love of brother for brother**
> **is as steadfast as the stars.**

Now if only people wouldn't assume that all those loving brothers were as queer as three-dollar bills, men could hug without having nightmares.

Director Clarence Brown spotted the rub. In his *Flesh and the Devil* (1927), John Gilbert and Lars Hanson play lifelong buddies who separate when one of them marries the woman they both love (Greta Garbo). By the end of the film, Garbo has slept with her husband's friend, precipitating a reluctant duel between the two men. Trying to stop them, she falls through the ice and drowns. At this the men throw down their guns, embrace and walk off into the sunset together, their arms around each other, their bond rejoined following the intrusion of a woman.

Clarence Brown spoke of the situation in an interview. "You can see my problem. How to have the two leading men wind up in each other's arms and not make them look like a couple of fairies?" It was a tough question. The primary buddy relationships in films are those between men who despise homosexuality yet find that their truest and most noble feelings are for each other. There is a misogyny here that goes beyond a simple hatred for women and things feminine. If the truly masculine man hated women—in the sense that he trusted only men as true friends—what then would be his reaction to homosexuals who are perceived to be "like" women yet are in fact male? It would be even more violent, it seems, for gays are the manifestation of what stands between men's complete love of other men and their acceptance of women as friends. Always wary that they might appear too effeminate and

Buddies Lars Hanson and John Gilbert in Clarence Brown's silent film Flesh and the Devil *(1927).* (British Film Institute)

therefore queer (like women), men have never been granted the full emotional potential that they might have had on film. This split is true of heterosexual relationships onscreen as well as potential homosexual relationships, but heterosexuality has not been made invisible because of it while male love has.

Most buddy films involve a group of men going off to fight a war or to conquer a wilderness—men's work, in which a female presence is superfluous but tolerated. In *Test Pilot* (1938), Clark Gable and Spencer Tracy play a pair of buddies who blow each other a ritualistic kiss each time they leave on a mission—for good luck. In William A. Wellman's *Wings* (1927), Richard Arlen and Charles "Buddy" Rogers have a more meaningful relationship with each other than either of them has with Jobyna Ralston or Clara Bow, both

Buddy Rogers and Richard Arlen in a scene from William Wellman's Wings *(1927).* (British Film Institute)

Richard Barthelmess and Cary Grant in Howard Hawks' Only Angels Have Wings *(1939).* (British Film Institute)

token love interests whom male adolescents all over America correctly identified as "the boring parts" of the movie. In fact Arlen and Rogers have the only real love scene in *Wings,* and Rogers learns the true meaning of love through his relationship with his buddy, just as in Howard Hawks' *Only Angels Have Wings* (1939) Cary Grant and Richard Barthelmess find satisfaction only in each other, despite the intrusive presence of Jean Arthur and Rita Hayworth. In *The Big Sky* (1952), it is with profound hesitation and to the ultimate detriment of the film that Kirk Douglas sends Dewey Martin back to his girl after the exciting comradeship they have shared in the great outdoors.

Joan Mellon, in her study of masculinity in the movies, *Big Bad Wolves,* says that the less violent men were in their film personas, the more likely they were to be interested in heterosexual love. Just the opposite has been true for homoeroticism. The perception of homosexual feelings as a brutal, furtive and dangerous force saw it flourish in films of male bonding and violence. Gentle men in the movies—Jimmy Stewart in any "Smalltown, U.S.A." picture or Spencer Tracy in *Father of the Bride,* for example—would never, even subtextually, approach such relationships or feelings. The concept of the gentle man who chooses to love other men does not exist in American film except as slapstick comedy. Stan Laurel and Oliver Hardy had the perfect sissy-buddy relationship throughout their long career, and it is naive now, looking at their films, to assume that they were not aware of and did not consciously use this aspect of their screen relationship to enrich their comedy.

In a film such as *Liberty* (1929), directed by Leo McCarey, the homosexuality emerged in traditionally comic ways, chiefly as farcical misunderstanding. Stan and Ollie have just escaped from prison, and in their haste they have put on each other's trousers. The running joke throughout the first half of the film is that each time they attempt to exchange trousers—in the back seat of a car, behind some crates in an alley, at a construction site—they are discovered by someone who thinks that they have been playing with each other. The French film critic André S. Labarthe maintained that *Liberty* "offers, to anyone who can read, the unequivocal sign of unnatural love." Yet this is the same, safe comic device that was used in Harold Lloyd films, when he found himself holding the hand of another man that he had thought belonged to a woman. But Laurel and Hardy, perhaps because of their adolescent behavior in general, often took such mistakes further than other comics did in their display of natural affection for each other. Their brand of unconscious affection was missing from the often brutal antics of Bud Abbott and Lou Costello or Dean Martin and Jerry Lewis (who were sometimes really cruel to each other).

In the films of Laurel and Hardy, their relationship was given a sweet and very real loving dimension. The two often wound up in bed together, and their wives were almost always portrayed as obstacles to their friendship. In a classic example of this, one with unmistakably gay overtones, they play a married couple complete with newborn baby in *Their First Mistake* (1932), a Hal Roach film directed by George Marshall. Ollie's wife (Mae Busch) complains that he sees too much of Stan and not enough of her, and the two friends discuss the situation.

Stan: Well, what's the matter with her, anyway?
Ollie: Oh, I don't know. She says I think more of you than I do of her.
Stan: Well, you do, don't you?
Ollie: We won't go into *that.*
Stan: You know what the trouble is?
Ollie: What?
Stan: You need a baby in your house.
Ollie: Well, what's that got to do with it?
Stan: Well, if you had a baby . . . it would keep your wife's mind occupied . . . you could go out nights with me . . . and she'd never think anything about it.

So they go out and adopt a baby. When they return home with it, they discover that Ollie's wife is suing him for divorce for "alienation of affections," having named Stan Laurel as "the other woman." The remainder of the film is a beautifully timed and performed domestic scene, with Stan and Ollie in bed and the baby between them. The scene climaxes when Stan reaches into his pajama top—as if reaching for a breast to feed the baby—and comes up with the baby's bottle, which he has been keeping warm.

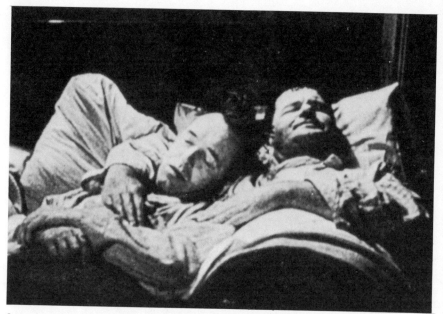

Laurel and Hardy in Their First Mistake *(1932)*. (University of California Press)

All this is charming, sometimes very funny and certainly of no great conse-quence. Yet when one suggests that there may be clues to homosexual behavior in the ways that Laurel and Hardy related to one another, it is as though one were attacking America itself. Charles Barr, in his study *Laurel and Hardy,* says that "there is something rather absurd about discussing this [the homosex-ual nature of *Their First Mistake*] seriously at all." In the often infantile, "pre-sexual" nursery world in which Stan and Ollie lived, Barr argues, such behavior would be "natural."

It is fast becoming evident, however, that there is no such thing as a "pre-sexual" age. Notice, too, that it is the "naturalness" of Laurel and Hardy's behavior that Barr and other critics choose to defend, not the sexuality. The homosexuality is unmistakably there; it remains only for people to say that *in this case* such behavior would be natural to fend off charges of unnaturalness in beloved film figures. And so it is indeed an attack on America itself to suggest that homosexuality is present in the Laurel and Hardy routines. In pointing these things out, one attacks the American illusion—the illusion that there is in fact such a thing as a real man and that to become one is as easy as changing one's name from Marion Morrison to John Wayne. The fact is that comedy has been able to comment on sexual roles more readily than drama could do only because people may dismiss it as impossible farce.

Neglected sissy-buddy relationships exist even in classic cartoons, and a look at Saturday morning television will discover a preponderance of sissy-bully plotlines. Walt Disney may not have liked hearing it, but there are gay overtones in the relationships of more than one pair of beloved animated figures of the classic years. In *Pinocchio* (1940), Honest John and Gideon, a fox and a cat, are best friends who procure lost boys for sale to an evil coachman who takes them to Pleasure Island. They seduce Pinocchio with the hit song "Heigh Diddley Dee" (the second line of which is "Heigh diddley day, an actor's life is gay"), and away he goes—twice.

In *Cinderella* (1950), everyone's favorite mice, Jock and Gus-Gus, volunteer to help finish Cinderella's dress in time for the ball. But they are quickly admonished by a female mouse to "leave the sewing to the women" and told to go find "some trimmin' " for the dress. Their relationship grows through their friendship in dangerous times, and later, when Cinderella describes how she was swept off her feet by the handsome prince, Gus-Gus, sighing evenly, puts an arm around Jock's shoulder and holds him close. After a minute, Jock realizes that they are sitting on a log at the side of the road in each other's arms, and homosexual panic seems to set in on the little fellow. Pulling away quickly, he gives Gus-Gus a quizzical look of wary scrutiny, as if to say, "Hmmm, there's something funny about this mouse." And there was. Just a few years after *Cinderella*, Tom Lee, a shy and sensitive student in *Tea and Sympathy,* would be told much more forcefully to "leave the sewing to the women." Everyone looked at Tom Lee sort of funny—and scratched their heads, too, just like Jock the mouse.

Again, these interpretations arise invariably from the fear of homosexuality, seldom from the fact of it. The expendability of women in buddy films was one reason for that fear. Heterosexual romance was often just a standard plot ingredient, thrown in at regular intervals because it *had* to be there, and

Bugs Bunny encounters a fey Oscar in Slick Hare.

lacking the emotional commitment that the filmmaker failed to give it. The real emotions in the movies, as well as in the movie industry, have always taken place between men. Men have been the important forces at work, both as instigators of all the action in the pictures and as instigators of the films themselves, by deciding what movies should be made and how. Subtexts presented themselves constantly but were left unresolved, just as the women waited around while the boys recreated their adolescent fantasies, unencumbered by an emotional commitment to anything but each other and a good time.

When screenwriter Gore Vidal discussed the script for *Ben-Hur* (1959) with director William Wyler, they concluded that the rivalry between Ben-Hur (Charlton Heston) and his boyhood friend Messala (Stephen Boyd) was insufficiently motivated by a single political scene in which Ben-Hur refuses to aid the Roman cause despite his friend's pleas. Vidal describes the problem.

I proposed the notion that the two had been adolescent lovers and now Messala has returned from Rome wanting to revive the love affair but Ben-Hur does not. He has read Leviticus and knows an abomination when he sees one. I told Wyler, "This is what's going on *underneath* the scene—they *seem* to be talking about politics, but Messala is really trying to rekindle a love affair," and Wyler was startled. We discussed the matter, and then he sighed, "Well. Anything is better than what we've got in the

Francis X. Bushman and Ramon Novarro in the 1926 version of Ben-Hur.

Stephen Boyd and Charlton Heston in the 1959 remake of Ben-Hur.

way of motivation, but don't tell Chuck." I did tell Stephen Boyd, who was fascinated. He agreed to play the frustrated lover. Study his face in the reaction shots in that scene, and you will see that he plays it like a man starving.

It was 1959, and the screen was on the verge of a new freedom. Vidal was saying that it *made sense* that the two men should be attracted to each other. Theirs was the most vibrant and interesting relationship in the film. Wyler later told Vidal, "The biggest mistake we made was the love story. If we had cut out that girl [Haya Harareet] altogether and concentrated on the two guys, everything would have gone better."

Howard Hawks always concentrated on the guys, and in his films things went better—better than in *Ben-Hur,* at least. Dealing almost always with close, dependent, emotional male relationships, his films were informed with a particularly schizophrenic sensibility with regard to maleness and the intrusion of women into its world. His early feature *Fig Leaves* (1926) is typical of the kind of male celebration that saw women as mothers or mattresses and took great care to deny any feminine implication in the closeness of comrades.

In *Fig Leaves,* Adam and Eve are swiftly updated from prehistoric to modern times. Adam, a plumber, complains to his helper that Eve, his wife, has taken up with a fashion designer named André because of her mindless passion for "something to wear," which the film defines as woman's chief problem through the ages. The two men discuss the handling of women ("Treat 'em rough, but don't kill 'em, you might need 'em fer somethin' ") and then take turns acting the part of the wife in order to illustrate various methods of dealing with her. Later they mimic André in the same way they had aped the wife. These sequences resemble the one in *Anchors Aweigh* in which Gene Kelly teaches Frank Sinatra to pick up a girl. Both are contemptuous of women and homosexuals; both see women as normal but only necessary. And, like Sinatra and Kelly in *Anchors Aweigh,* the men in Hawks' buddy films spend an inordinate amount of time preventing each other from actually getting laid or even spending too much time with women. As Sinatra purposely allows Kelly to sleep late and miss his date with Kathryn Grayson, so Robert Armstrong repeatedly starts brawls in order to keep his buddy Victor McLaglen away from the ladies in *A Girl in Every Port* (1928), a film which Hawks called "really a love story between two men." The title could well be ironic; the phrase "a girl in every port," a bravado claim, was almost always used facetiously. No sailor ever had a girl in every port, and every sailor was paranoid about the fellows' finding it out. In Robert Anderson's *Tea and Sympathy,* a study in masculinity, shy Tom Lee discovers that the classmates who taunt him because he has never been with a woman are every bit the virgin he is, only *they* don't need to prove anything and he does because he's not a regular guy. Tom Lee is the one who has to go out and get a whore and make sure everyone hears about it the next day.

In *Red River* (1948), Hawks' only use for Joanne Dru is to have her tell John Wayne and Montgomery Clift what we can already see. "Stop fighting!" she screams in the climactic scene. "You two know you love each other." Yet the nature of that love, despite the Clift screen persona's doing for the young Matthew what Garbo's did for Queen Christina, remained hidden. Probably the most homoerotic sequence in a Hawks film is the musical number "Is There Anyone Here for Love?" that Jane Russell performs in *Gentlemen Prefer Blondes* (1953). Russell is surrounded by muscular men in briefs who seem to be oblivious to her charms ("Doesn't *anyone* wanna play?") but are very interested in showing off their bodies to the choreography of Jack Cole.

The only acknowledgment of the homosexuality in buddy films has come from those critics who attribute the misogynist attitudes of such films to the covert gayness in them. When Joseph McBride and Gerald Peary, in an interview in *Film Comment,* questioned Hawks about "gay undertones" in his ·films, *Red River* in particular, Hawks told them it was "a goddam silly statement to make." And although Glenn Ford remarked in an interview that he and George Macready "knew we were supposed to be playing homosexuals" in *Gilda* (1946), director Charles Vidor laughed, "Really? I didn't know those boys were supposed to be that way!"

Montgomery Clift looks at John Wayne with stars in his eyes in Howard Hawks' Red River (1948).

"I was born the night you met me," Glenn Ford and George Macready in Gilda (1946).

Homosexuality as a viable option has been repressed both in the lives of men and in their work, and it is easy to see how directors could be blind to their own subtexts. The taboo against male intimacy is taken more seriously onscreen than it is in real life. Director Robert Aldrich, whose film *The Choirboys* (1977) deals extensively with the fear of homosexuality in its graphic portrayal of homophobia among the Los Angeles police, recognizes a traditional male reluctance to deal with such things.

That's an American reaction that is very easy to understand. I come from a very extensive athletic background, and I think that nobody examines that closeness in totally male groups put under any kind of pressure, whether it's war or athletics or the way the police must depend on each other daily for their lives. They don't examine what goes on between them, and then later, when they belatedly discover that there may be subliminal reasons, it frightens them, they resent it. They don't understand it, and it's not easy to face. The hardhat reaction is that if *this* was the emotional peak of their lives, they don't want it distilled by revisionist thinking. They can't afford the truth later, so they say, "Oh, no. That's not what I meant at all."

When buddy films returned in the late Sixties, the presence onscreen of homosexual characters was a perfect way of saying, Oh, no, this isn't what we mean at all. Homosexuals drew suspicion away from the buddies—it was yardstick time again. In John Schlesinger's *Midnight Cowboy* (1969), the relationship between Joe Buck (Jon Voight) and Ratso Rizzo (Dustin Hoffman) is lily pure. Their contempt for faggots and faggot behavior is well established in the course of their growing buddyhood and justified by the behavior of the "real" homosexuals in the film. When Joe Buck hustles a desperate-looking student (Bob Balaban) in the balcony of a Times Square movie house, we are being shown how pathetic such creatures are. The student, who has no money, ends up vomiting in the men's toilet in self-disgust and fear of retaliation.

When Joe hustles another pitiable spectre of the night, an aging, guilt-ridden Catholic (Barnard Hughes), the incident ends in violence and more self-hatred. As Joe is beating him, the old man mutters to himself, "I deserve this. I brought this about myself, I know I did. Oh! How I loathe life!" Joe's naivete and wholesomeness is contrasted with his seedy surroundings, and the film makes it clear who are the villains and who the innocent victim. The audience's sympathy is all for the virginal young man innocently drawn into the big-city web as he tries to raise the money to take his dying friend to Florida.

In an August 1979 interview in *Playgirl* magazine, Dustin Hoffman told how he thought the characters of Joe and Ratso would both hate blacks, being white trash from Texas and Italian white trash from the Bronx. In a restaurant scene, Hoffman suggested to Schlesinger, a black guy should come in and the two move away muttering "scum bags" or "niggers." Schlesinger replied, "My God, we're trying to get people to like Joe and Ratso. We'll lose every liberal in the audience." Instead, Ratso is vocally bigoted against gays in that scene, muttering "faggot" when a Times Square queen walks in.

Ratso delivers a devastating criticism when he attacks Joe's cowboy outfit and calls into question the innocence of this ultimate masculine ideal, one that had dominated the American screen in its formative years. "If you wanna know the truth," he shouts, "that stuff is strictly for faggots! That's faggot stuff." Wounded and confused, Joe shoots back in defense, "John Wayne! You're gonna tell me that John Wayne's a fag?"

This defines the fear. If there is no real difference between the cowboy hero and the faggot on Forty-second Street, then what remains of American masculinity? This scene comes closest to saying that the costume is only an image, as much a lie as all the other ways in which we force the movies to serve our dreams of an America that never really existed. To preserve a shred of "real" manhood becomes the goal of buddy characters, both in spite of their true feelings and because of them.

Joe Buck's reaction to the charge that his cowboy suit makes him a faggot was also the reaction of many critics when such films as *Butch Cassidy and the Sundance Kid* (1969), *The Wild Rovers* (1971) and *Zachariah* (1971) re-created the old tensions characteristic of films about exclusively male relationships. After all, who remembers Katharine Ross from *Butch Cassidy and the Sundance Kid*? In an interview, Paul Newman's wife, actress Joanne Woodward,

"Paul and Bob do *have a chemistry."* Joanne Woodward on Butch Cassidy and the Sundance Kid *(1969).*

Ryan O'Neal gets a piggyback ride from William Holden in The Wild Rovers *(1971).*

Buddy behavior is suspect. The National Lampoon
satirizes Michael Ritchie's buddy film Semi-Tough
(1977). (From the *National Lampoon Sunday Newspaper Parody.* Copyright 1978, National Lampoon, Inc.
Reprinted by permission.)

joked that "Bob [Redford] and Paul really *do* have a chemistry. Some day
they'll run off together and I'll be left behind with Lola Redford."

The male reaction was less whimsical and more phobic. The critic Richard
Schickel, who has consistently used the words *fag* and *dyke* pejoratively in
his reviews, refused to accept Joe Buck's relationship with Ratso Rizzo in
Midnight Cowboy as anything but a sham—and for all the wrong reasons.
He did not say that the film contained unconscious homosexuality, he said
that it was very conscious, as though the screenwriter and the director were
trying to put something over on an unsuspecting public.

It just doesn't work. One could accept mutually exploitative, explicitly stated faggery.
Trained the hard way in human misuse, one could imagine them using each other ill
in their agony. To what, however, can we attribute the pretty impulse that overtakes
them, converting them from dull louts (whom we have been encouraged to laugh at
most of the time) into tender comrades? How are we to accept the delicate suggestion
that if we will only look more closely at the top of the dung heap . . . we will find a
dear romantic pansy flowering there? Only as a fake, I fear.

Fear was the correct word. Schickel was afraid of the same thing that Joe
Buck and Ratso Rizzo were trying so hard to deny, that real men could have

a real romance. "It is not the hard truths that are difficult to take," Schickel wrote, "but the sweet nothings it disingenuously whispers in our ear that finally repel us."

To make matters worse, it was just about this time (1969) that gay men, themselves buyers of the American dream, rejected the sissy confessions of *The Boys in the Band,* opting for the macho drag of Joe Buck instead of fuzzy sweaters and teased hair, in order to prove that homosexual men could be just as butch as anyone else. (Which is true, of course, but why bother?) Instead of recognizing and destroying the worn-out myth of the real man, faggots adopted the solution of the traditional male. Just as Marion Morrison changed his name to John Wayne, they jumped on the bandwagon and became part of the parade. Throughout the Seventies the super-macho look was a dead giveaway for homosexuality. Straight men stopped wearing jeans and plaid shirts (for the battle lines had to be clearly drawn). As Archie Bunker said several times, "Jeez, I can't even tell the difference no more between boys and girls."

The fear of legitimate romantic relationships between men surfaced again in Jerry Schatzberg's *Scarecrow* (1973) and John Boorman's *Deliverance* (1972). The relentless naivete of buddies in the films of the Forties and Fifties was perhaps understandable, but in the excessive Seventies, when the love that dared not speak its name was becoming the lifestyle that didn't know

Four all-American men encounter unexpected difficulties on a trip down the rapids in John Boorman's Deliverance *(1972).*

when to shut up, it was a fairly ludicrous spectacle. When the brutally depicted homosexual rapes in buddy films of the 1970s invaded the world of our cheerful adolescent heroes, they were *shocked* to find that such acts could be performed. The mountain men who sexually abuse Ned Beatty in *Deliverance* are the savage, pre-civilized evocation of dark emotions that are alien to normal men and are locked away deep within our heroes at the start of their Huck Finn journey down the rapids. Where in most buddy films we have the label of homosexuality but not the fact of it, in *Deliverance* the reverse is true. An act that can be categorized as homosexual is performed on our lily-white all-Americans by persons who are not in fact gay characters but throwbacks to the pioneering mountain men of early America who saw pink and white city boys as reflective of the pansy life that caused homosexuality. The defilement of Ned Beatty's masculinity in a brutal act of forced sodomy has the effect of defiling the purity of the group's comradeship, which had been innocent of sexual relating. Thus Boorman's men were forced to consider homosexuality in spite of the taboo against discussing such a thing.

On the other hand, the brief homosexuality depicted in *Scarecrow* adds no insight or new awareness to the film. The joyous relationship between Al Pacino and Gene Hackman is only momentarily shattered by the intrusion of the "degenerate" prisoner (Richard Lynch) who tries (and fails, of course) to rape Al Pacino. Both Pacino and Hackman are baffled, as though neither had ever considered the possibility of such a thing's happening, though both, according to the script, had been to prison before. Well, there may have been lots of lesbianism in women's prison films, but there was no homosexuality at all in the Pat O'Brien and Humphrey Bogart prison films they saw as kids.

Stephen Farber, in his *New York Times* review of *Scarecrow* ("Just a Locker Room Fantasy"), said Pacino and Hackman's emotional reactions were an evasion of the most obvious implications of the film's theme. "The filmmakers," he wrote, "want to make absolutely certain that the audience won't mistake Al Pacino or Gene Hackman for a homosexual. Perhaps they protest too much."

For a while, protesting too much seemed to be the very subject of certain buddy films, including Michael Cimino's *Thunderbolt and Lightfoot* (1974), Robert Aldrich's *The Choirboys* (1977) and George Roy Hill's *Slap Shot* (1977), all of which employ a notable amount of open hostility, some of it unbelievably vicious, as a defense against the suspicion of homosexuality among their male characters. In *Thunderbolt and Lightfoot*, Cimino does a Ratso-and-Joe number on Jeff Bridges and Clint Eastwood, the same number he did later on Robert De Niro and Christopher Walken in *The Deer Hunter* (1978). At the beginning

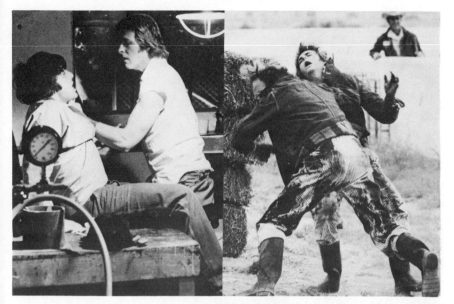

VIOLENCE ERUPTS behind prison walls when a degenerate prisoner played by Richard Lynch beats a fellow prisoner (Al Pacino) senseless, only to be brutally beaten in retribution by his victim's friend, played by Gene Hackman, in Warner Bros.' "Scarecrow," directed by Jerry Schatzberg and produced by Robert M. Sherman from a screenplay by Garry Michael White.

Printed in U.S.A.   COPYRIGHT © 1973 BY WARNER BROS. INC.   COMP L

Richard Lynch tries to rape Al Pacino and is beaten by Pacino's buddy Gene Hackman in Scarecrow *(1973). Note that the publicity refers to Lynch as a degenerate.*

of *Thunderbolt and Lightfoot,* Eastwood's baby blue eyes hit Bridges like a thunderbolt, and Bridges promptly lightfoots it into drag for the remainder of the film. Bridges is made to say to Eastwood such things as, "We've got to stop meeting like this, you know. After all, where there's smoke, there's fire."

This film is all smoke. Lightfoot, like Ratso, dies in the arms of his buddy, thereby preserving the purity of their unconsummated affair. In his review ("Tightass and Cocksucker") in the film newspaper *Jump Cut,* Peter Biskind shared Richard Schickel's homophobia and attributed the misogynist attitudes in *Thunderbolt and Lightfoot* not to the tiresome conventions of a misogynist genre but to the latent homosexual sensibility of the film. Biskind wrote that *Thunderbolt and Lightfoot* displayed "a frank and undisguised contempt for heterosexuality" and exploited "homosexual and working class attitudes towards women"—which he blithely assumed to be the same (all homosexuals hate women). Biskind's thinking is no different from Schickel's when he describes the "sentimentalization of homosexual passion" with which he says the film "humiliates and degrades heterosexual couples." Lightfoot must die, Biskind says, "because homosexual male love is still taboo, because society will not permit the consummation the film strains to achieve."

Exactly the opposite is true; the latent homosexuality in *Thunderbolt and Lightfoot* is itself misogynist, and it is the consummation of the love between

Jeff Bridges is all dressed up in Thunderbolt and Lightfoot *(1974), a movie for which he received an Oscar nomination.* (British Film Institute)

Eastwood and Bridges that the film strains *not* to achieve. Lightfoot's death is the only way to avoid it, just as, if Ratso Rizzo had not died on the bus to Florida, he and Joe would have lived happily ever after—and who would stand for that? Again, homosexuals—invisible in fact but not in theory—take the rap for the heterosexist woman-hating attitudes that permeate buddy films and characterize the attitudes of heterosexuals toward both gays and women, whom they consider indistinguishable.

Alan Parker's sensational screen version of *Midnight Express* (1978) went so far as to take an actual homosexual relationship from the Billy Hayes novel about his Turkish prison experience and "buddyize" it by going to great lengths to say, once again, "this is not what we mean." In a tenderly lit shower scene reminiscent of the woodsy setting served up by a rococo Vincente Minnelli for Tom Lee's seduction in *Tea and Sympathy,* Billy Hayes' close encounter occurs with all the solemnity of a church service. When Hayes (Brad Davis) gently but firmly rejects the loving caresses of his fellow prisoner in a gesture tender yet masculine, director Parker shows his audience that although our hero would bite out another man's tongue and spit it into the air in a spray of blood (something the real Billy Hayes did not do), he certainly would not stoop to loving another man (something the real Billy Hayes did do). And yet what homosexuality there was in the film eventually took the rap once again. Richard Schickel, writing in *Time* magazine, attacked the film for its romantic homosexual sensibility and the pretty way in which it was presented; at the same time, American audiences were cheering the film's violence and yelling "gross!" and "disgusting!" during the shower scene.

In an interview in New York's *Soho Weekly News,* the real Billy Hayes said, "I'm very happy that maybe somebody in the midwest who is freaked out by the very idea of homosexuality can look at that scene and feel the delicacy of it . . . after all, it's only love." Hayes would have opted for innuendo over invisibility, but he was overruled by Parker. "I wish," Hayes said, "that they'd let the steam in the shower come up and obscure the act itself instead of showing a rejection." Alan Parker, in the same interview, commented that a rejection was exactly what he wanted. "As a boring heterosexual director," Parker said, "I could approach that scene in the only way I knew how . . . it's the difference between being able to touch and not being able to touch." Yet in the scene in which Billy masturbates at the sight of his visiting girlfriend's breasts on the other side of a glass partition, they are unable to touch. The glass, installed by prison officials, presumably exists in real prisons. In the shower scene, however, it is Parker who erects the barrier in recognition of the fact that there was something that audiences did not want to see. "It was the clearest way," Parker said, "of showing the audience that he was not a homosexual."

All there was for Brad Davis and Nor-bert Weisser was to exercise a little foreplay in Midnight Express *(1978).*

In 1980 Parker did it again in *Fame,* a film about New York's High School of the.Performing Arts in which everyone is romantically involved or content with their work except the sad, frustrated, lone gay student played by Paul McCrane, who is the butt of the film's fag jokes.

The same defensive posturing exists in what might be termed lesbian buddy films. The post-*Alice Doesn't Live Here Anymore* "feminist" films that discovered that women could be friends almost always included a specific scene that made it clear that no sexual hanky-panky was implied. Claudia Weill's *Girlfriends* (1978) uses a lesbian roommate of Melanie Mayron as a way of saying that the friendship between Mayron and her best friend was not sexual. The "real" lesbian is there as an object lesson, another one of the drawbacks for single women living alone in New York, like cockroaches and drunks on the street. She moans and moons over Mayron until she is asked to leave.

A similar situation occurs in the distinctly non-feminist film *Sheila Levine Is Dead and Living in New York* (1975), directed by Sidney J. Furie. Sheila keeps meeting a pathetic, predatory lesbian in the elevator of her apartment building; finally, in hopes of getting rid of her, she jokingly tells the lesbian that she has a roommate who is just crazy about lesbians. It isn't true, of

Jane Fonda punches out John Glover when he dares to suggest that her relationship with Vanessa Redgrave in Julia *(1977) was a sexual one.*

course. It's just a practical joke on Sheila's roommate and a cruel one on the lesbian. The most violent defense of the purity of a female friendship onscreen occurs in *Julia* (1977), when John Glover indelicately suggests that Hellman and Julia have been sexually involved. For this insult Jane Fonda delivers a knockout punch that expresses more anger than she showed at the Nazi threat.

Comics and buffoons could get away with transvestism, double entendre and sexual ambiguity, but the heroes could not. As Andrew Sarris pointed out, in an article in the *Village Voice* on sex roles in film, it was always "the pretty boy leading men" in films who were "most vulnerable to snickers about their masculinity." However, Sarris also suggested that when actors went too far in role reversal, "crossing over into the domain of The Other," they deserved to be snickered at, that only those who got away with their masculinity intact had in fact pulled it off and were therefore worthy of praise. He characterized the female impersonations of the sound era—as opposed to the harmless essays of the silents—as "grimly defiant role reversals." This suggests that the men who performed them were in fact betraying something. The Ritz Brothers, Sarris says, were such professional sissies in the sound era that they "dishonored the Three Musketeers for all time." To what stage have we come if we must defend the masculine image of the Three Musketeers?

And so there is no discernible male homosexuality in the prison films of Cagney and Bogart because the hero cannot be sullied by such dangers. If affection between women in prison spills over into playful sexuality, so much the better for the male viewer. But men onscreen had to be constructed so that they could maintain important illusions about masculinity. Sissy comics—or, in the Sixties and Seventies, sissy scapegoats—were employed to protect heroism from defamation. In *The Choirboys* and *Slap Shot,* the same mechanism serves to exorcise homosexuality. The use of the words *cocksucker* and *faggot* by police and athletes in both films is ritualistic. (They are the same words the young toughs in *Rebel Without a Cause* might have used to accuse Sal Mineo's Plato if the Fifties had permitted such language.) Here the open use of such words serves as talisman against real homosexuality or the suspicion of it. *Slap Shot* screenwriter Nancy Dowd sees the vicious homophobia of her hockey players as an evil eye. "The proximity of the players is so much more intense than is usual for most men," she says, "that yelling 'faggot' at someone dispels the fear of having to admit the homoeroticism of their situation. They act like raging homophobes because they're constantly all over each other and can't admit that what they feel is love."

The physical expression of the love whose name nobody spoke cast a shadow over all feeling between men. In *The Choirboys* (1977), gays are talismans, fools or victims. The word *faggot* is a catchall, used for any candy-ass or homosexual. The gays in *The Choirboys* are MacArthur Park (Los Angeles) cruisers in the same way that *Midnight Cowboy*'s real items are Times Square cruisers, to be distinguished from Joe and Ratso. One aging queen in *The Choirboys* comes complete with pink poodle; stumbling on the naked policeman Tim McIntyre, who has been chained to a tree and abandoned by his buddies as a joke, the sissy does a Beulah Bondi routine, exclaiming in *Snake Pit* fashion, "Oh, my! A naked man chained to a tree! Am I dreaming?" He then becomes the target of a string of obscenities and promptly disappears from the film.

The other homosexual character in *The Choirboys* is an interesting one. A youngster of perhaps high school age, obviously confused and guilt-ridden about his sexuality, he cruises the park at night, apparently in terror of being caught. An affecting scene between the youth (Michael Wills) and a police sergeant (Burt Young) reveals both tolerance and confusion toward the evidence of homosexuality in so obviously normal a young man. Like an embarrassed father explaining sex to a young child, Young confesses, "Look, kid. This isn't something I understand. Do you promise me that if I let you go you won't

A faggot with a pink poodle stumbles on a naked cop chained to a tree in The Choirboys *(1977).*

do it again?" Do *it* again—the act becomes the orientation and vice versa. Homosexuality is something you "do" in the dark and like a bad habit, it can be broken. At the end of the film this same young man gets an accidental bullet through the head when he impulsively tries to aid a policeman who is having a nightmare about the war in Vietnam and instead becomes the target of the cop's delirium. Again, it is the classic formula: homosexual subculture equals violence. If the kid had not been cruising in the park, as the kindly old sergeant had warned him, he would not have been killed. Violence comes with the territory—that point is stressed so often and exaggerated so far out of proportion to any other aspect of gay life that its inclusion in the script of the film version of Gerald Walker's *Cruising* brought a storm of protest and rioting by gays in New York at the end of 1979.

Sometimes buddy relationships arose directly from an effort to avoid specific textual homoeroticism. Lewis John Carlino's original script for *The Mechanic* (1972), a film about an aging professional killer and his young apprentice, specified a homosexual relationship between the two male leads. The roles were summarily turned down by several actors, including George C. Scott, and the film ran into difficulty in its attempts to raise money until the overt homosexuality was deleted from the script. Charles Bronson and Jan-Michael Vincent finally agreed to star in the film if the sexual nature of the relationship was omitted. Sexual tension remained, however, especially in scenes in which the young apprentice first meets the killer and his hero worship becomes positively coquettish. Carlino described his feelings about the film.

The Mechanic is one of the major disappointments of my life. Originally it was a homosexual love affair between these two men. I wanted a commentary on the use of human relationships and sexual manipulation in the lives of two hired killers. It was supposed to be a chess game between the older assassin and his young apprentice. The younger man sees that he can use his sexuality to find the Achilles heel that he needs to win. There was a fascinating edge to it, though, because toward the end the younger man began to fall in love, and this fought with his desire to beat the master and take his place as number one.

Nobody would touch it. Actors wouldn't do it. They loved the story, but they wouldn't do the love scenes. It was very frightening to them. There's no way that people like George C. Scott or Charles Bronson are going to take chances like that. The picture was supposed to be a real investigation into this situation, and it turned into a pseudo James Bond film.

What was not omitted from *The Mechanic* and films like it was the sexual dynamic, which caused such critics as Vincent Canby of the *New York Times* to recognize that something more than simple male bonding was involved.

People say that there can be no such thing as a "gay sensibility" because the existence of one would mean that there is a straight sensibility, and clearly there is not. But a gay sensibility can be many things; it can be present even when there is no sign of homosexuality, open or covert, before or behind the camera. Gay sensibility is largely a product of oppression, of the necessity to hide so well for so long. It is a ghetto sensibility, born of the need to develop and use a second sight that will translate silently what the world sees and what the actuality may be. It was gay sensibility that, for example, often enabled some lesbians and gay men to see at very early ages, even before they knew the words for what they were, something on the screen that they knew related to their lives in some way, without being able to put a finger on it. Often it was the simple recognition of difference, the sudden understanding that something was altered or not what it should be, perhaps the role reversal of a Dietrich or a Garbo evoking a hidden truth about the nature of sexuality in general. Or it may have been the tone in James Dean's voice as he zipped up the jacket of the dead Sal Mineo in *Rebel Without a Cause* and muttered, "Poor kid . . . he was always cold." It was the sense of longing that existed in such scenes, the unspoken, forbidden feelings that were always present, always denied. It said, this has something to do with your life, and it was a voice that could not be ignored, even though the pieces did not fall into place until years later.

With no "real" homosexuals allowed onscreen in the Forties and Fifties, censors often looked for hidden meanings. Sometimes they found them even when the real thing was abundantly clear. While on the lookout for overt references to stereotypical homosexuality, censors missed the ephemeral emotional commitments to the kind of male bonding that had characterized couples since *Wings*. In Alfred Hitchcock's *Rope* (1948), Farley Granger and John Dall are the pretentious homosexual lovers who on a whim murder a former prep school classmate, believing themselves of superior intellect and not morally responsible to a crass society. It was the inconsequential dialogue rather than the specific relationship that caught the censor's eye. Arthur Laurents recalls that when he finished his screenplay for *Rope* he left England for New York, and while he was in America, the script was passed on by American censors. "*Rope* came from an English play called *Rope's End,*" Laurents explains, "and while I was in New York, the producer Sidney Bernstein took a few passages from the play and put them back into the script. So when it came back from the Hays Office, every one of those passages was circled, with the comment "homosexual dialogue" written in the margin. And do you know what they were? It was simply that they were saying things like 'My dear boy' to each

James Stewart confronts John Dall and Farley Granger with the evidence in Rope *(1948).*

"The most excitement-filled love story ever told" was about two homosexuals.

other, and the way the English talked was known as 'fruity' over here."

There were other, more covert homosexual relationships in Hitchcock films, among them that of Martin Landau and James Mason in *North by Northwest* (1959) and, more striking, Robert Walker and Farley Granger in *Strangers on a Train* (1951). But the director seldom commented on such aspects of his work. "We never discussed, Hitch and I, whether the characters in *Rope* were homosexuals," Laurents says, "but I thought it was apparent."

I guess he did, too, but it never came up until we got to casting. We'd wanted Cary Grant for the teacher and Montgomery Clift for one of the boys, and they both turned it down for the same reason—their image. They felt they couldn't risk it. Eventually John Dall and Farley Granger played the boys, and they were very aware of what they were doing. Jimmy Stewart, however, who played the teacher, wasn't at all. And if you asked Hitchcock, he'd tell you it isn't there, knowing perfectly well that it is. He was interested in perverse sexuality of any kind, and he used it for dramatic tension. But being a strong Catholic, he probably thought it was wrong. The homosexuality between the two men, after all, in *Strangers on a Train*, isn't in the script, yet it's there. Farley Granger told me once that it was Robert Walker's idea to play Bruno Anthony as a homosexual.

Walker's choice was particularly exciting in terms of the plot. The tension it created between his malignantly fey Bruno and Granger's golly gee tennis player, Guy Haines, heightened the bizarre nature of their pact. Bruno would kill Guy's unwanted wife, and in exchange Guy would murder Bruno's hated father. Bruno's homosexuality emerged in terms that would be used increasingly throughout the Fifties to define gays as aliens. His coldness, his perverse imagination and an edge of elitist superiority made him an extension of the sophisticated but deadly sissy played by Clifton Webb in *Laura*, Peter Lorre in *The Maltese Falcon* and Martin Landau in *North by Northwest*. A Bruno Anthony is what Hitchcock might have made of George Sanders' suave but lethal Addison DeWitt in *All About Eve* (1950), a Fifties film with another subliminally gay character, Eve Harrington. According to Ken Geist in his biography of Joe Mankiewicz, the character of Eve Harrington as played by Anne Baxter was conceived as a lesbian, a predilection only subtly suggested in a scene with Eve's boardinghouse roommate and again at the end of the film, when she impulsively invites an adoring young fan to spend the night with her. She is, of course, being taken in by a creature very much like herself.

Philip and Brandon, the lovers in *Rope*, were warped individuals who murdered out of a belief in their own moral and intellectual superiority, which they believed placed them outside the law. By existing outside the culture, such gays were able to deny explicit homosexuality while at the same time

Farley Granger is seduced by Robert Walker in Alfred Hitchcock's Strangers on a Train *(1951).*

Two of a kind: Anne Baxter and George Sanders in All About Eve *(1950).*

reinforcing specific stereotypes. This is how Oscar Wilde's *The Picture of Dorian Gray* could reach the screen in 1945, shorn of its more bizarre sexual implications while offering George Sanders ("I choose *all* of my friends for their good looks") as a symbol of sophisticated decadence. Such ghettoized characters presaged the gay-as-alien images of the 1950s and had their roots in the same anti-intellectualism and mistrust of difference that had characterized the shaping of Hollywood's image of the normal American man. In Frank Capra and Robert Riskin's original script for *It Happened One Night* (1934), for example, the character eventually played by Clark Gable was originally a Greenwich Village artist. According to Capra's autobiography, *The Name Above the Title,* nobody liked the Gable character until writer Myles Connolly said, "He must be one of *us.* Forget that pantywaist painter and make him a guy we all know and like."

The view of the homosexual as being alien to his own society was also present in the constant deletion of specific homosexuality from the screen adaptations of literary works in the Forties. In 1945, Billy Wilder brought Charles Jackson's novel *The Lost Weekend* to the screen with Ray Milland as the alcoholic writer Don Birnam. In Jackson's novel, Birnam's alcoholism stems from a complex variety of reasons that includes a father fixation and a false accusation of his having had a homosexual relationship with a college fraternity brother. (Other Jackson books had had gay themes; a subplot in *The Fall of Valor* involved a marine and a married man.) In Wilder's version of *The Lost Weekend,* however, the motivation for Birnam's drinking became a simple case of writer's block. Seemingly a victim of the same problems that would later beset Tom Lee in *Tea and Sympathy,* Jackson's Don Birnam is also "saved" by the love of a good woman. But in the film, Jane Wyman saves Ray Milland from his alcoholism, not from the cause of it. Paramount studio boss Buddy DeSylva stated the reason for the script changes: "If the drunk isn't an extremely attractive fellow who, apart from being a drunk, could be a hell of a nice guy, the audiences won't go for it."

Thus Milland's Don Birnam became as simplistically one dimensional as Hurd Hatfield's stoic Dorian Gray. Indeed, two little old ladies shopping on Third Avenue in *The Lost Weekend* point to Birnam on the street and cluck sympathetically, "Oh, there's that *nice* young man who drinks." But Birnam also becomes coyly and cruelly entertaining when drunk, and Milland's mannerisms suggest vaguely that his whispered problem might be rooted in greater psychological depths than the typewriter he keeps in his closet would indicate. A further hint that his closet might contain more than a typewriter comes with his mocking proposal of marriage to Nat the bartender. On being rebuked for his perversity, he says feyly, "Now, Nat. One more word and I shall have to consult our lawyer about a divorce." The scene is all the more disquieting when the viewer recognizes Milland's sissy voice from "If Men Played Cards as Women Do" in *Star Spangled Rhythm.*

An undertone of unnaturalness is retained in the film through Frank Faylen's caustic, sneering portrait of Bim, the male nurse who attends Birnam in the drunk tank during his delirium. Bim is lewdly homosexual and terrorizes Birnam with ambiguous suggestion. "Good morning, Mary Sunshine!" he intones sarcastically when they meet. "I'm a nurse. Name of Nolan, but my friends call me Bim. *You* can call me Bim." He asks for "honeyboy's name" so that he can notify the folks, and he takes the time to lovingly remind Birnam that "delirium is the disease of the night" before departing the darkened ward with a too sweet "good night." The inspired gothic innuendo of Faylen's performance left little doubt as to what Jane Wyman was really saving the hero from, and it was not writer's block.

The suppression of homosexuality, or the incorporation of it as something alien and sinister, plus the emotional tension created by the all-male dynamic in buddy films influenced homoerotic ideas and longings that achieved expression on the screen. Some repressed homosexual dreams and fantasies found that expression in underground film, where a scant measure of the gay subculture was reflected. In 1947, Kenneth Anger's *Fireworks* and Jean Genet's *Un Chant d'Amour* exposed two dazzlingly different visions of repressed homosexual desires, thwarted in real life and painfully exorcised onscreen. Anger, a high school student who had grown up on Hollywood's sanitized images, filled *Fireworks* with his hidden fantasies, complete with the bald sexuality inherent

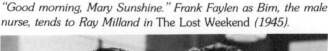

"Good morning, Mary Sunshine." Frank Faylen as Bim, the male nurse, tends to Ray Milland in The Lost Weekend *(1945).*

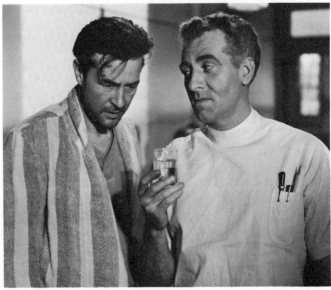

in the images of cowboys, test pilots and, in this case, sailors, images that dominated the dreams of millions. In a prologue to the film, Anger wrote:

In *Fireworks* I released all the explosive pyrotechnics of a dream. Inflammable desires dampened by day under the cold water of consciousness are ignited that night by the libertarian matches of sleep and burst forth in showers of shimmering incandescence. These imaginary displays provide a temporary release.

Anger dared to film one of his own wet dreams, and it brought the release of shattered silence, exposing illusions for the relative few who saw his work. The release from illusion as well as the necessity of that illusion is the subject of Genet's *Un Chant d'Amour*. In this case the need for fantasy grows from the cravings of men trapped in prison cells and driven to furtive homoerotic liaisons that desperately attempt to approximate tenderness and affection. Plaintive images of hands reaching through cell windows for symbolic union clash furiously with sadomasochistic visions of guards using dominance, submission, masturbatory fantasy and sex as power to get a little contact. *Fireworks* and *Un Chant d'Amour* are unforgettable reactions to the restrictions placed on the male role in society, told almost in pleading terms, on behalf of a subculture filled with unrequited passion and social despair. The films belied the half-truths of the commercial cinema and gave the secret dreams of a hidden minority a small, avant-garde voice. It was a large wilderness, however, and *Un Chant d'Amour* and *Fireworks* are rarely seen even today outside large cities with film forums and art theaters.

The secret signals and hidden signs of homosexuality in Hollywood features were the only frames of reference for most gays, who learned about themselves chiefly from movies that said that the whole world was heterosexual. The Mariposa Film Group's documentary *Word Is Out* (1977) shows that, as a result of this silence, most gays across America believed that they were the only ones in the world. Years later, *Fireworks* would help to pave the way for the legitimization of homosexual subject matter onscreen when Supreme Court decisions involving the film's exhibition pronounced it not obscene in spite of its homosexual material. But in the early and middle 1950s, the invisibility of homosexuality was enforced with an almost fanatical paranoia.

One line of dialogue in Betty Comden and Adolph Green's screenplay for *Singin' in the Rain* (1952) was penciled out by the censors because it gave "a hint of sexual perversion" between Donald O'Connor and Gene Kelly. When O'Connor gets the idea of dubbing the voice of Debbie Reynolds for the high-pitched, tinny voice of Jean Hagen in a proposed musical, *The Dancing Cavalier,* he illustrates his idea for Kelly by standing in front of Reynolds and mouthing the words to "Good Morning" while she sings behind him. When the song is over, O'Connor turns to Kelly and asks, "Well? Convincing?" Kelly, not yet catching on, takes it as a joke and replies, "Enchanting! What are you doing later?" The joke was eliminated.

The censor's notation on a scene from the film *Everybody's Girl* (1951) involved a similar reaction.

Eliminate the underlined in Reel One between showgirl and producer:

Producer: Did you ever have a fairy godfather?
Showgirl: No. But I have an uncle in Chicago we're not too sure about.

Pop psychoanalysis was rampant in the Forties and Fifties, and gays were increasingly being defined in psychiatric jargon both onscreen and off. Suddenly people began talking about dominant mothers and weak, passive fathers. The perversity of the outsider, the oddball or the alien screen character was very noticeable in an era of rigid conformity such as the 1950s. The equation between being different in any way and being homosexual was easy to see.

In Leo McCarey's *My Son John* (1952), Dean Jagger and Helen Hayes play the distraught parents of a young Communist agent (Robert Walker). When their suspicions about their son's activities are confirmed, it is an American tragedy. Suddenly they see their son as a shifty, unfamiliar "thing" with no respect for God or country, an unprincipled monster to whom it is impossible to relate as of old. The healthy family situation disappears. Walker's coldness, his superiority and his open contempt for his parents and their way of life conspire to create a perverse unnaturalness not unlike that of his sinister Bruno in *Strangers on a Train.* The parents' reaction on learning of their son's Communist activities is exactly the same as if they had discovered their child's homosexuality.

In a 1950 *New York Times* story, Guy George Gabrielson, Republican National Committee chairman, asserted that "sexual perverts who have infiltrated our government in recent years are perhaps as dangerous as actual Communists." By December of that year, 4,954 suspected homosexuals had been removed from employment in the federal government.

The presentation of lesbianism as an alien state of being emerged much more strongly in the Fifties in hard female characters who were seen as bitter reminders of the fate of women who tried to perform male roles. The strong women who fled their kitchens while men made the wartime world safe for democracy were turned back into dumb sexpots in the 1950s, and women who persisted in being independent were certainly perceived onscreen and off as outsiders, sometimes as even "things," foolishly competing in a man's world. Neurotic and cold, these steely gorgons hinted at a perverse sexuality that was never quite made specific. Their behavior was often pathological; they were seen as women trying to be men while in reality needing a man; they were grownup tomboys made to look pathetic and incomplete in their quest for status.

In 1950, Lauren Bacall's sophisticated Amy North in Michael Curtiz' *Young Man with a Horn,* Anne Baxter's cool and deadly Eve Harrington in Joseph L. Mankiewicz' *All About Eve* and Hope Emerson's sadistic prison matron Evelyn Harper in John Cromwell's *Caged* all shared unstated lesbian feelings and murderous impulses. Amy North's murderous impulses in *Young Man with a Horn* were aimed at the virility of Kirk Douglas. Described in the Dorothy Baker novel from which the film was adapted as having lesbian tendencies, the Amy North in the film is "a neurotic young girl who's tried everything." Unable to make a heterosexual relationship with Douglas work, she is finally taken with a young woman artist whose patron she becomes. The two women leave together for Paris. A shattered Kirk Douglas, left in the consoling arms of a wholesome Doris Day, tells Bacall at the kissoff, "You're a sick girl, Amy. You'd better see a doctor."

Lauren Bacall and her protégée in Young Man with a Horn *(1950).*

"Pipe the new fish." Hope Emerson as the sadistic matron Evelyn Harper in John Cromwell's Caged *(1950).* (Homer Dickens Collection)

The same kind of girl-nobody-can-tame coldness which characterized Amy North's contempt for men emerged as a contempt for humanity in Eve Harrington. In *All About Eve,* the acerbic critic Addison DeWitt calls Harrington "a killer" and tells her that they share a basic contempt for the human race. Harrington is certainly made to look "boyish" throughout the film, a sort of malevolent Huck Finn who betrays her friends to achieve stardom. Pushy and aggressive, she is described as being willing to "ask Abbott to give her Costello." The reason for her downfall, the same flaw that indicated Amy North's sickness to Kirk Douglas, was her lesbianism. According to writer-director Mankiewicz, her vulnerability in the last scene to another conniving woman is the result of physical attraction. Eve does not have the kind of generosity that led Margo Channing (Bette Davis) to take a waif like her under her wing. To ask Phoebe (Barbara Bates) to spend the night rather than take the subway home to Brooklyn could have only one motive, and it spells the beginning of the end for Eve Harrington.

Mannish, aggressive and a killer, the matron Evelyn Harper is another kind of user. The women's prison of *Caged* provides the most controlled and therefore the most specific kind of ghetto situation, one in which the sexual perversity of aliens is highly stereotyped. Amy North's sophisticated manipulation and Eve Harrington's stylish trickery occur in the civilized ghettos of the jazz and theater worlds; in the prison of *Caged,* where the pretenses of polite society are ripped away, there is an astonishing amount of lesbianism. The world of *Caged* is a total underworld, corrupting and brilliantly drawn. Like the reflections of homosexuality in the *cinema noir* of the Forties, lesbianism appears here as a product of an outlaw social structure—it comes with the territory. Evelyn Harper, the super-aggressive bull dyke, brutalizes the women while vice queen Elvira Powell (Lee Patrick) seduces them into prostitution with a sweet smile and a lecherous gaze.

All lesbians are outsiders, the films said, and in each film the myth of the predatory but lonely lesbian was reinforced. Yet overt homosexuality was seldom mentioned. Mervyn LeRoy's *The Bad Seed* (1956) omitted the "latent homosexuality" of Emory Breedlove that had appeared in William March's novel, and even Henri-Georges Clouzot's *Diabolique* (1955) changed lesbian lovers into a murder victim's wife and mistress. The only film of the 1950s to deal openly with lesbianism was a French melodrama that rejected such love as a valid emotional option. Jacqueline Audry's *Olivia* (1951) was given a sensational release in the United States as *Pit of Loneliness* (1954), the title chosen by the American distributors for its similarity to the title of the notorious novel *The Well of Loneliness,* by Radclyffe Hall, which had never been filmed. Scripted by Colette, *Olivia* offered hothouse lesbian passion in an upper class French girls' school. It was a perfect "shadow people" film for the Fifties. It featured dark doings in school corridors and ended in the obligatory tragic circumstances.

American censors assured the delicacy of treatment for which *Pit of Loneliness* was touted. One censor's notation read: "Eliminate in Reel 5D: Scene of Miss Julie holding Olivia in close embrace and kissing her on the mouth. Reason: Immoral, would tend to corrupt morals." The critics reflected the general tone of the advertising campaign, referring to "the love that dared not speak its name" and "the subject talked about in whispers." Nadine Edwards wrote in the Hollywood *Citizen-News:* "That there will be controversy surrounding the picture there is little doubt. Few will deny, however, that *Pit of Loneliness* carries with it an air of pathos and emotional tragedy—the only real outcome of such an unhappy and unnatural relationship."

The end of the film finds the older teacher renouncing her love for her student in order to save the girl from the disgrace of abnormal love. "All my life," she says, "I have had to fight these feelings within me." Her noble sacrifice on behalf of Olivia is seen as an act of civilized behavior, lesbian longings being freakish by any standards.

A look at covert lesbian behavior in films throughout the 1950s certainly bears out the neuroticism with which it was tinged onscreen. In addition to

Teacher comforts student in Pit of Loneliness *(1954).*

THE SECRETS OF A WOMAN'S
LOVE-STARVED SOUL!

COLETTE'S
masterful screen
drama...the off-
beat story of a
strange relation-
ship...condemned
by the world...
acknowledged
only in fanciful
dreams...
DISCUSSED
ONLY IN
WHISPERS

Pit of Loneliness
(1954)
THE DARING DRAMA OF AN UNNATURAL LOVE

Starring
EDWIGE FEUILLERE • SIMONE SIMON
Directed by Jacqueline Audry from the English novel, "Olivia" by Olivia • Written for the screen by Colette

the obvious lesbian allusions in *Caged, Young Man with a Horn* and *All About Eve,* other films depicting lonely, frustrated women often contained clues to lesbian leanings. In *Screaming Mimi* (1958), Gypsy Rose Lee almost certainly has a brief affair with a stripper who works in her club, the Gay and Frisky, which features a sadomasochistic strip scene unusual for 1950s Hollywood. Elizabeth Wilson, as the woman who finally takes charge of the life of Kim Stanley, a Marilyn Monroe prototype in *The Goddess* (1958), has repressed lesbian feelings for the star; in a final scene, Wilson fiercely protects her interests in Stanley in a fight with the star's former husband (Dane Clark) and their little girl. "You take care of your little girl, and I'll take care of mine," she tells him, adding, "I'll take good care of her . . . I kind of love her."

Nicholas Ray's neurotic western *Johnny Guitar* (1954) features a butch Joan Crawford and an even more butch Mercedes McCambridge in a series of confrontations that keep present-day gay audiences howling. But McCambridge outdoes *Johnny Guitar* in her unbilled appearance as a Chicano motorcycle tough in Orson Welles' *Touch of Evil* (1958). The character, unlike the other

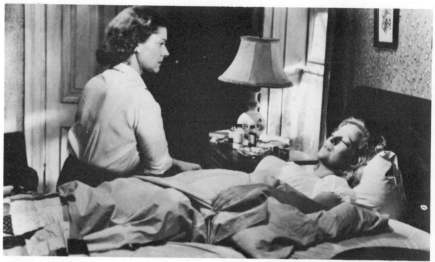

Elizabeth Wilson watches over her "little girl," Kim Stanley, in The Goddess *(1958).*

two girlfriends of the gang rapists, is almost undetectable as a woman, and she insists on staying in the motel room while Janet Leigh is raped. "Get out!" her boyfriend hisses. "No," she whispers hoarsely, "I wanna watch!"

Hilarious but instructive on the subject of crude stereotyping in the Fifties is the film *Children of Loneliness*, which appeared in 1953 and now seems to have disappeared completely. An independently produced documentary drama in the tradition of *Reefer Madness* (an hysterical 1930s film about the evils of marijuana), *Children of Loneliness* was actually made in 1939 but was denied a license for exhibition until the 1950s on the grounds that it was immoral. The film tells two stories, both accompanied by the interpreta-

Mercedes McCambridge (far right) was one of the boys who watched Janet Leigh being raped in Orson Welles' Touch of Evil *(1958), but her name is not in the credits.* (Cinemabilia)

tions of an onscreen analyst, a psychiatrist who "aids the police in cases of abnormal sexuality." In the first episode, Eleanor Gordon is about to succumb to the charms of her girlfriend, Bobby Allen. Eleanor works in an office with Bobby and is particularly susceptible to lesbianism, the doctor says, because she was "frightened by a man in her infancy" and cannot love in a normal way. In a confrontation scene in his office, the doctor tells Eleanor, "Let's be frank, Eleanor. What this girl offers to you is a false, barren substitute for the rich emotional life of a normal love. If you accept it, you will pay with misery, shame and despair. You should pity this girl. She undoubtedly belongs to that unfortunate class in whom this condition is congenital. She was born that way and there's nothing you or I can do for her. But *you* I can help."

Bobby Allen throws acid at Eleanor for spurning her advances. Eleanor throws it back and hits Bobby in the face. Partially maimed, Bobby rushes into the street and is killed by a speeding truck. The doctor introduces Eleanor to a fullback, whom she marries.

The second part of the film concerns Paul Van Tyne, an artist whose work a critic has judged "too feminine." Afraid that he can no longer conceal the truth of his abnormality, Paul seeks the advice of the doctor, who tells him that he "can never love as a husband because mentally he's a woman." Paul kills himself.

The film was "rejected in toto" by the censorship office in May 1939 with the comment, "As its title implies, the film is about sex perversion." In 1952 it was resubmitted by the distributor, Jewel Productions, and rejected once again. Finally the film passed the censorship board of review in 1953, but the censor's report stipulated several deletions, including one scene in a homosexual "cafe" set in Los Angeles in the early 1930s.

Delete entire cafe scene in which the following exchange takes place:

> *Eleanor:* What are these people?
> *Paul Van Tyne:* The Children of Loneliness! Nature's tragic mistakes, inverts, perverts and lesbians! Look at them—trying to escape from the fate to which they are condemned at birth, from the futility of their empty lives, from themselves.

Delete all views portraying acts of sexual perversion. These will include:

1. View of two women sitting on settee in embrace.
2. View of two men at table with hands joined, leaning forward, about to kiss each other.
3. Eliminate all views of homosexual couples and lesbian couples dancing together.

Advertisements *for* Children of Loneliness *and* Glen or Glenda?

Reason: Immoral and obscene. Also, there are certain scenes which add to the depressing effect of the film and are suggestive of immoral acts associated with homosexuality. I would therefore consider also the following eliminations:

1. Eliminate dialogue, "I will tell everybody about the dresses you own," in argument between Paul and former male model.
2. Scene in cafe where companion refers to dancer dressed as a woman as "he" and a "true artiste." It is felt that these pieces of dialogue are immoral as they refer to transvestitism and other acts of immorality which a homosexual might perpetrate.

Transvestism and transsexualism were used interchangeably with homosexuality and with each other in a similar low-budget epic of 1953, *Glen or Glenda? I Changed My Sex.* Produced in virtually the same documentary fashion as *Children of Loneliness* in order to cash in on the sensational sex change operation of Christine Jorgensen the previous year, the film starred Bela Lugosi as a divine being who preaches wise words from a large armchair. Surrounded by skulls, shadows and smoke pots that emit green vapor, Lugosi ponders aloud the mysteries of creation and assures the audience menacingly that "there are more things in heaven and earth than we know." He warns against tampering with the "natural order." Lugosi then introduces the familiar pompous psychiatrist, who relates the sad tale of a young man, Glen, who has an overpowering desire to wear female clothing. Glen is seen strolling down Main Street in broad daylight, wearing a sweater and skirt, with five o'clock shadow on his cheeks and lots of hair on his forearms. The aim of psychiatry, the doctor says, is "to save poor creatures like this one—four-time losers—and to help society understand that there but for the grace of God go all of us."

At first the censors rejected *Glen or Glenda?*, then they reconsidered and approved a version with three cuts.

1. A homosexual caressing the hand of another man as he is offered a light.
2. A man approaching Glen while he is dressed as a woman.
3. Dream sequence showing Glen tearing off his girlfriend's sweater.

The "dream sequence" was one in which Glen was suddenly seized with the uncontrollable desire to possess his girlfriend's white angora sweater. In a scene at the analyst's office, Glen's girlfriend learns about his problem and offers to help. "I don't fully understand this," she tells Glen, "but maybe we can work it out." She then gives him her sweater.

While *Children of Loneliness* and *Glen or Glenda?* may sound like films that belong on a midnight triple bill with *Pink Flamingos*, in their day they reflected prevailing opinion. In 1950, *Coronet* magazine called homosexuality "that new menace" and listed "glandular imbalance" as one of its causes. In 1956, *Time* quoted psychoanalyst Edmund Bergler (under Medicine) as saying, "The full-grown homosexual wallows in self-pity and continually provokes hostility to insure himself more opportunities for self-pity; he is full of defensive malice and flippancy, covering his guilt and depression with extreme narcissism and superciliousness. He is generally unreliable in an essentially psychopathic way and (unconsciously) always hates his family. There are no happy homosexuals." In 1954, *Commonweal* said, "the homosexual is a freak of nature as is the albino or the midget." Compared with *Time* and other national magazines, *Children of Loneliness* was a scholarly work on its subject.

The opinion of psychiatry that homosexuality is an illness was formally reversed in 1974 when the American Psychiatric Association stated that homosexuality, like heterosexuality, was not in itself a disturbance, but that there could be disturbed homosexuals just as there could be disturbed heterosexuals. In the 1950s, however, the shrinks ruled the day with opinions that had not come far from the thinking of those who had burned witches and heretics in the sixteenth century. The consensus of psychiatric opinion fed the legacy of sexual guilt and masculine doubt of the war years. In 1949, *Newsweek* had reported that "although army regulations forbade the drafting of homosexuals, scores of inverts managed to slip through during the war." Among the methods that induction psychiatrists used to detect homosexuals, *Newsweek* listed:

1. By their effeminate manner and dress.
2. By repeating words from the homosexual vocabulary and quickly looking for signs of recognition.

The fear of homosexuality emerged in several films of the late 1950s, notably in the first serious examination of sissyhood, Robert Anderson's *Tea and Sympathy,* which was brought to the screen by Vincente Minnelli in 1956. In other films, the pressure to conform, to hide any secret sensitivity out of fear of the word *queer,* was a popular subtext. Nicholas Ray's *Rebel Without a Cause* (1955) contained broad hints of alternative sexual behavior and the choices offered in the ritualism of gang members. In Jack Garfein's *The Strange One* (1957), perverse sexuality supplements the equally ritualistic behavior of cadets in a southern military school. In Joseph L. Mankiewicz' screen version of Tennessee Williams' *Suddenly Last Summer* (1959), homosexuality becomes evil incarnate, the symbol of a sterile decadence that is punishable by death. In all these films the homoeroticism of the chief characters is destroyed or discredited as being alien to normal life.

Natalie Wood watches over James Dean and Sal Mineo in Rebel Without a Cause *(1955). Was this a family?* (British Film Institute)

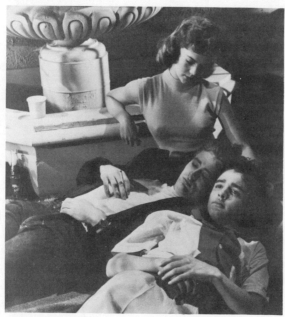

In 1963, Kenneth Anger's *Scorpio Rising* would use elements of all those films, especially *Rebel Without a Cause,* in its exploitation and exploration of "the masculine fascination with The Thing That Goes." Anger's homage to the motorcycle myth uses the violence, the decadence and the ritualism in tracing the path of boys and their toys to men and their machines—the sort of thing that film art catalogues refer to as "counterculture iconography."

Of the three troubled teenagers in *Rebel Without a Cause* (James Dean, Natalie Wood and Sal Mineo), it is Mineo's Plato who is the lonely, tormented sissy. Although he is not accused of it—unlike Tom Lee in *Tea and Sympathy*— Plato is the mama's boy, brought up by a smothering maid in the absence of his father. In his adoration of James Dean, he seeks a father more than a lover. But because Dean returns his feelings so blatantly, sparks fly. Dean's rebellious youth in crisis, a tender and courageous figure, is as loving toward Plato as he is toward Natalie Wood, and the three form a family relationship. Dean's Jim Stark is torn between society's guidelines for masculine behavior and his own natural feelings of affection for men and women. To act upon them in the case of Plato or any other man was forbidden, of course; even Jim explodes at finding his father (Jim Backus) in an apron.

Stewart Stern, the screenwriter for *Rebel,* has told how he drew on his own military experience to create parallels between gang behavior and the all-male dynamic that was present in wartime.

The gang in *Rebel Without a Cause* isn't much different from the army; both their rituals are tribal. The affection in gang behavior has to be hidden inside a different vocabulary, both spoken and unspoken, inside gestures and words which desensitized everything and made everything brutal. Also, they had to wear skins to keep the image intact—boots and leather. They had to put on a horse skin in order to feel defended against the discovery of their own sensitivity.

I don't know what other experiences in World War II were, but for us it was deliberate and conscious. We were told that the buddy system prevailed. The choice of a buddy was as or more critical than that of a bride. You'd be living in a kind of physical intimacy which was unlike any other. The classic David Duncan photos of buddies consoling each other, those who had lost their buddies, was very expressive of this. And what greater love song in those days than "My Buddy"? Men were having the experience of never having been so close to other men, and there was something of that love operating within the structure of the teenage gang whose members had left home, where there wasn't much love, to fight each other in the streets.

Fighting may have been a pretext for being close in *Rebel.* When Jim and Buzz decide to enter a "chicken" race to the edge of a cliff, a race in which Buzz will die, the two regard each other for a moment and question their participation in such an event. "We have to do something," they decide, and their encounter becomes the motivation for all that follows. Jim Stark refuses to deny his feelings, and in the screenplay Stern uses the character's guilt and grief over the death of Buzz as a weapon against conformity.

One of the things I wanted to show in *Rebel* is that underneath all the bullshit macho defense, there was that pure drive for affection, and it didn't matter who the recipient might be. There was a longer time in those days for young men to be in the warrior phase, where a lot of romantic attachments were formed before heterosexual encounters. My favorite moment in the film is not between Jim and Plato but between Jim and Buzz, who dies in the "chicken" race. It was tender and loving, and the killing of that boy, whom Jim had known for all of twelve minutes, motivated the entire last half of the film.

Rebel Without a Cause pleads a redefinition of manhood in the same way that *Tea and Sympathy* one year later would plead tolerance for "shy but normal" young men whose behavior sets them apart from the pack. Stewart Stern discusses the character of Jim Stark.

In talking to gang members, I realized that it was necessary to get through the barriers and redefine masculine behavior so that it was all right for a man to see tenderness as strength. The real power of Jim in *Rebel* was the opportunity he gave himself to choose and take the public consequences for an unpopular choice. He was willing not to dump all over Plato as a scapegoat. Even though we didn't get into that aspect of it, Plato was the one who would've been tagged as the faggot character. He hadn't shaved yet, and he had a picture of Alan Ladd in his locker at school. Jim was willing to forgo his own popularity to protect Plato.

The explosion of bottled-up feelings over this kind of emotional attachment kills Plato and Buzz, though Jim is left safely in the arms of Natalie Wood. Adult responsibility clearly includes settling down to a heterosexual relationship following the adolescent fantasies of youth. Homosexuality is considered "normal" until the end of adolescence; after that it is arrested development.

While no overt homosexuality emerged in *Rebel Without a Cause,* it could hardly be disguised, even by overvigilant censors, in Jack Garfein's *The Strange One* (1957), a film based on Calder Willingham's novel *End as a Man.* Although three scenes "indicating a homosexual relationship" between Ben Gazzara and Paul Richards were deleted prior to the film's release, it was enough of a Fifties psychological horror show to suggest strong sexual perversity without actually showing it. Gazzara plays a sadistic bully, Jocko DeParis, a highly unnatural presence among the all-American boys of a southern military school. Even his name juxtaposes clashing images of American virility and European dandyism. He engages in sadomasochistic games with freshmen cadets and holds several students under his evil spell. There is more than one dark hint that his interests in young men may have a sexual dimension that lurks beneath the surface of his cool manipulations.

In part because this intimation, frowned upon by the Code, could go nowhere, the military academy itself becomes an Old Dark House, populated with all sorts of goons and terrors. Cadet Simmons (Arthur Storch), for example, is a repulsive religious fanatic who does not date girls and refuses to shower with the boys because *"some* people are modest, you know." Gazzara shows Simmons an enema bag he keeps in his locker and then threatens him with a broom handle. Another cadet, aptly nicknamed Cockroach (Paul Richards), is obviously in love with Jocko, and here the censors intervened. Nevertheless, Cockroach does everything but buy Jocko a gold cigarette case. One explosively sexual scene shows Cockroach cleaning Jocko's sword with loving strokes. Ultimately Cockroach turns out to be a budding Sebastian Venable, a poet of sorts who imagines his oddness to be a product of his genius as a creative writer. He confesses shyly to Jocko that he has written a novel, *Nightboy,* in which Jocko is obviously the title character, whose activities are determined by Cockroach's erotic fantasies.

The moral is that one sickie can ruin an entire school. The honorable cadets eventually drive Jocko out of town, literally on a rail, in a scene whose righteous anger smacks of Ku Klux Klan tactics. The real key to Jocko DeParis and

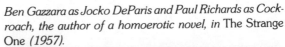

Ben Gazzara as Jocko DeParis and Paul Richards as Cockroach, the author of a homoerotic novel, in The Strange One *(1957).*

his threat—his sexual control over certain men—is never turned. "As a matter of fact," the director has pointed out, "there's still a bleep in the soundtrack when you see the film on television. At the end of the picture, Gazzara goes to a local cafe with the girl. Cockroach approaches them on the street and confesses his feelings to Jocko. The Johnston Office insisted that it be taken out."

Suddenly the "real" problem, the one that is never talked about in the film, becomes the ultimate culprit—because it seems to be the one subject that is so ostentatiously avoided. A review in *Time* said that audiences seeing *The Strange One* "will learn what goes on inside a sadist—mostly repressed homosexuality." But who is doing the repressing here? The author certainly made Jocko a sexually repressed character, but the sexuality that characters repress shows itself in their behavior in certain ways—ways that were then repressed by the censors.

A classic story of enforced repression is that of *Tea and Sympathy*. The play and the film have become so symbolic of the classic cure for homosexuality, the love of a good woman secured in the nick of time, that people forget it is the story of a shy heterosexual. Robert Anderson, who adapted his own play for the screen in 1956, uses the classic outsider image of the man who marches to the sound of a different drummer and must face the scorn of his contemporaries. Never in the film or in the play is it indicated that sensitive student Tom Lee (John Kerr) might actually prefer boys to girls. The subject here is the accusation of homosexuality, not the presence of it (at least not in Tom Lee). Lee's classmates call him "Sister Boy" because, like Jim Stark, he refuses to run with the pack. And Anderson, like Stewart Stern, was saying, "Look! This too is a man." Tom Lee likes Bach more than baseball and prefers the company of his housemaster's wife Laura (Deborah Kerr) to touch football with the guys on the beach. He is also clearly in love with the older woman, a fact that his male tormentors overlook because he does not fill the standard male role.

Most of the accusatory remarks about homosexuality were toned down for the Vincente Minnelli film. In the play, Tom is discovered swimming naked with a teacher who is also suspected of homosexuality. In the film, he is labeled a sissy because he is discovered sitting on the beach with a group of faculty wives, sewing a button on his shirt. Also muted in the film version is the repressed homosexuality of Tom's chief tormentor, the virile housemaster (Leif Erickson) who married Laura in order to prove *his* manhood. Erickson ignores Laura in favor of the young male students he coaches in both football and masculinity. *Tea and Sympathy* is about a heterosexual boy who is falsely accused of homosexuality by men whose sporting activities provide the most homoerotic action on the screen. In buddy relationships well established by his fellow students, Tom fits in as a scapegoat sissy. The film pleads tolerance, therefore, not for sexual deviation but for unfortunate heterosexuals who happen to be less than "masculine." At no time is homosexuality seen as a valid option for a real man. The message is that one cannot assume that a young man is homosexual just because he doesn't knock himself out playing football.

When Laura finally sleeps with Tom Lee, she is saving him not from a life of sissyhood but from his own fear that his fellow students might be right about his sexuality—a thought that has already driven him to attempt suicide. "To me, it was never a play about homosexuality," Anderson says. "When Leif Erickson hounds Tom Lee, he's really persecuting what he fears in himself." Thus *Tea and Sympathy* is the ultimate sissy film; it confirms what the creators and portrayers of sissies have always sought to deny, that the iconography for sissies and for sexual deviates is the same and that the one has come to *mean* the other.

While it was not about homosexuality, *Tea and Sympathy* served as a lesson for a generation of gay men who felt the sharp accusations of Tom Lee's tormentors not as shy heterosexuals but as terrified homosexuals. The film managed to describe some of what real homosexuals were feeling and experienc-

Tom Lee learns to walk like a man in Tea and Sympathy *(1956).*

ing in the 1950s while holding true to the cultural necessity of invisibility. Cultural necessity was in the hands of the Production Code, of course, and at no time was consideration given to making the homosexuality in *Tea and Sympathy* more explicit. Even the possibility that someone might actually be homosexual in real life was scotched from the film. Before the start of shooting, Deborah Kerr wrote Vincente Minnelli that "the Breen Office is very difficult about the homosexual angle, which is, I understand, their objection. Adultery is OK, impotence is OK, but perversion is their bête noire." In fact adultery was not OK, and it came under attack from the Catholic Legion of Decency. The already altered ending of *Tea and Sympathy* had to be made to reflect the necessary retribution for Laura's affair with Tom Lee. Thus the finished movie taught that instruction and initiation by an older woman was a positive thing but that at the same time such behavior could not be condoned.

The stage version ends as Laura, giving herself to Tom, undoes the top button of her blouse and says, "Years from now . . . when you talk about this . . . and you will . . . be kind." The fall of the curtain left the outcome of the encounter to the imagination of the audience. But this was not good enough for Hollywood. It filmed the seduction scene with an aura of hushed awe, like a church service. "The way the scene was shot, in the woods with the birds twittering and the special lighting," Robert Anderson says, "it looked more like the second coming of Christ than the first coming of Tom Lee." A sore-thumb epilogue then provides the morally correct ending that makes what has gone before acceptable to the Legion of Decency. Ten years later, at his class reunion, Tom Lee sports the largest gold wedding band ever held in close-up. He encounters his old housemaster, now bitter and alone, who gives Tom a letter from Laura. She writes that she was forced to leave her husband in disgrace because of what they did, and she says she cannot romanticize or excuse their sexual affair because it was "wrong." That word was used as a compromise for the word "sin," which the Catholic Church tried to pressure Anderson into using in the final screenplay. Anderson recalls a meeting with a group of bishops on the board of the Legion of Decency; one of them told him, "If you could only work the word 'sin' into that last scene, we would have no problem."

Tea and Sympathy was made too soon. The real issues raised by Anderson's play were dealt with more directly and with much humor in Claude Miller's *La Meilleure Façon de Marcher* (1976), which opened in the United States as *The Best Way* in 1978. In this film, the connection that society makes between homosexuality and sissy behavior is shown clearly. The relationship between two counselors at a boys' summer camp is parallel to that of Tom

Lee and his housemaster in *Tea and Sympathy*. The willowy, effeminate Philippe (Patrick Bouchitey), in charge of the drama group at camp, refuses to browbeat his students into mindless conformity, as does his friend Marc (Patrick Dewaere), the athletics coach. Marc catches Philippe in drag one day, and later he sees him kiss another man on the street. The film portrays the crucial days in their lives when Philippe's obvious homosexuality triggers Marc's misogyny and homophobia in a violent outburst. "I don't talk to people who take it up the ass," Marc tells Philippe. The same sentiment is expressed by the college professor in *Looking for Mr. Goodbar* when he tells Terry Dunn, "I can't stand having a conversation with a woman after I've fucked her." *Tea and Sympathy* implies that a hatred for women and a contempt for homosexuality go hand in hand, but *The Best Way* spells it out. At the end of *The Best Way,* an older Marc, now a real estate broker, shows Philippe and his new bride around an apartment in Paris. Marc sees that Philippe, though homosexual, has learned how to hide it, and he approves with a knowing smirk. "There are plenty of closets, Philippe . . . here and here and here."

The Best Way made the statement that *Tea and Sympathy* could not touch, and did it with whimsy. But *Tea and Sympathy* had paved the way. The zeal with which everyone had compromised to avoid giving offense backfired. *Saturday Review* said that "the movie demonstrates once more the old-hat nature of the Code," and *Time* said that "obviously the American public isn't old enough to know that there's such a thing as homosexuality." The end of the Fifties had brought the screen closer to actually speaking *its* name than ever before, and critics and audiences were practically yelling, "Say it, already; enough with the transparent innuendo!"

Tennessee Williams stepped forward to oblige with what became still another comment on the homosexual as alien. Twice before, plays of Williams had been brought to the screen with significant homosexual references deleted. In each case, the adaptors made sweeping statements claiming that the homosexual aspects of the play were unnecessary dramatically. In 1951, the "problem" that Blanche DuBois encountered with her husband was obscured for the screen version of *A Streetcar Named Desire;* in 1958, *Cat on a Hot Tin Roof* was shorn of the homosexual implications in the relationship between Brick (Paul Newman) and the dead Skipper. In both cases, the producers pointed out that homosexuality was not "the point" after all, that it was easily disposed of in favor of more acceptable explanations. Brick could not have sex with Maggie because he was still an adolescent.

Then, in 1959, two years before the Code was revised to allow homosexual subject matter on the screen, *Suddenly Last Summer* dealt with the subject as the kind of psychosexual freak show that the Fifties almost demanded. Treated like a dread disease, the homosexuality of Sebastian Venable, Williams' doomed poet, could be "inferred but not shown"—by special permission of the Breen Office. The resultant mixture of madness and cannibalism gave the film an unsavory, sick atmosphere that caused it to be approached with a pair of tongs by everyone involved. Katharine Hepburn, who played Sebastian's demented mother, Violet Venable, publicly expressed her distaste for the subject matter. According to director Joseph Mankiewicz' biographer, Ken Geist, Mankiewicz and Spencer Tracy, on location in Boston, spent the better part of an evening explaining homosexuality to Hepburn, but when they had finished, she flatly refused to believe that such people existed. In later years, she has been a vocal opponent of homosexuality, linking it with other "social ills" of society.

She need not have fussed so much about *Suddenly Last Summer.* The Breen Office, in a meeting with producer Sam Spiegel and screenwriter Gore Vidal, cut all direct reference to homosexual relations. "My script was perfectly explicit," Vidal says, "and then the Catholic Church struck." The Legion of Decency, after seeing that the necessary cuts were made, gave the film a special classification: "Since the film illustrates the horrors of such a lifestyle, it can be considered moral in theme even though it deals with sexual perversion."

Sebastian Venable, it was decided, would not appear in the flesh. According to Vidal, he was to be "a glimmer, an occasion for memory." With this decision, Hollywood achieved the impossible; it put an invisible homosexual on the screen.

In the January 1960 *Films in Review,* the critic Henry Hart discussed the genesis of *Suddenly Last Summer,* in which a young woman is used by her older cousin to attract boys when his mother becomes too old for that purpose. "It is said," Hart wrote, "that Tennessee Williams wrote *Suddenly Last Summer* when a psychiatrist advised him that for his own sake—not to mention society's—he had better stop denigrating normality and begin to expose the evils of homosexuality and its allied forms of vice." This Williams certainly did, whether or not the advice came from a doctor. Williams' tortured view of a failed homosexual artist and the people he victimizes with his abnormal desires is a classic horror story. Having used first his mother, in this case literally his mad creator, and then his cousin (Elizabeth Taylor) as bait for his affairs, the creature is finally destroyed by an angry mob of street urchins in a climax not much different from that of James Whale's *Frankenstein,* in which the peasants pursue the monster to the top of a hill, where fire engulfs him.

Sebastian Venable is presented as a faceless terror, a horrifying presence

The face of the demon: a publicity photo of Sebastian Venable, who is not seen in the release print of Suddenly Last Summer *(1959).*

among normal people, like the Martians in *War of the Worlds* or the creature from the black lagoon. As he slinks along the streets of humid Spanish seacoast towns in pursuit of boys ("famished for the dark ones"), Sebastian's coattail or elbow occasionally intrudes into the frame at moments of intense emotion. He comes at us in sections, scaring us a little at a time, like a movie monster too horrible to be shown all at once. The piecemeal images of his retreat through the "white-hot cobblestoned streets" as he is hunted by his grimy victims suggest that he must die, finally, at the hands of the society he has exploited and outraged.

Although Williams was credited with the screenplay of *Suddenly Last Summer,* it was written by Vidal and altered by Mankiewicz. "Sam Spiegel wanted Tennessee's name on the script with mine," Vidal says. "He convinced Tennessee he'd get an Academy Award for the script he had not written. So Tennessee took the credit. I contemplated suing, but Tennessee is a friend, and he said, 'Ah mean, Go-wuh, it *is* mah play,' to which I said, 'Yes, all forty minutes of it, but the other sixty are mine.' Besides, there was no doubt in the billing from whose brow sprang this gorgeous work. We were also not helped by Mankiewicz' ending—those overweight ushers from the Roxy Theater on Fire Island pretending to be small ravenous boys."

What emerged in *Suddenly Last Summer* was a *Glen or Glenda?* with a budget. It was a film with high moral tone that could not, in the end, explore its own subject. Henry Hart concluded that *Suddenly Last Summer* "exposes clearly the foremost causes of homosexuality and . . . points to one of the horrible fates that can overtake this particular kind of pervert." In fact the "cause" of Sebastian's homosexuality (no one ever asks what causes heterosexuality because no one is interested in stopping it) is certainly not explored in the film, which is concerned only with the effects of it—which are devastating to all. As for Sebastian's particular fate, it is unlikely that many homosexuals have died at the hands of cannibalistic Spanish-speaking street children. More have died at the hands of "fag bashers" in American cities.

The erosion of the power of the Production Code to maintain specific taboos had begun at the outset of the 1950s. Before 1953, no film rejected by the Code had ever had a commercial release. In that year, Otto Preminger's *The Moon Is Blue*, denied a seal of approval because of its light treatment of adultery (which does not actually take place in the film) and its use of the word *virgin*, was released without the seal and did very well at the box office. In 1956, Preminger again released a film on a controversial subject without a seal of approval. His adaptation of Nelson Algren's *The Man with the Golden Arm* graphically depicted drug addiction, in direct violation of Code precepts, and became highly profitable, earning receipts eleven times greater than its production costs.

Following the marked success of the two Preminger films, the Code was revised in 1956 to rescind the prohibitions against the use of narcotics, prostitution and miscegenation as film subjects. The enormous success of the British imports *Room at the Top* (1958) and *Saturday Night and Sunday Morning* (1960), both released in America without a seal of approval, further testified to the fact that the Code was too restrictive and essentially ineffective. The trend toward liberalizing the Code was helped along by a considerable drop in attendance at the movies, from seventy-five million people in 1950 to less than forty-six million in 1960. In a pamphlet on the Production Code written in the early 1960s, Bosley Crowther pointed out that "it was fashionable in the 1950s to boast, 'I haven't seen a movie in six months.' "

In early 1959, the California State Supreme Court, reviewing a case that involved a screening of Kenneth Anger's *Fireworks,* ruled that "homosexuality is older than Sodom and Gomorrah" and is a legitimate subject for screen treatment if handled properly. The ruling set aside the conviction of exhibitor Raymond Rohauer, who had been fined $250 and sentenced to three 'years' probation for showing *Fireworks* in 1957. Calling *Fireworks* "an attempt to convey, through impressionism, the homosexual attitude on life in general," *Variety* noted that the court opinion declared that "homosexuality is not to be approved of, but society should understand its causes and effects." Seven years later, after homosexuality as a subject had reached commercial film houses, Kenneth Anger's *Scorpio Rising* (1963) was finally released in theaters (albeit specialized "art" houses such as New York's Bleecker Street Cinema) and caused a similar commotion. Again the film was taken to represent homosexual life and attitudes in general. Andrew Sarris, reviewing *Scorpio Rising* in the *Village Voice* and noting that Anger parallels a sadistic homosexual orgy with footage from an old movie on the life of Christ, drew a homophobic conclusion. "Why the parallel with Christ?" he asked. "What else is there for beautiful homosexuals to experience after 30 but crucifixion?"

The handling of *Fireworks* and *Scorpio Rising* by the courts, the distributors and the critics suggested the way in which the Code would eventually change. There was far too much rampant, unchallenged homophobia, even in enlightened circles, for films with homosexual subjects to be viewed objectively, that is, on their cinematic merit alone. There would be no acceptance of the validity of homosexual subject matter, only a condescension to an amorphous "adult" audience that Hollywood was determined to reach without offending the bluenoses.

One of the last commercial films to have homosexuality removed from its script before the Code was changed was Stanley Kubrick's *Spartacus* (1960). Dalton Trumbo's screenplay contained a scene between Crassius (Laurence Olivier) and his young slave Antoninus (Tony Curtis), in which the older man

Antoninus (Tony Curtis) helps Crassius (Laurence Olivier) out of the bath in a scene cut from Spartacus *(1960). (Universal Pictures, collection Lincoln Center Library for the Performing Arts)*

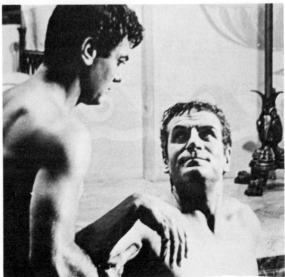

subtly establishes his taste for both men and women. In the climactic bathing scene, the two are talking about how to treat a woman, when suddenly Crassius seems to change the subject.

> *Crassius:* Do you eat oysters?
> *Antoninus:* Yes.
> *Crassius:* Snails?
> *Antoninus:* No.
> *Crassius:* Do you consider the eating of oysters to be moral and the eating of snails to be immoral?
> *Antoninus:* No, master.
> *Crassius:* Of course not. It's all a matter of taste, isn't it?
> *Antoninus:* Yes, master.
> *Crassius:* And taste is not the same as appetite and therefore not a question of morals, is it?
> *Antoninus:* It could be argued so, master.
> *Crassius:* Um, that'll do. My robe, Antoninus. Ah, my taste . . . includes *both* oysters and snails.

This exchange was cut, and the conversation about how to treat a woman was followed by the slipping away of Antoninus to join Spartacus and the other slaves in revolt. What is lost, then, is all indication of Antoninus' fear of being homosexually involved with Crassius, the fear that causes Antoninus to flee at that particular time.

Deletions such as this led producers and writers in the film industry to complain that the Code restricted their artistic freedom and prevented Hollywood films from competing in an adult market with foreign films that dealt openly with such subjects. The taboo against "sex perversion" was the single specific restriction on subject matter left standing at the beginning of the 1960s. Then, in the summer of 1961, the Mirisch Company, coproducers of William Wyler's *The Children's Hour,* waged a carefully orchestrated campaign to prepare the public for the inevitable. They let it be known that Wyler's second version of Lillian Hellman's play would restore to the script the lesbian implications. Although the film had been shot by August 1961, it was still being edited and would not be ready for some months, and of course the Code could not pass on the film until it could be screened. During this time, the Mirisch Company took every opportunity to indicate that they were dissatisfied with the Code position on sex perversion as a screen subject.

Meanwhile, in September, Otto Preminger—who had twice before defied the Code and appeared to take a special pleasure in doing so—announced that he was beginning to shoot Allen Drury's *Advise and Consent* on location in Washington, D.C., and said he would not soft-pedal the novel's homosexual episodes in his screen version. Preminger had reason to be pushy. According to Wendell Mayes, who adapted *Advise and Consent* for the screen, "It was always Otto's publicity game to break the Code, and he was successful at that game. You look at the record, and you will discover that many of the changes in the Code were a result of Otto Preminger's breaking the rules."

A debate was effectively begun on the merits of revising the Code to allow the onscreen treatment of sex perversion. The proponents of the change pointed out that the taboo against sex perversion was the last of the specific taboos, all the others having been dropped in favor of a Code that considered the taste and treatment of the subject matter of each film. There were many for whom the time was not yet ripe to do this, and there were also those for whom the time would never come. Some argued that to change the Code would bring down the wrath of what Vincent Canby, writing in *Variety,* termed "do-gooders and would-be censors all over the country" who were then pushing for an inquiry by the House of Representatives into the film industry and film morality. Canby quoted an unnamed "prominent screenwriter/novelist" who pointed out that William Wyler's first version of *The Children's Hour* had made a fine film as *These Three* in 1936 and that therefore "the use of the taboo subject in this subsidiary vein was unnecessary and rather capricious on the part of the filmmakers." It was clear that those who opposed the use of such subject matter did so because they perceived it as sexual material that would be ripe for exploitation. Canby's anonymous writer also attacked the work of Tennessee Williams, saying that the introduction of "bizarre undercurrents" in his work was simply a ploy to make the primary conflict in his drama "more exotic." In other words, why depict such things in drama or on film when we have learned that a play or a movie can be successful without them?

But the ball was rolling. In the fall, the Motion Picture Association of America said that it would "consider approving such references in motion pictures if the allusion to sexual aberration was treated with care, discretion and restraint." Seizing what was obviously the moment, Otto Preminger, ever the showman, used his appearance at a Washington Press Club luncheon in late September to stun the audience by announcing that the industry's Production Code had been changed to permit the tasteful treatment of homosexuality in order that he might be able to film *Advise and Consent.* The MPAA hotly denied that such a change had taken place, but less than a week later, on October 3, 1961, it approved the change publicly: "In keeping with the culture, the mores and the values of our time, homosexuality and other sexual aberrations may now be treated with care, discretion and restraint." Intimations that the change had in any way been the result of pressure by the Mirisch Company, Otto Preminger or other producers were flatly—but not convincingly—denied. Preminger et al. had won the battle.

In addition to *The Children's Hour* and *Advise and Consent,* Gore Vidal's *The Best Man* and Morris West's *The Devil's Advocate,* both with homosexual subplots, were under consideration by major studios. It seemed that the film industry, waiting to deal with this subject, had successfully put the squeeze on an already weakened Code. For producers knew that their films, like Preminger's *The Moon Is Blue* and *The Man with the Golden Arm,* would do well at the box office even if they were released without a seal. So the Code was changed in order to maintain some illusion of control.

The changes raised, for the first time, basic questions that no one wanted to hear asked. In an attack on the Code revision, an editorial in the *Motion Picture Herald* cited the three basic principles of the Code.

1. No picture should be produced which would lower the moral standards of those who see it.
2. Correct standards of life . . . shall be presented.
3. Laws—divine or natural or human—should not be ridiculed, nor should sympathy be created for their violation.

The *Herald* took the position that to allow sex perversion as a subject in motion pictures would violate all three basic principles because "homosexuality does not represent correct standards of life by any stretch of the imagination" and because dealing with homosexuals would "create sympathy for those who violate both Divine and human law by perverted acts." In casting aside the last specific taboo, the Code allowed motion pictures to portray all facets of life.

In an argument that remains the bottom line today, opponents of change insisted that there are some facts of life which it is harmful for people to know about at all. The whispered secret of *Tea and Sympathy,* they said, would now certainly be shouted from the housetops; the dark hints of *Suddenly Last Summer* would take over our screens in a flood of perversion and filth. In fact the dirty secret of old emerged on the screen in those newly enlightened times as a dirty secret, still a subject to be whispered about but not to be explored in a meaningful way. Homosexuality had come out of the closet and into the shadows, where it would remain for the better part of two decades.

In the 1960s, lesbians and gay men were pathological, predatory and dangerous; villains and fools, but never heroes. It was sideshow time. In *The Legend of Lylah Clare,* Rosella Falk played a cobra-eyed, dope-addicted dyke who had the hots for Kim Novak. In *Petulia,* Richard Chamberlain was a wife beater with a letch for young boys. Rod Steiger blew his brains out with a shotgun after kissing John Phillip Law in *The Sergeant.* Sandy Dennis died when a tree fell between her legs in *The Fox.* Homosexuals were the prime suspects in *The Boston Strangler,* rapists in *Riot* and hairdressers or queens in *No Way to Treat a Lady, Valley of the Dolls, The Producers, The Loved One* and countless stock comedies. Fear, hiding and self-destruction—the closet syndrome—were implicit in all these films. Homosexuality had become the dirty secret exposed at the end of the last reel.

Frightening
the Horses

**out of the closets
and into
the shadows**

The original ad campaign for William Friedkin's The Boys
in the Band *(1970).*

The Children's Hour is not about lesbianism,
it's about the power of lies to destroy
people's lives.

—William Wyler, 1962

The Sergeant is not about homosexuality,
it's about loneliness.

—Rod Steiger, 1968

Windows is not about homosexuality, it's
about insanity.

—Gordon Willis, 1979

Staircase is not about homosexuality,
it's about loneliness.

—Rex Harrison, 1971

Sunday, Bloody Sunday is not about the sexuality
of these people, it's about human loneliness.

—John Schlesinger, 1972

It was the first film in which a man
said "I love you" to another man. I
wrote that scene in. I said, "There's
no point in half-measures. We either
make a film about queers or we don't."

—Dirk Bogarde on *Victim*

In America we don't; that was the message of the MPAA barely a month
after its decision to revise the Code to allow homosexuality onscreen. Audience
and critical reaction to Tony Richardson's *A Taste of Honey* (1961) and Basil
Dearden's *Victim* (1961), both of which had opened in England by the time
of the American ruling, swiftly indicated the direction that American films would
take on the subject of homosexuals. In the spring of 1962, the two British
imports became the first films to apply for a seal of approval under the new
Code guidelines.

A Taste of Honey, adapted from Shelagh Delaney's play, presented its unkempt characters winningly. The friendship between Jo (Rita Tushingham), a pregnant and deserted working class waif, and Geoff (Murray Melvin), a lonely, effeminate homosexual, was portrayed with lyric tenderness. The appealing ugly duckling of a girl and the odd young man who acts "just like a woman" are cast as society's freaks, two unwanted creatures who enjoy their brief taste of honey together before being swallowed up again in the pain of being different in the real world. Geoff is pathetic, sexless, childlike. A nervous nellie with frightened eyes, he is the perfect nonthreatening male to help a shy girl on the road to womanhood—a man who will not mistreat her.

Geoff was harmless. Thus the film had no problem with the Code, and it was released immediately with a seal of approval. However, it was handled nervously in America. A study guide, prepared with the help of a church-affiliated film society and reprinted in *Life* magazine, quoted psychiatrists on the "causes and cures" of homosexuality. Geoff was perceived as a sick character, but his visibility, the very fact of his legitimacy as a character, was the irritant. Some American critics chafed like skittish horses, not yet really frightened but sensing something dangerous coming down the road. In England, the reaction to an increase of homosexuality onscreen was less agitated than it would become in the United States. The critic Dilys Powell wrote wistfully in the London *Times,* "I hope soon to feel the time has come to stop congratulating the British cinema on its ability to mention homosexuality."

American critics were neither amused nor amusing on the subject; they were openly hostile and expressed resentment at any kind of sympathetic treatment. Sympathy had come easily to *Tea and Sympathy*'s Tom Lee because, after all, he was not really queer. *A Taste of Honey*'s Geoff, on the other hand, was the genuine item, and this made a difference. Pauline Kael, calling Geoff "a sad-eyed queen," wrote sarcastically that liberal audiences now had a "new unfortunate" whom they could clasp to their "social worker hearts." It was not Richardson's sentimental approach to his characters that rankled but the very appearance of Geoff as a sympathetic character. Bosley Crowther, dissenting from a positive review of the film by A. H. Weiler in the *New York Times,* complained of Geoff's lack of villainy. "Certainly you'd think the grubby people who swarm through [the film] might shake out one disagreeable individual whose meanness we might despise," Crowther wrote. "The homosexual could do with some sharp and dirty digs. No one is more easily rendered odious than an obvious homosexual." In his search for villainy, Crowther ignored the easily despised meanness of the heterosexual sailor (Paul Danquah) who prompts Jo's pitiful condition in the first place and then abandons her. Instead, Crowther calls for the head of Geoff.

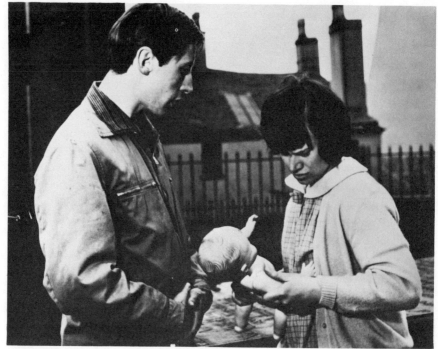

Murray Melvin, the "sad-eyed queen," with Rita Tushingham in A Taste of Honey *(1961).*

But a sad-eyed queen is no hero, and Geoff was no threat. The homosexual in Basil Dearden's *Victim* was an entirely different number, heroic enough to be a genuine menace. The key phrase in the Code's ruling, prescribing "care, discretion and restraint," was about to be clarified. *Victim* was a blackmail thriller that pleaded tolerance for homosexuals, the first commercial film to do so since the German *Anders als die Anderen* in 1919. The MPAA found *Victim* "thematically objectionable" on two counts and refused to grant it a seal without certain cuts. The film, the Johnston Office said, violated the basic precepts of the Code "through its candid and clinical discussion of homosexuality and its overtly expressed plea for social acceptance of the homosexual to the extent that [he] be made tolerable."

The first objection had to do with the spoken words *homosexual* and *homosexuality,* which had never before been uttered onscreen. In early 1961, before the new ruling on homosexuality, Sidney Poitier was allowed to deride a college student's lack of manhood by attacking his "faggoty" white shoes in *A Raisin in the Sun.* Now, in 1962, the Code fought to eliminate the nonpejorative "homosexual" from a film that was then doing well in Europe and was the sole British entry in the Venice Film Festival. The Code was answering the questions the *Motion Picture Herald* had raised about the basic contradiction in permitting homosexuality onscreen when to do so violated the precepts of the Code. In an official clarification of the October 3 ruling, the MPAA said that "sexual aberration could be suggested but not actually spelled out," a requirement that barred honesty and forthrightness and invited innuendo and slander. Thus "faggoty" was okay but "homosexual" was not. Although much was made of the refusal of *Victim*'s director Basil Dearden and his coproducer Michael Relph to cut the offending words from the soundtrack, it was clear that the real objections of the MPAA concerned the film's strong conclusion that homosexuals were victimized by society's laws. No cuts were made in *Victim*, and the film was released without a seal of approval two months after the liberalization of the Production Code.

The story of *Victim*, written by Janet Green and John McCormick, was shockingly explicit for its time. Green and Dearden had collaborated once before on a thriller with a social message; their film *Sapphire* (1958) built a neat murder mystery around the death of a black woman who had been passing for white. *Victim*'s story of homosexual blackmail was also about people who passed. For a unique difference between homosexuals and other minorities has always been that the homosexual had the option to "pass" simply by maintaining silence. The crucial need of the homosexual to hide is presented in *Victim*, which points out that ninety percent of all blackmail cases in England at that time involved homosexuals. The closet door had shifted uneasily on its hinges in the 1950s as homosexuality was discussed publicly for the first time in America, and now *Victim* sought to push the debate to a new level. The film portrays the screen's first homosexual character to choose visibility and thereby challenge the status quo. The issues of repression and enforced invisibility were equated, for the first time, with the law's relegation of homosexuals to a lawless subculture in which they became victims of their own ghostly status.

A plea for the legalization of homosexuality between consenting adults in private is implicit in *Victim*'s dramatization of one man's battle for understanding and tolerance. There are times when *Victim* says that being homosexual should be punishment enough for such creatures, that to hound them seems a pointless exercise. One tortured victim, a timid barber, offers "nature played me a dirty trick" as a reason to pay blackmail and "buy a little peace while I still have some time left." Powerlessness is seen as part of the mechanism of invisibility. There is silence because the law makes homosexuality illegal, and blackmail flourishes because there is silence. The police chief in *Victim* remarks to Dirk Bogarde, "Someone once called this law against homosexuality the blackmailer's charter."

"Is that how you feel about it?" Bogarde asks.

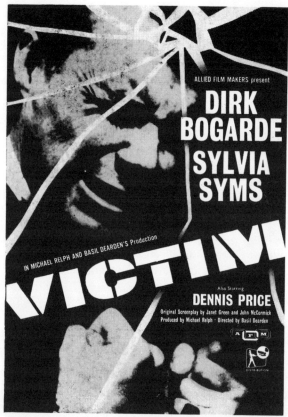

This advertisement for Victim *(1961)* showed a tortured Dirk Bogarde in a pose that does not appear in the film.

"I'm a policeman, sir," he replies. "I don't have feelings."

Victim creates a gay hero with credentials enough to get into heaven, let alone society. Like Sidney Poitier's superwhite super black in Stanley Kramer's *Guess Who's Coming to Dinner* (a summa cum laude big shot with the World Health Organization), Bogarde's upper middle class barrister in *Victim* is as clean as a whistle. Married to a loving and patient woman, Melville Farr has resolved to bury his homosexual feelings and has not been "active" for several years. His unexpected and personally unwelcome attraction to a working class youth (Peter McEnery) and their brief, sexless relationship is seen as a moral lapse. Farr is redeemed by the fact that he "wanted" the young man but never gave in to his "desires." When their affair is threatened with exposure through blackmail, the youth kills himself in an attempt to protect Farr's marriage and career.

The suicide turns Melville Farr into a hero in gay terms. Willing to sacrifice his reputation in order to "challenge the existing law" against homosexuals, he sets out to avenge the death of his friend by bringing the blackmailers to justice. Already an acceptable hero to some liberal audiences because he admits that homosexual acts are wrong and refrains from acting on his urges, he becomes a hero in the gay perspective because he is willing to lend a little dignity to his homosexual relationship by fighting to legitimize its existence. The situation in *Victim* offered the opportunity to explore the closet from both sides of the door. When Farr tries to enlist the aid of affluent homosexuals who are being preyed on by the same gang of blackmailers, the homosexuals practically form a posse to force him to "lay off." Farr assumes the role of the gay militant who is accused of rocking the boat; no other homosexual in the film so much as wishes him a furtive "good luck." And Farr is shocked when the meek barber tells him bitterly that he thinks the young suicide is "well out of it." The barrister, set against the paralyzing self-hatred of others like him, becomes ever more the shining hero.

A general distaste surrounded the filming of *Victim*. Reportedly the shooting was beset with overt hostilities on the part of crew members and production people. Bogarde recalls that the cast and crew were sometimes treated "as if we were attacking the Bible." One lawyer involved in preproduction contracts, Bogarde said, reported that he had wanted "to wash his hands after reading the script." For gays in the closet, though, it was one of the first indications on film of the knowledge of shared oppression. "I believe," Bogarde says, "that the film made a lot of difference to a lot of people's lives."

In America, *Victim* was given the serious art house treatment, but without a Code seal, and typed as a film that condoned homosexuality, it was shunned by the general public. Press reactions to the social issues raised in the film often obscured their reactions to the film itself, as though the topic of homosexuality were all-encompassing and capable of blinding critics in the analysis of other aspects of the work. Consider, for example, the criticism of *Time:* "[The film is] a coyly sensational exploitation of homosexuality as a theme—and what's more offensive—an implicit approval of homosexuality as a practice . . . nowhere does the film suggest that homosexuality is a serious but often curable neurosis that attacks the biological basis of life itself."

Victim touched a nerve and marked a turning point. The *New York Times* was quick to say that anyone who liked *Victim* had to be abnormal (just as critics in the Thirties had suggested that anyone who found lesbianism in *Mädchen in Uniform* was a pervert). The *Times* critic wrote, "How much [the film] will be appreciated and how much its pronounced sympathy for the victimized homosexual will be shared by the viewer will depend upon the individual's awareness and tolerance of the abnormality . . . while the subject is disagreeable it is not handled distastefully."

This type of film criticism remains with us. Critics, no matter how "liberal," continue to differentiate between straight and gay audiences, whether dealing with gay or non-gay films. The television critic Stuart Klein implied on the air that only gay people and gay critics would find *La Cage aux Folles* a funny film. When Woody Allen's *Annie Hall* opened in New York, Andrew Sarris wrote that he was glad to see a return of heterosexual romance to the screen—as if homosexual romance had become all the rage—worse, as if romance itself were somehow heterosexual in nature. (Why not just "the return of romance" to the screen?)

It is an old stereotype, that homosexuality has to do only with sex while heterosexuality is multifaceted and embraces love and romance. This is why the introduction of a gay hero in *Victim* ran counter to the popular conception of homosexuals. The film was seen as a challenge to heterosexual hegemony, and there was outrage at the social realities that now intruded on and crushed the illusions of earlier films made in simpler times. *Victim's* stark portrait of the pressures caused by hiding and the sense of despair of the homosexuals in the film (including the noble Farr) removed it from the category of films that dealt only with harmless, amorphous sissies; it made gays real. Farr's insistence on being both a homosexual and a real person mirrors the producers' insistence on using candid language in the film. On the one hand, the film was a regrettable legitimization of social issues perceived to be distasteful; on the other, it was a validation of the existence of homosexuals who were not comic relief for the majority. *Victim*, it seems, was a killjoy.

Pauline Kael bemoaned immediately the loss of "bitchy old queens like Franklin Pangborn and Grady Sutton" (whom nobody ever agrees were playing homosexuals) and despaired of the cinematic consequences of treating homosexuals "seriously, with sympathy and respect, like Negroes and Jews." She need not have worried; the equation of gay oppression with that of blacks and Jews is still under attack by liberals and conservatives alike, and the sissy remains with us today, albeit much changed. It soon became clear that while the Code might allow the use of homosexuality as a subject in films made in the United States, it intended to maintain some control over *how* that subject was used. "Care, discretion and restraint" meant, essentially, "treat it like a dirty secret." And that is what filmmakers did.

Heroes like Melville Farr were out of the question on the American screen. Deletions were made continually, under pressure or fear of public disapproval, whenever literary or historical material was brought to the screen. Strong suggestions in Peter Glenville's *Becket* (1964) of a sexual relationship between Thomas à Becket (Richard Burton) and King Henry II (Peter O'Toole), in a scene in which the two men sleep together, were condemned by American critics for damaging the heroic image of the two buddies' noble relationship. *Newsweek* attacked the source material, asserting that the playwright Jean Anouilh, "by descending to the realm of the psychiatric and implying a sexual attraction between the two, muddies the issues."

The issues were the eternal issues of masculinity and heroism and their preservation at all cost. Andrew Sarris, writing in the *Village Voice,* complained that "O'Toole plays the King as a lovesick Queen." (This attitude indicates why *A Taste of Honey* won a seal of approval and *Victim* did not.) For most people, homosexuality was inextricably bound to the idea of men acting like women—and that was bad, even dangerous, for heroes. Although, under the new Code, villainous homosexuals sometimes *wanted* the hero sexually, their homosexuality served as an illustration of their pathology and thus illuminated their villainy. In Peter Ustinov's *Billy Budd* (1962), the fatal attraction of Claggart (Robert Ryan) to the beauteous innocence of Billy (Terence Stamp) is both his problem and his eventual retribution. The attraction consumes him. Billy is pure and beautiful, seemingly unconscious of the feelings he engenders, much like Stamp's sexual angel in Pier Paolo Pasolini's *Teorema* (1968). Innocent and irresistible is how Melville created Billy Budd, and Ustinov left it that way. But the homoeroticism in the film comes as much from Stamp's angelic embodiment of Melville's Billy as it does from the lechings of the fascinated Claggart.

Other film characters were saved from self-knowledge by means of selective interpretation for the screen. Although Robert Bolt is credited with the screenplay for *Lawrence of Arabia* (1962), Michael Wilson, who wrote several preliminary versions, made some of the fundamental decisions regarding the film's approach to Lawrence's sexuality and shaped the use of homosexuality to indicate villainy. In an early synopsis, Wilson described Chapter 80 of Lawrence's book: "Lawrence [Peter O'Toole] goes out alone to scout the district of Derea on foot. He is picked up and arrested and taken before the Turkish bey, a sadistic homosexual [Jose Ferrer]. There follows here an account of the hideous night of torture and degradation he spends at the hands of the Turks."

This is the episode of which Lawrence writes, "the citadel of my integrity had been irretrievably lost that night in Derea." The problem for the filmmakers was how to interpret what that citadel was to Lawrence. Wilson's notes on the Derea sequence are illuminating.

Much has been made of this scene . . . as the key to the enigma of Lawrence. It seems to me that it becomes the key only if the question of homosexuality is placed

Peter O'Toole faces Jose Ferrer, the evil homosexual Turkish bey, in Lawrence of Arabia *(1962).*

at the center of the riddle—and this I have no desire to do. There is little to be gained from dramatizing the notion that Lawrence finally succumbs to the bey's advances . . . if Lawrence believed that he had strengthened his willpower to the point where he could endure any physical pain; if he was sure that his spirit could dominate his flesh (and thus, set him apart from other men)—and if he found that he too had his breaking point and finally whimpered for mercy—is this not enough for our story? This does not mean, of course, that we should omit any suggestion of the bey's homosexuality.

And so Lawrence's "citadel" was defined onscreen as his strength in being able to rise above other men, and its "irretrievable loss" came as a result of his admission of weakness under torture. His difficulties arise from nothing so long-lasting as homosexuality, which is represented in the film entirely by the evil bey. Thus an important by-product of the Code revision was the allowance of the American dream of staunchly heterosexual heroes to coexist with visible homosexuality so long as the two fought the classic battle and homosexuality and heroism did not occur in the same person. Again, the hero had to be "a hell of a nice guy or the audiences won't go for it." The hero still could not be queer.

Yet in a time when homosexuality was suddenly visible and villains could also be heroes, new choices soon became available. Perhaps the hero could not be a faggot, but he no longer had to be a hell of a nice guy. David Newman and Robert Benton's script for Joseph Mankiewicz' *There 'Was a Crooked Man* (1970) retained a sadistic homosexual prison foreman (Bert Freed) who has a prisoner flogged for spurning his sexual advances—in a film with a highly moral hero. But Newman and Benton's script for *Bonnie and Clyde* (1967) underwent drastic revision to accommodate a highly immoral hero. The sexual relationship between Clyde Barrow (Warren Beatty) and C. W. Moss (Michael J. Pollard), indicated by their biographers and included in the original Newman and Benton story, was erased when director Arthur Penn and producer-actor Warren Beatty joined the project. Newman describes the original treatment.

The first draft had a ménage à trois between Bonnie, Clyde and a third male character who was a different version of the C. W. Moss character. He was more of a dumb stud type, a conglomeration of three or four different drivers the real Barrows had used. In our research we came across references which suggested that several of these guys had been in a sexual thrall with Bonnie and Clyde. So in our first draft that seemed just one more thing which made them outside the structure of society. In fact, in the original draft, there was a shot of the three of them lying in bed together after having sex.

When Penn and Beatty came on the scene, this aspect of the story became a liability instead of an interesting asset. Beatty, it was decided, could play an impotent killer but not a sexually ambiguous one and still retain the audience's sympathy. Clyde's "problem" thus became the impotence that Bonnie Parker "cures" in a tender scene in the grass just before the final bloodbath. "We decided," Newman says, "that it would be off-putting to the audience and throw the picture out of kilter if we retained the sexual ambiguity. Plus, when Michael J. Pollard came along and his character was created, there was no sexuality at all because the part was rewritten especially for him."

As in *The Lost Weekend,* people wanted to deal only with updated "normal" American problems. There is never as much outrage at the sight of heroes who choose violence as there is absolute moral fury when a hero expresses unorthodox sexual feelings. The homoerotic aspects of the buddyhood of Truman Capote's two real-life killers of *In Cold Blood* were absent from the screen version directed by Richard Brooks in 1967. Misunderstood heroes driven to kill out of disaffection and frustration were fine, but homosexuality was clearly only for villains.

There has been speculation that an early version of the script for *Dr. Strangelove, or How I Learned to Stop Worrying and Love the Bomb* (1964) indicated that Peter Sellers' president of the United States was queer as well as incompetent. If so, it is a pity to have lost the added irony in a film so expertly satiric on the paranoia of the military concerning "preverts" in the ranks. The buddy relationship of soldiers in wartime was more sacred than that of western heroes or hip athletes. Just as Private Prewitt's homosexual episode in James Jones' *From Here to Eternity* was trimmed for Montgomery Clift's portrayal in the

1953 film version, soldiers ten years later were still protected from this particular intimation, even by extension. Carl Foreman's *The Victors* (1963) lost several scenes that would have indicated that American soldiers (George Peppard and George Hamilton) were sleeping with a young French male prostitute (Joel Flateau) and giving him food in exchange. As the Code said, it could be intimated but not shown. So while the Flateau character existed, it was a mystery to American audiences just who was patronizing the seemingly prosperous prostitute. (Probably the enemy!)

Similarly, Bryan Forbes' prisoner of war drama *King Rat* (1965), based on James Clavell's novel, was shorn of a subplot in which a prisoner acts as a surrogate woman by dressing in drag at camp shows, a routine that leads to a full-time cross-dressing situation that has sexual overtones. The prisoner comes to accept the female role to the extent that when the camp is liberated, he dons women's clothing once more and walks into the sea. According to Forbes, his script contained a sequence in which the character "actually underwent a sex change operation and, when the war was over, committed suicide." This episode did not survive the shock of the studio. "The sequence was removed in its entirety," Forbes says, "at the insistence of Columbia Pictures, in spite of the fact that it had always been in the script, which they either failed to read or didn't understand." The latter is more likely. A submerged, unstated homosexual attraction between the king (George Segal) and a young British officer (James Fox) is discernible but never threatening in the way that the deleted footage would have erased the line between male and female.

The hero-villain question persisted throughout the Sixties and well into the Seventies, with movie homosexuals increasingly falling victim to their own inherently villainous sexuality—the flaw that always destroyed them in one way or another. Self-hatred was the standard accessory with every new model. The "pioneer" films for which the change in the Code had been petitioned, the widely discussed "adult" dramas of the early 1960s, were barely an industry toe in the water, yet they revealed much for the first time. Three of the first four American releases to deal with homosexuality in a major way used it only as the subject of a false accusation made against ultimately heterosexual characters. The "dirty secret" angle was given full play in the media. Hundreds of articles appeared in newspapers and magazines describing the bold themes in such mature new films as *A View from the Bridge, Walk on the Wild Side, Advise and Consent* and *The Children's Hour. Life's* cover story, "The Outbreak of New Films for Adults Only," made it sound as though a new disease had been spotted; the magazine approached *The Children's Hour* with the headlines, "A Shocking Lie . . . A Terrible Secret!" William Wyler's first title for the

Audrey Hepburn and Shirley MacLaine are found guilty of having had "sinful sexual knowledge of one another" in a courtroom scene that was cut from The Children's Hour *(1962).*

TODAY at

WHAT MADE THESE WOMEN _DIFFERENT_?

Did Nature play an ugly trick and endow them with emotions contrary to those of normal young women? Or was it a child's vicious lie that caused them to live as objects of shame? Their's are powerful roles, magnificently played.

Only a child knew the real truth about her!

She learned how gossip can wreck a human life!

He refused to believe the horrible

Audrey *Shirley*

HEPBURN · MacLAINE

with the star of "MAVERICK"...

James **GARNER**

IN A **WILLIAM WYLER** PRODUCTION
(Who gave you "BEN-HUR")

THE CHILDREN'S HOUR

CO-STARRING
Miriam HOPKINS · Fay BAINTER
AND INTRODUCING
Karen BALKIN

Because of the mature nature of its theme.–this motion picture is recommended for adults only.

Released thru UNITED ARTISTS

BRONX
PARADISE
QUEENS
VALENCIA
MANHATTAN
ORPHEUM 86th ST. & 3rd AV.
83rd STREET
175th STREET
COMMODORE
DELANCEY
INWOOD
OLYMPIA
SHERIDAN
VICTORIA
116th STREET
BROOKLYN
46th STREET
ALPINE
CONEY IS.
GATES ..
KAMEO
KINGS ..
ORIENTAL
PITKIN ..
PREMIER
WESTCHESTER
MT. VERNON
NEW ROCH.
WH PLAINS

and

The original ad copy for the second film version of The Children's Hour *(1962) made the two accused lesbians freaks of nature.*

film was *Infamous!;* in England it was called *The Loudest Whisper.* Newspaper ads for the film were headlined, "Did Nature Play an Ugly Trick on These Women?"

The ugly trick was on the public, for the promise of forbidden fruit was fraudulent. In Sidney Lumet's adaptation of Arthur Miller's *A View from the Bridge* (1962), an Italian immigrant dockworker (Raf Vallone) is in love with his wife's niece (Carol Lawrence). In a fit of jealousy, he accuses her boyfriend (Jean Sorel) of being "not quite right," grabbing the youth by the shirtfront and humiliating him by kissing him on the lips in front of everyone. "That's what you are!" Vallone shouts, throwing him aside. The screen's first male-male kiss was an accusation of the behavior it was supposed to describe. If a man were to grab a woman and kiss her on the lips, shouting "That's what you are!" nobody would understand the accusation. (Was she accused of being a kisser?) But here the scene says that two men kissing represents not the act but the orientation—homosexuality, what Vallone calls "not quite right." Yet even by its own standards, the film presents nothing that is "wrong." The charges against Sorel are only that he knows how to cut a dress pattern and that he sings tenor. And so Vallone's character comes off as an old jock from *Tea and Sympathy* who is still yelling "Sister Boy!" at the sensitive but straight youth. Since there is no homosexual, the kissing scene is pure shock. The spectre of homosexuality is raised, but it remains as invisible as Sebastian Venable's gay ghost.

The lesbianism in *The Children's Hour* (1962) might have remained the

"That's what you are!" Raf Vallone (right) prepares to kiss Jean Sorel on the lips in Sidney Lumet's A View from the Bridge *(1962).*

same kind of spectre, a false accusation hurled at two "innocent" teachers by a vicious child, had it not been for an added touch of reality by Lillian Hellman. According to *Films in Review,* the idea for *The Children's Hour* suggested itself to Hellman when she read *Bad Company,* a story by a Scottish lawyer, William Roughhead. It told how two Edinburgh schoolteachers were accused of lesbianism in 1810 by a half-caste student whose grandmother then spread the libel and ruined the school. Similarly, Hellman's drama is the examination of how lies can have the power to destroy the lives of innocent people. And, as the director William Wyler pointed out, it could work on this level only if the lie were a pretty terrible thing. "The lie has to have such a devastating effect," he said, "that to be credible it must be appalling." So there is some *Tea and Sympathy* here, too, in that lesbianism is never considered a valid option. Homosexuality is the dirty secret.

But in the character of Martha Dobie (Shirley MacLaine) Hellman created the sudden revelation that comes to a woman who discovers the truth of her own lesbianism by means of a child's stupid lie. That self-revelation costs Martha Dobie her life—the first in a long series of suicides of homosexual screen characters. In a climactic confrontation scene, Martha traces the growth of her love for Karen Wright (Audrey Hepburn) from their schooldays. In a tortured monologue, filled with self-hatred, she expresses her own culpability. "I'm guilty!" she cries. "I've ruined your life, and I've ruined my own. I feel so damn sick and dirty I just can't stand it anymore." In a scene of the play that did not appear in the film, it is made clear that when Martha hangs herself following this confession, she does so not because a false accusation has ruined her life but because she has discovered that she really is a lesbian. It is not a lie that destroys Martha; it is the awful truth. Martha was guilty of being the alien thing everyone feared, and her "coming out" speech reflects the surprise and wonder she feels at this discovery. "There's something in you," she tells Karen, "and you don't know anything about it because you don't know it's there. I couldn't call it by name before, but I know now. It's there. It's been there ever since I first knew you."

It; the film did not name "it" either. In a courtroom scene cut from the final print, a judge finds Karen and Martha guilty of "having had sinful sexual knowledge of one another." In keeping with Code requirements, lesbianism existed in the film only by implication; the innuendos about child molestation are more explicit than those about the sexuality of the teachers. The accusing student's grandmother (Fay Bainter) orders the two women from her home, saying, "This *thing* is your own. Take it out of here. I don't understand it. I don't want any part of it . . . you've been playing with a lot of children's lives, that's why I had to stop you." Thus the lesbianism that Martha discovers in herself is the lesbianism defined by the drama, the desire of sinful sexual knowledge of another woman.

Martha's growing love for Karen, treated gently throughout the Hellman play, is thinly sketched in the film version. In an interview in 1976, Shirley MacLaine put the blame on Wyler.

Lillian Hellman hadn't just fallen out of her tree when she wrote *The Children's Hour* in the early Thirties. She had experienced a lot of it herself. In the play, scenes were developed so that you could see Martha falling in love with Karen and realizing why she was jealous of Karen's boyfriend . . . but when Wyler put it on the screen he cut those scenes out. He thought they would be too much for middle America to take. I thought he was wrong, and I told him so, and Audrey Hepburn was right behind me. But he was the director, and there was nothing we could do. Even so, I conceived my part as though those scenes were still there. I didn't want it to suddenly just hit her when the child tells the lie that maybe she could really be a lesbian and therefore she felt sick and dirty. Lillian had written a slow examination of one woman's personal growth in the area of falling in love with another woman. But Willie Wyler didn't want that, and that's why the story didn't work on film.

That is not what Hellman wanted, either—unless she intended to suggest that suicide equals personal growth. Martha was a doomed character, and the story did not work onscreen because the audience was denied the satisfaction of seeing Karen reunited with her boyfriend (James Garner) at the end. The close of the film offered a rare touch of dignity, but it was not a crowd pleaser. At Martha's funeral, Karen kneels at the flower-covered casket and whispers, "Goodbye, Martha. I'll love you until I die." As her estranged fiancé watches from a crowd of staring mourners, Karen walks past him and out of the cemetery, alone, her head held high.

According to the *Hollywood Reporter,* until two months before the film's final release date, Wyler wanted to tack a "new, upbeat ending on the picture. Instead of leaving Audrey Hepburn sobbing in the cemetery as of the present print, James Garner will follow her home." Although this alternative ending was not used, *Time* imagined its own happy ending and erroneously informed its readers that at the end of the film "Audrey Hepburn walks towards her boyfriend." Perhaps the *Time* critic saw what he wanted to see; others were out for blood. *Films in Review* attacked Hellman, Wyler and the Mirisch Company for "condoning lesbianism, albeit surreptitiously" because in the film MacLaine mentions those homosexuals "who believe in it, who have chosen it for themselves." After the two women have been destroyed by the child's lie, *Films in Review* said, "there is an explicit scene which asserts that those who *choose* to practice lesbianism are not destroyed by it—a claim disproven by the number of lesbians who become insane or commit suicide."

In fact *The Children's Hour,* while presenting a tragic figure, afforded the visibility of a real human being who discovered her true sexuality at a crucial moment in her life. The "condoning" of lesbianism cited by *Films in Review* involved Martha's reference to the survivors of her ordeal. "This isn't a new sin they say we've done," Karen says. "Other people haven't been destroyed by it." Martha thinks for a moment, then replies, "They're the people who want it. Who believe in it. Who have chosen it for themselves. That must be very different."

Karen and Martha referred unwittingly to a subculture that was still a twilight world of half-understood terrors. But not for long; Otto Preminger's *Advise and Consent* (1962), which followed *The Children's Hour* into release by only three months, presented homosexuality on essentially the same ground. Again, a false accusation and a dirty secret precipitate the suicide of the accused. But here, with Code approval, was the chance to show "the people who want it," of whom Martha Dobie had spoken. The story of political corruption, based on Allen Drury's novel, contains a subplot in which Senator Brig Anderson (Don Murray) is blackmailed by political opponents because of a homosexual incident in his army past with a fellow soldier named Ray (John Granger). In a sequence not found in the novel, Anderson, terrified by the snide accusations telephoned to his distraught wife, takes a night flight to New York to track down Ray. His search leads him to the apartment of a mysterious fat man who lives in a walkup surrounded by cats. The fat man obviously pimps for Ray, who has become a hustler of sorts. The young senator is directed to a local gay bar, one said to be fashioned after a popular New York haunt of the early Sixties.

The screen's first official gay bar, overloaded to create the desired effect of otherworldliness in a previously hidden subculture, is nevertheless quite tame compared to the more flamboyant versions of later films. As Anderson enters the dimly lit bar, he is confronted by three glaring, decidedly "arch" men, one of whom holds a cigarette grandly aloft. He walks past the three men, down a narrow hallway and into a room in which colored spotlights punctuate the darkness, revealing scenes of men sitting together at candlelit tables. The music, coming from a juke box, features the voice of Frank Sinatra.

Long alone . . .
I have sung the loser's song alone.

Let me hear a voice

A secret voice
A voice that will say
Come to me
And be what I need you to be . . .

Don Murray is shocked by his first glimpse of a gay bar in Otto Preminger's Advise and Consent *(1962). It was also a first for modern American audiences, and they were shocked as well.*

Anderson, visibly shaken, backs away and runs for the door. However, Ray has spotted him and follows, trying to explain why he has been cooperating with the blackmailers. "I was drunk," he shouts, "I needed money . . . you wouldn't see me, I kept calling!" There is a brief struggle on the street when Ray tries to stop Anderson from fleeing in a taxi, and Ray is thrown face down into a puddle of dirty water. Anderson speeds back to Washington, locks himself in his oak-paneled Senate office and slits his throat with a straight razor.

The "tired old sin" for which Brig Anderson dies is never named in the film. His grieving wife (Inga Swenson) knows the truth because she has seen the blackmail notes and photos of Brig and Ray, but she withholds the information lest it harm her husband's memory. His status as a hero depends on this because, like Shirley MacLaine's Martha, he too was once guilty, and in the gay bar he realizes this. He kills himself not because he is being blackmailed in Washington but because he has gone to New York and found people with whom he has something in common and is so repulsed that he sees no alternative to the straight razor. Thirteen years later, in Max Baer's *Ode to Billy Joe* (1976), another reflection of 1950s masculine mythology, Billy Joe McAllister (Robby Benson) suffers a similar fate and is protected in the same way by the girl who loves him (Glynis O'Connor). When Billy Joe jumps off the Tallahatchie Bridge because he had "been with a man—a sin against God and nature," his secret dies with him. "Can't have people thinking he died because of a *man,*" O'Connor says solemnly. "He's a legend around here now." And legends cannot be queer.

The bar scene in *Advise and Consent* dramatized the difference between Ray and Brig. The film virtually canonizes Brig for his dislike of Ray's surroundings. Look how the two young American soldiers turned out, the film seems to say; the one who was really straight became a senator of the United States, and the one who was really gay became a seedy hustler, a barfly and a blackmailer. The fat man, the cats and the cheap bar were necessary to make the distinction that had only been outlined in *The Children's Hour.* Ray and Brig illustrated the difference between someone who had "tried it" once in the army (where there is always a whine about no women and how loneliness can make a man weak) and someone who really wanted it. Preminger, unable to say "homosexual" in his script, had a field day with his graphic illustration of Ray's twilight world. Wendell Mayes, the screenwriter, noted that the sequence was created to spell out the nature of the blackmail threat on which the plot twist is based. "It was somewhat sensational in 1961, to be so open about a closed subject, and candidly, I suppose I dramatized it the way I did for its sensational impact."

Where *The Children's Hour* made brief reference to the twilight world and *Advise and Consent* visited it in New York City, Edward Dmytryk's adaptation of Nelson Algren's novel *Walk on the Wild Side* (1962) was set in the underworld itself, and the lesbianism of Jo (Barbara Stanwyck), the madam of a New Orleans brothel, was created to fit into it. In the three films, released in the same year, America returned to the archetypes with only a few concessions to modern times. Just as the briefly liberated films of the early Thirties had routinely represented gays as being part of various illicit subcultures, the evolution of Jo in *Walk on the Wild Side* indicated a return from ostrichlike silence to business as usual for Hollywood. The movies simply reflected what little they could identify of a hidden world and, in both pre-Code and post-Code times, saw homosexuals solely in sexual terms because that was what had always been sold. For more than thirty years people had agreed that "it" should not be talked about, and when the ban was lifted they picked up where they had left off. In 1962, however, *Walk on the Wild Side* was at liberty to define the sexual ghetto with greater frankness and precision. The Code allowed it. Therefore the brothel portrayed in the film, the screenwriter Edmund North points out, "was not a dance hall, as in the film version of *From Here to Eternity.* Our whorehouse was a whorehouse."

Stanwyck's Jo was the opposite of MacLaine's Martha, a villain, not a victim.

Jo's acceptance of her own lesbianism is part of her villainy. Any decent woman would kill herself, as Martha and Brig did, rather than open a whorehouse and prey on her girls. Like Ray, she was one of those "who have chosen it." When Jo lashes out at her husband with "What does *any* man know about the feelings of a woman?" it is supposed to explain—but not excuse—her man-hating lesbianism. Jo's sexual and emotional domination of Hallie (Capucine), her most beautiful whore, is central to the plot because it binds Hallie to prostitution and at the same time stands in the way of her chances for a normal relationship with her boyfriend Dove Linkhorn (Laurence Harvey). Jo's love for Hallie precipitates everyone's downfall. Hallie, a victim like Martha, dies when she is accidentally shot by one of Jo's minions, and Jo the villain is sent to prison ("Vice Queen Jailed"). Yet, according to North, "there was not the slightest hint of homoeroticism in Algren's novel. That relationship between Jo and Hallie, among others, was mine."

The marketplaces of various sexual ghettos widened routinely to accommo-

What the well-dressed lesbian will wear. Costume sketches for Candice Bergen's Lakey in Sidney Lumet's The Group *(1966) and Barbara Stanwyck's Jo in* Walk on the Wild Side *(1962).*

"Whores are a dime a dozen, but a good bookkeeper is hard to find." Shelley Winters zeroes in on Lee Grant in the film version of Genet's The Balcony *(1963).*

date new gay characters. A lesbian relationship involving another screen madam (Shelley Winters), in an adaptation of Jean Genet's *The Balcony* (1963), featured a kiss between Winters and her bookkeeper (Lee Grant) that earned the description a "lesbian letch" in *Variety's* review. In Sidney Lumet's *The Pawnbroker* (1965), Brock Peters played an imperious, sadistic pimp who is clearly having an affair with a man (whom *Newsday* called his "white underling"). These combinations of newly visible losers thrown together in the sexual jungles of major cities did not demystify homosexuality; they only paid tribute to its mysterious, lowlife nature. What disappeared was the restriction on saying "it" out loud.

Gore Vidal used the word *homosexual* in his screen adaptation of his own play *The Best Man,* directed for the screen by Franklin Schaffner in 1964. A political melodrama similar to *Advise and Consent,* but with fewer soapsuds, the film uses homosexuality once again as a blackmail threat, this time against a candidate for president of the United States (Cliff Robertson). The incumbent president (Henry Fonda) receives the information but refuses to use it because he knows it is not true. "If I thought he *was* homosexual, I'd use it in a minute," Fonda says, indicating that although he would not smear an innocent man, a homosexual president would be out of the question. The Code ignored the use of the word *homosexual* this time, but, according to Vidal, it insisted on one cut. "I had the old president react to the smear by saying, 'I don't care if he deflowers sheep by the light of the moon,' and the censors said, 'You can't say that—that's bestiality.' So I changed it to 'I don't care if he has carnal knowledge of a McCormick reaper,' and that was all right."

In the same period, America's obsession with defining homosexuality by its third syllable contrasted sharply with more human exercises from Europe. On the American screen the discovery of a character's homosexuality came most often as the shock of seeing the familiar suddenly turn alien, a ploy of classic horror films, like studying a pretty picture and watching it turn into a grinning skull. Revelation scenes abounded. *Bus Riley's Back in Town* (1965), written by William Inge under the pseudonym Walter Gage, contains this kind of lurking, sex-defined creature. A lecherous old undertaker puts his hand on the knee of all-American sailor boy Michael Parks who, like Brig Anderson before him, flees when he sees the face of the demon. But attitudes in European films were less relentlessly chilling, less grim. Maybe that is why the cool and sophisticated Lakey (Candice Bergen) in *The Group* (1966) ran off to Europe to be a lesbian, returning years later, complete with tailored suit and mysterious baroness (Lidia Prochnika) in tow. According to Pauline Kael, Lakey's lesbianism was handled with such "discretion that United Artists publicity men threw out the ad campaign they'd prepared to exploit it." But Mary McCarthy's heroines had the money to flee to Europe if necessary. Jonathan Katz' *Gay American History* recounts a conversation in which a lesbian says, "Lesbians are subnatural when they live next door to you and supernatural when they live in Paris and write books."

In such films as *The L-Shaped Room, The Leather Boys* and *The Family Way* from England and *This Special Friendship* from France, gays are portrayed in terms of nonsexual love as well as erotic love. Yet most of the homosexuals in these films faced heavy social or moral penalties, including the obligatory suicide in *This Special Friendship*. Nevertheless the situations were less hysterical than those in American films, and sexual acts did not form the framework in which the gay characters existed. Affection entered the picture, perhaps for the first time.

The L-Shaped Room (1962) portrays love as a many-gendered thing in a seamy London rooming house. Johnny (Brock Peters), a West Indian jazz musician, is painfully in love with the object of Leslie Caron's affections (Tom Bell) and lies in bed at night listening to the two of them make love and writhing in agony. But he is not suffering because he is homosexual; he has the blues because Tom Bell is not interested in him. (Bell, who describes Johnny as "a bit bent," later took the role of a homosexual on the London stage, opposite Ian McKellen, in Martin Sherman's *Bent,* a play about the Nazi persecution of homosexuals.)

Elsewhere in the rooming house lives a sweet old vaudevillian, a welcome contrast to Johnny's pain and spiteful behavior. Beautifully played by Cicely Courtneidge, she is full of song and dance and is cheerily interested in everyone else's business. She talks constantly of the "friend" with whom she once shared her life yet expresses contentment with her present solitary state. "A real love match it was," she tells Leslie Caron. "I've never wanted anything since." When Caron asks if "he" was in show business too, Courtneidge smiles and takes from the mantel a tiny framed photo of a woman. "This is my friend," she says gently. "It takes all kinds, you know, dearie." It is a coming out scene so much less painful than Martha Dobie's in *The Children's Hour*. But playing vaudeville in Brighton is not the same as teaching rich little girls in New England; show people are expected to be a bit odd.

The Courtneidge character does not appear in the novel by Lynn Reid Banks from which *The L-Shaped Room* was adapted. Bryan Forbes, the director, says he based her on "a woman I once met when I was an actor and on tour in England with Gertrude Lawrence. She was mostly my invention, drawn from personal observation, and it was my intention, for once, to present a sympathetic portrait of a lesbian's twilight world."

In terms of screen impact, the funny vaudevillian was a harmless old lady, slightly dotty, while the musician was a powerless, doubly cursed black homosexual. But Forbes made them people, even survivors in a sense, not guest freaks like the drooling undertaker in *Bus Riley*. In a way, the film says, "Well, even *they* have feelings," and in that sense the film can be seen as condescending, but it took the American screen another ten years to achieve that level of condescension toward homosexuals. Paul Mazursky's use of a token male homosexual couple in an otherwise heterosexual roundelay at the end of *Bob & Carol & Ted & Alice* (1969) looked forward to the Seventies with the teary-eyed acknowledgment that "What the World Needs Now Is Love, Sweet Love," and that included those silly faggots in their lavender silk shirts. Mazursky used a similar image at the end of *Blume in Love* (1973) when he showed a homosexual couple in the Piazza San Marco, a postscript that said with a gulp, "Yes, they too are loved," while Susan Anspach and George Segal embraced in the foreground.

In Sidney J. Furie's *The Leather Boys* and Bill Naughton's *The Family Way*, queerness emerges as the central issue in perceptive studies of masculinity. Both films show ways in which homosexual panic limits the feelings between men. In *The Leather Boys* (1964), young Reggie (Colin Campbell) leaves his wife Dot (Rita Tushingham) and their drab, disappointing marriage for the adolescent romance and excitement of a lawless alliance with his buddy Pete

(Dudley Sutton). Near the end of the film the innocent Reggie is confronted with Pete's homosexuality in a grim leather bar on the waterfront. Realizing that Pete and his friends are homosexuals, Reggie follows the tradition and runs like hell.

But Furie's film does not use homosexuality as a bogeyman; when Reggie runs away, he is not fleeing from the horror of the unknown or even the unthinkable. *The Leather Boys* illuminates the betrayal that Reggie feels. We see that he wants to escape what he imagines will be the same emotional responsibilities that he could not face in his heterosexual marriage. By popular definition, Pete's homosexuality brought "a woman" into the picture and destroyed the adolescent fantasy. *The Leather Boys* chooses to make the buddy relationship suddenly explicit and deliberately homosexual. In doing so it shows why the existence of physical homosexuality ruins the clean dream of the dime novel romance between men. The appeal of the buddy relationship for heterosexual men has always been that of an escape from the role playing of men and women—a safe, neutral emotional zone with no chance for confusion. The possibility that sex could intrude in such a relationship muddles the situation hopelessly. Reggie runs not from homosexuality but from what he sees as another kind of emotional commitment.

In its exploration of another kind of buddy relationship, *The Family Way* (1966) takes some of the issues raised by *Tea and Sympathy* a step further. When a shy young man (Hywel Bennett) fails to consummate his marriage to an equally nervous young bride (Hayley Mills) under his father's roof, speculation arises in the family regarding the lad's masculinity. The boy's father (John Mills) refers throughout the film to his "old pal, Billy Stringfellow," with whom it is clear he had the most satisfying emotional relationship of his life. Inseparable, they had enjoyed long talks and quiet walks along the beach; Billy had even accompanied him and his wife on their honeymoon. Then Billy disappeared one day, after a brief affair with the wife, and Mills never discovered the reason for his departure. Now, years later, he complains that his son is showing signs of sissyhood. "To think a son of mine can't prove his manhood!" he shouts, adding defensively, "There's nothing odd or queer about *me!*"

"Would you say," asks his wife (Marjorie Rhodes), "that there was something odd or queer about a fellow who went on his honeymoon and took his pal along?" But this is not sarcasm, it is tolerance. Answering the inherent question of *Tea and Sympathy,* she takes up the banner for her son. "And suppose he *were?"* she shouts at her husband, who is now lost in reveries of Billy. "Is it something to get *at* the lad for? Nature would've done it. A father should help and protect a lad like that—not turn on him like the mob when it sees

The last sequence in The Leather Boys *(1964), when Reggie discovers that Pete's friends are gay.*

somebody different." This is the only film speech in which a parent defends the possibility that a homosexual child might not be turned away from the fold. The mother's suggestion that queerness might be a natural thing, something one could live with, works here because the heterosexuality of her son is never really in doubt. It is the father's relationship with his friend that is at issue in the final scenes of the film, not the inadequacies of his son. Mills breaks down and cries when he sees finally how much like Billy his son has come to be. It is possible that his son is in fact the offspring of Billy; but Mills is crying for the adolescent freedom he lost when Billy disappeared. "Laugh about it when you're young," he mutters to himself, "but one day it will make you bloody cry."

At the end of Federico Fellini's *La Dolce Vita* (1960), a drugged transvestite hits the beach and screams, "By the end of the year 2000 the whole world will be homosexual!" To America, however, homosexuality was still something you did in the dark or in Europe—preferably both. Jean Delannoy's *This Special Friendship* (1964) and John Schlesinger's *Darling* provided slightly shocked American audiences with diverse gay experiences and even a few hints of the decadence that would be put to excessive use in American films of the early Seventies. The Delannoy film, based on Roger Peyrefitte's *Les Amitiés Particulières,* was a sort of male version of *Mädchen in Uniform*. It attacked

Two schoolboys in love in This Special Friendship *(1964).*

the authoritarianism of the Catholic Church, a favorite target of Peyrefitte. The innocent love between two schoolboys afforded one of the most natural and openly affectionate homosexual relationships ever filmed. The freedom and naturalness of the two boys' behavior was contrasted sharply with the fears of a repressed, self-hating homosexual priest who thinks their behavior (and his own) sinful. Although the younger boy (Didier Haudepin) kills himself by jumping from a speeding train, he does so because the priests have told him that his friend no longer loves him—a lie concocted in an effort to force him to leave school quietly. The idea of homosexual love is glorified here, and the Church is challenged on its condemnation of same-sex love.

This Special Friendship had a small success in the United States, drawing heavily on an increasingly visible gay audience that emerged in ghetto cities beginning in New York in 1967. In that year, critic Stuart Byron pointed out in *Variety* that Jean Genet's *Deathwatch,* then playing at the Bleecker Street Cinema, was the first film whose advertising was directed specifically at a gay audience. But while Jack Smith's *Flaming Creatures,* Kenneth Anger's *Scorpio Rising,* Genet's *Un Chant d'Amour* and the films of Maya Deren, Gregory Markopoulos, and others were being seen and discussed as the foremost experimental films of their time, Hollywood saw no such thing as a "gay" audience.

John Schlesinger's *Darling* (1965), which reached an enormous American audience (compared to that for *This Special Friendship*) and won an Oscar for actress Julie Christie, provided clues to the next logical step in the perception of homosexuality onscreen. Bisexuality was introduced, and although it was found to be more acceptable, it was still not considered "normal." Schlesinger's virile Italian waiter, who sleeps one night with Julie Christie and the next with her (happy, amiable, well-adjusted) gay photographer friend, was after all only a waiter in a foreign movie about decadent fashion models and their fey friends (whose chief concern, apparently, was to set the alarm clock to remind them to turn over in the Italian sun). This behavior was a threat to no one. Yet in the same year, 1965, there were big hassles over the character of a bisexual Hollywood actor to be played by Robert Redford in an American film.

Roland Curram cruises an Italian waiter in Darling *(1965) while Julie Christie pouts.* (British Film Institute)

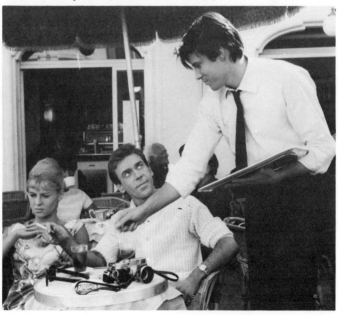

Gavin Lambert's script for *Inside Daisy Clover* (1966) underwent more than one major revision to avoid just the kind of freewheeling, unconscious bisexuality that Schlesinger had given his Italian waiter. The homosexual side of bisexual actor Wade Lewis is avoided altogether, and his bisexuality becomes the dirty secret. Redford's role as the screen star husband of the rising starlet Daisy Clover (Natalie Wood) was conceived originally as a homosexual character who marries Daisy Clover at the request of the studio—for appearances' sake.

But both Redford and director Robert Mulligan became nervous about the direction the role was taking and insisted on certain changes.

"I didn't want to play Wade Lewis as a homosexual, as the script originally had him," Redford told writer Jim Spada in 1976. "I wanted to play him as a guy who bats ten ways—men, women, children, dogs, cats, anything—anything that salves his ego. Total narcissism." The script was changed, and Wade Lewis became a bisexual.

But there was more nervousness as the shooting progressed, and again during the editing, and the new version of Wade Lewis' bisexuality became less and less specific. Lambert says, "We made the basic changes in the idea of the character of Wade and made him a sort of bisexual who keeps his bisexuality a secret, and I was quite happy with that. There were a lot of valid reasons for doing it, and it was marvelous for Redford." Consequently there is one telephone conversation in *Inside Daisy Clover* during which the secret of Wade's bisexuality comes out.

As the time drew near to shoot that scene, according to Lambert, "Mulligan got more and more nervous about the lines being too explicit, and several of them were cut, making it all not very intelligible." In the end the revelation of Wade's bisexuality was squeaked out in a postsynched line or two of dialogue, but all of Lambert's attempts to establish it visually failed. "I suggested one scene in which Daisy was having her breakdown and they all come to her bedroom one by one. When Redford arrived, I wanted a young man on the veranda behind him with never a word about why he was there. I think it would have made its point quietly. But it was vetoed. What pleased me about *Daisy Clover* was that even in its mutilated state, the film showed Wade as attractive and functional."

True; Wade Lewis, though of discreetly questionable sexuality at best, was a character cast in the traditional mold of the handsome Hollywood hero. Any tampering whatever with his sexuality represented a giant step away from that tradition. More than two dozen films used lesbianism or male homosexuality for a plot twist or as a major theme in the last years of the 1960s, and none of the gays were particularly attractive or even functional. Villains, of course, were cunning and functional, but they were all killed in the last reel. (As Lambert points out, if Wade Lewis had been totally homosexual, he would have had to kill himself at the end of the movie.) The gentle lesbian of *The L-Shaped Room* gave way in America to predatory neurotics and cartoon dykes; Johnny the West Indian jazz musician became Sidney Lumet's pimp in *The Pawnbroker*, a man who sells love for money. The cartoons and the caricatures continued.

A few changes were wrought by the increasing visibility of homosexuals in

American society. In the Sixties the subject of gays onscreen became more and more an examination of what was now being identified as the closet syndrome. All the homosexuals interviewed by Mike Wallace on *CBS Presents: The Homosexuals* in 1967 were seated behind potted palm trees, the leaves obscuring their faces. Stereotypes were heightened, but the growing diversity of new homosexual characters worked constantly against them. In her review of *Victim* in 1961, Pauline Kael had bemoaned the suffering in that film and longed for the good old days of Franklin Pangborn and Grady Sutton. She sensed that those characters and the shorthand they represented would disappear, and she was right. We no longer needed shorthand, though we hung on to the safety of the stereotype. "There is so much effort to make us feel sympathetic to homosexuals in *Victim,*" Kael wrote, "that they are never allowed to be *gay.*" This was like saying that there was so much effort to make us feel sympathy for blacks in *Nothing But a Man* or *One Potato, Two Potato* that they were never allowed to tap dance or eat a slice of watermelon. After all, the stereotype was the charm of such characters in the long view, and in a sense it is perfectly valid to mourn their passing.

It is common to wax nostalgic over one's lost cinema past, however stereotypical; the practice is perhaps even more common among members of a minority group that has been invisible in real life. Inclusion in the myth, even token representation in the American dream being played out onscreen, was of paramount importance, for it was confirmation that one existed. A visibility barely glimpsed through a pervasive illusion is doubly valued and certainly more memorable for those people who have never spoken aloud their very name. Homosexuals, cut off from society and from one another, have spent lifetimes growing up at the movies alongside heterosexual relatives and neighbors. Everyone learned the same dream, but gays appreciated the sexual joke more fully than the others, being able to see the illusion from both sides. For many the movies were where one learned to pass for straight, where one learned the boundaries of what America would accept as normal. Yet the movies shared an alternative truth. Early gay stereotypes in film were signals, testaments to the existence of others at a time when nobody was supposed to know that there *were* others. It was a screen reality that we now recall affectionately as the phenomenon which took place in the absence of gay visibility and was doomed to fade as gays found their voices.

In the documentary film *Word Is Out: Conversations with 26 Lesbians and Gay Men* (1977), Pat Bond, a former WAC, expresses this nostalgia for a stereotypical past. Having lived through the military witchhunts of the 1940s in Tokyo and police raids on San Francisco bars in the 1950s, she says, "I'll miss the excitement of the old gay world, somehow—of belonging to a secret place that nobody knew about but you. I'll miss that." It was comfortable, she was saying; everyone knew the rules, whom they were to be and what they were expected to do. In his affectionate interpretive history of blacks in film, *Toms, Coons, Mulattoes, Mammies and Bucks,* Donald Bogle says that "the essence of black film history is not found in the stereotyped role but in what certain talented actors have done with the stereotype." In the same sense, the characters created by Pangborn, Sutton, Horton, Webb and dozens of others brought a brief electric contact with the quicksilver truth and wrought a comic chaos that the social order suppressed. Each in his own style, they were signposts to a hidden gay experience where chaos was the norm. But what they reflected then is now dead.

Victim had revived the issue of politicizing homosexual visibility for the first time since the German propaganda films of the early 1900s. The jokes on which the old sissies had been based were no longer so funny; stereotypes lose their charm when they are examined too closely and their mythic foundations are challenged. They outgrow the naive values that gave them life. An alternative evolution was developed for the sissy, another option for the dyke. But the new options were no more attractive and even less universal than the old ones, and the stereotypes would be forced to live past their time for years to come.

When gays became real, they became threatening. The new sissies departed radically from their gentle ancestors; the dykes became predatory and dangerous. Lesbians were still creatures to be conquered or defeated, but now viciously so, as though they were other men. The charm and challenge of the early role-reversal comics, once the smug chink in society's armor, gave way to a subversive omnipresence. And the symbols gave way to the certainty that there actually were people who were queer.

While sober films would eventually take up some of the issues raised in *Victim,* the comic stereotype became a useful tool for putting homosexuality back in its place. As object lessons, officially defined as the opposite of normal, sissies and dykes throughout the 1960s were a nasty lot even when they were funny. They exhibited an abundance of the "meanness" that Bosley Crowther had found lacking in *A Taste of Honey*'s sweet Geoff. Once "it" had been named and had officially arrived onscreen, the whimsical creatures of old disappeared, to be replaced by the dirty jokes that neatly accompanied the dirty secrets of more serious films.

Popular sex farces and James Bond spy thrillers used sissies and dykes to prove the virility of cartoon heroes and to stress the sterility of homosexuality.

Crowther, reviewing *Goldfinger* for the *New York Times,* identified the super-masculine pose of James Bond as "what we're now calling homosexual sarcasm." There was plenty of room for sarcasm. In *From Russia with Love* (1963) and *Goldfinger* (1964), cartoon dykes are alternately killed and cured in the grand tradition of heterosexual solutions. In the former, Lotte Lenya's Colonel Rosa Klebb is old, snakelike, dangerous; a killer spy who makes cobra eyes at a young blonde agent on whom she tries to put the arm during a private interview. The young blonde, of course, is in love with James Bond, at whose crotch Klebb aims a spike-tipped shoe. Bond's castration is prevented when Klebb is shot to death by the pretty young thing she had tried to seduce. In *Goldfinger,* Bond conquers the beautiful Pussy Galore (Honor Blackman), a lesbian doll who comes to life complete with a coterie of beautiful Amazons. Sean Connery's Bond relishes the challenge that Ian Fleming describes so vividly in his novel.

[Bond] liked the look of her. He felt the sexual challenge all beautiful lesbians have for men. He was amused by the uncompromising attitude that said "all men are bastards and cheats. Don't try any hocus pocus on me . . . I'm in a separate league."

There is a preoccupation with sports terminology in the typical male definition of lesbianism; it also surfaces in Gordon Douglas' *Tony Rome* (1967), in which

Lotte Lenya as Colonel Rosa Klebb tries to put the arm on Daniela Bianchi in From Russia with Love *(1963).*

Frank Sinatra plays another kind of James Bond, a sexy private eye. Sinatra describes two lesbians as being "in the wrong ballpark" and therefore "out of his league" in the romance department. The solution is as much a cartoon as the problem. Bond is so much the "real" man that his seduction of Pussy Galore takes on a cosmic comic-book truth.

[Pussy] lay in the crook of Bond's arm and looked up at him. She said, not in a gangster's voice, or a lesbian's, but in a girl's voice, "Will you write to me in Sing Sing?" Bond looked down into her deep violet eyes that were no longer hard, imperious. He bent and kissed them lightly. He said, "They told me you only liked women." She said, "I never met a man before." His mouth came down ruthlessly on hers.

Lesbians who were of use in the service of male sexuality were those beautiful young women who could be variously defined to serve the fantasies of male conquest. Old crows like Rosa Klebb were messily dispatched, along with homosexual men and any other challenge to a James Bond hero. Wint (Bruce Glover) and Kidd (Putter Smith), two gay lovers who are not to be found in the novel *Diamonds Are Forever,* appear in the 1971 film version as gleeful killers. The pair even get to walk hand in hand into the sunset after they have blown up a helicopter. In the end, though, they are set aflame and toasted like the two marshmallows they really are.

Gays dropped like flies in the Sixties, and for as many reasons as there were tragedies. Sometimes the sexuality of lesbians or crazed gay men victimized others, threatening the status quo; sometimes it caused self-hatred enough to make them suicidal. Either way, the fray was thick with dead bodies, and few escaped to the relative safety of the closet. The question, as it applied to the portrayal of gays at the end of the 1960s, became one of visibility. Overt, active or predatory gays—including some particularly nasty sissies who would have been harmless thirty years before—were killed off. The repressed, tormented types usually committed suicide, and scattered cases were "cured" by sufficient attention from the opposite sex. Obvious cartoons were spared when they happened to be passing through only to provide color or to present a strong contrast to a sexy hero. Pathetic, lonely old lesbians were preserved if they were not wearing spiked shoes. Survival was an option only for nonthreatening characters, and almost all homosexuals threatened the heterosexual status quo by their very existence.

Lilith, The Haunting, The Night of the Iguana and *Seven Women* all featured lesbians who survive in a twilight world of neurotic repression. In Robert Rossen's adaptation of *Lilith* (1964), Jean Seberg is a mental patient who wanders blithely into an affair with an older woman (Anne Meacham) during their confinement in an institution. Lilith's acceptance of the lesbian attraction is seen as a consequence of her psychosis, a willingness to live in a constant state of sexual heat. Even so, Warren Beatty, supposedly a hospital trainee responsible for Lilith's mental health, insists on making love to her immediately following his discovery of the two women locked in an embrace in an old barn on the hospital grounds. Lilith is "set straight," and the cure of her psychosis presumes the cure of her lesbianism. Anne Meacham, the "real" lesbian, quietly disappears, just as Pussy Galore's lesbian lover Tilly Masterson (Tania Mallett) disappears from *Goldfinger* after Pussy is won over by James Bond.

Warren Beatty pulls Anne Meacham off Jean Seberg in Lilith *(1964).*

In *Lilith,* Jean Seberg was susceptible to the advances of Anne Meacham because Lilith was a sick girl and the affair took place in a mental hospital removed from the "civilized world." In *Seven Women* (1966) and *The Night of the Iguana* (1964), the action takes place in the desolate reaches of Outer Mongolia and in primitive jungles. Grayson Hall's repressed spinster in *Iguana* and Margaret Leighton's fanatical missionary woman in *Seven Women* have buried their lesbianism beneath religion and devotion to their work. In each case, they are tempted by an unsuspecting innocent who brings their latent sexuality briefly and dangerously to the surface. Both women are moralistic ogres whose predatory urges, unconscious and unrecognized, are quickly buried before they can do serious damage. In both films the childlike Sue Lyon is the catalyst.

In both films, too, there is inherent sympathy for these women who will never be fulfilled in a normal way. But in *The Night of the Iguana,* Tennessee Williams describes more fully the impact of the closet on Miss Fellowes (Grayson Hall), stressing the power of forbidden sexuality to destroy. When Maxine Falk (Ava Gardner), the earthy proprietor of the jungle hotel, lays Miss Fellowes out cold in the last scene, calling her a "dyke," the defrocked minister Shannon (Richard Burton) steps in to protect her. "Miss Fellowes is a very moral person," he tells Maxine. "If she ever found out the truth about herself, it would destroy her." Both Miss Fellowes and Leighton's missionary woman are saved by their ignorance. Never having to face the self-awakening that is forced on Martha Dobie in *The Children's Hour,* they are allowed to live. Unconscious lesbianism is its own punishment.

The same is true for Claire Bloom's neurotic Greenwich Village lesbian in *The Haunting* (1963). She gets her psychosexual jollies by hugging Julie Harris and blaming it on ghosts. But she is not predatory; she is just out of life's running. She professes no interest in actively seducing either Harris or an attentive Russ Tamblyn. The lesbianism is entirely mental, and her sterility leaves her at a dead end. The militaristic Rosa Klebb laid a hand on a blonde's knee and got shot, but Bloom merely returns to Greenwich Village—presumably where such characters are made. Lesbianism is rendered invisible because it is purely psychological. And since most lesbians were invisible even to themselves, their sexuality, ill-defined in general, emerged onscreen as a wasted product of a closeted lifestyle.

Creatures of repression are often fascinating characters because their whole lives are apt to be illuminated in a sudden brief moment of truth. The lesbianism of Calla Mackie, Estelle Parsons' lonely schoolteacher in *Rachel, Rachel* (1968), emerges all at once when she delivers an impulsive but passionate kiss on the lips of a shocked Joanne Woodward, local spinster. It is a touching and pathetic moment because she has been in the closet for years and is just as shocked as Woodward—who after an awkward time remains her friend in spite of the revelation. But "it" will never come up again; Calla Mackie has nowhere to go either. Like Miss Fellowes and Leighton's missionary, she is a highly moral person, almost fanatical in her religious beliefs. Each of these women has a motherly instinct that masks her untoward interest in young, helpless women. The formula is a remnant of the barely lesbian characters of the 1950s (such as Kim Stanley's motherly nurse [Elizabeth Wilson] in *The Goddess*) and it is with us today, representing one view of the closeted life.

In Robert Altman's *A Wedding* (1978), Geraldine Chaplin plays the "bride lady" who oversees the wedding reception from start to finish, making sure

Margaret Leighton represses her desire for Sue Lyon in Seven Women *(1966).*

that everything comes off on schedule. She thinks of her brides as "my only children" and, in a character switch, browbeats her female assistant mercilessly. She expresses her real feelings when she suddenly pulls an Estelle Parsons on the current bride. After the kiss, shocked for a moment by what she has done, she says the same thing that Parsons said to Woodward: "I didn't do that!" This is harmless dykery; the woman probably pulls the same pounce on all her brides and has developed it into a routine. Altman always creates characters who get their rocks off in strange ways, and gays who deny their own sexuality are invisible by choice and present no threat.

In the same way that lesbians measured the virility of a James Bond or enforced their own invisibility in serious drama, sissies measured the virility of Bond's humdrum generation while ensuring their own invisibility in serious films. In sex farces such as *That Touch of Mink, The Wheeler Dealers, A Very Special Favor* and *Any Wednesday,* heroes were sexual athletes who protested their masculinity too much. James Garner, Cary Grant, Jason Robards and especially Rock Hudson were the romantic leading men who played the field and ended up corralled. Along the way, they were contrasted persistently with any number of flamboyant decorators, art critics, hairdressers and aunties. In the Thirties and Forties, the "real" men were friends with the classic sissies; Fred Astaire and Edward Everett Horton had been affectionate with each other. But just as Eric Blore had stepped over the line and confused the issue when he told Leslie Howard "I love you" in *It's Love I'm After* (1937), more rigorous lines were drawn in the explicit Sixties. Sex became the dirty joke and homosexuality the added snigger.

Any Wednesday (1966) featured a gratuitous lisping interior decorator who comes and goes in a puff of lavender smoke, but the payoff was the reaction of Robards to a bogus intimation of homosexuality. His mistress (Jane Fonda) tells him that her fantasy is a roomful of balloons. "Wouldn't that be *gay?*" she asks. Robards snaps to attention at the word *gay* and puts his hands out in an automatic gesture of defense. "Oh, no!" he says firmly, "I never answer questions like that without my lawyer at my side."

In *That Touch of Mink* (1962), the paranoia is founded in psychiatry. Gig Young, a failed Romeo, regularly provides his psychiatrist with tips on the stock market. In one couch scene Young is distraught over losing Doris Day to Cary Grant, and he muses aloud about what he would do if he were a woman and a rich, handsome man offered *him* a trip to Bermuda and a mink coat. The psychiatrist hears only part of the monologue and concludes that Young is in love with Grant. He rushes to the telephone to call his broker. "Cancel my order!" he shouts. "My patient has developed some instabilities which make his judgment questionable."

The masculine insecurities of James Garner in *The Wheeler Dealers* and Rock Hudson in *A Very Special Favor* lead them to seize on yardstick sissies as pop psychology scapegoats for their problems with women. In *The Wheeler Dealers* (1963), Garner plays a Texas oil tycoon who spends his entire visit to New York City trying to seduce Lee Remick. It is the ancient story of the rugged cowboy who is disgusted by the weak men he finds in the big city, this time with Garner hooting and hollering like a dime-store Don Murray from *Bus Stop*. Constantly reminding "modern" businesswoman Lee Remick that it is "unfeminine" for a woman to engage in business, Garner points to the sissies in the movie as proof of the unnaturalness of the liberated world. Remick's boyfriend is a prissy art critic, an obvious fraud surrounded by little old ladies and hapless faggots in shiny silk shirts. Garner's objection to him and the rest of her "arty" friends is that they are a product of female emancipation. Only "masculine women," he says, attract such people.

In *A Very Special Favor* (1965), it is the old-fashioned father of a liberated woman who objects to her weak, passive boyfriend and enlists the help of what he considers a suitably virile replacement. Charles Boyer is the European father of psychologist Leslie Caron. Her boyfriend (Dick Shawn) used to be her hairdresser, and now she orders him about like a lackey. He follows closely on her heels everywhere, talking constantly of the baby they plan to have once they are married. Boyer, speaking with an old friend (Walter Slezak), shouts, "He's ridiculous! His only regret is that *he* will not be able to have the baby!" Slezak replies offhandedly that such a thing would be very difficult to arrange, but Boyer waves him aside. "Ahh," he sighs, "when you meet him, you will not rule out the possibility." In a similar scene in Carl Reiner's *The Comic* (1969), two old comedians (Dick Van Dyke and Mickey Rooney) discuss Van Dyke's effeminate son. "He'll make you a grandpa one of these days," Rooney says. "Don't you bet on it," Van Dyke snaps. Dick Shawn behaves so much like a woman that it seems he almost could have a baby, and Van Dyke's son is so pitiful a man that he could never have a woman. Same joke.

The answer to Boyer's prayers arrives in the person of the American businessman Rock Hudson. Hudson plays the standard model, a smooth but insincere ladykiller who talks with three women at once on different telephones—but only when someone else is in the room to appreciate how much of a man he is. Basically insecure, he really does not do well with women, and the constant strain of the pretense drives him crazy. His masculinity is on trial throughout the film, its authenticity under constant scrutiny. Boyer believes that Rock Hudson would make a fine husband for his daughter because he is everything that Dick Shawn is not. They decide that Hudson will pretend to be homosexual so that the therapist Leslie Caron can "save" him. Hudson sets up a hotel room liaison as a charade to fool Caron, using as his "boyfriend" not a man but a woman (Nita Talbot) in drag. At the last moment, Caron rushes into the room. "Stop! I'm trying to prevent you from making a tragic mistake. You were once a magnificent man." As she collapses in his arms, the scene fades to the birth of their first child, a boy.

The cure solution to homosexuality, popularized by *Tea and Sympathy,* was used in a flock of films, usually in a comic way but always with melodramatically serious overtones. People really believed that a good lay cured homosexuals. Otto Preminger's *Tell Me That You Love Me, Junie Moon* (1970) featured Bob Moore as Warren, a cripple who is homosexual because he was raised by a gay foster father (played in flashback by Leonard Frey). At the end of the film, Warren makes love with a black prostitute, a woman who is a hooker like his mother, and is summarily cured of his homosexuality—a fact that he gleefully shouts from a speeding car the next morning. In Robert Altman's *M*A*S*H* (1970), the well-endowed surgeon finds one morning that he "can't get it up" and concludes miserably that he "must be a fairy." He goes to his tent to commit suicide but in the middle of the night is visited by a young nurse, and in the morning he emerges to pronounce himself "cured."

In Mark Robson's adaptation of Jacqueline Susann's *Valley of the Dolls* (1967), Hollywood fashion designer Ted Casablanca (Alex Davion) is referred to throughout the film as "queer" even though the story indicates he is "bisexual." When superstar Neely O'Hara (Patty Duke) shows some interest in Casablanca, her husband (Martin Milner) remarks, "You sure are spending a lot of time with that fag."

"He's *not* a fag!" she screams. "And I'm just the dame who can prove it!"

In a kill 'em or cure 'em climate, violence by and toward homosexuals on-screen escalated at the end of the 1960s and became the keynote of the 1970s. Sissies were now cured, killed or rendered impotent in suitably nasty ways. Ray Walston's effeminate psychotic killer in *Caprice* (1967) reflects an unnatural fear that the world is about to become homosexual. Walston's Dr. Clancy, a cosmetologist, rationalizes that if women are made more beautiful, their husbands "won't want to kiss the bus driver in the morning"—something he sees as a widespread danger. He is later revealed as a murderer who likes to dress in women's clothing. Doris Day pushes him to his death from a balcony in a public building.

Ray Walston as the vicious transvestite killer kisses Doris Day on the set of Caprice *(1967).* (Homer Dickens Collection)

John Guillermin's *P.J.* (1968) featured George Peppard as the broken-down (but still sexy) private eye whose work takes him to an ominous gay bar and pits him against an evil queen. Summoned to act as bodyguard for the inevitable rich and beautiful woman, Peppard must first deal with her manservant, a classically turned out faggot named Shelton Kwell (Severn Darden) who peeks through curtains and is always preceded into a room by a puff of smoke from a long cigarette holder. After pointedly refusing to shake Kwell's hand, Peppard asks the mistress why she has chosen such an unlikely servant. "He isn't much," she admits, "but he sleeps in."

"Where?" shoots Peppard. "At the bottom of the garden?"

Unfortunately, Kwell is involved in a plot to murder his mistress, and he invites Peppard to meet him secretly at a club called the Gay Caballero. Guillermin's gay bar is one reason why so many people thought that the alien bar in *Star Wars* was a gay bar. The scenes in *P.J.* were typical of the gay bar buildup that the American screen had pushed for almost a decade. Filled with leather types wearing gold earrings, the place is a dark affair with tightly shuttered windows. The jukebox plays "The Halls of Montezuma" as Peppard is served a Scotch in a stemmed shot glass. Suddenly the music stops and the men at the bar turn and advance on him menacingly. Amused, Peppard asks, "Do any of you tomboys know a guy named Shelton Kwell?" The tomboys attack in force, but Peppard is ready for them, and he beats the daylights out of at least fifteen men, wrecking the place in the process. Our hero emerges from the battle none the worse for wear, sporting only a bloody nose and five artfully created fingernail scratches down one cheek.

All this gay activity did not go unnoticed. In June 1968, *Time* announced that the "third sex" was making a determined bid for first place at the box office. "Unashamedly queer characters are everywhere!" *Time* screeched, pointing out that most of the homosexuals shown so far were "sadists, buffoons or psychopaths." The power of the Code was at an end. In 1966, another drastic revision had divided films into those for mature and those for general audiences. Films such as *The Sergeant, Reflections in a Golden Eye, The Fox, The Detective* and *The Killing of Sister George* clearly contained "adult" material, and it became apparent that the Code had little or no control over them. John Huston's *Reflections in a Golden Eye* (1967) was released with a seal of approval despite the director's refusal to make a series of cuts requested by the Catholic Office for Motion Pictures and the MPAA. In spite of a C ("condemned") rating from the Catholic Church, the film gained wide distribution, something that could not have happened a decade earlier. *Variety* interpreted this as "a sign of increased independence on the part of Hollywood . . . and a decline in the importance of ratings to theatrical bookings."

One year later, in 1968, the Code was abolished altogether in favor of the "alphabet soup" rating system we have today. In January 1969, a *Variety* headline proclaimed, "Homo 'n' Lesbo Films at Peak, Deviate Theme Now Box Office." The explosion of "gay" films culminated in 1970 with the release of the film version, directed by William Friedkin, of Mart Crowley's stage hit *The Boys in the Band,* which coincided with the rebirth of the activist gay movement in America.

The onscreen exploration and exploitation of gay life in America was now carried out against a backdrop of vocal and visible homosexuals reacting publicly to their media image. On a June night in 1969, New York City police raided a Greenwich Village bar called the Stonewall. For the first time, gays fought back against the police, and there followed a week of nightly rioting. Less than a year later there were gay liberation groups in over three hundred American cities. Today there are more than two thousand such organizations in the United States alone, in small cities and towns, on college campuses and in almost every business and professional organization. The late 1960s and the whole of the 1970s saw a regurgitation of the closet syndrome in both commercial and independent films made by and about gays.

But gradually films by gays would begin to explore the gay lifestyle in personal terms, apart from the superstructure of a film industry interested primarily in economic return. The films *A Very Natural Thing, Word Is Out, Nighthawks, Outrageous!, The Consequence* and *Gay U.S.A.* evolved out of a consciousness seeded by gay liberation and shaped by the lies and distortions of most commercial cinema. At times the sex and violence that Hollywood attributed to the gay lifestyle were indistinguishable from the violence against gays in real life. Some films of the 1960s reflected the violence, and it was not always possible to separate the sad truth from the stereotypes.

Gay relationships continued to be shown as inherently violent. By making the lesbian relationship between Jill (Sandy Dennis) and Ellen (Anne Heywood) explicit in their adaptation of D. H. Lawrence's *The Fox* (1968), director Mark Rydell and screenwriter Lewis John Carlino exaggerated the results of that lesbian passion. A subtle, almost unconsciously lesbian affair between Jill and Ellen became on film a hotly explicit obsession that is broken up by the arrival of Paul (Keir Dullea), the "fox" for whom Ellen has an inexplicable attraction. The overstated sexuality in the film makes it a "will she or won't she choose normalcy?" tug-of-war between lesbianism and heterosexuality.

Lesbianism loses. At the end of the movie, the fox carries off his prize. A tree falls between Jill's legs, killing her, and Ellen goes off into the sunset with Paul. One lesbian is killed, the other cured. But because Sandy Dennis wore the dress and Anne Heywood the pants, American critics were confused at the denouement. Martin Gottfried, writing in *Women's Wear Daily,* expressed disbelief that Paul would be attracted to Ellen ("the bulldyke") over Jill ("the female lesbian"). "How," he asked, "could the feminine one be the real lesbian?" Pauline Kael, in a telling query, revealed that she could not conceive of a woman's preferring other women. "If Ellen isn't afraid of sex with men, what's she doing playing house in the woods with that frumpy Jill?"

Homosexuality, it seems, was still a matter of queers who imitated heterosex-

Anne Heywood makes love to Sandy Dennis in Mark Rydell's screen version of D. H. Lawrence's The Fox *(1968).*

The wages of sin: Sandy Dennis lies mangled beneath a fallen tree at the end of The Fox; *Keir Dullea and Anne Heywood walk off into the sunset.*

uality onscreen and off. In *Staircase, The Killing of Sister George, The Gay Deceivers* and even *The Boys in the Band,* heterosexual role playing was the rule. If there was such a thing as a defined gay behavior, it was not explicit onscreen even though it emerged often enough as camp.

John Huston's adaptation of Carson McCullers' *Reflections in a Golden Eye* and John Flynn's screen version of Dennis Murphy's *The Sergeant* dealt with the fate of repressed homosexuals who were at odds with the super-macho ethic of military life. The submerged emotions that had been given flesh in Kenneth Anger's *Fireworks* were here given the post-1950s Hollywood sledgehammer treatment. Both films explore graphically the fears of men who believe that they are freaks of nature and can no longer hide their true selves.

In *Reflections in a Golden Eye* (1967), Major Penderton (Marlon Brando) is a constipated closet case who sweats constantly and moons furtively over picture postcards depicting Greek statues of naked men. His repressed sexuality is seen as the triumph of his military training, and when it is set loose, it is responsible for the murder that climaxes the film. Penderton's sexual urges express themselves more fancifully in Huston's film than in McCullers' book, principally through Penderton's tortured reactions to crude fag jokes and a sadistic streak that is triggered by sexual frustration. Brando, who is said to have adopted Tennessee Williams' southern accent for his role as Penderton, follows a young private (Robert Forester) around the army camp at night, picking up discarded candy wrappers that he lovingly preserves along with his postcards. The most shocking scene shows Brando before a mirror, slathering makeup and cold cream over his face. Major Penderton's assumption of the female role through the use of cosmetics says more about John Huston's analysis of homosexuality than it does about Carson McCullers' version of sexual repression.

The simplistic rendering of Penderton's obsession matches the treatment afforded the character of the Filipino houseboy Anacleto (Zorro David), who is played as a screaming queen out of a Warner Brothers cartoon. He serves well as the visible result of the kind of sexuality Brando thinks he is hiding within himself. Anacleto is used consistently as sounding board for the kinds of ideas that have kept Major Penderton in the closet. The flighty creature is just what a mother might point to as an example of what could happen if a disobedient child did not stop playing with dolls. An officer (Brian Keith) says of Anacleto, "He wouldn't be happy in the army, but it would make a man of him." This pro-closet philosophy suggests that men can indeed be "made"—or at least approximated—and that homosexuality is merely a matter of effeminate behavior that can be altered with the right kind of training. The troubled Brando knows better, but he keeps the knowledge to himself. Lecturing on "leadership, strength, power and war," he tells the classroom of soldiers, "It is morally honorable for the square peg to keep scraping around in the round hole rather than to discover and use the unorthodox one that would fit."

In *The Sergeant* (1968), Rod Steiger's Callan is faced with the same dilemma as Brando's Penderton. After scraping around in the wrong hole for years, he suddenly encounters a perfect fit. So careful a film is *The Sergeant,* however, that it offers two hours of imagined foreplay, culminating in a sloppy kiss

Rod Steiger plants a tortured kiss on the lips of John Phillip Law in The Sergeant *(1968).*

and tragedy. Steiger approaches the object of his covert affections, one Private Swanson (John Phillip Law), the way spinsters Margaret Leighton and Grayson Hall approached Sue Lyon in *Seven Women* and *The Night of the Iguana*. When the two soldiers first meet, violins are heard on the soundtrack. Sergeant Callan is a homosexual Marty, his hands in his pockets, always hanging out with the straight guys, going along on their dates, secretly in love with them, waiting for the chance to pounce in a drunken moment. The ploy was immortalized by Mart Crowley in *The Boys in the Band* as the "Christ, was I drunk last night" syndrome.

Neither *The Sergeant* nor *Reflections in a Golden Eye* offers the possibility of homosexual relationships; they deal only in sexually motivated manipulations, spitefulness and petty jealousy, most of it unconscious and unexplored. The result is caricature. Steiger acts Sergeant Callan like a man possessed, pursing his lips maniacally and sweating buckets. When in the film's anticlimax he finally kisses the nonplussed Private Swanson, there is no culminating passion but rage and hatred for what the kiss represents. It is the accusatory kiss of *A View from the Bridge* all over again. In *Reflections in a Golden Eye*, Brando murders the young private when he discovers that his wife (Elizabeth Taylor) is the real attraction to the young man; he is betrayed by his own weakness. In *The Sergeant*, Steiger kills himself by blowing his brains out with a shotgun.

In each case, the gay character is killing what he sees as the source of his homosexuality. Both films insist that there is no option, no way out for these doomed people. They are driven by their fatal flaw. In an angry speech condemning the behavior of Anacleto, Brian Keith says, "We'd have run him ragged in the army. He sure would've been miserable, but anything would've been better than all that other mess—painting with watercolors and dancing. . . ." John Phillip Law sees Steiger go into the woods with a gun and realizes what is about to happen, but he makes no move to stop it. The virginal young private, hardly aware throughout the film that there is such a thing as homosexuality, knows enough finally to allow the suicide to take place unhindered. At the sound of the gunshot, he sighs in resignation; another doomed faggot has bitten the dust.

Eventually a new consciousness had to emerge from these dreary circumstances. For the rote suicide as solution to homosexuality soon looked like the worn-out stereotype it was. There was a subtle shift; the subject of films that dealt with gays became the ghettos in which gays lived. Where *Reflections in a Golden Eye* and *The Sergeant* had examined military closets, supercop thrillers such as *P.J., Tony Rome* and *The Detective* explored the seedy underworld of gay ghetto life, where homosexuality among the lawless was tolerated. *P.J.* and *Tony Rome* featured leather-jacketed killer gays and alcoholic lesbian strippers in a series of brief but sordid sequences that were designed to repel.

Some more serious implications of the closeted life were glimpsed in *The Incident* and *The Boston Strangler*, films that showed gays as victims of the law and the lawless. The physical and mental brutality that is visited so easily on creatures who are forced to spend their lives in hiding is illuminated in both films. In *The Boston Strangler* (1968), Hurd Hatfield plays Terence Huntley, a rich homosexual who is interrogated by detective Henry Fonda in a gay bar. "Whenever there are sex crimes," Hatfield tells Fonda, "the police crack down on us. When you're very rich and also gay, you're very vulnerable." An underground synonym for homosexual since the 1920s, the word *gay* had suddenly become acceptable in films (it was used again that year in *The Detective*). The vulnerability of closeted gays was elaborated on in both *The Incident* and *The Detective*, which also illustrated the Catch-22 nature of the trap that invisibility engenders.

In *The Incident* (1967), two mindless punks (Tony Musante and Martin Sheen) terrorize a subway car filled with people. But it is the lone gay passenger who is singled out first and tormented longest. Robert Fields plays Kenneth Otis, a man whose homosexuality makes him physically ill. At the outset of the film he tries—pathetically—to pick up a straight man (Gary Merrill) in a local bar and becomes sick in the john. It is a film that, while being repulsive, gives a sense of the alienation that results from being gay in a straight world. Fields' portrait of Otis is like Brando's Penderton; he almost shouts "Unclean!" as he walks the streets to the subway station.

Once the "Ride of Terror" (the title of the original teleplay) has begun,

Robert Fields as Kenneth Otis is tormented by Martin Sheen and Tony Musante in The Incident *(1967).*

Otis is victimized into trusting Martin Sheen, a psychosexual game player. Sheen allows Otis to think he is gay by smiling conspiratorially and touching him gently. One result of this early encounter is that Otis becomes the only terrorized passenger for whom no sympathy is created. As each rider in turn is attacked by the two youths, others make tentative attempts to offer help. The homosexual suffers alone. The lone comment is that of a male passenger who says to his girlfriend, "Ahhh, so what? So they found a queer." The homosexual is an outsider not only in his family and his neighborhood but on the planet itself, says the microcosmic vision of the film. He can expect none of the neighborly concern or simple human compassion that people share as a matter of daily life; he is not a part of the community.

In late 1967, screenwriter Abby Mann told the *New York Times* that "it's easier to be accepted in our society as a murderer than as a homosexual," and his next screenplay, for Gordon Douglas' *The Detective* (1968), had its roots in this observation. The film, set almost exclusively in the gay haunts of New York City's sexual underground, starred Frank Sinatra as a tough but liberal (educated) detective who is faced with having to solve the brutal castration murder of a wealthy homosexual (James Inman). Under pressure from his department to find the killer quickly and attain promotion, Sinatra uses the same kind of studied come-on that Martin Sheen had employed in *The Incident,* and he seduces a confession from an innocent gay beach bum (Tony Musante). Later Sinatra discovers that he has sent an innocent man to the electric chair just because he was in a hurry and any homosexual would do. The real killer (William Windom), a closeted homosexual who murdered to keep his secret, commits suicide. His written confession says, "I was more ashamed of being a homosexual than a murderer." The police cooperate in the suppression of the nature of his death because they do not wish to reveal the homosexuality of a prominent citizen. Thus the closet syndrome is held responsible for all three deaths of homosexual characters: an execution, a murder and a suicide.

In *The Detective,* Sinatra's search for the killer took him on a tour of the public sex hangouts of the New York waterfront. It was the most graphic coverage to date of the underworld of casual sex and violence that would become the dominant homosexual milieu on film throughout the Seventies.

As the Sixties came to a close, *The Killing of Sister George* (1968) and *The Boys in the Band* (1970) seemed to sum up and even type the gay experience for American audiences. Both films made detailed but divergent statements about the nature of the closet, and both were received as definitive portraits of gay life. Homosexuality was no longer a vague insinuation or the unexplored component of a tortured character. The lesbianism in *The Killing of Sister George,* John Lee noted in the *New York Times,* was "treated as a condition rather than an accusation." The "killing" in the film was not the death of homosexuality but the death of its visibility; the closet was at war with the flamboyance of Sister George herself. Homosexuality had become a fact of life, and Hollywood ballyhooed it as though the movies had invented it. Twentieth Century-Fox's full-page ad in the *New York Times* announcing the production of George Cukor's *Justine* listed the cast and concluded dramatically with, "And Dirk Bogarde as . . . The Homosexual." Bogarde in fact eventually played the heterosexual Pursewarden, but Cliff Gorman was featured as one of the nastiest sissies ever filmed.

Every attempt at portraying gays or the gay world was termed definitive. *Time* hailed *The Boys in the Band* as "a landslide of truths." Richard Schickel wrote in *Life* that *The Killing of Sister George* "recreates the whole lesbian world." Observing that the film "really penetrates the queer mind and milieu," Schickel said that *Sister George* would be sure to give its audience a "good sense of the demi-monde lesbians share with fags, prosties, etc." He said the picture was "tacky, tawdry, repellent and true."

The demi-monde in question was the Gateways Club, a lesbian bar in London at which director Robert Aldrich shot one scene for *The Killing of Sister George,* using regular patrons as extras. In spite of a strict press ban on the set, the scene was photographed by a still photographer and pictures appeared in a London daily and then in newspapers around the world. As a result, Aldrich says, a receptionist in a doctor's office was fired from her job because she was spotted in a photo. It was an ironic presage of the fate of the film's chief character.

In Aldrich's adaptation of the play, Beryl Reid's June Buckridge is a BBC

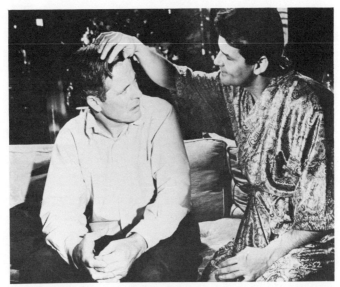

William Windom is about to murder a wealthy young gay man in The Detective *(1968).*

Susannah York, Beryl Reid and Coral Browne at the Gateways Club in The Killing of Sister George *(1968).*

soap opera actress who plays a cheerful country nurse, Sister George, on a weekly series. In private life, George is a loud, aggressive, butch lesbian whose alcoholic escapades and petty tyrannies precipitate her downfall. She loses both her job and her baby-doll lover (Susannah York) as a result of the reptilian interference of a predatory BBC executive, Mercy Croft (Coral Browne). George's crime lies not in being queer but in being so offensively butch about it, a dinosaur pitting herself against modern weapons. And Coral Browne's Mercy Croft was the newest thing in the hooded cobra look for lesbians onscreen that season. (Viveca Lindfors' domineering fashion photographer who preyed on Faye Dunaway in *Puzzle of a Downfall Child,* Capucine's bloodless lesbian spy who closed in on Suzy Kendall in *Fräulein Doktor* and Stéphane Audran's seductress in *Les Biches* were other examples of the excessive eyeshadow and dangling earring school of lesbian screen villains.)

The internal battle in *The Killing of Sister George* is one between the acceptable and the offensive gay lifestyles. The "killing" of Sister George is the process by which George's overt lesbianism is punished by forcing her into invisibility. "Look at yourself, you pathetic old dyke!" shouts Mercy Croft, belittling the tweedy George.

Though generally maligned as an offensive and nasty character, Sister George is in fact the only multifaceted woman in the film. The honesty and openness of her character, when set beside the cartoon treachery of the sleek and sophisticated Mercy Croft or the loveless opportunism of Susannah York's Childie, make George the more complete human being. Critics who pounced on George's domineering, somewhat sadistic role-playing with Childie and her small, middle class values and alcoholic jealousies, missed her emotional commitment to her lesbianism, that is, to being herself. When she suspiciously questions Childie about an affair with a co-worker, Childie snaps, "Not *all* girls are raving bloody lesbians, you know!"

George takes a slow puff on her cigar and pronounces, *"That's* a misfortune of which I am perfectly well aware."

George is clearly the only character in the film who is committed to being a lesbian—and the one for whom it is impossible (like the nellie Emory in *The Boys in the Band*) to hide it. She is also the only character in the film to love anyone in a nonmanipulative way and the only person with a sense of humor. Her description of the first time she saw Childie ("It was like standing in an enchanted wood") is the single love speech in the picture. Her tender and understanding relationship with a local prostitute suggests that her only real emotional contact or solace is with other outsiders. She goes to the prostitute's house because she needs a place "where I can cry." George's hilarious drunken assault on two nuns in the back seat of a taxicab and her barroom imitations of Sydney Greenstreet and Oliver Hardy are all naughty but funny indications of her unconventional nature, a nature that is eventually eclipsed and destroyed by people who are a bunch of fakes. The message for George is that only the fakes will survive, that she has no alternative to the closet.

"Sister George's loud behavior and individuality," Aldrich says, "are encompassed in her character, they're not a product of her lesbianism. She doesn't have to dress or act like that, but—fuck it—that's the way she wants to live. She doesn't give a shit about the BBC or the public's acceptance of her relationships. That's why they couldn't afford her. She didn't fit into the machine."

Because of what Mercy Croft calls George's "refusal to conduct herself in a decent, civilized manner," the Sister George character is killed off on the BBC, hit by a speeding truck while riding her motor scooter in the English countryside. Croft then seduces Childie away from George, leaving her without a job and without a relationship. Yet the final indignity is the theft of her openness. The only job offered the aging actress is the part of an animal on a children's series, a part that will require her to wear a cow's head for the duration of her television career. Alone at night in the deserted television studio, she spots the black casket that was used for the funeral of Sister George that afternoon. She lifts the lid, expecting it to be heavy, and discovers that it is made of light balsa wood. "Even the bloody coffin is a fake!" she cries, and in an impotent fury she begins to smash lights and props. Spent at last, she sits on a wooden bench on the set of a small country village and in the darkness begins to moo quietly, a sound that becomes a scream of despair. Sister George dies for our sins, and Mercy Croft gets the girl. The options are invisibility, assimilation or ostracism.

Aldrich's decision, in adapting the play to the screen, to make Coral Browne's seduction of Susannah York sexually explicit caused a furor. "After all," Aldrich said, "unlike the stage version, the picture had to play out the betrayal, and the story itself is so genteel, it's possible you could be sitting in Sheboygan and the film could be so 'well done' that nobody would know what the hell you were talking about." When she reviewed *The Children's Hour* in 1962, Pauline Kael noted that audiences felt sorry for poor Martha Dobie because she and Karen "don't really *do* anything, after all," and Kael added parenthetically, "I always thought that was why lesbians needed sympathy—because there isn't much they *can* do." Six years later, when Aldrich released *The Killing of Sister George* with 119 seconds of footage showing exactly what lesbians could do, Kael's review of the film was titled "Frightening the Horses."

The seduction scene was cut from *The Killing of Sister George* in several states, including Connecticut and Massachusetts, where it was found to be in violation of obscenity and licensing laws. Yet the film's X rating was not a reflection of the offending scene, which Aldrich finally offered to cut for an R rating.

After a disastrous screening in New York at the Ziegfeld Theater, I called my old friend Jean Dockerty, who was the head of the Code Administration, and said to him, "Okay, I'll make the cuts."

"It's too late," he said to me, "Jack Valenti said that it gets an X no matter what you do to it."

The X was based on subject matter alone. So there was a curtain in front of that picture. No matter how good it was, it was dirty because it was an X film. *The Pom Pom Girls* was an X, and *The Killing of Sister George* was an X. No difference. And the whole idea of having ratings to let us compete with foreign filmmakers in an adult market went right down the toilet.

Aldrich's movie was as much a scapegoat as its heroine was. The film had begun shooting under the old Code system, which involved having a seal of approval or not, and it completed shooting under the new rating system. To release the film without a seal would not have had the stigma that an X rating eventually took on. It was also a transitional time for the movies. Technically, *The Killing of Sister George* was given an X rating on theme alone. Yet less than a year later, *Midnight Cowboy* won the Oscar for best picture of the year in spite of its X rating. Then, early in 1970, *Variety* reported that the MPAA, in a landmark decision, had given *The Boys in the Band* an R rating in spite of what it called "homosexual dialogue."

The Boys in the Band (1970), with its "landslide of truths," became the most famous Hollywood film on the subject of male homosexuality. Viewed in the press and by the public as a "serious study" of gay men, Mart Crowley's Off Broadway play was transferred to the screen by director William Friedkin with its original nine-member cast. The film was a "special" project in Hollywood, and it was handled with a fidelity to the text that was more appropriate to a *Long Day's Journey into Night*.

Andrew Sarris, in his review of *The Killing of Sister George,* observed that "you can't make tragedy out of abnormal psychology." But he ignored the fact that most tragic figures in literature and history were indeed abnormal by society's standards and that in reality both *The Killing of Sister George* and *The Boys in the Band* are tragedy. Most heterosexual critics wear blinders when it comes to homosexuality onscreen; they tend to see the very theme as abnormal. The review of *The Boys in the Band* that appeared in the *New York Times* was headlined, "Crowley Study of Male Homosexuality Opens"— which sounds like the description of a documentary.

The author, who also wrote the screenplay, says the film was approached with a pair of tongs in Hollywood. The film industry had homosexuality under a microscope, and there was a hush, as though some great advance were about to be made. "It was a very taboo subject in Hollywood," Crowley says, "and it still is. When we were filming it, it was considered this very liberal New York theater project, and nobody wanted to get too close."

On the strength of a classy set of New York stage reviews and its billing as a comedy despite its dead serious intent, *The Boys in the Band* was taken for gospel in an America populated by people who had never met a live homosexual in their entire lives. The film presented a perfunctory compendium of easily acceptable stereotypes who gather at a Manhattan birthday party and spend an evening savaging each other and their way of life. The "landslide of truths" consisted ultimately of some jumbled Freudian stabs at overly protective mothers and absent fathers and lots of zippy fag humor that posed as philosophy. Yet in spite of itself, Crowley's passion play was part catharsis and part catalyst. His characters were losers or borderline survivors at best, but they paved the way for winners.

Although it was difficult to see this clearly in 1970, *The Boys in the Band* presented some attractive and functional gay men who formed an implicit challenge to the stereotypes exploited in Emory (Cliff Gorman) and Harold (Leonard Frey). The film was not positive, but it was fair. The heterosexual Alan (Peter White) can easily despise the nellie Emory because he is everything a faggot is supposed to be, a "butterfly in heat." Alan even comes to pity the battered sissy in the end. But what scares Alan and the audience, what they could not come to terms with or understand, is the homosexuality of Hank and Larry (Laurence Luckinbill and Keith Prentice), who are both just as queer as Emory yet "look" as straight as Alan. The possibility that there could be nonstereotypical homosexuals who are also staunch advocates of a working gay relationship is presented by the two lovers throughout the film. And they are the two characters most often ignored by critics and analysts of the film. It is Larry who speaks of rejecting heterosexual concepts of marriage and creating a relationship with "respect for one another's freedom, with no need to lie or pretend." At the end of the film, Larry and Hank win the telephone truth game, that Michael (Kenneth Nelson) has viciously devised, when they call each other and say "I love you." It is when Larry and Hank express affection for each other physically and verbally that the audience and the lone straight party guest are most uncomfortable.

In contrast, Michael's inability to deal with his own homosexuality is exposed as old-time movie melodrama, and Harold's final, equally melodramatic speech puts it in perspective.

You are a sad and pathetic man, Michael. You are a homosexual, and you don't want to be, but there's nothing you can do to change it. Not all your prayers to your God. Not all the analysis your money can buy in the years you have left to live. You may one day be able to know a heterosexual life. If you want it desperately enough. If you pursue it with the fervor with which you annihilate. But you will always be homosexual as well, Michael. Always. Until the day you die.

The speech captured the essence of self-hatred and summed up a generation of gay men who were taught to blame all their troubles on their homosexuality. In the end, Michael's self-hatred and his inability to function became as antiquated as Harold's keeping his marijuana in a Band-Aid box in the medicine chest so that he can flush it down the john if the police should arrive. Michael's crying jags and old-movie fantasies shed light not on his homosexuality but on the falsehoods and illusions of Hollywood dreams, the dreams that had taught homosexuals that there were no homosexuals in polite society.

Laurence Luckinbill as Hank and Keith Prentice as Larry in a scene not used in The Boys in the Band *(1970).* (Mart Crowley)

When Clive Barnes called *The Boys in the Band* a homosexual play, he was right. It was a homosexual period piece just as *Green Pastures* was a Negro period piece. But blacks are visible and gays are not, and Hollywood was not moved to change a whit by all this hysteria in the gay drawing rooms of Manhattan. Yet *Boys* moved homosexuals throughout the country. The internalized guilt and self-hatred of eight gay men at a Manhattan birthday party formed the best and most potent argument for gay liberation ever offered in a popular art form. It supplied concrete and personalized examples of the negative effects of what homosexuals learn about themselves from the distortions of the media. And the film caused the first public reaction by a burgeoning gay rights movement to the accepted stereotypes in Crowley's play.

Protests by gays did not dispute the existence of such stereotypes, but they were quick to point out that the view was one-sided and that the exclusive depiction or representation of any group of people by a minority stereotype is called bigotry. *The Boys in the Band* was a play about homosexuals and a homosexual play. It was a work that sprang from the subculture itself and represented bitter reflection. Society treated it as though it were a scientific expedition, but in fact it was an inner journey for countless gays who snapped to attention when confronted with the pathos of Michael's sickening routines. Many of the stereotypes put forth by Crowley were myths that gays had accepted and even fit themselves into because there appeared to be no alternative. At the beginning of the 1960s, two British films about the life of Oscar Wilde could not even be shown in the United States because the Code had not yet been revised. The audience for *The Boys in the Band* included gay people who had grown up thinking that they were the only homosexuals in the world. The film explored passing and not being able to pass, loving and not being able to love, and above all else, surviving in a world that denied one's very existence. But it did so before an American public that was at the stage of barely being able to mention homosexuality at all. It was a gay movie for gay people, and it immediately became both a period piece and a reconfirmation of the stereotypes.

The film industry showed no sign of seeing *The Boys in the Band* as anything but a diversion in a business that was always on the lookout for a novel angle. During the Seventies Hollywood did not relinquish the stereotypes of the Crowley play but moved steadily toward solidifying them. It was the gays in the audiences of 1970 who would eventually form a rebuttal to the homosexual party guests, and their voices would grow louder with each passing year.

"Nobody would try to pass Michael off as having today's consciousness," Crowley admits. "All the negative things in the play are represented by Michael, and because he's the leading character, it was his message that a very square American public wanted to receive." And did receive. The internal chaos of Michael, a guilt-ridden Catholic, forms the focal point of the reaction to the gay lifestyle throughout the story. The *Catholic Film Newsletter* said that the film "comments with wit and passion on the desolation and waste which chill this way of life . . . with all its anxiety, bitterness, depression and solitude."

It is the Roman Catholic Michael who utters the play's most famous line, "You show me a happy homosexual and I'll show you a gay corpse." The author gathers together one Jew, one black, one Wasp, one midnight cowboy, one nellie queen and a married man and his lover to react to Michael's torment. When gays reacted publicly, Friedkin said, "This film is not about homosexuality,

Chris Sarandon as Leon (patterned after the real-life Liz Eden), the transsexual lover of a gay bank robber in Dog Day Afternoon *(1975).*

it's about human problems. I hope there *are* happy homosexuals. They just don't happen to be in my film." Nor have they been in any other major American release before or since.

If nothing else, *The Boys in the Band* illuminated the fear and ignorance that surrounded homosexuality in America. And while it was considered the pinnacle of Hollywood's commitment to the exploration of such "adult" themes as homosexuality, it was in fact a freak show. The 1970s would continue to reflect the freak show aspects of homosexual villains, fools and queens. The most successful film of the decade that dealt with an openly gay homosexual, Sidney Lumet's *Dog Day Afternoon* (1975), was the ultimate freak show, a film that used the sensational side of a true story to titillate a square audience. The decade that began with regurgitations of *The Boys in the Band* and the riots that sparked the gay liberation movement would end with more public violence over the filming of another William Friedkin movie, *Cruising* (1980), marking the first time gays rose up and rioted in the streets in reaction to the making of a motion picture. And the hero still could not be queer.

Struggle

fear and loathing
in gay Hollywood

*Hitler, Anita Bryant and the Ku Klux Klan featured as
the common enemy in a scene from Arthur J. Bresson,
Jr.'s* Gay U.S.A. *(1978).* (Distributed by Kit Parker Films,
Carmel Valley, California)

The Boys in the Band is not about homosexuality.
—William Friedkin, 1970

Cruising is not about homosexuality.
—William Friedkin, 1980

Gay people will die because of this film.
—Leaflet protesting
the filming of *Cruising*

An accumulation of scenes from the 1970s presents a depressingly homophobic picture of attitudes about lesbians and gay men onscreen.

※

A campus revolutionary in *Getting Straight* (1970) shouts at teacher Elliott Gould that "in a few months the military-industrial complex will have us all in concentration camps in Arizona."

"Don't knock Arizona," he shouts back, "it's a great state. They have the lowest incidence of lung cancer and homosexuality."

※

In *Rafferty and the Gold Dust Twins* (1975), Sally Kellerman tells Alan Arkin that she and her sidekick MacKenzie Philips met in the lesbian section of the state prison. He freezes and does a slow stare, his eyes widening.

"Oh, shit," Kellerman laughs, "don't worry. I'm a woman."

※

In Stig Bjorkman's *Georgia, Georgia* (1972), Roger Furman plays the gay road manager of actress-singer Diana Sands. While on tour in Sweden, Sands' partiality to white lovers is attacked by a group of black Vietnam veterans as an abdication of her responsibility to her race. Furman is pointed out as a further example of her betrayal; his being a faggot distorts the image of the black man. "Get a real man," they tell her.

※

In *Valley of the Dolls* (1967), *Play It as It Lays* (1972) and *Funny Lady* (1975), relationships between gay men and strong show-business women are exploited but never examined. The homosexual pet of the female star is used as a punching bag by the real but insecure men who surround her. Roddy McDowall's Bobby in *Funny Lady* was the fag chorus boy adopted by Streisand's Fanny Brice. James Caan insults and degrades him throughout the film, calling him a "pansy."

In an interview after the film opened, McDowall said, "The relationship of a big female singer and a gay man could have been explored here, especially since fag hags are such a staple in tinseltown. I know I could have done without all the insults Bobby had to endure from Billy Rose, although I must say James Caan did them very expertly."

※

When the director James Goldstone ordered June Allyson to report to work on *They Only Kill Their Masters* (1972) dressed as a lesbian, she showed up wearing her son's football sweatshirt. Goldstone added a Peck's Bad Boy smudge of dirt to her face, and she was all set. The film featured Allyson as a lesbian killer and contained such lines as, "Isn't a pregnant lesbian a contradiction in terms?"

June Allyson as a killer dyke in They Only Kill Their Masters *(1972).*
(Homer Dickens Collection)

※

In John Huston's *The Kremlin Letter* (1970), George Sanders cavorts as an ancient drag queen while a beautiful but deadly black lesbian spy seduces the daughter of a Russian diplomat for hidden cameras. In Joseph McGrath's *The Magic Christian* (1970), Yul Brynner in drag sings Noel Coward's "Mad About the Boy" while the fag jokes fly in a viciously homophobic film. Martin Balsam plays a prissy, toupeed antique dealer who is described as a "sex deviate" in Sidney Lumet's *The Anderson Tapes* (1971); the character, a thief and a coward, is strictly for laughs.

※

In *Freebie and the Bean* (1974), a transvestite killer (Christopher Morley) is cornered by James Caan in a ladies room for a fight to the finish. After getting in a few licks, he gets splattered against the walls—as much for assuming male aggression as for assuming female attire.

In *The Eiger Sanction* (1975), Jack Cassidy plays a killer fairy who can "change a nine dollar bill in threes" and has a despicable little dog named Faggot. Cassidy is left to die in the desert, though the pooch is saved (lest the film be accused of cruelty to animals).

※

In *Theatre of Blood* (1973), Robert Morley plays a homosexual theater critic who dies when he is forced to eat his two poodles, who have been baked in a pie in the same fashion that a Roman empress's two sons were served to her in Shakespeare's *Titus Andronicus*. In *Play It as It Lays,* despondent film producer Tony Perkins dies in star lady Tuesday Weld's arms after swallowing a handful of sleeping pills. She understands. Other gays died violent deaths in *The Day of the Jackal* (1973), *Swashbuckler* (1976), *The Laughing Policeman* (1973), *Busting* (1974), *Drum* (1976) and *The Betsy* (1978).

> Basically, it goes like this:
> Every time a minority culture
> starts to affect the mass sensibility,
> the mass has to water things down
> a little bit . . . gayness is even scarier
> to people than femaleness or blackness.
> So it has to be denied now. At least
> for awhile.
>
> —John Lombardi,
> "Selling Gays to the Masses,"
> *Village Voice,* June 30, 1975

For lesbians and gay men in America, the Hollywood horror show was a part of life in the 1970s. In spite of the dramatic and increasingly vocal visibility

George Sanders whoops it up as a San Francisco drag queen in John Huston's The Kremlin Letter *(1970)*.

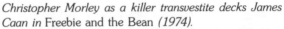

Christopher Morley as a killer transvestite decks James Caan in Freebie and the Bean *(1974)*.

of gays, prompted by the gay rights movement, the film industry stuck to stereotypes. The gay audience, recently defined as a "new" market by publishing, music and the theater, was courted by every medium even when the courting was not expressly acknowledged. Plays, books, magazines, even television shows presented a steady stream of diverse characters, real and fictional, who challenged gay stereotypes even in the face of a political backlash. But not motion pictures.

In 1968, *Time* speculated that Hollywood was "using" homosexuality more and more as a subject because it had "run out of conventional bad guys," and the evidence bears this out. It became clear early in the 1970s that the exploration of gay issues onscreen was not big box office. However, the incorporation of newly visible gay stereotypes from the newly visible ghettos in a screen language for the Seventies was routine. The few instances of vague stirrings of consciousness in the mainstream cinema were insignificant alongside the mass stridencies of abysmally offensive sops to a bigoted public.

About the same time as *The Boys in the Band,* there appeared a low-budget feature, *The Gay Deceivers* (1969), directed by Bruce Kessler and released by Fanfare Productions. An "animated" live-action cartoon version of California gay life, *The Gay Deceivers* offended almost everyone, including homophobic critics who wrote that the film was viciously anti-gay. The film told the story of two normal, all-American boys (Larry Casey and Kevin Coughlin) who evade the draft by pretending to be homosexuals—and are then forced to "live like homosexuals" when they are put under surveillance by an army investigator. The publicity material for the film, prepared by Harold Rand & Company, used the words *fag, queer* and *deviate* to describe the gay characters in the film; it advertised the comedy as a "slice of gay life."

Our heroes move into an all-gay apartment complex in Los Angeles, composed of tiny, doll-like cottages decorated in lavender and puce and complete with round beds, mirrored ceilings and plaster Greek statues—in fact the decor of most strictly heterosexual motels in America. The saving grace of the film is the comic performance of Michael Greer as Malcolm, the landlord. Greer not only wrote his own role as a flamboyant queen (complete with Bette Davis imitations) but apparently rewrote the screenplay in places, making it "funnier and less homophobic than was intended" wherever he could. "It was also one of the few films," said Greer, "in which the gays didn't end in suicide or insanity." It was a good example of gay humor used in an oppressive situation. Malcolm was a stereotype with a sense of pride, but he could not counteract an essentially homophobic film. The script was loaded with references to gays as child molesters, the scum of the earth and the cause of the fall of every civilization in recorded history. The twist at the end of the film is that the two recruiting officers turn out to be gays who are successfully keeping straights out of the service. "We don't want *their kind* in the army, do we?" one of

*Michael Greer as Malcolm DeJohn in
The Gay Deceivers (1969).*

them asks, fingering the other's ear. The message: "they" are everywhere.

Homosexuality was almost never incidental or second nature to a screen character; after all, sexuality was always the reason for using a gay character in the first place. In fact, except for the hitchhiking funny lesbian ecology freaks (Helena Kallianiotes and Toni Basil) whom Karen Black and Jack Nicholson pick up in *Five Easy Pieces* (1970), Buck Henry's incidentally gay lawyer to David Bowie's alien in *The Man Who Fell to Earth* (1976) and Robert Altman's unobtrusively integrated, happy lesbian couple (Heather MacRae and Tomi-Lee Bradley) in *A Perfect Couple* (1979), American cinema was unable to portray gay characters without their being sex-obsessed or sex-defined.

Only twice, both times incidentally, has a serious American film dealt with homosexuality as a family issue or even suggested that homosexuals might be someone's children. In Gilbert Cates' *Summer Wishes, Winter Dreams* and in Robert Mulligan's *Bloodbrothers,* the alienation of gay children from their parents provides vignettes that ring true but lack focus in their own contexts. In *Summer Wishes, Winter Dreams* (1973), the homosexuality of Joanne Woodward's son (Ron Rickards) is seen only in terms of how the revelation affects her present mid-life crisis, as one more token of her failure as a wife and mother. In the end, she comes to terms with it. Her son, who does not commit suicide or go insane, moves to Amsterdam with a lover and refuses to see his parents until they can deal with him as he is. He turns their inability to see him as a whole person into their problem, a family matter, not his problem.

In *Bloodbrothers* (1978), deeper meanings are hidden in the subplot of a gay son (Bruce French) who refuses to see his rough, immigrant father, even when a friend of the family (Paul Sorvino) pleads with him. There is a mixture of righteous anger and stubborn pride in the son who demands to be seen on his own terms. It was only a brief scene, but it was not exploitative, and it pointed a way out of stereotyping. In the same film, Richard Gere plays a heterosexual offspring who is in essentially the same boat. He does not want to join his father in the construction workers union, preferring instead to act as counselor for youngsters at a day care center. "That's woman's work!" his father shouts. It is easy to imagine the trials of a gay son in the same situation. For Gere, the heterosexual outsider, it will be tough; for the gay jewelry salesman, impossible and painful. Cinema has not yet taken the homosexual as alien and shown where that alienation comes from. The family as we know it needs to be examined onscreen in radically different terms. That is why Altman's lesbian couple in *A Perfect Couple* are special, because the film sees them as a family.

The movies await permission from the world-famous general public before they will portray gays as a fact of life. And the self-hatred of gays in the film industry is as much at fault as the ignorance of that general public. Commercial film turned its back on the possibilities almost immediately. Within two years after the release of *The Boys in the Band,* more than a dozen features dealing with homosexuality emerged. Some, like *Staircase* and *Fortune and Men's Eyes,* were major studio releases whose financial and critical failure warned Hollywood away from substantial projects on the subject. Others, such as Mervyn Nelson's *Some of My Best Friends Are . . . ,* Christopher Larkin's *A Very Natural Thing* and Rosa von Praunheim's *It Is Not the Homosexual Who Is Perverse But the Society in Which He Lives,* were low-budget independent features that, in widely different styles and perspectives, attempted personal analyses of the lives of people in a sexual ghetto. These films were not seen by a wide audience, but they served as litmus paper for a newly formed gay liberation movement that was trying to come to terms with the implications of feminism, role playing and sexual stereotyping that existed in the portrayals of ghettoized gays.

The problem then and now is how to explore on film the gay ghetto and its implications without embracing and seeming to reinforce the stereotypes that exist and flourish there. Gay audiences, in the Seventies somewhat visible and vocal, could see and understand the use of stereotypes as a tool for self-exploration, but most viewers would accept all images of gays on film as true representations. Gays who condemned both *Staircase* and *Some of My Best Friends Are* . . . as examples of unliberated films were correct, but the stereotypes were used differently in each. Pre-liberation reinforcements of the "old" gay lifestyle were and are valid on film because they reflect the facts of gay life in most areas of the United States. The majority of lesbians and gay men in America are still straight-identified people, people trapped in roles they were taught to assume without their being given an alternative. When motion pictures do not reflect the alternative, they simply reflect the majority. This leaves us in the middle of transition. Many gay activists wanted the film industry to "skip a step" and omit the painful but necessary public exploration of a once hidden subculture, especially if that exploration were to be conducted by a misinformed majority. But films with good or ill will toward gays, independent and commercial, explored the same ratty turf relentlessly throughout the Seventies, seeing only the readily visible poles of the gay community—the sissy at one end, the leather-jacketed macho violence of the waterfront sex bar at the other. Gays who wanted films about people in the middle forgot that movies will not reflect what America cannot see. Lesbian couples living in a suburb of Denver and gay men who are corporate executives and share a townhouse in Boston are hardly visible in the fabric of the culture.

Gay liberation made the early mistake of asking Hollywood to begin reinforcing the myth that homosexuals are just like heterosexuals except for their attraction to members of the same sex. To "ask" Hollywood for anything is a waste of time for any minority group; to ask that a reflector of society show lesbians and gay men as being part of rather than being outside the social norm when they have not yet become a visible part of it is unreasonable, contradictory and destructive to gay life and liberation. Most gay people would like to forget the reasons why they have always been considered outsiders and simply start afresh. But that is not only impossible, it is damaging. From the early 1970s, when the gay movement first began to formulate an ideology, to the violent public protest in 1979 over the filming of a potentially dangerous film, *Cruising*, middle class gays in America have sought to have it both ways. They do not want to see the sexual ghetto life of most large American cities portrayed as the only side of the gay world, but at the same time they are unwilling to affiliate themselves as homosexuals in order to demonstrate the reality to the rest of America.

The closeted gay sensibility that apes heterosexual values (and often spitefully puts them down) created an alternative even less attractive than the spray of stereotypes let loose in most films. The gay cult film *Something for Everyone* (1970), often shown on a double bill with *The Boys in the Band,* is a good example of the way in which a gay audience is lured into supporting a negative image of itself in response to an attractively homoerotic but ultimately destructive sensibility. Hal Prince's film, an adaptation by playwright Hugh Wheeler of Henry Kressler's *The Cook,* idealizes the "homosexual affair" between Michael York and Anthony Corlan as though it were the only shred of true love in this thin black comedy. In fact there is no love at all. Prince even has the two men kiss on the lips, a move that got the picture an R rating but failed to mitigate the unsavory circumstances surrounding their cheap, bogus passion.

York plays an evil opportunist who will stop at nothing to possess Orenstein Castle, owned by the Countess Orenstein (Angela Lansbury) and her two children, Corlan and the oddly shaped Jane Carr. The film makes use of all the stock camp mannerisms and stereotypical gestures famous from the days when homosexuals were either flamboyantly outrageous in public or married with two children and passing for straight (except for weekends in the city). In other words, the film presents gayness as a matter of style. Angela Lansbury's countess is an Auntie Mame with a partial stroke, and York is her homoerotic but necessarily bisexual Patrick Dennis. He also has the appearance of an *Adonis* magazine model of the Fifties, and we get to look at his pretty legs in lederhosen and watch him seduce the countess' willing son. But the payoff is dangerous and retrogressive. York sleeps with everyone in sight to achieve his goal, and he murders half a dozen people before Jane Carr finally outsmarts him. York's homosexuality is a part of his evil, an immoral tool used to gain power, yet the film makes it attractive for a covertly gay audience.

The same audience thought that Michael York's decadent bisexuality in *Cabaret* (1972) was liberating and refreshing when in fact his homosexual side in that film was used to the same effect as in *Something for Everyone.* Joel Grey's master of ceremonies in *Cabaret* can be a creep because no one has to like him, and Inger, the transvestite at the Kit Kat Club, can be a more honest character because he is only local color. But Michael York's Brian is the hero. Brian represses his homosexual feelings throughout the film, and when he does sleep with the baron (Helmut Griem), the act is seen by everyone in the film as a fall from grace. Before Brian and Sally Bowles (Liza Minnelli) can get married, she calls it off—largely because she fears he might "slip" again and wind up in a gay bar, returned to his old bad habits. Christopher Isherwood, who wrote *The Berlin Stories* on which *Cabaret* was based (in a roundabout way) and whom the character of Brian is supposed to represent, has said, "I felt as though his homosexual side was used as a kink in the film—like bed wetting—and that he was really supposed to be basically heterosexual."

Homosexuality is seen as the same kind of kink in Herbert Ross' *The Last of Sheila* (1973), another film whose attitudes toward homosexuality come from a hopelessly closeted mentality. Written by Stephen Sondheim and Anthony Perkins, it is another instance of Hollywood and Broadway dragging homosexuality back to the realm of the dirty secret. In a long weekend game played by various Hollywood types on a luxury yacht, each is given a slip of paper with a secret about another player written on it ("I am an alcoholic," "I am a shoplifter," "I am a hit and run driver," "I am a homosexual"). The object of the game is for the guests to match the correct "crime" with the correct player. The homosexual turns out to be the screenwriter (Richard Benjamin), who once slept with host James Coburn early (as they say) in his career. (Nobody is ever *really* homosexual in Hollywood on Hollywood; it is always something that people "tried once" when they were nobody.) Benjamin is now married to Joan Hackett, having furthered his career with his dirty secret.

Variety said, "The picture's very premise is a red herring, predicated as it is on the assumption that these film industry friends would keep such banal secrets from one another . . . the chief victim is Richard Benjamin, whose true confession scene with Joan Hackett (in which he reveals an early homosexual liaison with Coburn) drew laughs at the Cannes Festival showing."

People who think that homosexuality is like bed wetting have often made films in which homosexuality is presented as erotic and attractive yet morally reprehensible. In his review of *Something for Everyone,* John Simon postulated that "disguised homosexuality" was a distorting factor in the film's treatment of heterosexual love, making it look sordid and unappetizing in comparison to the homosexual affair, which was done lovingly. The reverse could also be claimed; how many films have made homosexuality look seedy in order to serve a heterosexual concept of normality? Simon does make the point, however, that such "covert slanting" could be remedied by allowing the homosexual to come out in the open. "I think," he wrote, "that the lion's share of our indignation should be directed at society, which through obsolete laws begets needless falsifying strategies and concealment." In fact there is no conscious falsification in such films; there is simply no room in such people for the equation of homosexual love with natural emotion. Everything is falsified in a situation in which gays accept their own oppression and become contributors to it.

Simon makes it sound as though gays in the closet sit up at night, plotting to proselytize homosexuality in cunning but covert ways. Yet most people in the closet are afraid of their own homosexuality and are unable to accept it. They believe it to be just as abnormal as they have been taught. Anything "covert" that manages to escape from them does so unconsciously and quite naturally. The situation may be somewhat pathetic, but that is the product of self-hatred and an overriding consciousness of the heterosexual norm of which such people want desperately to be a part.

The syndrome of ghettoization maintains the separation of gay and straight life. Thus closeted people are said to lead "double" lives. And most often it is the work of closeted homosexuals or homophobic heterosexuals that lampoons the gay ghetto mentality with little or no insight. The same people are often responsible for the witchhunting mentality that produces periodic purges such as the ones which appeared regularly in the *New York Times* in the mid 1960s, hysterically identifying sinister and corrosive homosexual influences in "our" theater, as though gays were taking over while nobody was looking. There is not a whit of understanding in such rantings about the nature of gay solidarity or the reality of gay history or the dynamic of enforced ghettoization.

In Richard Rush's *Getting Straight* (1970), one of the examining professors on Elliott Gould's dissertation committee is a raving fool who has a nervous breakdown while insisting that F. Scott Fitzgerald was a homosexual. In Herbert Ross' *The Goodbye Girl* (1977), an antifeminist and homophobic film, a super-swishy Off Off Broadway director (Paul Benedict) insists on the homosexuality of Shakespeare's Richard III and forces Richard Dreyfuss to play the part in lavender robes, "like a California fruit salad—the king who wanted to be queen." It is particularly degrading to homosexuals to witness the creation of a gay character who forces his narrow, kitschy vision of life on everyone around him. The irony is that the opposite has always been true; society has always told everyone in sight that everyone else is, was and always will be exclusively heterosexual.

Stanley Donen's *Staircase* (1969), adapted from Charles Dyer's stage play about two aging homosexual barbers, is a heterosexual story cast as a gay tragedy. It is *Who's Afraid of Virginia Woolf?* crossed with *The Boys in the Band*—just what a heterosexual might do to try to prove the straight fantasy that Edward Albee's play is really about two homosexual couples. (How else could this unmarried playwright know so much about *their* lives?) What comes out in *Staircase* is "Nobody Loves You When You're Old and Gay"—not even yourself. Harry (Richard Burton) and Charlie (Rex Harrison) have been together for twenty years. For two hours they moan and piss about their sad, wasted lives, never showing a sign of love or affection. We are meant to feel sorry for them, but after all their time together there is no sign of an emotional attachment between them, no indication of a commitment to the relationship. When they do cling to one another, it is in loneliness and desperation, emotions that have been used to characterize homosexual relationships in film and literature for a century. Throughout the film Charlie and Harry repeat how much happier they would have been if only nature had not played them such a dirty trick. Harry keeps reminding Charlie that at least *he* was once married and has a child ("a privilege denied most of us"). Homosexuality, not loneliness, is their central problem, and no solution is possible. The exploration of self-hatred among homosexuals was valid, and it is still being done effectively by

Stanley Donen directs Rex Harrison in the fine art of faggotry for a scene with Richard Burton in Staircase *(1969).*

openly gay filmmakers, but *Staircase* says only that the problems of Charlie and Harry are insurmountable because they are the wrong sex for each other.

Archer Winsten, reviewing *Staircase* in the New York *Post,* was at a loss to define the potential audience for such dismal concerns. "It's knee deep in pathos," he wrote, "but not the kind that makes you want to help. You have the feeling that this is something beyond cure. It will continue after they're dead. It has got to end badly for them . . . the future has got to be worse." Charlie and Harry represented the sum of gay and non-gay thinking on the subject of gay life as imitation of the heterosexual pattern. The vision of a working gay relationship that is not based on the assignment of male and female roles—advocated by Larry in *The Boys in the Band*—will apparently have to wait its turn, for heterosexual relationships on film have only just begun, in the 1980s, to reflect that possibility. And gays were deemed "wrong" for the dream in the first place. In *Who's Afraid of Virginia Woolf?* at least the battered George and Martha have some hope. Even without their phantom son as a crutch, they're willing to try together, "just us." They are a man and a woman. But Charlie and Harry are cheap imitations. They represent the rotten side of the romantic dream, and they could not survive for a moment without their illusions. "You can't call *me* a poof!" Charlie cries, shivering in a graveyard. *"I'm* married, I am. Nothing poofey about me. No, sir. I'm normal." Trying to be normal is what makes Charlie and Harry so miserable, and that is what the film is all about. Homosexuals have been shown on film as victims of their own twisted values and misunderstandings of the nature of human relationships, but the responsibility of the dominant culture for instilling those values is never explored, even in films *about* the dominant culture. This is one reason why openly gay filmmakers are essential; no one else will confront the reality.

In a review of *The Sergeant,* Pauline Kael told the story of a gay friend. (Almost every time Kael reviewed a film with a homosexual theme, she told about a gay friend; after a while it came to be something of a George and Gracie routine.) This gay friend regularly stared at a certain young man in his nightly cruising area but would not approach him for fear of being rebuffed or even beaten up. Some time later, Kael's friend finally approached the man and told him how afraid he had been of speaking to him. "Gee," the guy replied, "I wish there was someone *I* could feel that way about." Homosexuals, Kael concluded, are all looking for "the real man they don't believe they are," and when they think they have found him, he turns out to be a homosexual— a sissy—like themselves. And so the search continues.

It does not take a private eye to figure out that most gay men do indeed buy the same sexist myths that straight men accept. Hollywood has always been the principal cheerleader for heterosexual role playing as the inevitable norm. Everything else is queer. Homosexuals cannot be real men, and real men cannot be homosexuals. We all have been taught this, and the movies have reinforced it as the truth. Nevertheless the realization that homosexuals have been taught to hate themselves for not being "normal" was news to Hollywood. Once homosexuality became a fit subject for screen treatment, it was open season. The movies made gay self-hatred an inherent part of the species, but they never explored their own sexual attitudes or how they affected Kael's pathetic friend. The definitions of lesbians as not quite women and gay men as less than men remained as firm in commercial film after the fact of gay liberation as they were before it. Mainstream cinema simply explored the self-hatred that was a result of some of its own early teachings.

Village Voice film critic Stuart Byron was one of the first openly gay writers to tackle the issues of gay liberation as they were raised in the commercial cinema. In a *New York Times* article in July 1971, "Finally, Two Films Which Deal with the Issues of Gay Lib," he noted that thus far the gay movement was one without a formal philosophy, much like the women's movement was before the publication of *Sexual Politics.* (If one exists now, it is certainly Dennis Altman's *Homosexual Oppression and Liberation.*) Byron identified two emerging issues of gay liberation as ones raised (but not explored) in Luchino Visconti's film based on Thomas Mann's *Death in Venice* (1971) and Harvey Hart's *Fortune and Men's Eyes.*

In Visconti's version of the composer Aschenbach (Dirk Bogarde), Byron saw Pauline Kael's constant cruiser, dominated by a heterosexual vision of his own homosexuality and therefore unable to relate to the young Tadzio as anything but a sexual object (an "ideal of beauty"). Society's age-old proscription against sex for the sake of sex and the nonprocreative nature of homosexuality, Byron reminded his readers, have kept homosexual oppression going since

Dirk Bogarde as Aschenbach reaches out for Tadzio, his ideal of beauty in Death in Venice *(1971).*

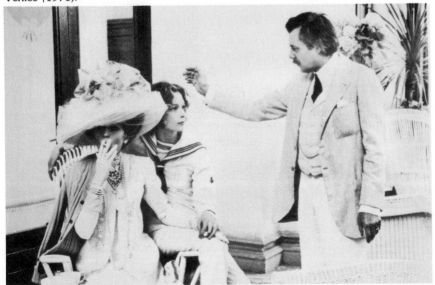

prehistoric times. Homosexual relationships necessarily lie outside the boundaries of permissible sexual relations and have always been viewed as exclusively sexual and nonproductive. The necessity of maintaining heterosexually oriented roles also forces Aschenbach to turn himself into a female sex object, dyeing his hair and painting his face pathetically for the "hunt"—like Brando in *Reflections in a Golden Eye,* who thought that to be homosexual was to be like a woman. In Aschenbach's dye-streaked face, Stuart Byron identified questions for gay liberation: Do homosexuals accept such role playing? If they do, how will gay liberation break down the belief in this dominant ideology and free gays as well as straights from such restrictions?

In the January–February 1978 issue of *Film Comment,* critic Robin Wood pointed out that "the dominant ideological norms of the society in which we live are . . . marriage and the nuclear family . . . between them they offer homosexuals the terms on which they might be acceptable—the aping of heterosexual marriage and family, complete with poodles as children." Wood further suggested, in his article "The Responsibilities of a Gay Film Critic," that by "asking" for admission to society and to the mainstream cinema at this time, homosexuals were asking for acceptance from that society and therefore implicitly accepting society's terms. The belief that society has the right to accept certain kinds of behavior implies a belief that society may also prohibit certain behavior. And the behavior that society most often prohibits is that which falls in the area between marriage, family and fidelity that homosexuals usually occupy—the area of "promiscuity," or having numerous relationships. Both Byron and Wood looked to the women's movement and to the gay movement to define relationships that were free of society's sexual role playing. They asked both movements to defy society's automatic repression of what is usually labeled "permissive" or "promiscuous" behavior; further, they asked that we not look to mainstream cinema to reflect a radical vision of sexuality. As the critic Noel Purdon wrote in *Cinema Papers* in 1969, "mainstream cinema will no doubt continue its boring shuffle towards sexual liberation," but gays should look elsewhere for an alternative vision of human relationships.

Byron's second example, *Fortune and Men's Eyes* (1971), raises these very issues and proves that the commercial American cinema was and is in no shape to take them on. *Fortune* takes place in a Canadian prison where situational homosexuality requires that homosexuals be either active (masculine and powerful) or passive (feminine and powerless). Byron noted that these were major problems for gays to work out; he also said, and for the first time, that gays need to work them out in the context of the sexual politics of the outside world that they consciously or unconsciously parody. Therefore, the attitude represented in such a line as "Isn't a pregnant lesbian a contradiction in terms?"—a joke in a straight film about gays—must be recognized not simply as a negative view of lesbianism but as the product of the sexual attitudes that form it. The sexism of the dominant culture makes Pauline Kael's gay friend think he must be a real man—or meet one—in order to fulfill his idea of a relationship. In fact the very existence of lesbians and gay men disproves the belief that personality is either male or female. Yet this existence has been first repressed and then redefined by our culture, along with all other alternatives to fidelity, monogamy and heterosexuality.

In *Fortune and Men's Eyes*, Rocky (Zooey Hall) is the "old man" who keeps young Smitty (Wendell Burton), a first timer, as "wife." When Smitty, urged on by the drag queen politician Queenie (Michael Greer), wipes the floor with Rocky and thereby reverses their sexual roles, Rocky kills himself. It is a question of manhood, a question for gay liberation. In Richard Brooks' *Looking for Mr. Goodbar* (1977), there is an ugly and offensive sequence in a parking lot between two gay men, one of whom (Tom Berenger) later kills Theresa Dunn (Diane Keaton). Their argument is clearly about Berenger's confusion over his own homosexual role. *"You're* the nellie!" he screams at his lover, "not *me.* I'm a pitcher, not a catcher! Don't you ever forget that." His disgust

Producer Lester Persky was responsible for turning Fortune and Men's Eyes *(1971) into a sexual peep show with scenes such as this of mass rape.*

with his "female" role eventually leads him to commit murder; unable to prove that he is not queer, he goes crazy. A society that demands that we play one sexual role and one sexual role only is the problem, not the solution. Because movies continue to reflect male and female role playing in both homosexual and heterosexual relations, gays can never measure up—they are not "real" to begin with, they are seen only in terms of heterosexual images. No matter that the havoc caused by role playing has devastated relations between men and women as well as between members of the same sex; homosexuals are Harrys and Charlies, queer imitations of the allegedly healthy norm.

Fortune and Men's Eyes went out of its way to reflect onscreen this kind of slavish imitation of society's roles by changing the basis of John Herbert's play (seemingly with the cooperation of the author) from a comment on sex as power to an exploitation of sex as a matter of gender identification. If director Jules Schwerin had not been removed from the film and replaced with Harvey Hart, the film might have reflected a deeper understanding of the sexual politics that were the basis of Herbert's stage play and of the role playing that a prison environment engenders. The play made the point that in this kind of situation the system seized upon and used sex as a weapon against everyone, that all became victims of the institution. Herbert's play, first produced Off Broadway by David Rothenberg in 1967, was an across-the-board plea for prison reform, and it used the homosexual feelings of its four principals integrally. Rocky did not commit suicide in the play because the play was not about the tragic implications of the passive homosexual role. The play focused on the dehumanization of all four principals by the emotional demands of their roles and their environment. The film, however, made the time-honored equation between homosexual discovery and suicide. It said that role playing in itself was so intolerable as to require suicide—like that of the British soldier in *King Rat* who walks into the ocean because he had "become" a woman and could not face the scorn of society.

When *Fortune and Men's Eyes* was produced on the stage a second time, by Sal Mineo in 1969, nudity and simulated sex were added and the play drew large gay audiences in major cities. Jules Schwerin, who had optioned the play in 1967 after seeing the David Rothenberg production, had no such ideas. Heavily involved in prison reform, Schwerin wanted the prison itself to be the culprit. A lot of unused footage from his version of the film focused on the prison building as a malevolent character that swallowed up its victims. "I was not interested in exploiting homosexuality," Schwerin insists, "it's not why I became interested in the play." According to *Variety*, Schwerin presided over thirty-one days of shooting on the MGM production in Quebec City and was then dismissed by the studio at the request of producers Lester Persky and Lewis Allen. Hart, who had directed William Inge's pseudonymous *Bus Riley's Back in Town* (1965), finished *Fortune* and received screen credit. What emerged seemed like a story about a country club for sadomasochistic homosexuals, backed by a Galt MacDermot score of country and western hijinks more appropriate to a *Bonnie and Clyde*. Persky's concept for the film was more in line with Mineo's stage interpretation, and Schwerin is convinced that Persky won the author over to his point of view. "Persky wanted only a kind of sex fantasy," Schwerin says. "He began to intrude on my direction day by day. He wanted a great deal of nudity and was interested only in the exploitation element. Any time I tried to inject humanity or tried to make the characters seem like the victims they really were, Persky would object. When I tried to show Queenie as a sympathetic and ultimately mutilated man, Persky kept saying, 'You're losing the funny drag queen quality.' "

Persky and MGM had their way. The advertising campaign for *Fortune* told the story: "What Goes on in Prison Is a Crime" meant homosexuality. "Let's face it," Persky told Robert La Guardia in *After Dark*, "we're saying something important here. I think what goes on in prisons is a terrible thing. Homosexuality is OK in some gay bar in Greenwich Village, but in prison it's forced on young people." A worse distortion of playwright Herbert's original intentions cannot be imagined. MGM wanted a picture that exploited and condemned homosexuality at the same time. When Schwerin first approached MGM with the property, they asked, "What makes you think you can direct this picture, seeing as you're not homosexual?" He told them he did not think it mattered whether a homosexual directed the picture or not. "They wanted a picture *about* homosexuality," Schwerin says, "because they perceived—wrongly, I think—that this was going to be the new hot subject." Persky seemingly wanted, and eventually got, a covert homoeroticism for a burgeoning "gay market," and everyone was happy but Schwerin and the gay liberation movement.

The movement, however, by now included film critics who wrote regularly from an openly gay perspective. Reviewing *Fortune* in the *Village Voice*, Richard McGuinness wrote, "The film has an unliberated, craven homosexual personality. I won't try to pin this mentality to its proper origins—writer, director, players—about which I am not knowledgeable, but to its incapacity for sincerity, its subversiveness; to the fabulous, epic bitchiness of the institutionalized faggot. Gay and proud it is not. Elusive, self-destructive and cruel it is." As for the advertising campaign, Byron added in the *New York Times*, "It's true. Homosexuality is still a crime in 45 out of 50 states." London critic Jack Babuscio put it best; comparing representation of the consequences of sexual repression in *Fortune and Men's Eyes* with Genet's *Un Chant d'Amour,* he wrote, "Genet's silent celebration of homoerotic love and sexual fantasy goes far further than the sadly compromised film version of John Herbert's play. Genet . . . challenges the morality of his audiences. The real prison, he seems to be saying, is within. It is the flesh that resists the pleasures of homosex in the celluloid cage."

> **Laden with every type of fag character, today's audiences with this leaning should find it fascinating fare. For more normal patrons, the going may be tough.**
>
> —Review of *Some of My Best Friends Are . . .* in *Variety*

The epic bitchiness of the institutionalized faggot and Lester Persky's contention that "homosexuality is OK in some gay bar in Greenwich Village" merged in Mervyn Nelson's *Some of My Best Friends Are . . .* (1971). This ghetto melodrama resembles the little theater production that the patrons of a gay bar might put on for their friends: a plea from the inside for the understanding and tolerance of ghettoized and exploited people. The oppression of gays by the very institutions that offer them a temporary haven is the subject of the film. But it is explored only superficially and ultimately gives way to the soapy possibilities of an all-stops-pulled evening at a gay bar, the Blue Jay (whose name is reminiscent of New York's famous "bird circuit" of the 1940s). It is Christmas Eve in this gay Grand Hotel, and the film witnesses the sad plight of two dozen or so characters who are exploited by the heterosexual superstructure around them. *Some of My Best Friends Are . . .* was originally titled *The Bar,* and Nelson retained over the credits the song "Where Do You Go?" about the predicament of people allowed to congregate safely only on someone else's terms and for a price.

Everything in the film points to the ways in which heterosexual society limits gay activity; few films have done this so well. Gerald Hannon, writing in *The Body Politic* about Edouard Molinaro's *La Cage aux Folles,* says that that film shows, in the surrender of Albin and his lover Renato to the every wish of the heterosexual son, how the entire history of homosexuality in a heterosexual world has been one of "small accommodations, concessions, sacrifices made by us so that their world might have its way." And that is what Mervyn Nelson shows in his film, but he does it almost by accident. He defines the ghetto from without, criticizing only the society at large and never his own characters for their passive acceptance of their victimization. The Blue Jay is run by a

Mafia underling who pays protection money to the police and confides to a cop, "These fags paid for my daughter's first communion party."

There are so many characters in *Some of My Best Friends Are . . .* and they are so briefly sketched that it is difficult to take them seriously. But they are sincerely conceived, and like Mart Crowley's characters, they date the iconography of their world, the gay bar ghetto. In fact much of the fascination of Nelson's film lies in the portrait it paints of the classic pre-liberation bar scene. It is almost as if the guests at Crowley's party were so miserable because their alternative was the Blue Jay. Yet the film never makes concrete connections between self-hatred, political oppression and apathy. It is conceived and played as a gay disaster movie that features great cameo performances, and it happens like an accident from which one cannot look away. Gay life on the town turns out to be a bunch of disenfranchised losers huddled around a blowtorch for the warmth and holiday spirit they cannot get from the families who have forsaken them. The film is epic tack.

A television actor tries unsuccessfully to have sex with a woman under the opening credits. Later, in the bar, he blurts out, "Why can't I just ball a chick? Why can't I do that?" His speech sets the tone for all the other children of loneliness who measure themselves always in terms of the straight norm. In a dark booth, a middle-aged man tells his Swiss ski instructor lover that he takes hot showers after their encounters to try to "wash off" his homosexuality—so far with no luck. The ski instructor wears more blue eye shadow than Rue McLanahan as Lita Joyce, the evil fag hag. In love with the handsome airline pilot who has thrown her over for a cute fashion photographer, Lita spitefully telephones the photographer's mother (Peg Murray) and tells her that her son is spending Christmas Eve in the arms of a man at a gay bar. The mother rushes to the Blue Jay in the snow, a shawl over her head, and finds her son on the dance floor in the arms of the pilot. She slaps him across the face, yelling, "It's dirty, dirty, dirty!" and says that as far as she is concerned he is dead, he is never to come home. For comic relief, Fanny Flagg plays Mildred Pierce, the hatcheck girl ("You know, honey. Like Joan Crawford on the late late show?") and Sadie the cook is jazz singer Sylvia Sims, playing a Jewish mother who will not turn her boys away or declare them dead ("You boys make me feel just like a queen"). Carleton Carpenter plays a prissy neurotic soul with only one line of dialogue ("Noel"), and the late Candy Darling gives the best performance in the film as Karen, the sloppy drag queen who dreams of being a real woman and is beaten to a pulp in the john by a hustler (Gary Sandy) who compulsively denies his homosexuality.

Some of My Best Friends Are . . . does not lay the blame on self-hatred.

The patrons of the Blue Jay bar chant "We Believe in Fairies" to raise the spirits of lovesick waiter Nick De Noia in Some of My Best Friends Are . . . *(1971).*

It says that gay people hate themselves enough already, that people should pity them and leave them alone. In the last scene, the ski instructor lies drunk beneath a table. The bartenders lock up and are getting into their car when one of them says, "Oh, shit, we have to go back inside. There's a faggot under one of the tables."

"Oh, leave him there until morning," the other says. "Where else does a faggot have to go?" The end credits roll.

Like *The Boys in the Band,* the film is an enlightening period piece that has lost its power to offend; it should be seen again, especially by gay audiences. When the film first opened, it was striking to note that gays had little empathy for the characters in Nelson's film. That should be different now. As a camp disaster movie, the melodramatic clichés of the Blue Jay have become grist for self-satire. Sluttish fag hags like Lita Joyce and punching-bag transvestites like Karen now populate the animated features of Ralph Bakshi and the films of John Waters, along with the likes of Divine, Snowflake and three-hundred-pound black lesbian schoolteachers from Baltimore. The characters in *Some of My Best Friends Are . . .* were the movie fantasies of gay bar queens who, though they are now cartoons, were too close to the shrill truth for many people at the end of the 1960s.

If *Some of My Best Friends Are . . .* was a Ross Hunter soap opera in drag, then Rosa von Praunheim's German film *It Is Not the Homosexual Who Is Perverse But the Society in Which He Lives* (1971) was the political reaction to its bourgeois values and goals, an attack on those who tried to gain entrance to the system that oppressed them instead of trying to change it. Defining the gay ghetto as a state of mind, a product of internalized heterosexual values, Praunheim takes a dime-novel story about one man's journey to liberation and uses it to assail media-created romantic illusions, capitalist principles and sexist role playing. The film chronicles the coming out of David and follows him through various options of the gay world, including street cruising, the bar life, a monogamous relationship and a hippie collective in which he engages in deep discussions of the nature of gay oppression. A narrator describes the condition of gay people and issues a call to arms.

Fags use culture as a means of getting together. In a sensuous atmosphere of exaggerated formality, they soon let their masks fall. Lifelong disappointment in love has made many of them cold and inhuman so that the partner is now seen only as a sex object . . . most homosexuals are in white collar, service-oriented jobs because they don't want to get their hands dirty and are afraid of hostility from blue collar workers . . . we have to become erotically free and socially involved.

The film was brought to New York on a minuscule budget after the German government refused to subtitle a print with grant money obtained for that

An aging, helpless faggot is beaten up by local toughs outside the men's room he has been cruising in Rosa von Praunheim's It Is Not the Homosexual Who Is Perverse But the Society in Which He Lives *(1971).*

purpose. It played first at the Museum of Modern Art and then, explosively, at the Gay Activists Alliance headquarters, an old firehouse in Soho. The film infuriated most American gays with its highly dogmatic, almost dictatorial litany of accusations lodged against bourgeois homosexuals and their self-destructive lifestyle. An intense confrontation between the filmmaker and an angry gay activist audience was videotaped and is now shown as an appendix to the original feature. In 1972, American gays expected a gay liberation film from Germany; instead they discovered that Praunheim had made a film which attacked them mercilessly, exposing a sterile gay subculture that fostered dreams of movies like *Love Story* turned into a "Bruce Doesn't Live Here Anymore" liberation fantasy.

New York Times critic Vincent Canby called *It Is Not the Homosexual* a "militantly Marxist call for an end to gay oppression," but he misunderstood the audience for whom it was intended. As Stuart Byron pointed out, *"Variety* and the rest of the straight press always review Rosa's films as if they were for a straight audience, and they're really for the gay community." This is borne out by Praunheim's second feature, *Army of Lovers, or Revolt of the Perverts* (1978), which was screened at the 1979 Los Angeles Filmex. *Variety's* critic threw up his literary hands in disgust, complaining that Praunheim spotlighted the very aspects of homosexuality that give the gay movement a bad name. To give the gay movement a good name, it seems, would require a film to disagree with Praunheim's politics, for politics is what his films are about. Rosa von Praunheim makes home movies for the gay movement.

Army of Lovers, a subjective view of the gay movement in America, charts the progress of what Praunheim sees as a losing battle. His images form a picture of a movement talking to itself. For the most part, *Army of Lovers* examines the stridencies of political and social extremes within the movement, telling its story through a series of interviews interspersed with newsreel footage, still photo montages and snippets of marches and rallies as well as agitprop gay theater. Some of the footage, like that of America's largest gay demonstration which took place in San Francisco in June of 1977, is dynamic and inspiring. The still photos by Bettye Lane capture some of the most vivid and emotional moments in the history of the movement; they include views of the crowds outside the Stonewall in Greenwich Village on the night of the 1969 riots. Another sequence, in color, shows the press conference at which a gay activist hits Anita Bryant in the face with a cream pie, followed by clips of Bryant in a silver dress hitched over her knees, singing and dancing to "You Are My Lucky Star."

But a heavy hand is at work everywhere in the film. There is no pretense to objectivity, even toward internal gay politics. "Radicalism died in 1973," a grim-voiced narrator intones while onscreen the former executive director of the National Gay Task Force, Bruce Voeller, is seen on the street wearing a suit and tie. NGTF is described, conversationally, as "a conservative, elitist organization"—and it is quite clear that some socialist gay activists would like to chop off a few hands. No love is lost in *Army of Lovers*.

Further, there is an underexplored yet powerful antifemale dynamic in both of Praunheim's films on the gay movement. They approach the issues of gay liberation from a distinctly nonfeminist point of view. Feminism, effeminism, lesbianism and lesbian separatism are dispatched in perfunctory and self-serving ways. Sequences in *Army of Lovers* that depict effeminate behavior, the macho gay "clone" look and the cult worship of superstar women by gay men give rise to violently conflicting emotions among both members of the audience and the people in the film but are never fully discussed by the filmmaker. The best example of this in the film was the appearance of disco star Grace Jones at a gay rally in New York. Jones, worshipped by the gay men in the crowd for her rendition of "I Need a Man," sung with her breasts bared, infuriated most lesbians in the audience, who saw her appearance as an insult to women perpetrated by a gay male mentality. The only comment is that of a lesbian who shouts, "All men are alike after all!" Praunheim, onscreen, looks properly ashamed.

The films of Praunheim offended American gays more than a film like *Some of My Best Friends Are . . .* because they said that all the worst clichés were founded in truth and then challenged the gay movement to do something about it. Praunheim attacks the dominant culture as the source of gay oppression, but he goes on to say that since most homosexuals embrace that culture, they invite censure. Praunheim described the problem in an interview with a Montreal gay publication, *Le Berdache*.

It's too easy to show homosexuals as victims. To get out of the situation of a victim you have to struggle. Gays have been used to hiding and playing a passive role. They are also very passive politically. Most gays are very conservative. They vote for governments that will protect the status quo. To push gays into action you have to confront them. When they saw my films, many gays felt hatred and anger for the first time, though it was directed at me myself and at the films. But that's the reaction I wanted. It's a very important step forward. I think Anita Bryant was one of the best things that has happened for the cause of gay liberation. She forced even conservative gays to come out of their closets. But now self-criticism has to be pushed even further. No sentimental shit about gays as poor little victims.

He was right, too, but nobody wanted to hear it. The middle class gays at whom Praunheim aimed his message never heard a thing; they were too busy hailing the decadence of Bob Fosse's *Cabaret* as a step in the right direction and warmly approving *Sunday, Bloody Sunday.*

In 1979, another West German film, Wolfgang Petersen's *The Consequence* (1977), won rave reviews from mainstream American critics by using precisely the kind of melodramatic theme Praunheim was talking about and depicting gays as poor victims of a society that refuses to leave two men to love each other in peace. *The Consequence* portrays the attempts of Martin (Jurgen Prochnow) and Thomas (Ernst Hannawald) to build a life together, attempts that are thwarted, exploited and betrayed at every turn by gays and straights alike. Petersen said he made the film to "tell the private love story of two people who happen to be men and whose relationship is systematically destroyed by their environment, which gives them no chance. In this way, perhaps, it just might be possible to change public sentiment; it's only a hope. I don't know if it will happen."

The Consequence told a melodramatic love story and got away with it because the quality of the acting and the taut, gripping direction avoided clichés and made the story believable and moving to large audiences. Although no American film has yet approached the kind of gay love story that Petersen tells in *The Consequence,* Salvatore Samperi's *Ernesto* (1979) and even *La Cage aux Folles*

Jurgen Prochnow and Ernst Hannawald share one of their rare peaceful moments in Wolfgang Petersen's The Consequence *(1977).*

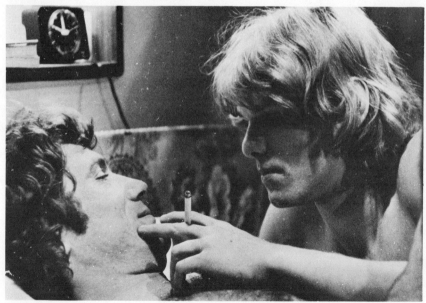

(in its own quaint way) are gay love stories told with different points of view. But these films suggest that the one big film that most gays are waiting for will never come. Films about gay life, especially those made by openly gay filmmakers, have had the burden of having to redress all the misinformation, the stereotypes and the myths of society that have accumulated through the ages. Every film is expected to be "the" breakthrough film, but it will not happen that way. Gays are realizing finally that the myths will be exploded one by one, in small ways, in big films and small films.

In 1973, one American gay liberation love story was expected to rival *Gone With the Wind* in scope and popularity and solve the problem of oppression in the bargain; its failure left its director, a pioneer, bitter and disillusioned. Christopher Larkin's *A Very Natural Thing,* the first film on a gay liberation theme intended for commercial distribution, attempted to deal with some of the issues raised by Rosa von Praunheim. In his introduction to the film, printed in the program handout, Larkin described its genesis.

The idea for a film about gay relationships and gay liberation themes came out of my own personal reaction, on the one hand, to the mindless, sex-obsessed image of the homosexual prevalent in gay porno films and, on the other hand, to the debasing caricatures and slurs about gay people and gay life coming out of the vast majority of commercially oriented films.

Originally titled *For as Long as Possible,* the film examined the options available to gay couples on society's terms and asked a question that ultimately could have only Praunheim's Marxist answer. How do two men who will not play society's game define a relationship that is not based on roles? *A Very Natural Thing* attempts to leave behind marriage, fidelity and monogamy and instead reinforces them. While the film came about as a result of the impact of the gay movement on Larkin and his co-author Joe Coencas, it was dismissed as trivial soap opera by the establishment press and generally savaged by gay liberationists for its romantic illusions and a lack of radical conviction.

David (Robert Joel), an ex-seminarian, teaches school in New York City and settles into a monogamous relationship with Mark (Curt Gareth), a straight-identified insurance salesman. Their meeting, courtship, marriage and breakup are examined in the first half of the film. As documented by Larkin, their romance is a long and deliberate *Love Story* parody in which the two go to the opera, roll in the autumn leaves in Central Park, watch each other shave in the morning and ape every heterosexual movie cliché about love and marriage. Mark's refusal to be possessed and David's nagging insecurities end the relationship.

Robert Joel and Curt Gareth as a traditional married cou-ple in Christopher Larkin's A Very Natural Thing *(1973).*
(New Line Cinema)

In the second half of the film, David explores the alternatives. Promiscuous sex at bathhouses and orgies on Fire Island are as unsatisfying to him as his pervasive loneliness. In a sequence filmed at the 1973 gay pride rally in New York's Washington Square Park, David meets Jason (Bo White), a divorced photographer who helps him to begin to redefine his perceptions of the nature of gay relationships. After establishing that there should be no promises, no expectations, only a commitment to explore each other, the film ends with the two running naked in the surf at Cape Cod, a slow-motion sequence that bore the brunt of the outrage and criticism directed at the film. Freedom from the assumption of roles in an unstructured relationship is difficult to express on film in a lyric way without attracting brickbats, but Larkin knew this, and he consciously chose to see romance as the bottom line.

Too many people, both straight and gay, see gay relationships as sad, necessarily transient sadomasochistic parodies of heterosexual marriages which cause nothing but unhappiness to the parties involved. This is simply not true. I wanted to say that same-sex relationships are no more problematic but no easier than any other human relationships. They are in many ways the same and in several ways different from heterosexual relationships but in themselves are no less possible or worthwhile.

Consequently, because of Larkin's insistence on couching his message in such relentlessly romantic terms, the film infuriated the very people who were fighting for such a redefinition on the political front.

Neither porno nor commercially oriented, *A Very Natural Thing* had such massive advertising and distribution problems that it made little impact, though it is still screened regularly, in series on homosexuality in film, as a breakthrough movie. The New York *Post* called it "an argument rather than an entertainment"; Judith Crist wrote, "If the gay lib movement wants its own mediocre movie preachment—here it is."

Critics who lambasted the film for being preachy saw the very use of gay characters in a romantic context as being preachy. In an interview in *Christopher Street* magazine, Debbie Reynolds asked her gay audience to remember for whom movies are really made.

(Interviewer) Gay people have never really felt that their lifestyle was presented on the screen because all the people in the movies are supposed to be heterosexual. It's like we don't exist.

(Reynolds) Yes, but I think you have to realize, really now, that the majority of people are *not* gay and that mass audience is out there. If you're a producer and you want to make pictures to make money, you make pictures to appeal to what we call the norm or the straight audience. Unless a producer had a wonderful and interesting film, a poignant and understanding story, but they haven't done it, have they?

John Schlesinger's *Sunday, Bloody Sunday* (1971) was a poignant, understanding and interesting story, but it did not sell to a mass audience. It has consistently been cited since as an example of a "good gay film" that failed to make it at the box office, "proof" that homosexuality is not a money-making proposition in movie terms. The problem, however, was in the packaging. *Sunday, Bloody Sunday* was a talky, introspective British production that was in no way an American mass audience picture. In fact there seems to be very little room in the American market anymore for the "small but interesting" film. According to producers and writers, this is now the specialty of movies made for television. Every theatrical film has to be a *Grease* or a *Star Wars* because the studios will now make only two or three films a year instead of ten, and each one has to be a smash hit. Americans who saw it seemed not to understand *Sunday, Bloody Sunday,* though they took their cue from the highbrow critics and respected it. Others, unable to figure out what it was "about" in spite of the glowing notices, stayed away in droves.

"This film," Schlesinger said, "is not about the sexuality of these people." The people in question were a homosexual doctor (Peter Finch), a heterosexual career woman (Glenda Jackson) and the bisexual artist (Murray Head) with whom they were both in love. And Schlesinger was right; *Sunday, Bloody Sunday* was not about sexuality. But it was a film in which alternative sexuality was taken for granted, something that gay activists had been asking for all along. It was a film about human relationships and how they do not always match our ideas about what love ought to be. Everyone in the film settles

Peter Finch and Murray Head kiss passionately in John Schlesinger's Sunday, Bloody Sunday *(1971).*

for something less than he or she had hoped for or been taught to expect—except the bisexual, whose sexuality is viewed as part of his youthful noncommitment to anyone or anything but his work. When Head runs off to America at the end of the film, leaving Jackson and Finch to fend for themselves, it is clear that their lives will continue though they are trapped in resignation. In the end, they realize, one is always alone.

When Glenda Jackson belittles her parents' marriage, her mother tells her, "The trouble with you is that you're looking for 'the whole thing.' There is no 'whole thing.' You just have to make it work." Murray Head already knows this, but he never gets credit for knowing it. He is not really noncommitted; he has made his choices both sexually and professionally. Yet his bisexuality is seen as a lack of fidelity, in the same way that Michael York's bisexuality in *Cabaret* is seen as a betrayal. Both Finch and Jackson are more interesting characters than Head because they are given the kind of solid values with which the audience can identify. They are committed to romantic stability which the film defines as good health. The ability to make a choice is seen as a necessity. Head chooses both men and women, and that is against the rules: it is no choice rather than a new choice.

The film presented a happy ending for a homosexual character whose dull resignation is not the product of his gayness. Finch tells the audience in a closing monologue, "People say to me, He never made you happy. And I say, But I *am* happy. Apart from missing him. All my life I've been looking for someone courageous and resourceful. He's not it. But something. We *were* something." The speech has little to do with homosexuality, but it does say that gay relationships are not nothing. And *Sunday, Bloody Sunday* said something even more universal and important, that "the whole thing" that Jackson's mother spoke of is an illusion. Like the cold, metallic connections made by the telephone equipment at the beginning of the film, people connect randomly, hoping that their system of relating will not break down before they can connect and find a way to make it work together.

America hated *Sunday, Bloody Sunday*. One kiss exchanged between Head and Finch caused even more of a stir than scenes that showed them in bed together. Male-male relationships are defined in terms of sex, yet in many minds affectionate love between men is out of the question. And this was the first affectionate kiss onscreen between two men that was not a device or a shock mechanism. It drew gasps from audiences wherever it played, and because of it many theaters would not book the film at all. The London press quoted singer Shirley Bassey, a friend of Peter Finch, as complaining that at a screening the kiss had made her sick to her stomach, forcing her to leave the theater. The flood of gay films that followed *The Boys in the Band* into release in 1970 revealed many similar instances of latent homophobia among actors, writers, directors and critics.

Actors have always resisted playing homosexual roles lest they be typed— especially those actors who are gay in private life. Some performers have even expressed strong moral convictions against playing such roles. As Louise Brooks discovered, her role in *Pandora's Box* (1929) led many people to believe that she really was a lesbian. In the 1960s and 1970s, these consider- ations came into the open in company with the subject matter. Suddenly actors were discussing not their own sexuality but the drawbacks of playing homosex- ual parts. When Beryl Reid appeared on the Johnny Carson show to publicize *The Killing of Sister George,* she was compelled to reiterate that she was not in fact a lesbian, for the press had been focusing its questions on her sexuality rather than on the film. Angela Lansbury, whom Robert Aldrich ap- proached originally to play the title role in *Sister George,* turned him down politely but made her feelings known the next day in a widely distributed interview with Earl Wilson. According to Aldrich, her comments were "best described as unfortunate. She said, 'Oh, *who* could possibly play those charac- ters?' and expressed great distaste for 'what those women are.' It was a total putdown of the project and was quite unnecessary. You don't have to play the part. It's a free country."

Lansbury, quoted by Keith Howes in London's *Gay News* in 1976, said, "I didn't want to play a lesbian at that time. Not very many women played recognizable lesbian roles in 1968, and that had a bearing on my decision. Now, of course, I think that the truth is filtering down to all of us, but I still don't think I'd play the part."

Susannah York had the same trouble playing Childie in *The Killing of Sister George* that Alice Roberts had had dancing the tango with Louise Brooks in *Pandora's Box* in 1929. A year before shooting began on the film, Aldrich flew to Dublin, where York was making a picture on location, to discuss the role with her. He told her that her accepting the part included the understanding that she would play the seduction scene as written because he intended to direct it following the script as closely as possible. York agreed. "She knew it was going to be difficult," Aldrich said, "but she had wrestled with that before I got to Ireland, and everything was fine.

A year later, on the day we were to shoot the scene, she came to me in the morning and said, "I can't do it," and I said, "Susannah, I really want you to like me. But there's no fucking way you're not going to do this scene, or you'll just never work again." Now that's not the nicest thing in the world to say to someone. But, after all, she missed her chance to say no a year before in Ireland. So she did it. You must understand that she's a great actress, but this was terribly painful for her. It was an ordeal. And then, when I saw the footage, I realized that it wasn't erotic enough. So I said, "I'm sorry, Susannah, it isn't enough." This depressed her. But when she saw the footage, she agreed that it wasn't good enough. Finally, she asked me if she could do those scenes alone, without Coral Browne on the set. So I said, "Okay, but if it doesn't work, we have to shoot it with Coral." It worked. She was sensational. But you must see that this was not an unprofessional thing for her to do. There's a conventional resistance to doing that sort of thing.

The resistance was widespread. Producers, directors, writers and actors talked constantly about how certain films were "not really" about homosexuality but were about loneliness or human relationships or anything that was universal enough to quash the identification with homosexual subject matter. The reactions of the press, the public and especially the defensive actors were instructive. Anne Heywood, after playing Ellen March in *The Fox*, found it necessary to tell the press, "I've played murderers, but I've never killed anyone." Cliff Gorman and Leonard Frey both accepted effeminate homosexual roles immediately following their success in *The Boys in the Band*, Gorman in *Justine* and Frey in *Tell Me That You Love Me, Junie Moon*. Since then both have spent a lot of time trying to shake the gay image. Gorman told the press, "If I play a psychopath, it doesn't mean I'm a psychopath." Actors dragged out baby pictures as though they had to defend themselves against the charges. Jane Wyman complained that in the 1960s she was offered only "lesbians and axe murderers" and added, "I won't play lesbians, honey. Not this kid."

When the program notes for the New York stage production of *Staircase* stressed the heterosexuality of the actors, *The Villager* noted, "The playwright, the two actors and the director are married and ostensibly happy. The fact that the actors are not homosexual gives their acting strength. You realize it *is* acting." When a homosexual actor plays a homosexual, then, it is not acting because all homosexuals are alike and can be played only as stereotypes; when a heterosexual actor plays a heterosexual character, it is acting because heterosexuals are different individuals and can be played as people. When Rex Harrison and Richard Burton played Charlie and Harry in the film version of *Staircase,* a circus of innuendo and fag humor surrounded reports of the filming in both the print and the electronic media. The sight of two virile actors, each with ample heterosexual credentials, lisping and mincing for the benefit of newsreel cameras, was a way of saying, Look; they are really only acting.

From on location in Paris, Liz Smith reported in the *New York Times* that Rex Harrison, "never known for his tolerance of the lightfooted members of his profession . . . patiently let a grassroots American press junket tear at his vitals over the very idea of a masculine movie star and an Oscar winner playing a pervert." One member of that press junket asked Richard Burton how he intended to "disguise his magnificent voice to make it homosexual."

Later, Burton asked Liz Smith, "Are they even vaguely aware that some of the greatest voices in the theater belong to homosexuals? They frighten me. Because they're supposed to be the intellectuals, and I suddenly realize that they're the audience for this film. I have never known anyone who took great exception to homosexuals that there wasn't something very wrong with that person himself."

When Perry King accepted the role of a gay man in Paul Aaron's *A Different Story* (1978), his friend Sylvester Stallone warned him, "Don't play no faggots." According to Elizabeth Ashley in her book *Actress,* George Peppard, offered the script for the film adaptation of Carson McCullers' *The Heart Is a Lonely Hunter,* was advised by his agent to turn it down because "the part was a weak man, possibly a homosexual and it would ruin [his] career." Robert La Tourneaux, who played the midnight cowboy in *The Boys in the Band,* found that out too late. He says he lost the lead in Paramount's *Love Story* to Ryan O'Neal because of his role as a hustler. "I was too closely identified with homosexuality," he told James Wechsler in the New York *Post.* "Charles Laughton played every kind of part but never a homosexual. People knew he was gay, but his public image never betrayed his private reality. So he was safe. I wasn't safe." In 1979, singer Michael Jackson turned down the part of the gay dancer in the film version of *A Chorus Line* because, according to *Jet* magazine, "People already think I'm that way—homo—because of my voice, and I'm not." The British actor Peter Finch was infinitely more secure.

When a London *Times* reporter asked him how he could possibly bring himself to kiss a man onscreen in *Sunday, Bloody Sunday,* Finch replied, "I just closed my eyes and thought of England."

America closed its eyes. It was easy to see why gay actors feared playing homosexual roles and why straight actors worried about their box office appeal. For Hollywood the gay world was still strictly a place to search for sex and to encounter violence. In *The Day of the Jackal* (1973), Edward Fox is an assassin who picks up a man at a gay bathhouse and uses him and his apartment to hide out from the police for a few days. Unfortunately, the man sees Fox's picture on a television news program and is routinely shot to death. He is killed not because he is a homosexual, but because, as a homosexual, he frequents places where one is likely to meet unsavory and dangerous characters. If you hang around gay bars and baths, you are likely to get bumped off— and you were probably asking for it. In *Looking for Mr. Goodbar,* Terry Dunn courted the same kind of sexual violence by frequenting singles bars and bringing home strangers. Yet no one suggested that her behavior represented the heterosexual lifestyle or that Terry Dunn's heterosexuality was to blame when she got knocked off. No, she is killed by a repressed homosexual who lets her have it when she laughs at his failure to perform in bed. So, even in a film about the underground of heterosexual cruising, it is the homosexual wanting to be a real man who commits the violence out of frustration and rage at not being accepted by the heterosexual majority.

Because so few films have been made that presented any aspect of homosexuality at all, and because the majority of those films that did dealt only with the sexual ghetto, filmmakers tended to sound hollow when they responded to the protests of gay activists by suggesting that they were simply capturing the truth. Peter Hyams' defense of his film *Busting* (1974), which is about two vice cops (Elliott Gould and Robert Blake) who bust homosexuals, was that since it was a film about vice cops, his characters would naturally meet only the sleaziest people. Yet this was the *only* popular context in which homosexuality was ever shown. The opposite of Richard Burton's weakling Harry in *Staircase* was at the other end of the spectrum, the violent killer Vic Dakin, whom Burton portrayed in Michael Tuchner's *Villain* (1971). Again, the trouble was not that the film failed to paint a vivid and interesting portrait of a quite plausible thug but that there was nothing to indicate the diversity of the gay population that lay between Charlie and Vic. Lesbians and gay men remained as closeted onscreen as they were in real life.

The black exploitation films *Cleopatra Jones* (1973) and *Cleopatra Jones and the Casino of Gold* (1975) used lesbians (played by Shelley Winters and

Stella Stevens) as dope pushers and gang leaders. *Mandingo* (1975) and *Drum* (1976) saw male homosexuality as a white man's disease visited on black men to enforce a racist powerlessness. In *Drum,* John Colicos played an evil white slaver who raped and mutilated black men. His character was no less a cartoon than Snowflake, the black transvestite in Ralph Bakshi's animated feature *Coonskin* (1975). Snowflake, described in the script as a "lousy, no good queer," likes to get beaten up by real men and spends his time having sex in the back of a trailer truck on the waterfront. Such films said not only that the homosexual life was synonymous with sex and violence but that this was the norm, that homosexuality *belonged* in the sexual ghetto because it was an abnormal manifestation of love.

One film escaped this trap by walking a thin line. Thomas Rickman's script for *The Laughing Policeman* (1973) seems to have changed in response to some gay activist visibility. In an early version of the screenplay, Walter Matthau was a homophobic detective who says, "I've been on the homicide detail for eight years. You know who commits the most vicious murders? The ones you can't believe? Homosexuals." But in the released version of the screenplay, Matthau is a liberal cop who comes up against the homophobic Bruce Dern in almost every scene. When Dern suggests that they arrest a suspect on the ground that he is a closet case, Matthau says impatiently, "You miss the point. Things are different today. Homosexuals don't hide anymore, they demonstrate." That was the first acknowledgment in a commercial film that a gay liberation movement existed in America.

In an excursion outside the San Francisco gay ghetto, where most of the action of *The Laughing Policeman* takes place, Dern and Matthau discover that one of the victims of the mass slayings touched off at the start of the film was a lesbian whose lover (Joanna Cassidy) works as a nurse in a city hospital. The lesbian who was killed, it turns out, was an innocent caught in the crossfire. Dern's scene with the nurse is lively and inventive, and he reports back to the office, "The nurse turned out to be a happily married dyke—nothing we can do about that . . . any of us." Only in its depiction of a gay bar did *The Laughing Policeman* succumb to the temptation to pack the whole gay world into one garishly lit room. Consider the description of the scene in Rickman's original script, one of the few scenes that director Stuart Rosenberg did not change.

INT. Gay Bar–day

Two young men are dancing to raucous rock music on a stage behind the bar. They are muscular and not obviously effeminate except that their eyes are made up, they wear false eyelashes and the briefest bikinis. Their pubic area is painted with phosphorescent paint so that it is all that is seen when the lights are turned off. The place is crowded—a strange mixture of transvestites, hustlers, rough trade and very square businessmen.

Leather men and transvestites, oil and water in any real-life gay bar, are always chummy in movie bars. The same distortion occurs in *Busting*, which takes a much more homophobic look at the subculture. And these films were just two in a string of features that offset gays as villains only with gays as victims.

Positive gay characters were often proposed but seldom made it to the screen. Thomas Rickman recounts one incident.

In my first movie job, I was asked to rewrite *Kansas City Bomber* for Raquel Welch. I wrote a completely new script which included the subplot of a young roller derby girl who fell in love with Raquel. The intent was to show that such a relationship could be as normal as any heterosexual one. Raquel's character was to be sympathetic to the girl even though she found that she couldn't return her love. When this draft went to the MGM hierarchy—James Aubrey was president at the time—word thundered down that "no dykes would be in the same picture with Raquel." The script was later rewritten by someone else and all references to lesbianism removed. However, the lesbian character remained, metamorphosed into a whiny, somewhat superfluous roommate.

In two articles that appeared a year apart in the *New York Times*, "Let the Boys in the Band Die," April 8, 1973, and "Why Do Gays Want to Bust *Busting*?" March 3, 1974, Arthur Bell, a founder of the Gay Activists Alliance, fired a broadside at the film industry for its images of gays in films. "Our revolution came late in 1969," Bell wrote. "But our stereotypes continue. Our screen image is alive and sick and in need of a euthanasic ending and a liberated beginning." Citing such "swizzle stick" token gays as René Auberjonois' passive but bitchy gossip in *Pete 'n' Tillie* and Tony Perkins' suicidal film producer in *Play It as It Lays* as recent examples, Bell said that films since *The Boys in the Band* were "stereotypical of the progression of late 1960s and early 1970s films written and/or directed by homosexuals who have not been willing to come out of the closet or by heterosexuals who are either unconscious of what they're doing or homophobic enough to want to perpetrate age-old stereotypes that gay is bad, an equivalent to black is ugly and one which the gay movement is working to obliterate."

While Matthau and Dern in *The Laughing Policeman* search for a murderer in a gay bar, Gould and Blake in *Busting* raid another gay bar simply because it is there. The bar scene in *Busting* requires the same suspension of disbelief as the bar scene in John Guillermin's *P.J.* There is a wild fracas in which Gould and Blake are attacked by scores of men but emerge with only a few scratches and one nasty bite ("That greasy faggot took a chunk out of my leg!"). Since the film is about vice cops, the homosexuals they try to entrap in public rest rooms are equated with the homosexuals with whom they tangle at the bar—people whose lives are defined as lawless. On the other hand, *The Laughing Policeman* shows that there are homosexuals who live outside the ghetto both physically and psychologically.

When Arthur Bell attacked *Busting* in 1974 as a distortion of gay life, he was not claiming that the particular scene Hyams chose to portray did not exist but that the movies, by focusing exclusively on this one aspect of gay life, told a lie. Responding to Bell's *New York Times* article, Hyams pointed out that the gay bar used in the film was a real gay bar and that the extras in the scene were patrons of that bar who were told to dress and behave as they normally would. Looking at the scene, it is hard to believe this, but Hyams insists, "these are facts . . . they may not be pleasant facts, but this is true." However, Hyams claimed that his film illustrated and illuminated the nature of gay oppression by showing how badly the court system treats gays, and he cited a scene in which a transvestite is humiliated by a judge. But the transvestite, the hustlers, the leather men and the glitter queens of Hyams' world are neither approached nor shown as three-dimensional characters. We know nothing about them beyond their sexual orientation. Their oppression does not move us to view what happens to them as oppressive. They are criminals—fair game—and they are easy targets in comedy or tragedy.

In Alvin Sargent's screen adaptation of Paul Zindel's *The Effect of Gamma Rays on Man-in-the-Moon Marigolds* (1972), directed by Paul Newman, Joanne Woodward is made to yell "Faggot!" at her next-door neighbor because he is not interested in her. The word does not appear in Zindel's play. Toney Brealond played the "swishy" (*Variety's* adjective) gangster's aide who is belittled in Mark Warren's *Come Back Charleston Blue* (1972). In Woody Allen's *Sleeper* (1973), a swishy gay couple have a swishy gay robot. In *The Tamarind Seed* (1974), Dan O'Herlihy played the evil homosexual British minister in Paris. In *For Pete's Sake* (1974), Barbra Streisand was $1.80 short at the supermarket checkout.

> *Streisand:* But how can $31.46 fit in one bag?
> *Snippy Faggot Cashier:* Well, no one is *forcing* you to *eat*, madam. Put back the roast.
> *Streisand:* Here. Take back the Fruit Loops. You should really enjoy those.

In *Magnum Force* (1973), Clint Eastwood as Dirty Harry tangles with a group of suspiciously gay fascist rookie policemen. At the climax, when a cop dressed in black leather and a crash helmet kisses his dead buddy on the lips, Eastwood blows him away in disgust. Even in François Truffaut's *Day for Night* (1973), Jean-Pierre Aumont's positively presented relationship with a young lover ends in tragedy, the lover killed in a pointless car crash.

Occasionally films revealed some measure of truth about the nature of gay life, but this almost always happened by accident, and the inherent possibilities were never explored. The gay American Indian Littlehorse (Robert Littlestar) in Arthur Penn's *Little Big Man* (1970) suggested but did not pursue the alternative cultural vision of homosexuality held by the Human Beings—not of outcast but of unique, almost sacred position in the tribe. The attitudes of Native Americans toward homosexuals in their tribes is discussed at greater length in Rosa von Praunheim's *Army of Lovers* in a conversation between third world gays on a Manhattan rooftop.

Robert Littlestar as Littlehorse, the gay Native American, with Dustin Hoffman in Little Big Man *(1970).*

Sometimes a satiric talent proved that homosexuality could be funny without being offensive. In Billy Wilder's *The Private Life of Sherlock Holmes* (1970), a Russian ballerina wishes to engage Holmes as her bodyguard/lover, a position declined by Peter Tchaikovsky because "women were not his glass of tea."

Holmes: Well, I *had* hoped to avoid the subject but you see . . . ah, Watson
            and I have been bachelors for several years and ah . . .
Ballerina: Come to the point!
Holmes: The point, madame, is that Tchaikovsky was *not* an isolated case.
Ballerina: You mean . . . Dr. Watson? *He* is your glass of tea?
Holmes: If you want to get picturesque about it.

Critics carped about Wilder's refusal throughout the film to have Holmes
deny his homosexuality, even at the hysterical urgings of a mortified Watson.
But whenever homosexuality became the principal subject of a film, genuine
humor was replaced by fag humor. In *The Ritz, Norman, Is That You?* and
even the enormously successful *La Cage aux Folles,* homosexuals are essentially
buffoons who soothe an audience's sense of superiority by portraying gays
as weak, powerless sissies just like those of the Thirties, if without the charm.

The Ritz (1976), Terence McNally's wacky Broadway farce about a Cleveland
garbage man who eludes his Mafia brother-in-law by hiding out in a New
York City gay bathhouse, lost a lot of steam in the transition from stage to
screen. The one-joke situation traps a straight man in gay surroundings but
provides no comic insight or surprise in the way *La Cage aux Folles* occasionally
does because the characters in *The Ritz* are all looney tunes. The story is
that McNally saw Rita Moreno doing her Puerto Rican chanteuse routine at
a party and decided to write a play for the character. Onstage it was a piece
of fluffy provincialism that emerged from a very sassy New York gay sensibility
born in the days when Bette Midler sang at the Continental Baths and straights
met gays in humorous circumstances that produced some funny moments.
Onscreen, director Richard Lester fails to get any of the real jokes. He directs
as though the existence of gays in such a place were joke enough. His pacing
has two speeds, one hundred miles an hour and full stop; if pregnant pauses
were elbows, the audience would have black and blue ribs. After each laugh
is signaled, the picture screeches to a halt so that unsophisticated audiences
can get it. Lester was sure that the famous general public needed time to
catch up with McNally's snazzy farce, and he knew as well that the public
would not accept a film about a gay bathhouse unless the homosexuals were
comic.

George Schlatter's *Norman, Is That You?* (1976) may have been the first
pro-gay fag joke. Schlatter combined what looked to be good intentions with
a production that only a hack could love and a solution that nobody could
believe. The short-lived Broadway comedy about the parents who discover
their son's lover and gay lifestyle on a weekend visit went on to become a
big dinner theater hit, and it is easy to see why: it plays both ends from the

Dennis Dugan and Michael Warren as the young lovers in Norman, Is That You? *(1976).*

middle, refusing to make any comment on the situation for fear of offending someone. The black lover is butch, obviously the "husband"; the white lover is nellie, obviously the "wife." Just like us, George! The homophobes can identify with Redd Foxx's Neanderthal reactions, and gays can bask in the glory of the script's revelation that Stephen Foster, dead 112 years, was a homosexual.

In June 1973, *Variety* reported the first in a series of meetings between gay activists and representatives of the film and television industries to "discuss the treatment of homosexual figures and homosexuality in U.S. made theatrical and television films." The Gay Activists Alliance had requested the meeting with the Association of Motion Picture and Television Producers to protest "false and derogatory depictions of lesbians and gay men" and to suggest that there were ways "to put the pros and the cons of the gay lifestyle on film with no loss of audience appeal or consequent revenue." In the summer of 1973, the Gay Activists Alliance, in cooperation with the National Gay Task Force, released a set of guidelines.

Some General Principles for Motion Picture
and Television Treatment of Homosexuality

1. Homosexuality isn't funny. Sometimes anything can be a source of humor, but the lives of twenty million Americans are not a joke.

2. Fag, faggot, dyke, queer, lezzie, homo, fairy, mary, pansy, sissy, etc. are terms of abuse. If you don't want to insult, the words are gay, lesbian and homosexual. That doesn't mean that nobody on film can use a dirty word, but if you have rules about kike, wop, spic, nigger, etc., use them for fag and dyke.

3. Use the same rules you have for other minorities. If bigots don't get away with it if they hate Catholics, they can't get away with it if they hate gays. Put another way, the rights and dignity of homosexuals are not a controversial issue.

4. Stereotypical people do exist. But if such a minority of any group receives exclusive media exposure, that's bigotry. Until a broad spectrum of the gay community is expressed on film and the stereotypes are put into perspective, their use is damaging.

5. Homosexuality is a natural variant of human sexuality. It is not an illness, nor is it a problem for the majority of gays who are happy to be what they are. If all blacks or Jews or Irish or Chicanos were portrayed as anguished, oddball or insane, they'd be angry too. Gays are angry.

6. If you are doing a drama or a comedy or a talk show about homosexuality, you have an obligation to do your homework and free yourself from the myths.

7. There is a wide variety of available themes concerning the place of homosexuality in contemporary society and the range of gay relationships and lifestyles. Many of these can provide entertainment for a broad, general public. Gays do not want to return to media invisibility.

8. A permanent board of consultants consisting of gay men and women is available to the industry. But there are gay people all around you in your jobs. It is up to you to provide a climate in which they feel free to speak out openly.

Television, which is subject to regulation by the Federal Communications Commission and to the reactions of its advertisers to vocal public opinion, was more vulnerable to this type of activist pressure than was the motion picture industry. Television programming, scheduled for nearly twenty-four hours a day, was in constant need of social issues with which to deal, homosexuality among them. A film may have to be a hit, but when a television show flops, there is always next week and another subject, so experimentation was encouraged. Pressure by gay liberation directed the course that television would take regarding the presentation of homosexuality for the American viewer, and it succeeded in obtaining a more balanced and certainly more prolific dialogue on television than in film.

In 1972, Norman Lear's lovable bigot Archie Bunker encountered homosexuality for the first time when he discovered that one of his drinking pals, a former football player, was gay. President Richard Nixon watched the episode at the White House and pronounced it "distasteful" because "it made a good man look like a fool." It was not clear whether the president referred to the shocked Archie Bunker or the football player.

In that same year, ABC took the first important step in the portrayal of average gays on television. A two-hour movie of the week called *That Certain Summer* told the story of a divorced man (Hal Holbrook) who decides to tell his fourteen-year-old son (Scott Jacoby) that he is gay when the boy comes for a weekend visit. The son is hostile to the presence of his father's lover (Martin Sheen), and when Holbrook finally gets around to explaining the situation to him, the boy runs away, unable to deal with it. The story was a trifle mild for gay liberationists; while it received rave reviews in the straight press, some gay writers condemned it for being too tentative and overly cautious. The impetus for the idea, according to the screenwriters Richard Levinson and William Link, came from "the fact that a homosexual friend of ours mentioned that his son was coming to visit him. We knew he had been married, but we didn't know he had children, and it struck us as an exciting idea for a story."

The major objections of the gay activists were political ones, for most agreed that the film was an artistic success. The two lovers did not touch each other "enough"; they were "too" middle class. When at the end of the film Holbrook tells his son that he is gay, he says, "A lot of people—most people, I guess—think it's wrong. They say it's a sickness, that it's something that has to be cured. I don't know. I do know that it isn't easy. If I had a choice, it isn't something I'd pick for myself." This speech was savaged by gay liberationists, and not without cause. Although, as writer Merle Miller pointed out in a supportive article in the *New York Times,* "some people *do* say it's a sickness," the motivation for the speech was basically homophobic; it was imposed on the script for "balance." (Some homosexuals pointed out that the entire body of American film and television previous to *That Certain Summer* could surely serve as balance.) Levinson tells how the speech came about.

The reason for inserting those lines into the script was a meeting we had with two psychiatrists in the employ of ABC. Their feeling was that somewhere in the script we had to introduce a character—in their words, either an Archie Bunker or a policeman—who would give voice to prevailing public opinion. Meaning that they were reflecting a corporate concern over the fairness doctrine. They felt that we were taking a pro-homosexual stand and that the opposing view had to be aired. We strongly resisted, disagreeing with them totally, but finally we decided to have the homosexual himself, rather than some bigot imposed on the story, tell his son the harsh truth, that some people think homosexuality is a sickness—some people *do*—and that if he had his choice, he wouldn't be a homosexual. We justified this in our minds by feeling that in a racist and bigoted society, it is simply more comfortable being rich, white and straight than poor, black or gay.

The fairness doctrine, however, worked both ways. The National Gay Task Force invoked it on behalf of gay rights and won several battles in a row, establishing on television something that had never existed in films, an advocate-

Hal Holbrook, Scott Jacoby and Martin Sheen form an explosive triangle in Lamont Johnson's made-for-television film That Certain Summer *(1973).*

versus-bigot situation. In 1974, the *Policewoman* episode "Flowers of Evil," which portrayed the lesbian owners of an old-age home as predatory killers, was attacked by the gay movement and a rerun of the episode was halted. In 1975, when *Marcus Welby, M.D.* scheduled "The Outrage," a drama about a teacher who sexually molests a fourteen-year-old boy, NGTF learned of the plot before the show was aired and succeeded, by means of a nationwide letter-writing campaign, in discouraging advertisers from buying time on the show. NBC inserted lines in the script to explain the difference between homosexuals and child molesters, and it had to run its own promotional ads during the hour-long telecast. The show was never scheduled for rerun. As a further result of the publicity engendered by the protest against "The Outrage," the public was informed that the majority of child molesters in this country are heterosexual males who attack young girls, usually members of their own families.

Each battle incited new debate on long-closeted issues. In the same way that Walter Matthau had become an advocate pitted against Bruce Dern's bigot in *The Laughing Policeman,* television created a pro and con situation whenever a homosexual topic was aired. Putting the words *fag* and *lezzie* in the mouths of Archie Bunker and other obvious bigots categorized those terms in the public mind as unacceptable and made homophobia a concrete threat that involved the slander of increasingly real people. Within a very few years, beginning in 1972, television presented a more vibrant and diverse portrait of gay America than had been seen in the entire history of American film.

The first television show to portray homosexuals was the dramatic police series *N.Y.P.D.* in 1967. (Before that the only "gay" character on television was the strange fellow who appeared during every Milton Berle Show and said, *"I'm* with *you."*) In a story about a police officer tracking down a black-mailer of gay men, *N.Y.P.D.* featured a gay character, used the word *homosexual* for the first time and characterized homosexuality as "an area of human activity feared and detested everywhere." Speaking of a gay suicide, a gay businessman tells the police, "If he was a homosexual, it's easy to see why he would kill himself."

Nothing more about homosexuality appeared on the home screen until *That Certain Summer* five years later, but with that the barriers seemed to be lifted. By the mid 1970s, lesbian or gay male characters, often in the context of issues first raised by the gay liberation movement, had appeared on virtually every situation comedy, drama and talk show in prime time television. *All in the Family, Rhoda, Maude, Barney Miller, M*A*S*H, Baretta, Kojak, Phyllis, Mary Hartman Mary Hartman, The Bob Crane Show, Carter Country, The Bob Newhart Show, Family, Medical Center* and scores of others featured gay characters, and most continue to do so. Gay life in America has been the subject of local and national documentary shows each year, and television movies such as *Sergeant Matlovitch Versus the U.S. Air Force* and *A Question of Love* were based on the real-life struggles of gay men and lesbians.

In 1976, as part of its Bicentennial salute to great Americans, CBS aired a dramatization of the life of Walt Whitman that starred Rip Torn as our nation's poet laureate and Brad Davis as his lover Peter Doyle. Thus a poet whose masculine pronouns were often changed to feminine ones by people who tried to suppress the evidence of his homosexuality was presented as a gay man on national television. Two stunning television dramas, *The Naked Civil Servant* and *The War Widow,* were positive evocations of the lives of gay characters, real and fictional. Both shows infused their central characters with a sense of history and of their role in that history as strugglers for sexual freedom. Both shows uncovered with romance and humor a hidden part of the gay experience.

Although Quentin Crisp's story, *The Naked Civil Servant* (1977), was not the dream of a gay liberationist, gays admired and respected Crisp's defiant lifestyle enormously. Crisp makes public hay of the fact that he is not a gay militant, but he may in fact have been one of the first gay activists in his own passive way. A man who dyed his hair, wore eye makeup and painted his lips and nails, a man who refused to deny his homosexuality, Crisp was a revolutionary soon after the turn of the century. In revealing his life and

John Hurt (left) as Quentin Crisp finds others who are like him in The Naked Civil Servant *(1977).*

opinions in print and on film, he is himself an implicit challenge to the myth; the stereotype speaks. *The Naked Civil Servant* said that flamboyant, overt homosexuality was heroic and the struggle to remain different in a conformist world was admirable.

Harvey Perr's *The War Widow,* shown on PBS television in 1976, was the story of a woman who falls in love with another woman while her husband

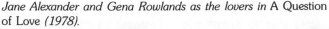

Jane Alexander and Gena Rowlands as the lovers in A Question of Love *(1978).*

is fighting in World War I. Her decision to leave her husband and her young daughter, to choose a lifestyle that was violently condemned at that time, was shown to be cataclysmic. Thus her courage is striking yet understandable. "To leave all that I know," she tells her lover, "for what I cannot even name when I am alone and there is no one else to hear. . . ." This defined the plight of countless women discovering their true sexuality and having the courage to face the unknown. The ending of *The War Widow* encapsules those women who left small towns all over the world for the anonymity and safety of larger cities where they could be with their own kind and begin to be the people they truly were. The necessity to leave behind family, tradition and comfort, to accept ostracism and disgrace, was devastatingly portrayed. But these were stories of survival, and the message was that gays were survivors.

Yet not one gay hero emerged on the movie screen. In the 1970s, heroes who were gay in original source material were made heterosexual for the screen—just as their counterparts had been altered in the 1940s and 1950s. Gay fiction is now big business, but not one lesbian or gay literary hero has been successfully transferred to the screen. Film projects based on the life of gay tennis pro Bill Tilden and on James Kirkwood's novel *Good Times/Bad Times,* announced repeatedly in the trade press, have not materialized. According to Andrew Sarris, the Tilden project was dropped because of "nervousness about its unsavory nature." The producer Ray Agayhan tried for three years to get a film version of Laura Z. Hobson's *Consenting Adult* off the ground in Hollywood. The story of a mother who must come to terms with her son's homosexuality, "it was turned down by all the major studios with enormous promptness," according to the author. Hobson could sell Hollywood Jews in 1947 with her *Gentleman's Agreement,* but she could not sell Hollywood gays in 1979. "They're scared to death of this one," she said.

Deletions have been common. The lover relationship between the characters played by Roy Scheider and William Devane in William Goldman's *Marathon Man* was simply not retained in John Schlesinger's 1976 screen version. *An Unmarried Woman* (1978) lost the references that established the lesbianism of the Jill Clayburgh character's fictional therapist. When Casablanca Filmworks tested its disco film *Thank God It's Friday* (1978) in the Midwest, producer Kenny Friedman studied the reactions of audiences to the inclusion of one gay male couple on the dance floor amidst a sea of heterosexual couples. He found that "the gays got it, and the straights never saw a thing." Which is exactly what he wanted; he found that general audiences are unwilling to see gays, and he made it easy for them. Had there been negative reaction to the scene, it would have been dropped.

Roy Scheider and William Devane in John Schlesinger's Marathon
Man *(1976). Their love relationship, present in William Goldman's
novel, was obscured in the film version.*

Herbert Ross, who has made some of the most homophobic films to come
out of Hollywood, excised from *The Turning Point* (1977) a subplot involving
a long-term gay relationship between the artistic director of the dance company
(James Mitchell) and the ballet master. The screenwriter Arthur Laurents describes the situations.

It wasn't even a question of saying anything. It was my feeling that it was dishonest
and lacking in texture to do a film about the ballet world and not have homosexuals.
I mean, it's a known fact, and it couldn't be safer. And all I did, really, was that you
saw the two of them together and they were very nice with each other. And I felt
that was enough. You wouldn't have to say anything else. But the director Herb Ross
absolutely avoided all of this, wouldn't have them touch or anything.
    Also, there was a scene that was shot and never used that was crucial to the gay
couple and crucial to Shirley MacLaine and her husband. It was at the party in the
beginning of the film. There were four men sitting around very late. There was MacLaine's
husband Wayne, Michael and his lover and a dancer named Freddie (Scott Douglas)
who was drunk and bitching about his wife. He was saying how she was after him to
dance on television and make more money and so forth. Suddenly he says, "I don't
know why I got married," and he turns to Wayne and asks, "Why did you get married?"
and there's just silence.
    Wayne turns to Michael for help, and Michael says to Freddie, "Well, why *did* you
get married?" and Freddie says to the two lovers, "Oh, I don't know. Why did you
two get married?" It set up the two lovers, and it also said something very strange
about this one guy who wouldn't say why he got married. It was relaxed intimacy
and very good, but it was all cut. Everything became aggressively macho because of
Baryshnikov.

Aggressively macho was a good phrase for the late Seventies. Instead of relaxed intimacy we got characters like Warren Beatty in *Shampoo* (1975), a heterosexual hairdresser who allows the husbands of his customers to think him queer so that he can seduce their wives. When Jack Warden asks his wife Lee Grant whether Beatty is a fairy, she asks why he wants to know. "Because I'm thinking of doing business with him, and I'm thinking he's too flighty, irresponsible. That's why I asked if he was a fairy." Grant does not deny it. The same old jargon about homosexuals being unstable had been used fifteen years earlier in *That Touch of Mink,* and in 1975 Hal Ashby's film was not much hipper, though it was dirtier, for it used women in as smarmy a way as it used fags. The role that won Lee Grant an Oscar was that of a mother who arrives home to discover that her daughter has just had sex with Beatty; she is so turned on that she insists on sex with him immediately. Beatty, of course, "acts like a fairy" only in the presence of a husband, when he is trying to get off the hook. And whenever Warden touches Beatty, he recoils when he remembers he is touching a fairy. Warden's reaction could have been a comment on the uptightness of heterosexual men when they are around gays; instead it reinforces such reactions.

More insightful—though depressing as hell—was Paul Mazursky's *Next Stop, Greenwich Village* (1976), in which Antonio Fargas is brilliant as Bernstein, a black homosexual of 1950s Greenwich Village. Here is a good example of a stereotype treated in an interesting and inoffensive manner. Fargas' Bernstein, who by his own description has been "brutalized physically and mentally," hides behind a phony name and a phony attitude. Mazursky is so good at evoking the period that we understand in some measure how gays like Bernstein coped with their self-hatred in the 1950s and survived because they found a tolerant pocket of civilization to inhabit. Bernstein has no gay friends in the film; he is accepted by sympathetic straights who in their own minds are just as weird as he is. The only gays he seems to know are the tricks (usually straight "trade") he picks up offscreen.

Fargas played another memorable gay character in *Car Wash* (1976), and this time his character, again a stereotype, shows an uncharacteristic militancy that is both funny and challenging. He also has the audience cheering for his outrageous Lindy, a transvestite with a great mouth on his shoulders. When the black militant Abdullah suggests to him that he is just another example of how the white man has corrupted the black man and robbed him of his masculinity, Fargas enunciates with expert timing, "Honey, I'm more man than you'll ever *be* and more woman than you'll ever *get.*"

Such scenes are gratifying, and they would be revolutionary if they were

"I met him on the subway this afternoon, and I think I'm in love."
Antonio Fargas (right) as Bernstein sits next to a Swedish sailor
in Julius' bar in a scene from Next Stop, Greenwich Village *(1976).*

used in anything other than a comic context. But Lindy is only a cartoon, like Snowflake the black transvestite in *Coonskin;* their effect in the end was just that of the safe sissy who ruled the day in the topsy-turvy situations of Thirties comedies. Serious films dealing with the real world presented not Lindy but the battered Bernstein. *The Turning Point* would not even admit

Antonio Fargas as Lindy, "more man
than you'll ever be and more woman
than you'll ever get," in Car Wash
(1976).

to homosexuality in the ballet world, only to its possibility, which is something to be disproved through marriage to a woman. Arthur Laurents relates some of the contentions during rehearsals.

Shirley MacLaine and Herb Ross were even fighting what little gay mention there was in the script. Shirley said, "Oh, I don't know why it has to come up at all," and Herb Ross said that he didn't think Wayne was gay at all but was just very handsome and was always being approached by choreographers with the promise of a part, and I said, "That's total bullshit, and you know it." In the case of *The Turning Point*, two fears were operating. One was personal, which you find a great deal in Hollywood among actors who—let's be charitable and say they are ambivalent—and the second is that Hollywood is behind the times in this area.

Yet emotion once condemned in men as feminine is now possible in a heterosexual hero. In order for a hero to exhibit such emotion, however, his sexuality must never be ambivalent. Only Al Pacino's performance as the gay bank robber in *Dog Day Afternoon* gave evidence that a sexually ambiguous character could also be a likeable hero. Jon Voight's paraplegic Vietnam veteran in *Coming Home*, Kris Kristofferson's gentle yet manly rancher in *Alice Doesn't Live Here Anymore*, John Travolta's disco dancer in *Saturday Night Fever* and Jeff Bridges as Sally Fields' understanding husband in *Norma Rae* are all unimpeachably heterosexual, yet they represent breakthrough ideas for men in general.

In *Saturday Night Fever* (1977), Travolta is the only one of a gang of teenagers who thinks it stupid to taunt a faggot on the street. (Such taunting has become epidemic over the years as gays have become more readily identifiable.) Travolta's bedroom wall sports a poster of Al Pacino as the gay bank robber in *Dog Day Afternoon,* and Travolta imitates his hero when he yells, "Attica, Attica!"—a line from *Dog Day* that linked the oppression of blacks and gays. It is interesting that when one of the young women in *Saturday Night Fever* expresses her devotion to David Bowie, her boyfriend draws the line.

"That faggot!" he says.

"He's *not* a faggot!" she screams back. "He's bisexual."

"Yeah, so he's half faggot." In this case, sexual prejudice follows ethnic prejudice; the boyfriend might have been talking about someone who was half Jewish or half black or half Chicano and saying that the "white" half was good and the other half objectionable.

From *Cabaret* to *Hair,* bisexuality has been used to disguise or legitimize homosexuality. The emphasis is usually placed on the heterosexual, as though the homosexual were the "quirk" that Isherwood talked about and "real" sexuality was something that neurotics took excursions from occasionally. In *Hair,* a musical number such as "White Boys" can serve as a delightful burlesque in a gay vein, but when an army psychiatrist asks Woof if he is homosexual, Woof says, "I wouldn't throw Mick Jagger out of bed, but no, I'm not homosexual." Like Mick Jagger, bisexuality is freaky. In *Dog Day Afternoon,* when Sonny's straight accomplice Sal complains that the television news reports are calling him a homosexual, Sonny says, "Ahh, Sal, what do you care? It's only a freak show to them." And that was all the movie was to middle America, a freaky, only-in-New York story that made a fair two-hour yarn but failed to touch their lives.

A good measure of what society will allow can be found in Paul Aaron's *A Different Story* (1978), a film that tells the tale of a lesbian (Meg Foster) and a gay man (Perry King) who unexpectedly and quite naturally fall in love with each other. It may be significant here that neither of them is found to have a particularly healthy or stable gay relationship to begin with. He is the kept boy of a famous music conductor, and she is having a relationship with a neurotic, jealous and firmly closeted schoolteacher (Valerie Curtin). King's life is presented as one in which gays are the kind of people described by Rosa von Praunheim in *It Is Not the Homosexual,* that is, wasteful and boring. Foster's life is ruled by her lover's constant fear that they will be "found out" and she will lose her teaching job. (Curtin is in analysis and bursts into tears in public at the drop of a hat.) King's only other social life seems to be with the men he picks up at the baths. So when the two fall in love, we are happy because they are the most attractive and functional people in the film and the heterosexual lifestyle seems at first to be the answer to all their problems. It even solves King's problem with the immigration authorities because, being Danish, his marrying an American would allow him to stay in the country, and his evil and exploitative ex-lover is about to blow the whistle on him.

As written, directed and played, the film really is about two people who fall in love. Nevertheless, gay activists were correct to protest the film because for most American audiences it reinforced the notion that gays can "go straight," and further, that it is better to do so. When Albert cheats on Stella, we are led to think that another man is with him in the shower. When we discover that it is a woman, we are reassured because he has not in fact returned to his bad habits. In a certain sense, the film says that people are basically heterosexual and that their homosexuality is expendable.

Could Paul Aaron have directed a really different story? Perhaps a film about two heterosexual husbands who suddenly and quite naturally fall in love with each other? "Could I have done that movie today?" Aaron asks.

Meg Foster and Perry King as the lesbian and gay man who fall in love in Paul Aaron's A Different Story *(1978).*

"No, not yet. But it'll happen soon. It has to." That is the current verdict. The people responsible for *Midnight Express* said that their hero could not be gay yet either. Not yet; but it will happen. Like director Alan Parker of *Midnight Express,* Aaron says, "I just knew that I wanted this movie to be as much of an acceptable movie as possible in the sense of wide distribution. I didn't want to make *Outrageous!*"

Richard Benner, an openly gay director, made *Outrageous!* (1977), and in many ways it was the different story that proved that a good gay film could be made cheaply and achieve commercial success. In fact its success easily eclipses that of the Aaron film while saying much more revolutionary things. Robin Turner (Craig Russell) is a slightly overweight Toronto hairdresser for whom "there are three things in life, sex, movies and my career." The career is Robin's dream of dazzling the world as a female impersonator. Robin's best friend Liza Connors (Hollis McLaren) is a certified schizophrenic who has run away from a mental hospital to try to live in the real world, to prove that the dead voices she hears inside herself are wrong when they tell her that she is dead too. Robin understands Liza; he too has voices inside him, and he knows there is no place in the real world for a hairdresser who wants to be Tallulah Bankhead.

Robin appears at a local bar as Bette Davis and is a smash. But because he is spotted by a customer of the beauty salon, he is fired from his job. "These women don't want to think they're being touched by a fag," his gay boss says. "It's one thing to be gay, but doing drag . . ." Robin and his friends have heard this before. "He wants to liberate the denim faggots and lock up the satin queens," says Robin's friend Perry. Robin decides that they cannot lock up his characters the way they locked up Liza, and he packs his feathers and heads for New York City.

Outrageous! presented Craig Russell in a more believable *A Star Is Born* than Barbra Streisand's version; at the same time it raised issues that were vital to gay liberation. The unspoken battle in gay life is the one between the denim faggots and the satin queens, the same battle that has characterized the nature of homophobia through the years, the fear of men appearing feminine. Many gay people have believed that stories about drag queens and schizophrenics can do nothing for the gay "image." Likewise, some gay extras working on the movie *Cruising* railed against "fluff" in an article in *Mandate* magazine in 1979. Their roles as macho men in the film, they said, would prove that they were just as masculine as any straight man. (There is a lot of desperation to appear masculine in that attitude.) Nonetheless most gays, like most straights, have opted for an acceptable image and will continue to do so. In *Outrageous!* after the hasty departure of a young hustler from Robin's bed, he asks Liza, "Do you know what it's like to see a really good-looking guy and *know* that all he sees is drag queen?" Some people look at *Outrageous!* and all they see is drag queen. Others see Robin and Liza, two people who, like Sister George, refuse to pay for their being different by dying.

With the help of the Canadian Film Development Corporation, Richard Benner made *Outrageous!* for only $160,000. It was his first feature film, it became a big hit and Benner was hired to direct *Happy Birthday Gemini* (1979), the film version of Albert Innaurato's long-running Broadway comedy *Gemini,* starring Rita Moreno, Madeline Kahn and David Marshall Grant. The play has a funny and touching gay subplot, and the film adds a scene in which father and son (Robert Biharo and Allen Rosenberg) confront the son's homosexuality. In the film, the father makes it clear that if his son is gay, it is okay with him as long as he is happy and not miserable like a lot of heterosexuals are. What was an ambiguous relationship between the son and his girlfriend in the stage production is also cleared up in the film when the two decide that they will remain just friends—an improvement over what Benner termed the cop-out of the Broadway show. "If it's real and honest," Benner says, "people will go to it. People who underestimate the intelligence of the audience

are always in trouble, and I think William Friedkin's *Cruising* proves it."
  Benner is determined not to give America the same old heterosexualized vision of gay people.

I won't fit reality to a political end. I am so *bored* with normal-looking people, whether they're gay or not. And besides being boring, it's a big lie to tell all those people out there that what we want is the same lifestyle as theirs, the same suburb, the same house; to adopt children and live like *them*. It's just a big lie. It's the way we dress ourselves up to make ourselves more comfortable with our straight friends.

  Eventually Hollywood must swallow the differences if gays are to be made safe for screen treatment. In order to be integrated into the American dream, gays will have to become as American as apple pie. When this happens, there will be films that do not portray lesbians or gay men as outsiders because they will be inside. Meanwhile, the transition is difficult and interesting to watch. Homosexuality, after all, remains a libelous charge that requires a strong defense. Remember, Miriam Hopkins said in *The Children's Hour,* "Friendship between women, yes. But not this insane devotion. Why, it's unnatural. Just as unnatural as can be." It is the same attitude that prompts Jane Fonda, in *Julia,* to punch out the guy who suggests that her relationship with Vanessa Redgrave is a sexual one.

  All cinematic statements that view gay people as politically oppressed people are being made by openly gay filmmakers in independent productions. In all probability, Hollywood will "Americanize" homosexuality and the gay lifestyle in its films just as it has incorporated everything else into American life onscreen. Samuel Goldwyn's solution to the filming of *Well of Loneliness,* to make the lesbian an American, was a prophetic one. And it will mean the loss of a certain uniqueness. Just as Diahann Carroll played a very white black lady in the television series *Julia,* gays will appear first as background, then—scrubbed up—as tokens and finally as acceptable versions of what the world has always wanted to believe. It will not necessarily be the truth, but it will be an acceptable lie, and the cash registers will ring.

  The tried and true homophobic formulas seem to have run their course, largely because of the increasingly violent protests that gays have brought to Hollywood's door. In the last years of the 1970s, all the old clichés came to a head with several productions that either defamed or ignored gays in traditional ways. *Can't Stop the Music* (1980), directed by Nancy Walker, is a big-budget disco film about the meteoric rise of a popular music group, the Village People. Producer Alan Carr demanded swift retractions from the Hollywood press in 1979 when it was reported that *Can't Stop the Music* was a "gay themed" film. Even though the Village People, regardless of their individual sexual orientation, are clearly a group with a gay attitude and an outlook shaped by a gay subculture, the filmmakers took great pains to erase any implication of gayness in their film. *Can't Stop the Music* chronicles the rise of the disco group against the backdrop of a love affair between Bruce Jenner and Valerie Perrine. Like *Thank God It's Friday,* the film concentrates on the real people—the heterosexuals—and relegates any gay presence to the periphery, for fleeting use as color. This is the safe, commercial position; it will be breached only by filmmakers with courage and vision.

The *Front Runner* is a good example of the potential breakthrough film that so far no one has had the guts to make—the most celebrated failure to produce a film from gay fiction. Patricia Nell Warren's best seller is about a young, handsome Olympics runner and his love affair with his coach. The novel was originally optioned for the screen by Paul Newman, who intended to play the coach and perhaps direct the film. For almost five years he could not elicit an acceptable screenplay. "I'm not ready for a cop-out," he told *Blueboy* magazine in 1977. "I won't tolerate this project being turned into a watered-down love story or substituting a female for the runner, as has been suggested by people who should know better." Finally Newman dropped his option, and in 1979 several producers announced their intentions to film *The Front Runner* from a screenplay by Jeremy Larner. In Warren's novel, the young runner Billy Sieve is shot to death just before reaching the finish line at the Olympics; in the Larner script, he wins the race but not the coach. "Gay people don't need any more screen martyrs," producer Howard Rosenman said. "We're cutting the assassination and making it a love story." In the script, the coach decides that he and Billy are in an impossible situation, and they agree to part after the Olympics for reasons that are not entirely clear.

The resistance to any legitimization of gay relationships onscreen is clearly the culprit. Stories that place gays in the mainstream of American life challenge heterosexual hegemony and dispel the myth that gays are people who live only at the fringes of society. According to John Watson of the Los Angeles *Times,* the reason such films have a tough time getting produced is that "closeted gays within the industry obstruct positive gay projects."

This observation is borne out by the experience of producers Arnie Reisman and Ira Yerkes, who spent four years trying to sell a screenplay of Rita Mae Brown's best-selling *Rubyfruit Jungle* to every major studio and independent in the country. Studio representatives all agreed that it was an important and exciting film, but nobody would touch it. Brown's protagonist, Molly Bolt, is a winning and attractive lesbian Huck Finn, a southern white kid who grows up in the backwoods knowing that somehow she is different. Defiantly, but with great warmth, she challenges the world to love her. The reader of the novel cannot help but love her; she is a hero. A Columbia Pictures executive told Reisman that they might consider doing it if the story were made tragic. A gay studio head sent word that if he were out of the closet, he would do it. A representative from Twentieth Century-Fox said she thought it was a very important film that needed to be made, but "not by us." Yerkes says, "I was told three times in one week in Hollywood, 'I *hope* somebody has the guts to make this picture. But find somebody with balls, not me.'"

Meanwhile, Gordon Willis had the balls to make *Windows* and William Friedkin had the nerve to film *Cruising.* And each had the money and the backing of a major studio. *Windows* (1980) is the story of a psychotic lesbian killer (Elizabeth Ashley) who is in love with a straight woman (Talia Shire). Ashley hires a goon taxicab driver to assault Shire in hopes of turning her off men and perhaps driving her into Ashley's arms. Shire plays a recently divorced woman who seems unable to live without a man and who does such stupid and careless things as going out alone at night. She ends up in the arms of the detective who saves her from Ashley in the nick of time. *New York* magazine film critic David Denby pointed out that *"Windows* exists only in the perverted fantasies of men who hate lesbians so much they will concoct any idiocy in order to slander them."

William Friedkin's *Cruising* (1980) was based on a 1970 novel by a *New York Times* editor, Gerald Walker, that portrayed the process by which a New York City policeman, assigned to capture a psychotic killer of gay men, becomes aware of his own homosexuality and commences murdering gays. The novel, while exploiting the socially instilled self-hatred of an unstable character, is homophobic in spirit and in fact; it sees all its gay characters as having been "recruited," condemned to the sad gay life like modern vampires who must create new victims in order to survive. The gay characters in the novel are all filled with self-hatred and a hatred for the people who "turned" them gay (the blame usually falls on the first man with whom they had sex). Walker's killer intimates that the homosexual lifestyle is an inherently violent one—not that the cruising scene is violent, but that to be homosexual is to be violent.

In 1969 William Friedkin said, *"The Boys in the Band* is not about homosexuality," and in 1979 he said the same thing about *Cruising.* Yet he used the Greenwich Village ghetto and scores of gay extras—as did *Can't Stop the Music*—to make a film about a series of grisly murders patterned not on Walker's book but on the killings of gay men that had been reported widely in the press in the late 1970s. Friedkin's screenplay incorporated the locales and the modus operandi of several real-life Greenwich Village murders, and Friedkin consulted in prison with Paul Bateson, who was convicted of killing *Variety* critic Addison Verrill and had once had a bit part as a medic in Friedkin's film *The Exorcist.*

Al Pacino dances at an all-night sex club in his search for a killer of homosexual men in Cruising *(1980).*

The killer in Friedkin's *Cruising* knifes his victims to death during or immediately following sex, and the film opens with a shot of a gangrenous severed arm floating in the Hudson River. The late-night sex scene in the after-hours clubs becomes, in *Cruising,* the only game in town for gays. Al Pacino, who plays the cop, immerses himself in the sex-obsessed underground of heavy leather and sadomasochism. As the film wears on, he becomes agitated and restless, a state brought about by his own sexual identity crisis, though his motives are never explored or explained. When he finally locates the killer, he stabs him, which puts the killer in the hospital under police custody. Pacino's assignment is over. However, there follows the murder of Pacino's gay next-door neighbor (Don Scardino), who was the only relatively happy gay in the film. It is implied that Pacino himself has committed this final murder, and the film ends with him gazing in a mirror.

In a statement to the press, the director-screenwriter Friedkin said that he was not sure who the real murderer was and that, furthermore, he did not consider the murderer to be homosexual. A more likely conclusion is that Friedkin deliberately obscured the identity of Scardino's killer in conscious or unconscious response to the wave of protest that arose in the summer of 1979, when he began shooting. Gays who protested the making of the film maintained that it would show that when Pacino recognized his attraction to the homosexual world, he would become psychotic and begin to kill. So Friedkin avoided that situation by leaving the ending of the film ambiguous.

Yet Friedkin realized that his film said what gay activists claimed it said, and he added a disclaimer to all prints of the film.

This film is not intended as an indictment of the homosexual world. It is set in one small segment of that world, which is not meant to be representative of the whole.

The disclaimer is an admission of guilt. What director would make such a statement if he truly believed that his film would not be taken to be representative of the whole? Protest leaflets against *Cruising* said, "People will die because of this film." In November 1980, outside the Ramrod Bar, the site of the filming of *Cruising,* a minister's son emerged from a car with an Israeli submachine gun and killed two gay men.

There were no disclaimers on Paul Schrader's *American Gigolo* (1980), or on any of the other homophobic films that emerged at the beginning of the 1980s. *American Gigolo* was about a male prostitute (Richard Gere) who "didn't do fags." The only gay characters in the film were a lesbian pimp, a black pimp, a murderer and a closet case who hates women and has his wife beaten while he watches. Jacques Scandalari's *New York After Midnight,* still editing at the end of 1980 and with uncertain prospects, was another film shot in the gay ghetto. A straight woman discovers that her husband is gay; the discovery triggers psychotic tendencies, and she murders eight gay men in Greenwich Village. Producers, directors, writers and actors continued to state in the press that they could see no trend toward anti-gay attitudes in motion pictures—and, moreover, that they had not considered such attitudes offensive in the past.

Before the making of *Cruising* in 1979, protests against films that were perceived to be dangerous to gays had always taken place after the opening of the film. Just as blacks had rioted in Harlem in 1915 to protest D. W. Griffith's racist *Birth of a Nation,* gays had gone to movie houses across the country to picket such films as *The Boys in the Band, Some of My Best*

Friends Are . . . and *The Gay Deceivers.* In Germany in 1973, the Homosexual Law Reform Group led a violent protest against Ulli Lommel's *Tenderness of the Wolves.* Lommel's film, produced by Rainer Werner Fassbinder, told the true story of Fritz Haarman, whose life had inspired several films, among them Fritz Lang's classic *M* with Peter Lorre. Haarman was gay, not straight, and Lommel's film exploits the grisly child molester and killer as a human vampire who picked up boys, molested them sexually and drained their blood. He then used their bones in soup and sold their flesh to a local butcher shop for sausage meat. The response of Fassbinder and Lommel to the protest resembled Friedkin's response to protests in New York in 1979. "But this is the truth," they said. Fassbinder told London critic Jack Babuscio, "What I am after is an *open* realism, one which allows for an emotional identification with characters which society has taught us to despise."

In essence Friedkin agreed, saying of *Cruising,* "I'm trying to present a portrait of a group of people who get their sexual kicks in ways that society doesn't approve, but I'm making no personal judgment of these people." Gay activists responded that the judgment was being made nonetheless by a misinformed and already prejudiced society and by a Hollywood that seldom portrayed any other aspect of gay life and thus created a climate for backlash and repression. *Cruising* was the last straw in a long stream of Hollywood horrors. Coming as it did in company with *Windows* and *American Gigolo,* it acted as catalyst for a massive nationwide protest of the Hollywood treatment of gays. The

A seduction scene from Ulli Lommel's Tenderness of the Wolves *(1973).*

protest was disorganized and violent yet energetic and effective, and it drew media attention not to the mediocre films lambasted by most critics but to the issue of violence against lesbians and gay men in America. "We are not asking for censorship," said Ronald Gold, a former *Variety* reporter ar i media consultant for the National Gay Task Force. "We are asking Holl wood to use the same system of self-censorship they apply to other minorities. Nobody would dare to do a film about a group of organized black men whose objective is to rape white women. We always find ourselves in the position of having to play civil libertarian to a bunch of bigots who want their constitutional right to express their hatred of us."

The issue was not one of censorship but that of a minority group's taking the lead in securing the right to defend itself against what has become a national pastime—attacks on gays by gangs of marauding teenagers in every major city in the United States with a gay ghetto. Just as rape was once joked about by men and even women, "queer bashing" has a patina of legitimacy as a result of its being silently sanctioned by courts, police and parents who consider that their children are simply a little wild. The victims seldom come forward for fear of disclosing their homosexuality, and the game goes on. The protests against *Cruising* were a fight for the recognition of the problem—in a real sense, a fight for survival.

The bottom line is the nature of the film industry itself. The overwhelming majority of filmmakers are looking for a hit. Some who work in commercial film grow as people, and it is possible to discern in them a thinking, flexible mind at work. In mainstream cinema, there will always be saving graces. Woody Allen's *Manhattan* (1979), for example, is not a case of Is it good for the lesbians or bad for the lesbians? Woody Allen has consistently taken a stab at a gay joke or theme. Sometimes, as in *Sleeper,* it is offensive. But sometimes it is charming, as in *Love and Death* (1975), in which he muses aloud, "I wonder if Socrates and Plato took a house on Crete during the summer?" You can like or dislike the lesbian characters in *Manhattan,* and you can even argue that Allen is neurotic in his reaction to them, but it is an argument you would win quickly. Allen is neurotic for a living, and *Manhattan* is a great film.

On the other hand, there are those who will always see homosexuality only as a crude joke. Carl Reiner made fun of rape in *Where's Poppa?* (1970) by having a man rape a cop in drag for laughs. The next day the cop sends him a dozen roses. Reiner's film *The One and Only* (1978), which starred Henry Winkler as Gorgeous George, was just as viciously homophobic and was based on the same familiar anti-woman and anti-gay stereotypes.

More and more, films seem to echo the generalizations and myths of yesterday. Blake Edwards' *"10"* (1979) uses homosexuality and promiscuity as the stuff of adolescence, habits to be discarded when one is ready to face adulthood and maturity. Dudley Moore's gay friend and collaborator Robert Webber, who tries to hang on to his youth through his lover, a young beachboy, ends in tatters as the film closes, unhappy and alone, while Moore returns to his stable marriage and lives happily ever after. The same sentiment—that homosexuality is a bid to stay forever young—is present in Franco Brusati's *To Forget Venice* (*Dimenticare Venezia*, 1979), in which two gay couples reach maturity and leave their childhood home to face the adult world. But in Brusati's film there is an honesty and a respect in dealing with the gay characters and their sexuality that is missing entirely from *"10"*. The Edwards film, like Gilbert Cates' *The Last Married Couple in America* (1980), features homosexuality only to make a point about heterosexuality, the latter being considered the norm. With a bid for a return to the good old values of the American family, it may be that the true Americanization of homosexuality depends on the assimilation of it into the mainstream. Nancy Walker's *Can't Stop the Music* treats the Village People, a disco group that has built its reputation on gay fantasies and stereotypical drag, as an in-joke—which most of the straight teenagers who loved *Grease* fail to get. "It's a gay movie for straight people," Arthur Bell wrote. "No. I amend that. It's a stupid gay movie for stupid straight people."

One of the few tender moments between lesbian characters in American movies. Alexis Smith and Melina Mercouri in Jacqueline Susann's Once Is Not Enough *(1975).* (William S. Kenly, Paramount Pictures)

It is a crazy business. Guy Green's film *Jacqueline Susann's Once Is Not Enough* (1975) featured Alexis Smith and Melina Mercouri in one of the most positively approached lesbian love scenes ever, and theirs was certainly the healthiest relationship in the film. Bette Midler's lesbian scene in *The Rose* (1978) was a disaster. With the best of intentions, she told *People* magazine, she really threw herself into the scene so as not to make it seem tentative or forced. When her manager saw the rushes, there were cries of "I told you! No tongue kissing!"—and the scene was completely reshot. Frederick Forrest, whose character, as critic Stuart Byron has pointed out, is the moral bellwether of the film, takes it in stride when Midler sleeps with other men but goes nuts when he catches her with a woman.

The same sort of moral outrage is pandered to in the ads of Herbert Ross' *Nijinsky* (1980), which chronicles the life of the legendary ballet dancer (George De La Pena) and his relathionship with the impresario Sergei Diaghilev (Alan Bates). The first ten minutes of the film, according to the advertising, were "the most shocking ten minutres in film history." The sequence turned out to be De La Pena kissing Bates through a silk handkerchief—an echo perhaps of another shocking kiss, in *Sunday, Bloody Sunday* almost a decade earlier. Hollywood's next big gay project in the 1980s was to be the film version of Lucian Truscott IV's *Dress Gray,* in which the pivotal plot element is the murder of a gay West Point cadet. Herbert Ross was signed, then taken off the picture; another director with a big hit at Paramount was offered it and turned it down because "in light of *Cruising,* its time was past." Eventually *Dress Gray* was produced as a television mini-series in which the homosexuality of the murdered cadet became the shocking revelation at the end of the last reel.

Yet the most insightful and important films—gay films, not simply films about gays—are those which have been made in struggle, by small groups of people and against tremendous odds. Ron Peck and Paul Hallam, the director and producer of the British film *Nighthawks* (1978), spent five years in planning and raising money for their film about a gay teacher (Ken Robertson) who spends his nights cruising in bars and discos and having one-night stands. *Nighthawks* provides an almost documentary look at the nighttime scene and the ritualistic life of one man who is beginning to realize that he leads two separate lives. In the climax of the film, the students in his geography class ask him if he is "queer," and he tells them he is gay. The dispassionate view of London gay nightlife allows a gay male audience to experience the hunt as more than a passive spectator. There is an uncanny feeling that each member of the audience is himself cruising, recognizing a look, a gesture, a glance, then realizing it is meant for the character in the film, through whose *eyes* we are looking. No slick and sensational Hollywood peep show, *Nighthawks* is a good, perceptive film with modest intentions, and it succeeds without compromising its scope for commercial reasons.

While William Friedkin was on New York's streets filming the blood-and-guts Holywood version of the gay underground, *Nighthawks* opened in New York and got what turned out to be better reviews than *Cruising* would get six months later. Several mainstream critics, including Janet Maslin in the *New York Times* and David Denby in *New York* magazine, singled out *Nighthawks* as a film that managed to examine gay nightlife with sensitivity, intelligence and a respect for its main character. In his program note on the film, director Ron Peck wrote, "The film only shows one part of the gay scene . . . it does not cover everything as many people may wish it did. But such a hope or expectation is only a reflection of the dire situation in which there are so few films with or about gay characters. Almost any film starts off with the burden of trying to redress an imbalance, to make homosexuality visible in the cinema. We need hundreds of gay films, not half a dozen."

When in 1975 Peter Adair first conceived a documentary film to be called *Who Are We?* he intended to redress an imbalance by throwing light on a largely ignored part of gay America. *Who Are We?* eventually became *Word Is Out,* an assemblage of conversations with twenty-six lesbians and gay men, subtitled *Stories of Some of Our Lives,* a landmark film. *Word Is Out* made a beginning at answering the question, Who are these different people and what are they doing here? Using more than two hundred videotaped interviews with gay people from all over the United States, Peter Adair, Lucy Massie Phoenix, Rob Epstein, Veronica Selver, Nancy Adair and Andrew Brown turned Adair's original question into an electric piece of history. At each step in the development of the film, the interviews were screened for groups of gay people in various cities, and their comments and suggestions were incorporated into the shaping of the film. In a real sense, the gay community made *Word Is Out.*

The film reveals a sense of longing, a nostalgia for a lost time, in the conversations with those gays who broke their silence to talk about gay life in America. The diversity of the people in the film is stunning. Whitey tells how her psychiatrist put her on a diet of three green salads a day to cure her lesbianism and how, at age eighteen, she was sent to a state hospital where she spent eight years simply because she was a lesbian and her parents did not know what to do about it. Pat Bond, a former WAC, reminisces about the recruiting office in Davenport, Iowa, where she first signed up. "I remember I went down to the Blackhawk Hotel where the recruiting sergeant was. She sort of looked like all my old gym teachers in drag. Stockings, little earrings, her hair slicked back, and *very* daintily done so you couldn't tell she was a *dyke*. But *I* knew. I remember when I came staggering into the mess hall with my suitcase, I heard a voice from the barracks say, 'Good *God*, Elizabeth, here comes another one!' " David sits in a field of daisies in Springfield, Massachusetts, and tells of breaking the news to his father that he was gay. "I asked him if he was ready for a heavy conversation, and he said, 'Let me grab a cigarette.' I told him to grab the whole pack." Roger, a Boston actor, talks about growing up gay in the 1950s. "They fought the Second World War, and then they said, Okay, this is what we fought for—fit into it. And then they got old." Linda sits on a porch in North Carolina and recalls her college days. "I was the American dream daughter . . . cheerleader, prom queen, straight A student, president of the honor society . . . I was miserable. I hated it."

The two-hour journey of *Word Is Out* is filled with instant recognition for gays. The people in the film point up the remarkably common experience of growing up gay in America, a straight world. Elsa Gitlow, a seventy-seven-year-old poet, says, "If there was ever any problem with my being lesbian, it was the loneliness, the fact that I didn't know anyone else like me. Where were the others, if there were any?" George says, "It was 1952 and I took a Greyhound bus to San Francisco with thirty dollars in my pocket. I ran into a policeman and said, Where's a gay bar?" Whitey says, "I had heard about Greenwich Village, and that's where homosexuals were supposed to be. So I got on a train." These stories are the threads of gay history; together they tell how obscure people found each other and finally themselves in their attempts to form a community.

When for the first time two men kissed onscreen, Raf Vallone's accusatory *"That's* what you are!" burned a hole in the consciousness of an invisible gay audience. The movies, gays thought, had spoken their name. For it is not gay actors or gay characters but the *idea* of homosexuality for which gays have searched in films, almost always in vain. But the decision to make visible the gay lifestyle is irrevocable, and eventually the movies will have to reflect the diversity of gay existence.

Invisibility is the great enemy. It has prevented the truth from being heard, and it will continue to do so as long as the celluloid closet is inhabited by lesbians and gay men who serve Hollywood's idea of homosexuality. In 1975, a group of producers and directors, some of them reputedly closet gays, walked out of a screening of Robert Aldrich's *The Choirboys*, reportedly because of its anti-gay language. "Those guys who walked out are some of our most successful directors," Aldrich says, "and if they're walking out but not talking in public about why they walked out, then they're not the ones who are going to make the breakthrough films about homosexuals. No fucking way. They're going to stay in the mainstream and direct action pictures. It's the old joke: I'm on board, pull up the ladder."

There never have been lesbians or gay men in Hollywood films. Only homosexuals.

Taking the Game Away from Hollywood

finding a voice
and facing
a backlash

Gary Oldman as British playwright Joe Orton and Alfred Molina as his lover Kenneth Halliwell in Stephen Frears' Prick Up Your Ears.

There is no such thing as a gay sensibility and it
has an enormous impact on the culture.

—Jeff Weinstein

The Celluloid Closet may not be an altogether valid title for the updated edition of this book, because homosexuality is no longer in the closet either on or off the screen. Indeed, since the first edition of this book was published in 1981, more than a hundred films have dealt with gay issues or featured gay characters. Yet this increased visibility of lesbians and gay men is extremely tenuous and has occurred chiefly in independent films and in the very few mainstream films designed for grown-ups. The rampant homophobia that made this book necessary in the first place is still a key element in most mass audience features.

The first edition of this book concluded, too superciliously for some, that there have never been any lesbians or gay men in the movies—only homosexuals. This exaggeration, a semantic affront to some, was meant to point up that Hollywood films, content with easy laughs and cheap social comment, have perpetuated a lazy, stereotyped idea of homosexuals in the place of realistic characters who happen to be gay. Homosexuals are a compendium of media-created stereotypes. Gays are a diverse group of real people.

Images found on our television and motion picture screens cannot be viewed in isolation from the political climate of the nation that produces them. A vocal minority of right-wing religious fanatics in America, similar in style and viewpoint to the Nazi youth groups found in Germany just before Hitler took power, have been permitted to set the terms of the political debate regarding the existence of gays in society and have used the AIDS health crisis to exploit anti-gay prejudices that already existed. Dangerous political extremists like Lyndon LaRouche, Jerry Falwell and New York's Archbishop John J. O'Connor have fostered the fiction that homosexuality is simply chosen behavior; an act, not an orientation. Such behavior is then termed sinful or illegal, creating a partisan moral issue where none should exist.

Choosing to ignore that people are gay in the same way that people are short or blond or left-handed is a useful political stance that keeps homosexuality controversial, justifying ancient religious superstitions and centering political debate on whether homosexuals have a right to exist at all. In Hollywood films, therefore, homosexuals have not been people; they have been a dramatic device used to shock and sell.

A group of people cast as immoral by religious leaders and illegal by the Supreme Court become natural targets for ridicule in the popular media. This is why a film like Glenn Jordan's *Mass Appeal* (1984), the only mainstream film to touch upon the debate about homosexuality within the Catholic Church, is so fraudulent. The story of a young priest (Zeljko Ivanek) who admits to his superior (Charles Durning) that he has had homosexual experiences has a responsibility to deal with the issues alive today in a battle that rages between the traditional church and the forces of change. Instead, the film is a facile, cowardly vehicle for Jack Lemmon to twinkle as a lovable old priest who learns a lesson in humility if not tolerance.

Open violence against gay people in America has reached epidemic proportions, fueled by films that encourage young people to believe that such behavior is acceptable. In Paul Schrader's *Hardcore* (1979), George C. Scott beats up a gay man. When he asks a police lieutenant (Peter Boyle) if he will be arrested for it, Boyle replies, "No, they don't care about some faggot hustler." The simple message is that you can beat up a queer and the police won't do anything. Which is perfectly true today. Films that expose bigotry are necessary but in most films that portray anti-homosexual bigotry, the bigots are the heroes.

The relative success of a few independent gay-themed films may seem at odds with the almost hysterical homophobia of the mainstream media. Yet it is partially because of the success of such films and gay visibility in general that we are experiencing such a violent backlash.

In the same week in which *Parting Glances, My Beautiful Laundrette, Desert Hearts* and *Dona Herlinda and Her Son* opened in New York, the news magazine show *20/20* did a segment on the national increase in gay bashing, which has risen in some cities by almost ninety percent. Film critic Stanley Kauffmann, reacting to this, wrote in the *New Republic,* "Suppose that in these days of the smash success of *The Color Purple,* '20/20' had shown a segment about the tarring and feathering of blacks, about black lynchings. One's sense of reality would be at risk. For a moment after the tv segment I almost felt I had to check the calendar."

The AIDS crisis is only a small factor in the rise of such violence. Increased gay visibility has trod on the central nervous system of American life. The inevitable acceptance and integration of gay people into society will change both the dominant and the gay cultures profoundly and we are in the midst of a battle over those changes. In the popular arts, the topic of homosexuality is preserved as the last taboo; any mention of it onscreen is still considered daring. So no matter how vile or offensive the onscreen action may be, producers can congratulate themselves on their courage in choosing to deal with such a controversial topic at all. The casual treatment of lesbians and gay men is still not a legitimate concept for most filmmakers, who are either consciously opposed to it or simply don't think about it at all.

In popular films, anti-gay prejudice may be more prevalent now than at any other time in our history. Never have Hollywood screenwriters felt so secure in their belief that it is acceptable to insult homosexuals, and nowhere has fear and hatred of gay people been more evident than in commercial, mainstream motion pictures, which reflect and encourage the prejudices of their intended audience. The same producers, directors and screenwriters who socialize with gay people and give money to support research for AIDS allow the films they create to foster a climate of panic and fear.

This craven, ignorant behavior is largely a matter of economics. In 1940, Hollywood producers, many of whom were Jewish, refused to make films that attacked either fascism in general or Nazism in particular simply because they feared losing box office revenue from countries like Germany, Austria and Poland. It was not until America was officially at war that studio heads allowed producers to openly portray Nazis onscreen and reflect anti-German senti- ments. By this time, of course, Hitler had already kicked most major American studios out of Germany and banned their films anyway. According to Otto Friedrich in his book *City of Nets,* only Jack Warner had the courage to make anti-Nazi films in the Forties and was attacked by other studio heads for rousing the ire of the German embassy in Washington and jeopardizing the industry's foreign profit margin.

This behavior is directly analogous to the situation we have today in which producers might be privately opposed to homophobia and institutionalized fag bashing but are afraid to hurt their profits by offending the sensibilities of the Christian lobby and conservative elements in the mass audience with films that challenge their prejudices. It's easier to underestimate the general public and bow to religious pressure than to take a stand.

Paramount Pictures recently cancelled production of Martin Scorsese's *The Last Temptation of Christ* because of letters received from right-wing funda- mentalist Christian groups expressing outrage that an artist would be "al- lowed" to make such a film. One of the objections to the project cited by protestors was the completely manufactured assertion that Scorsese intended portraying Jesus Christ as a homosexual. At the same time, the most vicious anti-gay dialogue and situations go unchallenged by these alleged Christians.

Examples are almost too numerous to catalogue. In the few months before this update was completed, virtually every major release took a cheap shot at homosexuals. *The Name of the Rose* (1986) ignored the historical evidence of early Christian tolerance toward homosexuals amassed by scholar John Boswell to give us a monk with "unnatural lusts for boys" who is morally condemned. The violent death of the monk, even though only one of a series of murders in the film, leaves us with nothing but another in a long line of dead faggots.

Dean Stockwell's menacing pimp in David Lynch's *Blue Velvet* (1986) is easily read as gay, especially if you accept that Lynch is showing us the 1950s. Jerzy Skolimowski's *Lightship* (1986) contains a much more explicitly homosexual villain. *Crocodile Dundee* (1986), in which a transvestite is the butt of an extended cruel joke, reaches young people with traditional stereotypes in the pre-teen stage. There is a cartoon gay villain in *The Great Mouse Detective* (1986) and a sissy cat in Steven Spielberg's *An American Tail* (1986), a blatant ripoff of the Cowardly Lion in *The Wizard of Oz*. Most of these films were released within a month of each other.

The use of the word *faggot* has become almost mandatory. Outright slurs that would never be tolerated in reference to any other group of people are commonly used onscreen against homosexuals. Consider a sequence from John Hughes' *Weird Science* (1985) in which a gang of toughs invades the home of two nerdy students. "I want you and your faggot friends out of here in ten seconds," screams one of the kids. Make the characters black and translate that line to "I want you and your nigger friends out of here in ten seconds." Unless such a line was clearly put into the mouth of an unsympathetic bigot, it would never reach the screen. Yet anti-gay dialogue is most often given to the very characters with whom the audience is supposed to identify. This is particularly offensive in a film like Robert Townsend's *Hollywood Shuffle* (1987), a comedy meant to attack negative stereotyping of blacks in Hollywood films. The anti-Semitism and homophobia contained in Townsend's film is all the more offensive because it is so seemingly unconscious. Townsend complains that in order for blacks to make it in Hollywood they are expected to shuffle. Then he creates gay characters who are shuffling, stereotypical hairdressers and wardrobe queens. In a script which points out that Hollywood forces blacks into Uncle Tom roles, every other word is *fag*. In such a context, bigotry is blithely reinforced and legitimized by the very people who should be most sensitive about it.

Homosexuals are powerless by virtue of their unwillingness to be publicly identified. This makes them fair game. Scores of films use fag jokes and gay villains in venomous and gratuitous ways. In George Miller's *The Road Warrior*, (1982), barbarian punk homosexuals on motorcycles symbolically threaten not only the decency of the family but the future of the surviving post-nuclear society as a whole. Symbols for a decadent destruction of moral values become homosexual in nature. Someone made the decision to link the destructive characters with homosexual iconography and nobody challenged it.

In Rod Daniel's *Teen Wolf* (1985), Michael J. Fox confides to his best friend that he has something important to say about himself. "You're not gonna tell me you're a faggot, are you?" asks his friend fearfully. "No," replies Fox, "I'm a werewolf." His friend is greatly relieved. Better a werewolf than a faggot.

In Ron Howard's *Night Shift* (1982) Henry Winkler ends up in prison and mutters to himself, "Well, I guess I can't sink any lower than this." He then notices an effeminate homosexual inmate at the other end of the cell and says, "On second thought I guess I could."

In Howard Storm's *Once Bitten* (1985), in which Cleavon Little plays the (literally) deathless stereotype of a prissy, mincing gay vampire, screenwriters David Hines and Jonathan Roberts felt comfortable with phrases like *homo* and *rump rangers* in addition to a particularly atrocious shower scene in which a dozen students become hysterical and race around yelling, "Fags in the showers!" Undeniably homoerotic, such scenes serve to lull a gay audience into complacency about their own oppression.

Much of this is classic defensiveness on the part of people who are out to give a generation of yahoos the illusion that there aren't any queers either behind or before the cameras. One of the most homophobic popular films of 1985 was written and directed by a gay man with a desperate need to be one of the boys. Anti-homosexuality is still the best cover for a closeted gay. By the fag jokes in all three versions of *Porky's,* both versions of *Meatballs* and similar films popular with young audiences, teenagers are reassured that the guys we're dealing with are regular fellas; all-American boys who may pal around together and grab ass in the showers, but not faggots.

There is a shocking disparity between real-life gays and the popular conception of such people onscreen. The problem used to be that most gays in real life chose to remain hidden and so their diversity remained hidden as well. While the majority of lesbians and gay men are still in the closet, there are nevertheless a sufficient number of openly gay people in America today to provide alternatives to the old stereotypes. Yet purely mythological gays have proliferated on the screen, perpetuating menacing stereotypes that threaten heterosexual society much more than any reality.

A preponderance of fictional homosexual villains and fools has abetted a nervous backlash against something that doesn't even fully exist. Thus, in Jeff

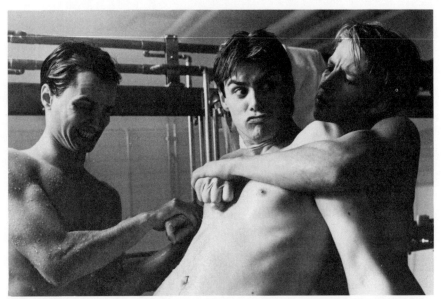

Skip Lackey, Jim Carrey, and Thomas Balatore in the shower scene from Once Bitten *(1985).*

Kanew's *Tough Guys* (1986) Kirk Douglas, representing both the good old days of gangsterdom and the golden age of movies, emerges from prison after thirty-five years and discovers that his favorite local saloon is now a gay bar when a guy approaches and asks him to dance. That the situation is entirely unrealistic and the gay bar like no gay bar in existence on the planet today is proof only that real gay people don't exist in the minds of those who continue to see homosexuality simply as a comic device or a symbol of what threatens us most. The moronic message in *Tough Guys* is that homosexuality didn't exist in the Forties; the world was better then.

As we have seen innumerable times, the world was also better when homosexuals knew their place. *Tough Guys* director Kanew is also responsible for *Revenge of the Nerds* (1984), in which Larry B. Scott plays Lamar, an effeminate black homosexual in dancing tights whose limp wrist actually helps him win a javelin-throwing contest against a bunch of jocks. In fact, *Revenge of the Nerds* presented a rare opportunity for genuine social satire based on a group of teenaged outcasts. Instead, it took four story developers and two screenwriters to come up with the same tired stereotypes we've been seeing since the turn of the century.

Similar throwbacks continue to turn up in dozens of films in which the sexuality of the characters seems tossed in for a quick sight gag. The evidence that Hollywood continues to recreate virtually the same scenes over the years is overwhelming. In John Landis' idiotic *Spies Like Us* (1985), two Russian soldiers going off arm in arm into the woods is a cheap sight gag reminiscent of the old joke in a Thirties comedy in which two guys find themselves arm in arm on a dance floor by accident.

Roddy McDowell's bitchy fag gossip columnist Rex Brewster in Guy Hamilton's *Evil Under the Sun* (1982) and Stuart Pankin's Ronnie, the flaming faggot secretary to Shelley Long in Charles Shyer's *Irreconcilable Differences* (1984), are cardboard nellie acts so ancient they have long beards. The only gays present in Mike Nichols' ultrasophisticated milieu in *Heartburn* (1986) are two caterers at a wedding who amusingly discuss recipes. They're comic servants used in the same way blacks were forty years ago. Similarly, in Sidney Lumet's *The Morning After* (1986), a film that superficially comments on racism and anti-Semitism, gays are reduced to minstrels—faggot pets of an aging actress who provide comic relief from a murder mystery.

In both *Police Academy* and *Police Academy 2*, the Blue Oyster gay bar is a running gag. For realism, each scene shot there features leather guys dancing the tango. The culminating face-off between the gays and the Hell's Angels is right out of John Guillermin's 1968 film *P.J.*, in which dozens of gays are no match for a few real men.

Robert Vincent O'Neil's *Angel* is the story of a teenaged prostitute, which Vincent Canby called "one of the top sleazemobiles of 1984." The prostitute, played by Donna Wilkes, has two friends—Mae, the pathetic old drag queen played by Dick Shawn as though he were Jack Lemmon in *Some Like It Hot*, and Susan Tyrell as your basic alcoholic crazy lesbian landlady. This film feeds the traditional vision of gays as outcasts who inhabit only the nether world of illicit sexuality, a view evoked by Richard Schickel, in 1968, when he wrote in *Life* magazine that Robert Aldrich's *The Killing of Sister George* gave audiences a good sense of "the demi-monde lesbians share with fags [and] prosties."

In the shy, asexual fairy department, Paul McCrane reprised his tortured little gay boy from *Fame* in Tony Richardson's *Hotel New Hampshire* (1984) as Frank, the brother who we were told is gay but who never does anything about it except act lonely. Just as in *Fame*, McCrane's character is the only one in *Hotel New Hampshire* without a love interest. It is also significant that the gay character was dropped when *Fame* became a television series, to avoid having him actually relate to other people every week. Here again, an opportunity to do something positive was lost. McCrane simply played the character as an average guy who happened to be gay. It was the timidity of the script that disallowed any development of his character beyond a trite formula.

In John Schlesinger's flop comedy *Honky Tonk Freeway* (1981), four gay guys in a jeep are tossed into a scene in a grand hotel on the highway simply to show off a bumper sticker that reads "Honk If You're Horny" and throw around a few jokes about crab lice, continuing a tradition in which gays are defined entirely by their sexuality.

We even got an update on the perennial lesbian vampire routine in Tony Scott's *The Hunger* (1983). Boy, does Hollywood love those lesbian vampires. The film was so chic that Vincent Canby said, "If Bendel's made movies, this is what they would look like." Catherine Deneuve's affair with Susan Sarandon was described by critic Carlos Clarens as "Richard Avedon's notion of Midnight Blue." The movies are just in love with the rapacious lesbian.

Lesbians in recent popular films have remained predatory twilight creatures, often hopelessly in love with heterosexual women. Those who come on to Pia Zadora in *The Lonely Lady* (1983) and Tracy Camila Johns in Spike Lee's *She's Gotta Have It* (1986) are minor annoyances, like ants at a picnic. The ridiculous leather-clad inmates of women's prisons in *Reform School Girls* (1986) and *Chained Heat* (1983) illustrate not true lesbianism but situational homosexuality used as high camp. It's funny up to a point but if all heterosexual women were consistently portrayed in such ways, how funny would that be?

In William Friedkin's *To Live and Die in L.A.* (1985), lesbianism is a kinky sideline enjoyed by the counterfeiter's girlfriend and it is used solely to heighten the decadence of the milieu. In Neil Jordan's *Mona Lisa* (1986), lesbianism is the key to a mystery. Cathy Tyson is the prostitute searching for the young girl she loves but there is no relationship between them in the film; lesbianism is just a plot device that drives Bob Hoskins' passion for Tyson.

Male homosexuals are more visible and more numerous but equally ridiculous. Martin Brest's *Beverly Hills Cop* (1984) and Joel Schumacher's *St. Elmo's Fire* (1985) illustrate how serious the situation has actually become. These films say that gay people are less than a joke; that they don't even exist today except in the minds of gag writers and nervous adolescents. The humor of Bronson Pinchot in *Beverly Hills Cop*, whether his characters are gay or not, is gentle and affectionate. But when Eddie Murphy bluffs his way into an exclusive men's club by pretending to be a homosexual who has just been diagnosed with herpes simplex 10, the humor is neither gentle nor affectionate, and this is why Pinchot nearly stole the film from Murphy. Murphy uses his characters to ridicule and the mockery is an end in itself, an impulse that columnist Armand White in the New York *Daily News* correctly terms "the naive insensitivity of a kid with no heart and no mind . . . a deeply offensive presence in American movies."

The herpes simplex 10 joke is in particularly bad taste in light of the AIDS health crisis, and Murphy, who conceived and wrote the sequence, is not alone in his insensitivity. Hugh Wilson's *Rustler's Rhapsody* (1985), a film based entirely on an extended fag joke about masculine insecurity, contains a saloon sequence in which a frontier doctor discusses a strange new disease affecting only single men, clearly a metaphor for AIDS used to provoke the cheapest kind of laughter.

AIDS has turned up as a joke in more than one film. In Jean-Jacques Beineix' *Betty Blue* (1986), a writer is first insulted by being told that his writing is faggy and finally receives a rejection letter telling him that his work has "all the symptoms of AIDS." Audiences reportedly found this hilarious.

In the usually very sensitive Paul Mazursky's *Down and Out in Beverly Hills*, Bette Midler screams, "Don't! You'll get AIDS!" when her husband gives mouth-to-mouth to the drowning Nick Nolte. Not only is the fear medically inaccurate, perpetuating the kind of mindless panic researchers have been trying to avoid, but it's unnecessary and offensive, making people with AIDS in the audience feel even more like outcasts than they have already become at the hands of a panic-stricken, misinformed society.

Even when mention of AIDS in a script occurs naturally, it is used as a pop reference thrown in simply because the issue is in the news. In Sidney Lumet's *Power* (1986), reporter Julie Christie mentions journalistic speculation that retiring U.S. senator E. G. Marshall has AIDS. In Denys Arcand's French-Canadian film *The Decline of the American Empire* (1986) the sole gay character is a pathetic cipher for the insecurities of the heterosexual characters around him. Additionally, he is a sexual compulsive who has an affection for twelve-year-old boys and we are led to believe that he has AIDS because there is blood in his urine—something which isn't even a symptom of the disease. In Woody Allen's *Hannah and Her Sisters* (1986), Barbara Hershey, in a casual cocktail party conversation, mentions that her dentist has a lot of gay clients and is now wearing rubber gloves for fear of AIDS. Neither reference pays off in any significant way. Perhaps Allen meant to point up the irony of this present heterosexual society. No matter that this reflects a truth. A larger truth is that AIDS is not being dealt with in any significant way in commercial cinema.

Without indicting Mazursky or Lumet or Allen in particular, one must ask the question in regard to all of these films, who's minding the store? Certainly Midler could have refused to speak such dialogue in *Down and Out in Beverly Hills*. All she had to do was say to Mazursky, "Listen, I can't say this; it's offensive. Why don't we change it?" Certainly there are gays among the thousands of screenwriters, directors, stars, producers and executives in Hollywood who read these scripts. Yet the same people who would refuse to insult other groups keep silent when the slur is anti-homosexual, either because they are homophobic themselves or because by speaking up they may brand themselves homosexual. The only other explanation is that such things simply never occur to them. There is a kind of defensive fear operating in Hollywood today, partly a result of the AIDS crisis, which almost dictates anti-homosexual attitudes.

St. Elmo's Fire, written and directed by Joel Schumacher, is a case in point. A film about adolescents with an adolescent point of view, it's an inconsequential brat pack flick masquerading as a film about adults. As in most films, everyone who really matters is straight. The guys have indiscriminate sex with every woman in sight, treat their wives and girlfriends like less than zero and throw temper tantrums when they're sexually betrayed. It's no surprise, then, that the issue of homosexuality is raised in equally infantile ways. Andrew McCarthy plays a writer for the *Washington Post* who is suspected of being homosexual because he hasn't had a date with a woman in over a year. This predictable and extremely tired act turns out to be the same show we've seen since the 1930s: McCarthy is actually in love with his best friend's girl, a dilemma that explains his celibate state and melancholy demeanor. The bogus homosexuality serves the same function it did in films like *The Front Page,* in which real men suspect intellectual poets and writers of being sissies so that we the audience may learn the lesson that real men can be sensitive without actually being queer.

This is a problem shared by most coming-of-age comedies that feature gentle adolescent heroes. In Harold Becker's *Vision Quest* (1985), for example, Matthew Modine is such a well-mannered little sweetheart that, in order to let us know he isn't queer, there is a scene in which another guy grabs his crotch simply so that he can flee in terror. The female counterpart of Modine's character is a butch Kristy McNichol in Ronald Maxwell's *Little Darlings* (1980); she is accused of lesbianism by the other girls at summer camp and must lose her virginity to prove them wrong.

Similarly, the tame, affable hero of Jerry Schatzberg's *No Small Affair* (1985), played by Jon Cryer, is taunted by his classmates for being a shy photography bug. The scene is reminiscent of *Tea and Sympathy,* representing a trend back to the caves. "I've got this friend," says Cryer's high school classmate. "His name is Bruce. He wants to take you to the dance on Saturday night. You can flip a coin to see who wears the dress." That short speech echoes virtually every thoughtless stereotype about gays left over from the 1950s, and the fact that they are still being blithely incorporated into contemporary films indicates a total lack of sophistication or resourcefulness on the part of supposedly intellectual screenwriters like Charles Bolt and Terence Mulcahy.

The gay-baiting dialogue in *No Small Affair* is given to a fool who is eventually humiliated by our hero when Cryer romances Demi Moore, a sophisticated older woman. This means nothing because the fool is proven wrong, crushed by the fact that Cryer is really straight. If Cryer had been gay, would he have deserved all that abuse? Probably so. When a character is gay, it is the hero who makes the fag jokes. We like the hero. When the character in question is straight, the bigots are simply proven wrong. We still like the hero. The hero is always straight and the straight guys are always our friends. The gay character always loses.

The actual homosexual in *St. Elmo's Fire* is—surprise!—a minor character who is an interior decorator played by Matthew Laurence. A walking limp wrist who lives across the hall from Demi Moore, he emerges from his apartment actually carrying a perfect frozen cocktail with a strawberry on the rim of the glass. In no time at all it is clear that the decorator is in the film only to establish that Andrew McCarthy is not queer. "Here!" the film is saying, "this is what a real queer looks like—and he's definitely not one of the inner circle of shit-kicking heteros with whom we are meant to identify." When a fight breaks out in the local bar, the faggot throws up his hands and screams, "I just had my nose fixed!" When Demi Moore tries to kill herself, all the "guys" are hard at work trying to save her life while Ron the decorator runs around in the hallway whimpering, "What's going on?" When Andrew McCarthy asks a street hooker why she thinks he's gay, she replies hastily, "Because you always act *strange* and I never see you with a girl." Schumacher treats homosexuality as a joke and a problem because that's the way Hollywood wants it and Schumacher wants to work in Hollywood.

Homosexuals are convenient scapegoats but their shabby treatment is only the most ostentatious aspect of a wider problem—that the diversity of American life has never been reflected in popular films. There are virtually no black faces on the American screen, and those we see are the faces of clowns— Richard Pryor, Whoopi Goldberg, Bill Cosby and Eddie Murphy. Even by Hollywood's box office standards, Billy Dee Williams should have been another Clark Gable after *Lady Sings the Blues* was released. Yet there are no black romantic leads of either sex in Hollywood. Nor do we see Asian faces at the movies today except in *Year of the Dragon* as psychopathic drug runners or nymphet newscasters. As recently as 1981, a Caucasian played Charlie Chan in a popular comedy, *Charlie Chan and the Curse of the Dragon Queen.*

It is equally rare to see old people on the screen and when we do, they're portrayed as lovable children, as in Ron Howard's *Cocoon* (1985). How realistic is it, then, to expect to see incidentally gay characters woven into the fabric of films that reflect an industry dedicated to serving white, heterosexual teenagers?

For the increasing numbers of adult moviegoers who have begun to see Hollywood as an amusement park for adolescents, the alternative visions of foreign and independent productions have become more attractive and more accessible. A decade ago, most independently made films, especially those addressing gay issues, didn't have the remotest chance of a healthy commercial release. Today, films like Stephen Frears' *My Beautiful Laundrette* and *Prick Up Your Ears,* Donna Deitch's *Desert Hearts* and Bill Sherwood's *Parting Glances,* each made for less than a million dollars, have reached wide audiences, while elephantine turkeys like George Lucas' $46-million *Howard the Duck* sink without a trace after only a few weeks. Of course, a good film is a good film, whether made in Hollywood for millions of dollars or by an independent on a shoestring, but good films are the exception rather than the rule in Hollywood and the independents have been taking up the slack. This situation has created a climate in which a mass audience can now be exposed to good films that happen to include gay characters who are neither gratuitous nor offensive.

A turning point of sorts was reached in 1980 when there was a tremendous amount of controversy surrounding William Friedkin's *Cruising,* which many gay people correctly perceived to be deeply homophobic at the conceptual level. By the end of the film, in which Al Pacino plays a New York policeman trying to track down a killer of homosexuals, we are led to believe that Pacino himself has become homosexual through his intimate contact with the gay world. In addition, the unavoidable conclusion is that Pacino also becomes a murderer of gays, having killed the gentle homosexual (Don Scardino) who lives in his building. The audience is left with the message that homosexuality is not only contagious but inescapably brutal.

Actor-director Don Scardino, looking back on the film, says, "I found the murder of my character more morally reprehensible than anything else because I was playing an average guy who happened to be gay. So what the film ended up saying is that no one is safe. The point of the movie should have been that when you suppress sexuality of any kind, heterosexual or homosexual, it can foster violence. We're not taught to handle growing up gay in this society, so we engender violence against it. *Cruising* had the opportunity to say that and it didn't."

Friedkin's response to criticisms of *Cruising* on the grounds that it was gratuitously violent was, "But this is the truth. It happens." Yet there is a difference between exploiting violence to attack a group of people and using that violence to make a legitimate point. That there is no aspect of human activity, no matter how violent or repulsive, that cannot be dealt with onscreen fairly is proven in Penelope Spheeris' *The Boys Next Door* (1986), which, unlike *Cruising*, explores the violence engendered when a young man's suppressed homosexual feelings turn to uncontrollable rage and does so concretely, so that the connection is clear.

The premise of the film—that ordinary guys can turn out to be killers—is undermined by the fact that Maxwell Caulfield and Charlie Sheen are a couple of weirdos who are about as ordinary as the Manson gang. They are the school outcasts. No one will have anything to do with them because they are so strange. But in the exploration of Caulfield's character, Spheeris illuminates the kind of hatred that can be triggered when natural desires are forbidden.

Unfortunately, *The Boys Next Door* reinforces the fiction that violence is committed against gays most often by other gays or by those who are sexually confused and threatened by their own latent homosexuality. While it is true that teenagers are sexually insecure in general, most often in American society it is the confident heterosexual bigot who attacks homosexuals, usually for religious reasons.

In the opening sequence of *The Boys Next Door*, Caulfield is contrasted with a gay high school classmate named Tom, who's as free as Caulfield is bottled up. Tom gets a laugh when he announces he's going into modern dance after graduation and makes a sarcastic remark about Caulfield, drawing a murderous stare. As the puzzle of Caulfield is pieced together, almost every incident betrays his insecurity with his own homosexuality. He kidnaps a dog named Bon Bon. "What a pussy-fucking name for a dog," he says. "A dog needs a name like Boner the Barbarian!" At the beach a young girl calls him queer and he flies into a rage, trying to run her down with his car. At one point he turns to Charlie Sheen and says tentatively, "I don't want you to think I'm queer or anything but you *are* my best friend." Shortly afterward, when Sheen is having sex with a woman, Caulfield pulls them apart and murders her, obviously in a jealous rage.

Eventually the two pick up a gay guy at a bar, L.A.'s The Revolver, called The End Zone in the picture, and go back to his place, where Caulfield brutally murders him. After the murder, a homophobic police officer viciously interrogates the dead man's lover, oblivious to his grief. Kenneth Cortland played Duane, the distraught young lover, magnificently. It was his first screen role.

"Penelope Spheeris never discussed with me how to play a gay person," says Cortland. "She was interested only in the emotional truth of the character. As far as playing a gay character? I never thought about that. I saw it as an opportunity to play a great scene my first time out. I didn't have any time for fear. Actors who are afraid shouldn't be acting."

Spheeris drew on her own experience in creating Duane's pain for the screen. "Right before I started working on that picture," she says, "my brother was killed in a motorcycle accident. He was hit by a drunken driver. My brother was gay. So when I was directing Kevin for the way he felt when that homophobic cop started questioning him, I tried to relate it to how my brother's boyfriend felt when he died."

There was no such truth in *Cruising*. *New York Times* critic Vincent Canby, reviewing the film, said, "Homosexual activist groups which have been protesting the production of *Cruising* on the grounds that it would present a distorted view of homosexual life were right. *Cruising* is a homosexual horror film." The monster in Friedkin's horror film is homosexuality itself. Everything in the film conspires to present gay life as menacing. The background music accompanying the homosexual scenes is loud, intimidating rock, while the score when Pacino is with his girlfriend is a Boccherini violin suite. The fact that Pacino's girlfriend ends up in the last shot trying on his leather gear says that this lifestyle is seductive and contagious, threatening to what's good in the world. Usually, when gay people complain about this sort of thing their concerns are dismissed as partisan, but this time everyone complained because the evidence was too overwhelming to ignore.

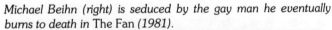

Michael Beihn (right) is seduced by the gay man he eventually burns to death in The Fan *(1981).*

Another horror film, Edward Bianchi's *The Fan* (1981), is strikingly similar to *Cruising,* especially in the iconography of its killer. Michael Biehn, the introverted psycho in *The Fan,* shares with Richard Cox, the first killer in *Cruising,* an intense obsession with—believe it or not—Broadway musical comedy. By some twisted logic these shy theater queens suddenly become raving, knife-wielding maniacs. As soon as we spot the soundtrack album from *Gypsy* in their cluttered apartments, we know who the killer is. We get everything but a New York *Post* headline screaming, "Ethel Merman made me gay!"

Cruising turned out to be one of 1980's biggest yawns, prompting *New West* critic Stephen Farber to conclude that the film would be remembered "not as a scandal or an outrage but as just another lousy movie." It wasn't the only lousy movie to exploit gays that year. Gordon Willis' *Windows* had already presented Elizabeth Ashley as a psychotic lesbian killer whose repressed emotions led to violence. The violence isn't a general problem. It's seen as an intrinsic part of the lesbian terrain.

In the same year, Bill Persky's *Serial* provided the kind of cruel comedy that has traditionally constituted the alternative to violence in Hollywood's dealings with gays. Based on Cyra McFadden's heterosexual ripoff of Armistead Maupin's *Tales of the City, Serial* concerns itself chiefly with the faddish lifestyles of a group of pea-brained Marin County swingers. The film is permeated with hatred for gays and could easily have been written by Jerry Falwell. *Serial* urges us to admire its hero (Martin Mull) for blackmailing a homosexual businessman (Christopher Lee) into helping him rescue his daughter from a cult. Lee is the leader of a grotesque homosexual motorcycle gang named "The Road Reamers" and is in love with the local guru, played by Tommy Smothers. Sally Kellerman's ten-year-old son is in analysis with a crackpot shrink who gives him a Gay Bruce doll that comes in a box shaped like a closet. Eventually the kid kills Gay Bruce "because he's a fag." Probably the most telling sequence is one in which Tuesday Weld's best friend comes out as a lesbian. Weld tells her matter-of-factly, "You know—gay or straight—you're still a cunt." *Serial* was, as critic David Denby pointed out, the perfect antifeminist, homophobic statement to usher in the age of Ronald Reagan.

Meanwhile audiences in 1980 were still laughing at the adventures of Zaza and Renato in the sequel to the popular farce *La Cage aux Folles.* The lovers, referred to in *Variety* as "the Abbott and Costello of gaydom," were warm and charming, endearing themselves to audiences by their genuine affection for each other. They were also two faggots who knew their place and threatened no one. For *La Cage aux Folles* to succeed with mainstream audiences it was necessary to avoid any genuine homosexual passion. Hence, the gay-ness was sublimated into outrageous mannerism and decor. "Isn't it peculiar," wrote David Ansen in *Time* magazine, "that in a movie that celebrates a long-lasting lovers' marriage, we never once see the lovers kiss?"

A gay reading of *La Cage aux Folles,* one that escapes most audiences, shows that in fact the film is about passing for straight and the accommodations gays make, large and small, each day of their lives in order to meet the expectations of the straight world. The scene in which Albin attempts to affect John Wayne's masculine walk, under the tutelage of his lover, is out of *Tea and Sympathy,* in which Tom Lee is taught by his college roommate how to walk like a real man so that the other guys won't make fun of him. The slapstick humor of the film overshadows the serious issues, however, which are apparent only to those in the audience who have experienced such conflict in their own lives.

A poorly made film got progressively worse with each sequel. The second part, released in 1980, is a confusing espionage caper in which Zaza is made to jump out of a cake looking like Ethel Merman. Part 3, released in 1985, is a hideously boring piece of crap, put together by no less than five screenwri-ters, in which Zaza must marry a woman in order to cash in on an inheritance.

Some critics were enchanted. Richard Schickel called the original the *Guess Who's Coming to Dinner* of the Eighties, and Pauline Kael, wearing the blinders she keeps in her top drawer for reviewing gay films, noted that "gay

Cartoon from Christopher Street's *May 1981 issue.*

activists haven't been obstreperous about the film because it deals—affectionately—with transvestites . . . who can hardly be considered representative of homosexuals." When gay people protest their own bashing in the popular arts, they're being obstreperous, like annoying mosquitos who have no business invading one's living room.

What Kael failed to see is that although there are individual gay activists, there is no such group of people. What does it mean if you ask whether or not white people liked *Star Wars?* Nothing. It's as absurd as when, after a riot in Greenwich Village during the *Cruising* demonstrations, a journalist asked a single gay, "Why can't you control your people?" Kael makes it sound as though gay reaction passes through some sort of central clearing office. In fact, most gays, like most straights, did enjoy *La Cage aux Folles*; both groups could feel superior to the bigots and the drag queens in the film.

Such was also the case with Peter Yates' *The Dresser* (1983), based on Ronald Harwood's long-running play about the relationship between a Shakespearean actor (Albert Finney) and his effeminate dresser. Tom Courtenay's lavender-tinted prissiness captured the hearts of audiences and some critics because here was another gay character who threatened no one and for whom everyone could feel sorry. A great deal of meaning was attached to the relationship between Courtenay and Finney as well as to the film, which David Denby termed "a cruelly sentimental movie about unrequited love." In fact, the film contains no viable relationship. Tom Courtenay is little more than a pathetic, spinsterish pair of pursed lips for whom the theater is a safe refuge from a world with which he could never cope. There was nothing new, daring or insightful about the creation of such a character; he was simply a melodramatic first cousin to John Hurt's doe-eyed timid faggot in *Partners.*

There is a false assumption abroad that gays, especially politicized ones, don't want to see effeminate homosexuals portrayed onscreen at all because they represent negative stereotypes that have been overworked. In fact, it is the politicized lesbians and gay men who appreciate the radical politics of drag. Closeted gays are threatened by it. It's true that flaming queens have been beaten into the ground onscreen but that doesn't mean that they can't be portrayed fairly in both serious and comic contexts. All stereotypes are based on a germ of truth and there's no reason why sissies shouldn't be created for the screen with some attention to character and human insight. Effeminate homosexuals are individuals just like role-playing dykes; they can be explored, parodied, laughed at and laughed with. But we have to know who they are or they're just symbols for failed heterosexuals.

Michael Blakemore's *Privates on Parade* (1982) and Peter Medak's *Zorro,*

George Hamilton as Zorro's brother Bunny in Zorro the Gay Blade
(1981).

Dennis Quilley (center) as Captain Terri Dennis doing Carmen Miranda in Privates on
Parade *(1982).*

The Gay Blade (1981) are worlds apart in quality and intent, but both employ classic sissy stereotypes and both avoid offensiveness by examining the clichés and using them in turn for humor and pathos. Sequences that could have easily been offensive in Zorro, The Gay Blade are gently humorous. There is no cruel edge to the humor, which more often than not sends up people's ideas about gay stereotypes instead of using them to wound. Zorro's brother Ramon, also known as Bunny, is the real hero of the film, saying to an adoring crowd at one point, "Remember, my people, there is no shame in being poor . . . only in dressing poorly." There's a gay sensibility operating here that emerges more in the point of view than in the possible sexuality of the creators. When a local priest gets smart with Bunny, he casually says, "Father, I have heard that many of your brethren in the church are actually sissy boys." Bunny is an asexual sissy who presents no threat but, like Robert Preston's Toddy in Victor/Victoria, he possesses style, defiance and freedom, traits almost always denied such characters.

Privates on Parade is not a silly film. In fact, it's almost unbearably poignant, especially for gays. The story of a theatrical troupe of drag queens during wartime provides a forum for examining cultural and sexual stereotypes when an effeminate homosexual, played by Denis Quilley, is trapped in a macho culture that is innately hostile to him. The film is a bitter satirical farce that shows real affection for its gay characters without nervousness or boring rhetoric. What emerges from the experience is human and universal; we are exposed to qualities in stereotyped gays never before revealed or explored in the movies. When real war and real killing come to upset the flaming queens decked out in their Carmen Miranda drag, we find that effeminate men are just a diverse group of men. Some of them show courage and some of them show fear. They display neither emotion because they are gay but because they are people.

The protests against Cruising and the simultaneous emergence of films like Windows and Serial created a serious debate centered on the treatment of gays in film as less than people. Although it had virtually no effect on the Hollywood establishment, the debate gave direction to gay and lesbian filmmakers who, in the coming years, would make their own statements.

In a telephone conversation with the late Arthur Bell, reported by Nat Hentoff in Inquiry magazine, Larry Marks, Vice President for Production and Marketing at Paramount said, "I can feel the effects of the demonstrations [against Cruising] already. Industry people will be more careful about gay lifestyles and the kind of gay ingredient that should be in a script. To use a cliché, what you've done in New York is raise consciousness."

Others held that Hollywood had no consciousness to raise, and history has proven them right. *New York* magazine's David Denby, for example, was less optimistic than Marks about Hollywood's ability to mature and reflect anything but its own interest in formula box office hits. Speculating eloquently on the future of gay imagery on screen, Denby wrote, "The lesson of *Cruising* is not that gays have to fight Hollywood but that they should give up on Hollywood. Yes, give up on a rotten system and make better films here in New York. The money is here, the talent is here—why not find a script that gets the scene right and then produce it independently? With real dedication, a good movie can still be made for about a million dollars. Take the game away from Hollywood! What revenge could be sweeter than that?"

It would be only a few years before such films would begin to emerge in America, but this process had already begun in Europe, where independent filmmakers are more often subsidized by television stations and governments. Two strikingly different films, Frank Ripploh's *Taxi zum Klo* from Germany and Salvatore Samperi's *Ernesto* from Italy, opened in the same year as *Cruising* and *La Cage aux Folles II,* providing contrast to both the tragic and comic aspects of those films.

Michelle Placido and Martin Halm begin their clandestine affair in Ernesto *(1979).* (International Spectrafilm Distribution Inc.)

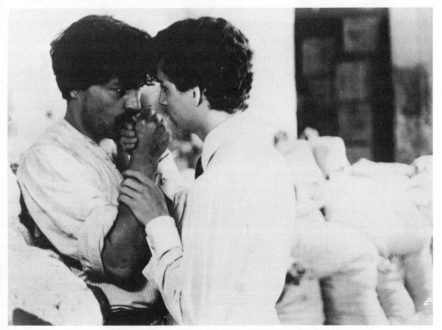

Made in 1979, *Ernesto* was given its American premiere at the New York Lesbian and Gay Festival in 1980 but was ignored by the mainstream press until its short commercial run in 1984. Based on the novel by Umberto Saba, the film is set in Trieste in the early 1900s. The pampered seventeen-year-old son (Martin Halm) of a mercantile Jewish family is described as a socialist with a capitalist stomach. His natural homosexual urges are smoothly subverted by the pressures of conforming to a bourgeois social structure. *Ernesto* contains one of the most sexually explicit sequences of homosexual passion ever filmed. Yet after his first erotic encounter with a stevedore (Michele Placido) at the grain warehouse where he is a clerk and a brief fling with the male half of a pair of beautiful twins (both played by Lara Wendel), he is married off by his family to the twin sister. The final shot of Ernesto's winking face at the wedding is meant to indicate that neither marriage nor time will subdue the rebel in him.

While Samperi's film rather fancifully uses homosexuality as a metaphor for one's place in life, Frank Ripploh's *Taxi zum Klo* is completely autobiographical and told from a deeply personal gay point of view. In direct contrast to the heterosexual voyeurism of *Cruising*, Ripploh's film, which won the Max Ophuls prize in 1981, covers virtually the same underground sex scene with wit, charm and unsentimental passion.

Frank Ripploh (right) goes out on the town in Taxi zum Klo *(1980).*

Cartoon which appeared in The Soho Weekly News *during the* Cruising *controversy* (T. Hachtman)

Taxi zum Klo was that rare combination of great personal filmmaking and controversial political insight that made it the first popular post–gay liberation film to break through to mainstream audiences, especially in Germany. Ripploh and his real-life lover Bernd Broaderup played themselves, focusing on the sexual issues of contemporary gay life from opposite points of view. Broaderup, the monogamous homemaker, wants fidelity and a quiet life of casseroles and television watching. Ripploh, a high school teacher, wants freedom and fast-lane promiscuous sex. He puts on drag or leather at the drop of an earring and marks his students' papers while cruising public toilets. He even leaves a hospital bed in one scene to take a taxi to the local john for a quickie with a stranger. Made for about $50,000 in 16 millimeter, Taxi zum Klo was Jerry Falwell's worst nightmare and a bigger hit than Cruising.

Taxi zum Klo was revolutionary in the sense that it ignored politically correct questions about the "positive gay image" some gay activists want projected to the public. The majority of gay characters on the screen have been portrayed as morally reprehensible simply because they are homosexual. Taxi zum Klo disposed of the issue of homosexuality completely. The ideas in the film become Ripploh's ideas, not those of gay people. "I hate problem movies," commented Ripploh in an interview. "I wanted to show the audience both happiness and sadness because that's how life is."

Like Taxi zum Klo, Stephen Frears' Prick Up Your Ears (1987) freaked out a lot of people. Based on John Lahr's biography of British playwright Joe Orton, Prick Up Your Ears focuses on the relationship between Orton (Gary Oldman) and his lover Kenneth Halliwell (Alfred Molina). In many ways, it is the story of the rage engendered when a "wife" plays grudging helpmate to a creative husband. Thanks to a witty, sacrilegious script by Alan Bennett, Prick Up Your Ears becomes the ultimate Orton black comedy. Joe Orton's credo was "Reality is the ultimate outrage." By simply filming this twisted, tragic love story without any special regard for the fact that it happens to be about two men, Frears points up the truths he first touched upon in My Beautiful Laundrette: a good story is universal and sexuality doesn't matter if one creates real people instead of stereotypes.

In Prick Up Your Ears, Frears contrasts the unequal sexual and intellectual relationship between Orton and Halliwell with that of author John Lahr (Wallace Shawn) and his wife (Charlotte Woodehouse). Instead of saying that gays are just like heterosexuals and share their problems, Prick Up Your Ears focuses on the fact that in many ways, the opposite is equally true. Straights are often just like gays—or more simply that relationships are just like relationships.

No intelligent person who sees *Prick Up Your Ears* will think that all homosexuals are compulsively promiscuous or psychopathic killers. Bigots and morons will says such things in any case. When Frears was told by a journalist that the sex scenes in public rest rooms were probably the first of their kind in a commercial film he was shocked. "Oh, my goodness," he said, "I suppose that's true." It had never occurred to him to think in those terms. This is the difference between a filmmaker like William Friedkin who shoots something *because* it will shock some people and Frears who doesn't even notice the shock value. "I don't know what the demographics of the audience are," says Frears, "but one makes movies for people like oneself—people who are intelligent and interested." It's worth noting that both Friedkin and Frears are heterosexual and that this sort of gift has little to do with sexual orientation.

Homophobia affects everyone. Heterosexuals who don't like gays and gays who don't like themselves may argue with the sexual politics of *Prick Up Your Ears*. Straight homophobes will think it immoral and disgusting to show such things. Self-hating gays will fall into the "Is it good for the Jews or bad for the Jews?" argument. The bottom line is that no one should have to fear making honest films because one true life story might be used as a weapon against millions by a few fools.

This is not the case with mass audience features. Frears sees a good story, not an issue which is controversial. For Hollywood and network television, movies about homosexuals remain problem films. The Hollywood trap is that the success of a film is judged by whether or not it reaches a mass audience. The gay activist trap is that a film is judged by whether or not it succeeds in persuading that audience to accept homosexuals. Neither of these barometers is valid or important. Both views encourage the making of films in which acceptance of homosexuals is begged based on the notion that they are just like everyone else. Such ideas demand films that are designed by committee to reach the largest numbers of people in the most inoffensive manner. This will never be the answer. There is no reality or tension in such films. The point is to reflect life in an interesting way and learn to live with the personal, idiosyncratic truth of an individual artist no matter who gets freaked out by it.

The mini-cycle of so-called gay films that emerged from Hollywood in 1982 satisfied no one. Films like *Making Love, Personal Best, Victor/Victoria* and *Partners* were too straight for gay audiences and much too gay for conservative straights. Arthur Hiller's *Making Love* (1982) has been described as the genre's landmark film, the first attempt to "deal" with homosexuality in a big-budget, mainstream movie for a mass audience. Once again, if you're going to make mainstream gay films, you stress that gays are basically just like straights. Yet this is a false premise that never works. You can't plead tolerance for gays by saying that they're just like everyone else. Tolerance is something we should extend to people who are not like everyone else. If gays weren't different, there wouldn't be a problem, and there certainly is a problem.

Making Love is a coming-out film about a rich, white, handsome doctor (Michael Ontkean) who must confess to his beautiful wife (Kate Jackson) that he is in love with a man (Harry Hamlin). When Hamlin makes it clear that he isn't interested in settling down but prefers to play the field, Ontkean finds himself a rich architect and marries the guy.

Termed a timid rehash of Fifties soap operas, the film was trounced by most critics as strictly formula. Yet the gay press, grateful no doubt for any liberal mainstream film that treated gay people favorably, lavished praise on the film for its daring. By Hollywood standards, *Making Love* was daring. As critic Robin Wood pointed out, it featured two handsome and popular male stars believably falling in love, taking each other's clothes off and going to bed together. It was also the first time in commercial film that a serious gay couple were permitted a happy ending. Hollywood thinks that's radical and that's its mistake. If that's all a film is about, it's boring.

As industry analyst Stuart Byron said in *American Film* magazine, *Making Love* opened very strong at box offices across the country, proving that the

Michael Ontkean and Harry Hamlin in Making Love *(1982).*

subject itself is not a turnoff to people. Business dropped off after a week because word of mouth had it that *Making Love* was a dull film. The problem was that openly gay screenwriter Barry Sandler, who went on to write a radical and brilliant script for Ken Russell's *Crimes of Passion* the following year, had been straitjacketed by the dictates of commercial film. As in other so-called pioneering films about minorities—*Guess Who's Coming to Dinner, Gentleman's Agreement*—the minority in *Making Love* is presented in terms wholesome enough to win the Good Housekeeping Seal of Approval. Both *Making Love* and *Taxi zum Klo* grew out of personal gay experience. Ripploh was free to put a radical vision on the screen and Sandler was not. This is why the Harry Hamlin character in *Making Love* must disappear from the film. He won't settle down and behave like Hollywood's idea of heterosexuals.

There are a few films that grow out of an emotional and passionate need for personal gay expression. In 1983, Arthur J. Bressan, Jr., released one such film—*Abuse,* an American independent as radical as Ripploh's *Taxi zum Klo.* A film about violence against children and the love affair that blossoms between a thirty-five-year-old gay filmmaker and a fourteen-year-old boy, *Abuse* was made for $27,000 and turned down by thirty-five distributors before being picked up by Cinevista, which also distributed Ripploh's film. Rejected by Filmex, the New York Film Festival and the Chicago Film Festival, *Abuse* finally premiered at the Berlin Film Festival, where Bressan was called "America's most closely guarded secret." Shortly afterward, *Abuse* opened at New York's Plaza Theater.

Abuse is a triumph of content and style, telling an important, dramatically gripping story in an uncompromising fashion without sacrificing sexual politics or pandering to a mainstream audience. Larry Porter (Richard Ryder) is a gay film student doing a project on child abuse for his graduate thesis. Raphael Sbarge, who later played one of Tom Cruise's buddies in *Risky Business* and now stars in a popular television sitcom, is Thomas Carroll, an abused youngster who becomes the focus of Porter's film. Eventually, with Carroll as the aggressor, the two fall in love. When it becomes clear that Carroll's parents will probably beat him to death if he remains at home, he and Porter run away together to San Francisco.

Abuse caused controversy both in and out of the gay community, raising as it did issues of intergenerational sex, power and the definition of child abuse. Bressan didn't shrink from any point of view on those topics. He included in his film voices that maintained that Porter was, in fact, abusing Carroll in the same pattern as his parents, setting up a situation in which an older person holds power over a youngster not fully aware of his situation. The audience was given sufficient lead to go beyond that perspective. Some critics also managed to avoid inflammatory rhetoric and hysteria. Judith Crist called *Abuse* "a fascinating film . . . an exploration of child abuse from the child's point of view." In the New York *Post,* Rex Reed wrote, "The surprising thing is that Bressan . . . has miraculously managed to tie all of these controversial elements together until they fit beautifully, avoiding clichés, raising his audience's consciousness, and providing us all with an arresting film of astonishing power, solid emotional impact, and first-rate entertainment."

Bressan, who began making films in 1972, is an openly gay filmmaker who consistently sets out to challenge the gay status quo. "For a moviemaker there is nothing better than making a movie that has something of yourself in it," he told the New York *Native.* "I worked on *Abuse* for two years, from conception to completion. It took four weeks to shoot and a year to edit. The actors deferred their salaries and both stars invested in the film when things got tight. The rest of the money was raised from friends."

Bressan's next project was *Buddies* (1985), the first feature film about AIDS. It was shot in nine days and tells the simple story of a gay man dying of AIDS and how his assigned volunteer "buddy" from the "gay center" copes with his illness and death. The film, however, goes far beyond the AIDS crisis and examines the foundations of gay love and desire, which transcend politics. Robert (Geoff Edholm) is dying of AIDS. His life has been one immersed in an era of gay political action. At first he doesn't even like David (David Schachter), the gay yuppie who volunteers to be his buddy out of a sense of community responsibility. Their brief relationship, however, illuminates the emotional intensity of present-day gay life better than any disease-of-the-week, made-for-television drama could ever hope to.

"When you're in a theater where *Buddies* is about to go on," says Bressan, "and someone says, 'Will the people with AIDS in this theater stand up' and forty-five people stand up including your cameraman, you feel very small. This film has changed me drastically. I really have so little empathy for the bullshit left in the movie world. If I never make another movie, *Buddies* will be a fine way to leave. Once in a while a filmmaker gets to make a movie that's not about his career, a film where everything configurates to help you make a positive statement. It's about life, people, death, feelings. That's what movies are about."

Outside of the independent arena, there is no idiosyncratic gay vision on the screen. The idea that nobody is ever really homosexual is pervasive, and gay artists in Hollywood translate their experiences into heterosexual language. Nor are gay people portrayed with fidelity to the truth; it is historically

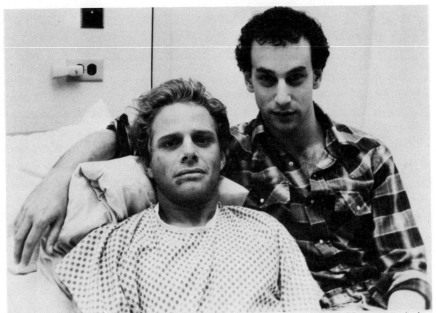

Geoff Edholm and David Schacter in Buddies *(1985).* (Photo C. H. Montagna; Arthur J. Bressan, Jr.)

true that celebrated figures who were lesbian or gay have invariably been either portrayed as heterosexual on the screen or neutered sufficiently to shift the focus away from the importance of their sexuality to their lives.

This hasn't changed. Gillian Armstrong's *My Brilliant Career* (1979) is based on the novel by celebrated Australian writer Miles Franklin. In the film, Sybylla Melvin (Judy Davis) is pictured as a strong-willed woman who refuses twice to marry a gentle, handsome man (Sam Neill) because she is committed to her work. Most critics commented on the implausibility of her choice and the lack of sufficient motivation for it. "Perhaps director Armstrong sees something in Sam Neill's Harry Beecham that would doom this marriage from the start," wrote critic David Chute, "but she hasn't conveyed it."

It was not "something" in Sam Neill's character but in the character of the heroine that was omitted from Armstrong's film as well as from the novel on which it is based. In an exhaustively researched piece by Michael Bronski called "The Story Behind the Movie," which appeared in *Gay Community News* in 1980, it is revealed that, in fact, the real Miles Franklin spent most of her life in relationships with women. It is Franklin's own discretion that kept the truth from her adoring public during her lifetime, but it is Armstrong's disinterest in exploring the real woman that perpetuates the deception for filmgoers. Feminism, yes. Potential lesbianism, no.

The same impulse to protect the image of a beloved national figure made

Paul Schrader's *Mishima* (1985) a fascinating esoteric piece of filmmaking, which, nevertheless, avoided dealing directly with its subject. Schrader illustrates Mishima's life both in black-and-white flashbacks and in dramatizations of three of his novels recreated in color using high-definition video. Yukio Mishima ran a small private army and was a militant right-wing cult figure bent on restoring the glory of the emperor. He was also a homosexual with a taste for bloody sadomasochistic fantasies and an erotic fascination with death, including his own. Before granting Schrader permission to film her husband's life story, Mishima's widow forbade the director to deal with his homosexuality or explicitly with his death. This, reported Vincent Canby in the *New York Times*, was "a little like making a movie about Pearl Harbor without identifying the nationality of the attackers."

That the complexity and cultural context of Mishima's homosexuality were necessarily simplified for Western audiences is explored in an exhaustive interview with director Schrader conducted by writer Larry Mass in the New York *Native*. Pointing out that Mishima was a self-negating, self-hating, closeted homosexual, Mass suggests that Schrader intentionally intellectualized his sexuality, making him "comfortably masculine and believably heterosexual," unlike his androgynous counterpart played by Ryuichi Sakamoto, David Bowie's erotic focus in Nagisa Oshima's *Merry Christmas, Mr. Lawrence*.

"Have you really told us the truth about Mishima," asked Mass, "or rather the kind of truth that would be most acceptable to his heterosexual admirers, or to Mishima himself?"

"There is much truth to what you say," replied Schrader. "I personally think Mishima's homosexuality was more important than the film portrays it . . . in order to get permission for the novels from Madame Mishima, I had to agree not to show anything I couldn't document. Since my interest was not to do Fassbinder's Mishima, I agreed."

Although Schrader did create a multilayered vision of a complex political and sexual creature and although legal problems probably prevented him from making a more accurate film, gay people are invariably left with a vision of homosexuality tailored for heterosexuals. And there's always a perfectly good reason for it.

In the popular arena, *Making Love* was a gay film for straight people. It focused on coming out as a family problem, an approach it shares with made-for-television films like *An Early Frost* and *Consenting Adults*. In such cases, the question is never "How was the film?" but "How were the ratings?" In 1985, *Life* magazine did a cover story on AIDS announcing that the disease was "now affecting the rest of us," meaning heterosexual society. It was

Gena Rowlands and Aidan Quinn in An Early Frost *(1985).*

as though no one had considered that the reader holding the magazine might be gay. In the same way, television films like *Consenting Adults* and *An Early Frost* subtly say that there are no homosexuals, only a homosexual problem.

In *An Early Frost* we see how AIDS affects a young man's mother, father, sister, brother-in-law and grandmother. There is no consideration given to the fact that this is happening to him—not them. In *Consenting Adults* we see how a handsome young jock's coming out of the closet affects his mother, his father, his sister and his college roommate. When the latter learns of his buddy's homosexuality, he says, "I don't believe this is happening to me!" Such films are about the real people in our society, the straight people. Gays are the problem they have.

Exceptions are rare and follow the same commercial/noncommercial patterns as do motion pictures. *Welcome Home, Bobby* was a singularly fine attempt to deal with a gay high school student on network television. In the equivalent of the independent arena, cable's Showtime has produced the series *Brothers,* featuring two gay characters and a variety of realistic situations handled courageously and unself-consciously.

Most television movies are made by liberal heterosexuals who mean well but are limited in their efforts by the demands of the medium. Prime time soap operas, on the other hand, are aimed at a moron mentality and aren't even well meaning; they seem manufactured by greedy little children exploiting sensational themes for a general public composed of supposed bigots. The gay character on Dynasty isn't even a gay character. He's a sexually confused cipher through which the audience is taught that no one is ever really gay; gayness is just self-indulgent behavior, a plot covenience that can be changed weekly to achieve a high number of sexual permutations.

A 1986 episode of Hotel dealing with fag bashing is similarly gutless. Jan-Michael Vincent is made to come to the rescue of an army buddy who he has just learned is gay. Vincent renews his macho credentials by wiping out the evil fag bashers for his fey friend and the show ends with him telling his buddy, "I'm sorry. We can't be friends anymore. I was brought up not to accept this sort of thing." The show has it both ways. The makers of Hotel get to make their idea of a social statement while reaffirming the prejudices of its targeted audience. Jan-Michael Vincent is the hero. He was brought up not to accept homosexuals. The viewer gets to admire the heterosexual's courage and masculinity and at the same time sympathize with his dilemma in being unable to accept a gay friend. The gay character, of course, isn't a regular on the series and disappears after one episode so that we don't ever have to deal with him again. Gay viewers are consistently put in the untenable position of having to endure insults or accept well-meaning but misguided efforts to treat them as a social problem without actually dealing with their lives.

This kind of casual exploitation is carried to its ultimate conclusion in Robert Towne's Personal Best (1982), in which Olympic hopefuls played by Mariel Hemingway and Patrice Donnelly have a lesbian affair. By portraying lesbian passion as an adolescent rite of passage, Towne can move Hemingway along the road to adulthood and into a heterosexual relationship without sacrificing the steamy erotic sequences between women that heterosexual men have traditionally enjoyed. As usual, there's only one lesbian, rather than two or more who interact socially and comfortably. By abandoning Patrice Donnelly's character of Tory completely, the film shows us that the real action is about the heterosexuals. "According to this movie," wrote Rex Reed, "lesbianism is just something you catch in the locker room, like athlete's foot."

In fact, Personal Best did what Steven Spielberg was criticized for not doing in The Color Purple (1985). For Alice Walker, lesbianism, which is never called that in the novel, is the catalyst through which Celie discovers her capacity to love another human being, gets in touch with her own beauty and is able to seek her independence from Mister. Yet the criticisms of Spielberg were valid because he took a sexually explicit love affair in an existing work and, by his own admission, sanitized it into a series of chaste kisses to beg acceptance from a mass audience. "According to Steven," said Whoopi Goldberg, "mid-

Patrice Donnelly and Mariel Hemingway in Personal Best *(1982).*

Whoopi Goldberg as Celie and Margaret Avery as Shug in the bowdlerized love scene from The Color Purple *(1985).*

dle America simply would not sit still for me on top and Shug on bottom, so we made it less explicit. This way we won't offend anyone."

Properly conceived and executed, the lesbianism in *The Color Purple* might have been a rare screen instance of women relating to each other on their own terms. This is what was missing from *Personal Best.* Like most depictions of lesbianism in popular culture, the sexual sequences in the film are a male fantasy; two childlike women innocently exploring each other's bodies so that a male audience can get hot.

If, at the end of *Personal Best,* both women had preferred each other over the men in the film, audiences would have been profoundly disappointed, as they were with John Sayles' well-intentioned lesbian coming-out film *Lianna* (1983). A lesbian version of *Making Love,* Sayles' film is about a wife and mother who leaves her family for another woman. *Lianna* basically presents lesbianism as a refuge from the hostilities of heterosexual life. Lianna's husband is such a bastard that the film gives the viewer the idea that if men weren't so odious, women wouldn't turn to each other. The same situation occurs in George Kaczender's *Chanel Solitaire* (1981), a soap opera biography of Coco Chanel in which the famous designer's affair with Misia Cert is explained away as a momentary diversion when her longtime lover leaves her to marry another woman.

"Any director who makes a grainy, amateurish home movie about lesbians in Hoboken," wrote Rex Reed of *Lianna,* "must have a death wish. This may be the most sensitive, balanced and sobering view of lesbians the movies will ever give us. It is 100 times better than *Personal Best.* But . . . don't lesbians ever have any fun? *Lianna* is a sad, humorless, thoroughly depressing downer."

For fun, we turn to the tried and true portrayal of the male homosexual as screaming queen. Blake Edwards' *Victor/Victoria,* released in 1982, was a crowd pleaser. It was the most entertaining and colorful of films dealing with gays to emerge in the period. Much of the pleasure generated by *Victor/Victoria* came from Robert Preston's delightful, liberated performance as Toddy, the witty, outrageous and unrepentent gay best friend of Julie Andrews. Preston's character brought audiences back to the innocent days of the pre-Code 1930s, when gay characters and straight characters were friends in a fantasy world where a musical number made everything rosy.

Unfortunately, Edwards' cowardly handling of the sexual politics in *Victor/Victoria* stopped short of any radical statement the film might have made. A love affair between Toddy and James Garner's bodyguard, played by Alex Karras, could have been revolutionary. Instead, the one shot of the two in bed

Jane Hallaren and Linda Griffiths in John Sayles' Lianna (1983).

Alex Karras confesses his homosexuality to James Garner in Victor/Victoria (1982).

together shows them fully clothed, propped up primly like two maiden aunties. Thus, a rare chance to eroticze the asexual sissies of the Thirties was lost. Besides, given Toddy's ostentatiously randy dialogue, the scene doesn't ring true. It looks fake. It's a punch line to the joke that burly ex–football star Karras is gay.

Edward's biggest mistake was not trusting his audience. James Garner falls in love with Julie Andrews, thinking that she is a man. He can't understand why he's attracted to another guy. Refusing to believe that she isn't a woman, he hides in her bathroom and watches her undress. It is only when he is absolutely sure that she's a woman that he kisses her, saying, "I don't care if you *are* a man." That scene would have been daring and truly unique if it had come before Garner discovered Andrews' true sex. Edwards could have let his audience see a heterosexual man kissing what he thought was another man simply because he felt he was in love. But that would have pushed the audience too far. For all of its high-flown dialogue about heterosexual insecurity with homosexuality, *Victor/Victoria* is as straight as the values it pretends to challenge.

Blake Edwards may not be a radical but at least his heart was in the right place. James Burrows' *Partners* (1982) had no heart at all. Written by Francis Veber, who did the screenplay for *La Cage aux Folles*, this comedy of a straight cop and a gay cop infiltrating the gay community in order to catch a killer was insensitive to the point of slander. World-class homophobe Ryan O'Neal was chosen to play the straight cop. As the gay cop, John Hurt is a terrified closet case who can't even hold a gun without dropping it or raise his voice above a timid whisper. He spends all his time mooning over O'Neal and sweating profusely because he's been thrust into an openly gay situation.

Inquiry magazine critic Stephen Harvey put it best when he said "Picture this: A lot of Jews have been murdered and a gentile cop is teamed up with a Jewish cop who's fixed his nose and changed his name and they go into this mysterious Jewish community and every Jew they find is pushy, foul-mouthed, vulgar, greasy, aggressive and a gold digger."

Partners was yet another opportunity to create a breakthrough film in which a gay man and a straight man learn something from each other in a funny, human situation. Once again, the filmmakers refused to trust their audience, going instead for cheap laughs. "Hollywood's latest crime against humanity in general and homosexuals in particular," wrote Rex Reed in the New York *Post*, "is a dumb creep show called *Partners*—stupid, tasteless and homophobic, this sleazy, superficial film implies that gay cops cannot be trusted to work with straight cops because they might fall in love with them." David Ansen noted in *Time* magazine that *Partners* brought back "the good old days when homosexuals were protrayed as swishy fruits, leering queens and pathetic spinsters." Putting a finger firmly on the root of the problem, London's *Daily Mail* critic said, "The cinema seems to be having an even tougher time coming to terms with homosexuality than the society whose attitudes it's supposed to reflect." Ideally, of course, the cinema shouldn't have to reflect anyone's

Ryan O'Neal and John Hurt pretend to be gay lovers in Partners *(1982).*

attitudes except those of the person making the film. It is because filmmakers are terrified to challenge the bigotries of their audience that we are confronted repeatedly with mindless banalities.

Sometimes it's easy to please the crowd and also score political points. Hector Babenco's *Kiss of the Spider Woman* (1985), based on the 1978 novel by openly gay writer Manuel Puig, presents a homosexual exotic enough to be distanced from practically everyone in any audience. William Hurt, playing Molina, became the first actor to win an Oscar for a homosexual role. The film tries and fails to create the missing ingredient of *Partners,* the transformation of a gay man and a straight man through their understanding of one another.

Raul Julia as Valentin and William Hurt as Molina in Kiss of the Spider Woman *(1985).*

Babenco, whose 1981 film *Pixote* is a brutally realistic look at the cruelties of street life for abandoned children in Brazil, subtly alters Puig's novel to meet the expectations of the audience.

Kiss of the Spider Woman is the story of the relationship between cellmates in a South American prison. Molina (William Hurt) is a thirty-seven-year-old effeminate homosexual window dresser jailed for molesting a minor. Valentin (Raul Julia) is a professional journalist incarcerated for his radical left-wing activities under a fascist regime. Puig's novel is about the definitions of masculine and feminine behavior and what, if anything, those definitions have to do with sexuality. Molina spends his time spinning tales from old movies for Valentin, who, in turn, tries to politicize Molina. In the end, Valentin and Molina make love and Molina—for love, not politics—becomes a martyr to Valentin's cause. Audiences feel safe because this is not just a story of two men who fall in love and have sex. There is redeeming political significance to justify the affair.

The film version leaves out perhaps the most crucial aspect of Puig's novel, Valentin's realization that homosexual men needn't adopt the sexist attitudes widely held by heterosexual men about women. In a long passage of dialogue in the novel, Valentin challenges Molina's destructive, masochistic identification with the cinematic downtrodden female, telling him that there isn't any reason why gay men shouldn't take the active sexual role as well as the passive. In the film, Valentin changes in a radical way under the influence of Molina, but Molina changes in a way that confirms sexist assumptions about gender roles. Molina's courage in taking on a dangerous political role is seen as making him more masculine. In a world in which *Roget's Thesaurus* lists *effeminate* as a synonym for *cowardly,* it isn't surprising that we admire the drag queen who breaks out of his assigned role. He dies in the end like one of his old movie queens, never understanding the significance and profundity of Valentin's true growth.

"*Kiss of the Spider Woman,*" wrote J. Walcott in *Texas Monthly,* "is essentially a homosexual wish fantasy about how the love of a real man, however brief, can be transforming—purifying." Much of this is cultural. In societies in which there is a strong macho ethic, sexual role playing is as basic to gay life as it is in the dominant culture. Films like Eloy de la Iglesia's *The Deputy* (1978) and Paul Verhoeven's *The Fourth Man* (1983) share with *Kiss of the*

Syndicated cartoon which appeared after the release of Kiss of the Spider Woman *(1985). (L.A.* Herald*)*

Spider Woman an exploration of gay passion in terms of its basically unrequited nature. In all of these films we are presented with gay men who obsessively try to seduce straight (real) men and come to grief over it.

In *The Deputy,* a rising star in post-Franco politics meets up with a straight

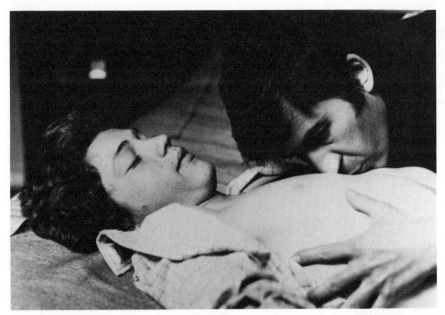

Congressman Roberto Orbea (Jose Sacristan) embraces his young lover Juanito in El Diputado (The Deputy) *(1978).* (Award Films)

WRONG

René Soutendijk and Jeroen Krabbe in The Fourth Man *(1983).* (International Spectrafilm Distribution, Inc.)

adolescent working for a group of fascists who have set a trap for the "faggot politico." Like Istvan Szabo's *Colonel Redl* (1985), it's a film about the lengths people will go to in order to disguise their true nature, using homosexuality as a fatal flaw. The Achilles' heel of the hero in this type of film is often homosexuality, which eventually betrays and destroys him. John Mackenzie's *The Long Good Friday* (1979) makes a lieutenant of an underworld kingpin homosexual simply so that he can be dramatically murdered while cruising a public bathhouse. His sexual desire leads him to his death.

The Fourth Man, taken from a novel by ostentatiously gay, right-wing Catholic Gerard Reve, is about a gay writer who gives a lecture in a coastal Dutch town, spends the night with a mysterious woman and stays to meet his doom simply because he cannot stay away from the woman's heterosexual lover with whom he is obsessed. It's a film about the consequence of obsessive sexual desire that paints women as predatory creatures and homosexual men as helpless victims of their own lust. Homosexuality itself, not the individual homosexual character, is seen in these films as obsessively sexual in nature.

Rarely in the last few years have lesbian or gay characters appeared naturally and incidentally in major motion pictures that were not "about" homosexuality. James Coco twice played gay men attached to strong female movie stars, as Marsha Mason's best friend in Glenn Jordan's adaptation of Neil Simon's *Only When I Laugh* (1981) and as Elizabeth Taylor's sidekick in the 1986 television movie version of James Kirkwood's *There Must Be a Pony.*

In both cases, the homosexuality of his characters is implicit and secondary to the main action. "In *Only When I Laugh,*" says Coco, "there was never a big deal made out of the fact that Jimmy Perino is gay. The only time it comes up is when Marsha Mason says to him, 'Why don't we get married?' and he says, 'Because I'm gay and you're an alcoholic and we'd have trouble getting our kids into a decent school.' I would never play a gay character who is an outrageous gay stereotype. We've had enough of that and I'm just not interested in doing it. Sometimes you'll hear people saying that to play a gay character is a career killer but it isn't true. I haven't stopped working. If it's honestly done and you can find the heart of the character, people will not only accept it, they'll respond to it."

In *There Must Be a Pony,* however, the single concrete reference to homosexuality was changed substantially by the producers from what it was in the novel in order to insert a judgment where none existed. In Kirkwood's novel the Elizabeth Taylor character, a woman with a young son, is casually comfortable with her friend's sexuality. In one scene, when he repeatedly calls her "sweetie," she cries, "Oh, stop with the sweetie, already. The next thing you know, Josh will be running around saying, 'Get you, Mary.' " In the television

James Coco as Jimmy Perino, the gay best friend of Marsha Mason in Only When I Laugh *(1981).*

film, Taylor instead worriedly asks Coco, "Do you think Josh is gay? Somehow, I'd feel guilty if he were."

It wasn't the first time a Kirkwood novel was altered out of nervousness about homosexual content. In 1982 Paramount filmed *Some Kind of Hero* with Richard Pryor, excising a key sequence in which he has a gay affair with his buddy during the war.

"I wrote the screenplay originally," says Kirkwood, "and that scene was in it. Originally the film was written to be Neil Diamond's first movie but that didn't work out. Diamond got cold feet about doing a movie at all at that point and backed out. When Pryor was eventually chosen the studio was adamant about removing the sequence in which he and his friend Vin fall into that sort of violent sexual relationship in jail during the bombing raid. I tried to fight for it but once you sell something to them you have no control. No matter what you say, they do what they want, which is why I have become so totally disenchanted with having anything to do with that medium."

Yet another Kirkwood project, Broadway's *A Chorus Line,* which he wrote with Nicholas Dante, turned up on screen minus most of the groundbreaking monologue that told of a gay dancer's relationship with his family. "When it was first presented to audiences on the stage," said director Sir Richard Attenborough to the *New York Times,* "it was shocking. But in 1985 to be shocking you would have to deal with AIDS."

Here it becomes clear that Attenborough thinks the entire gay monologue is intended to shock, instead of seeing the two gay characters in the line (played by Cameron English and Justin Ross) as just two people with a story to tell. The original intention was not to shock but, for a change, simply to include the gay component of Broadway theater. Actor Justin Ross who played Greg says that the producers were initially nervous about keeping his character gay at all, feeling that one gay in the film was enough. "They took me aside before my reading," said Ross, "and told me, 'By the way, he isn't gay anymore. So try to play him as straight as possible and not as a homosexual.' When I asked what that meant, they said I should think of Tyrone Power or some debonair movie star. I feel in general, they played down the sexuality of every character in that film because they were going for more of a family audience."

Author Kirkwood sees Attenborough's reactions to the gay characters as so much nonsense.

"We were talking about the reason a person's whole life has influenced their character and their background in *A Chorus Line*," says Kirkwood. "AIDS doesn't even enter into the context in which we brought up the sexuality of those people. It might have had some validity if the director had said to the dancer, 'How do you feel about your sex life in these days of the AIDS crisis?' but that was never a part of the concept. They sure fucked that one up."

Cameron English (second from right) as the gay dancer in A Chorus Line *(1985).*

With one exception, the few instances of incidental, seemingly unconscious homosexuality onscreen since 1981 have been minor sequences. In a nice touch, Steven Spielberg's *Raiders of the Lost Ark* (1981) contains a moment in the opening sequence in which a preppy-looking student in Harrison Ford's archeology lecture casually drops an apple on his desk on the way out of class. An almost imperceptible scene in Peter Weir's *The Year of Living Dangerously* (1983) reveals that Australian journalist Wally Sullivan, played by Noel Ferrier, is in love with a young Asian man. In Sidney Lumet's *Garbo Talks* (1984), Harvey Fierstein has a gentle scene as a gay man on Fire Island who tries to help locate Greta Garbo. Robert Joy has an effective scene as Dianne Wiest's gay suitor in Woody Allen's *Radio Days* (1987). When Joy bursts into tears for his departed lover upon hearing the song "I'm Getting Sentimental Over You," Wiest reacts first with disappointment and then tender understanding. "It's a beautiful song" she says, touching his hand. In Stanley Jaffe's *Without a Trace* (1983), Keith McDermott plays the boyish and sensitive housekeeper of a woman whose son has been kidnapped. As J. Hoberman pointed out in the *Village Voice*, this film is so worried about gay baiting that it takes an hour for a false clue to be followed and the gay character arrested, even though he is a natural suspect. James Bridges' *Mike's Murder*, made in 1982 but not released until 1984, features Paul Winfield as a sympathetic gay man who has a theory that the Moral Majority is funded by the Mafia so that they can keep certain activities sinful and clean up on illegal dealings.

In Martin Scorsese's *After Hours* (1985), the two leather guys kissing passionately in the background of a scene in a Soho bar are as incongruous as everything else encountered by Griffin Dunne in the film. He's fallen down a rabbit hole and nothing is treated as more unusual than anything else. Another sequence in the film illustrates how occasionally a potentially offensive character is altered by the intervention of an actor or a director during shooting. The sequence in *After Hours* in which Dunne picks up a gay man named Mark on the street was challenged by the actor playing the young gay, changing the scene considerably.

Robert Plunket, author of the novel *My Search for Warren Harding*, played Mark. "When the script first came to me," says Plunket, "the character of Mark was a man wearing leather and an earring, cruising the streets of Soho. This was supposed to be the first time he'd ever encountered another man. I thought that it was highly unrealistic that a guy dressed like that would be having his very first encounter with another guy. There was also some humorous dialogue which was inappropriate—a straight person's idea of the way gay people talk. I said all of this to Marty Scorsese and he was very open to

Noel Ferrier (center, with cigarette holder) as the gay Australian journalist in The Year of Living Dangerously *(1983).*

Harvey Fierstein (left) as Bernie in Garbo Talks *(1984).*

In the background: Joel Jason and Rand Carr as the two leather numbers in After Hours *(1985).*

simply letting me do what I wanted with Mark. It became a much simpler, truer scene." This verisimilitude was bolstered by the additional casting of gay playwright Victor Bumbalo as one of the gay tenants of the apartment building Dunne is accused of burgling. These scenes made *After Hours* the least homophobic of Scorsese's films.

A similar incident affected the way one of Goldie Hawn's roommates looked and behaved in *Protocol* (1984). Actor Grainger Hines, who played Jerry, says the director Herb Ross wanted the two guys to be unoffensive. "In fact," says the actor, "I wanted to do little corny things like put on an earring and Ross said, 'Absolutely not. I want you just the way you are,' so I didn't change my attitude or my personality at all." The difference when an actor is not instructed to "play gay" is that instead of a homosexual stereotype, what emerges is a person who happens to be gay.

The only major character in a mainstream film to achieve this level of casual realism in recent years was Cher's Dolly Pelliker in Mike Nichols' *Silkwood* (1983). Screenwriters Nora Ephron and Alice Arlen based Dolly Pelliker on Karen Silkwood's actual roommate Sherri Ellis, who has consistently evaded questions about her sexuality in the press ("I'm a virgin like everyone else in Oklahoma"). Dolly's lover Angela, played by Diana Scarwid, was entirely created by the scriptwriters. With its portrayal of Dolly Pelliker and her girlfriend Angela, *Silkwood* is the best example we have of a film that is not about lesbianism yet presents lesbian characters who are perfectly integrated into a story without condescension, explanation or self-consciousness of any kind. The two characters could just as easily have been heterosexual, except they're not.

This kind of choice, rarely made by filmmakers, was explained simply by director Nicholas Roeg, who created the character of David Bowie's incidentally gay lawyer for Buck Henry in *The Man Who Fell to Earth* (1976). When Henry asked, "Why is my character gay? Why am I playing a homosexual?" Roeg replied, "Why not? There are homosexuals."

Nora Ephron's attitude about creating Dolly Pelliker was equally unselfconscious. "We never asked ourselves, 'How do we write a lesbian?' " she says, "or 'How do we write Oklahoma people who work in a plutonium plant?' We believe that people are much more like each other than they are different from one another. My experience is that when factory workers are having coffee in the morning they talk about who was on Johnny Carson last night. That's a truth everyone can relate to; people are people."

Like the two lesbians in Robert Altman's *A Perfect Couple*, Dolly Pelliker is different but conceived as a family member, in direct contrast to the protrayal of most gays as alien to society and to the individuals around them. "The

A tender moment between Meryl Streep and Cher in Silkwood *(1983).*

secret of the film," says Ephron, "is that it's about a family. We saw it as being about Drew and Karen and Dolly and into their lives comes this issue about radioactivity. So we had this triangle in place in the house and Angela comes into the middle of everything. If Dolly fell in love with Angela, it didn't seem to us that it would be any different from what would happen when one person brings another person into the house and causes a series of constant irritations. Dramatically, it gave us something to play Karen's burgeoning political awareness off of so that the whole middle of the movie isn't spent with her running around saying, 'What about the radioactivity?' "

It is unfortunate that in Dolly Pelliker we have an ultimately sad individual who seems to fall hopelessly in love with women she can never have. Not only is Karen in love with a man but Angela eventually leaves Dolly to go back to her husband. The departure of Angela also serves the dramatic structure of the film; she is there only to bring tension to the midsection of the film and ultimately has to go. This paints Dolly as a loser who will probably never find happiness with another person. This wouldn't be an issue at all if there were a variety of lesbian characters on the screen. But we still don't have a lesbian couple who make it through to the last reel in a mainstream movie. Apart from Donna Deitch's *Desert Hearts,* an independent film, we also don't have a lesbian heroine. What if Karen Silkwood had been a lesbian?

About the real-life lesbian experiences of Karen Silkwood herself, ignored in the film, Ephron says, "Karen was very sexual and pretty much up for grabs. She certainly had a couple of experiences with women. The question was, did we want to do that in the film? I don't actually believe that this was a major issue with Karen. She was a heterosexual woman who'd had a few lesbian experiences. I believe this. The major issue in her life was that she had given up her children and found, in her crusade, a means of redemption. The real question is, if, hypothetically, Karen Silkwood had actually been a lesbian, would we have done that on film? I don't know. If she weren't only a slightly unbalanced woman who'd given up her children but a slightly unbalanced lesbian mother who'd given up her children, who knows how the audience might have reacted? Meryl Streep does have the ability to be what she has to be and not lose the affection of an audience so it's possible it might have worked."

Cher seems to have the same effect on audiences. Additionally, the private lives of women are not as suspect when they play lesbians as those of male stars are when they play gay men. There is seldom the degree of speculation about the lesbian sexuality of famous women that there is about male stars. The explicit sexuality of two men onscreen is also more offensive and upsetting to audiences than lesbian sexuality, which is why *Personal Best* contained confident erotic love scenes played in the nude while *Making Love* held its breath for a single kiss between Ontkean and Hamlin. The male counterpart of *Personal Best* would actually be a film version of Patricia Nell Warren's *The Front Runner,* about a coach who falls in love with a young Olympic runner. Although the book was on the bestseller lists of the *New York Times, Time* magazine and the *Los Angeles Times* for more than three months, none of those publications chose to review it. For ten years Paul Newman tried unsuccessfully to get a movie project off the ground. It was turned down by every studio because of the male love scenes. In 1987, plans were continuing to produce the film independently with Grant Show, star of ABC's *Ryan's Hope.* A feature story by Kim Garfield in the *Advocate* documented the consistent homophobia encountered by producer Jerry Wheeler in attempts to cast the role of the coach. "Suddenly, agents weren't returning our phone calls," said Wheeler. "We would get responses like, 'We don't want our client playing a fag.' " Women making love is a male fantasy; men making love is not—and men still run the industry.

There is no mainstream motion picture in which two men do anything more sexual than kiss each other, and even that simple act is still approached with trepidation by filmmakers and greeted with cries of outrage from audiences and critics alike. When John Schlesinger was about to shoot the kiss between Peter Finch and Murray Head in *Sunday, Bloody Sunday* the camerman turned to Schlesinger and said, "John, is this really necessary?" This nervous reaction is not confined to motion pictures. According to Richard Thomas, his kissing Jeff Daniels in the first act of Lanford Wilson's *Fifth of July* on Broadway drew such loud comment from audiences that several times during the run he was forced to bring down the curtain and begin the play again.

In Sidney Lumet's *Deathtrap,* neither Christopher Reeve nor Michael Caine plays his character stereotypically gay, partially because their sexual orientation is a key element in the surprise ending. Yet choosing to have their love affair revealed through a passionate kissing scene that was not in the original play must have been a calculated error. "The sight of Michael Caine kissing Christopher Reeve," wrote Peter Ackroyd in the *Spectator,* "is enough to make the most jaded of us sit upright in our seats."

The reaction of audiences was more violent. The same spectators who cheer the most disgusting forms of violence are horrified by a single kiss between two actors. "I heard that a preview audience in Denver booed the kiss," says Christopher Reeve, "and that was reported in *Time* magazine, thus ruining the plot for millions of people. We later referred to it as 'the ten million dollar kiss' as an estimate of lost ticket revenue." As for playing gay characters, Reeve simply says, "I think the problem is with other people. I've been used to straights playing gays and vice versa all my life so it seems pretty ordinary to me. People aren't freaked out by homosexual characters on the stage or the screen if they emerge as compelling, real people that the audience can identify with on other levels."

This is exactly the kind of character Hollywood refuses to present, preferring

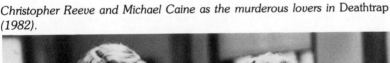

Christopher Reeve and Michael Caine as the murderous lovers in Deathtrap *(1982).*

instead to endlessly recreate the shocking and sensational one-dimensional stereotypes with which it has become comfortable. British actor Daniel Day Lewis, who played Johnny, the punk lover of a Pakistani laundry owner in Stephen Frears' *My Beautiful Laundrette* (1986), told the *Los Angeles Times,* "We all expect to play both straight and gay sooner or later—except when we work in Hollywood."

The presence of more than a few gay characters on American screens, even in a minimally positive context, continues to provoke a backlash. As soon as three or four films with gay themes open within months of one another, we are treated to critical and popular reaction that would lead people to believe that the gays are taking over. This absurd notion is fueled by the hysteria of the right-wing religious lobby. Gary Jarmin, a spokesperson for a group called the Christian Voice, for example, told a reporter for *20/20* in 1985, "There must be homosexuals within the industry who have made the decision to portray this subject more than ever before, otherwise why would it exist?"

If gays are, in fact, "taking over," then why are most films so viciously anti-gay? The tiny minority of closeted gay people within the entertainment industry are the least likely to push for more positive depictions of gays on the screen for fear of personal exposure. When the independently produced *Parting Glances* opened to rave reviews, made a lot of money and ended up on CBS Fox Video, director Bill Sherwood suddenly got a lot of calls from Hollywood. "I couldn't believe it," he says. "All these gay people at Twentieth Century-Fox and TriStar and Disney will quietly call me and say that they're fans of the film. They're the type of gays who have made themselves a part of the corporate structure. They're out there but they don't do a fucking thing." It is more often liberal straight producers like Daniel Melnick, responsible for getting *Making Love* off the ground, who can safely propose such films.

According to John Sayles, the reaction of potential investors to his proposed filming of *Lianna* was, "Oh, no! Not another one of those!" It was as if, says Sayles, "there were hundreds out there instead of only two or three out of thousands." It is clear that the smallest step toward positive depiction of lesbians and gay men on the screen is cause for alarm. "As soon as you have a little gay action on the screen," says *Parting Glances* director Bill Sherwood, "critics start reviewing heterosexual films by saying, 'Well, for *once* we have a heterosexual movie to see,' as though we haven't seen millions every year for a century. One little hiccough of positive gay films and they act like it's a deluge."

The gay menace is almost always defined as a threat to the sexual values of the majority. In a way, this is true. Integration of a variety of lesbian and gay characters into motion pictures should challenge the sexual values of society and change them. Such a situation would not "create" more gay people; it would simply allow that portion of the population that is gay to live more openly. Yet the alteration of the sexual values of the dominant culture is too often portrayed in a facile manner, pointing to a destructiveness of human values rather than to a positive integration of people who are different into a more casually tolerant society.

In Bertrand Blier's *Tenue de Soirée* (1986), released in the United States as *Ménage*, the dangers of men assuming the sexually passive role are vividly if moronically outlined. When Gérard Dépardieu has an affair with Michel Blanc, it turns them both into ostentatious transvestite whores. The fear of homosexuality is the fear of losing male power and becoming like women. In the case of *Ménage* there is no real statement made. One gets the idea that Blier, unsure of how to end his film, said, "Let's put Dépardieu in drag. That ought to be amusing." Yet the idea that sex between two men is dangerous remains.

Gender specificity has become an obsession. America has returned to the pioneering values of the real men who conquered the wilderness. *Crocodile Dundee*, with its rough Australian hero, brings us back to that frontier, replacing the American Western that has disappeared. When Paul Hogan grabs the crotch of a transvestite to reveal his actual gender comically, he's exercising his male power to expose a pathetic imitation of womanhood. In a later scene, he also grabs the crotch of a woman, making the point that it is also the male prerogative to inspect the meat. Homosexuality is seen as a threat to the supremacy of men over women and an abdication of the power conferred on men as a birthright.

David Rabe's play *Streamers*, which was adapted for the screen in 1983 by Robert Altman, takes place in an army barracks at the dawn of America's involvement in Vietnam. The play explores the psychological damage done to American men by their obsession with masculinity and their collective fear of death, madness and homosexuality. Unfortunately, Altman directs Mitchell Lichtenstein to play the homosexual character as such a flaming, sophisticated queen that the question of whether or not he is really homosexual, essential to the drama, doesn't exist. The root of heterosexual fear of male homosexuality is in the fact that anyone might be gay. Straight men aren't theatened by a flamboyant faggot because they know they aren't like that; they're threatened by a guy who's just like they are who turns out to be queer.

Probably the only subversive presence in the American media currently challenging assumptions about gender specificity is Pee Wee Herman. It is precisely because Herman is so outrageous that he is so subversive. A children's comic whose material is based on the revenge humor of a sissy wounded by bullies all his life, Herman is such a kid himself that at first you don't notice he's performing in a full face of makeup with bright red lipstick. His first feature-length film, *Pee Wee's Big Adventure* (1985), considerably tones down the sexual innuendo so blatant in his first appearances in nightclubs and, especially, his HBO special, "The Pee Wee Herman Show." On the latter there was direct sexual dialogue between Pee Wee and a handsome blond mailman with sexy legs and a leering gay attitude.

On his Saturday morning children's show, Herman often does quite dangerous gay-related material. Recently, he and another male character were married and even had a kissing scene. "Pee Wee is anti-Rambo," said Barry Walters in the *Village Voice*. "He argues against compulsory polarization of the sexes by summoning up a child's androgyny. Being just a kid allows Pee Wee and his pals to play with gender codes unnoticed, and therefore all the more subversively."

If Pee Wee Herman were a typically masculine-looking comic using the same material, it would provoke outrage. Milton Berle always wore a dress when doing gay humor. Pee Wee is safe because he too performs in the guise of a creature people don't recognize as serious. Paul Reubens, who plays Pee Wee, is almost never interviewed outside his Pee Wee persona. The most he would say to an interviewer on the subject was, "I just want kids to know that it's okay to be different."

For most of society it is definitely not okay to be different. Difference is, in fact, the enemy. In a *New York Times* piece on Richard Green's book *The "Sissy Boy Syndrome" and the Development of Homosexuality*, writer Jane Brody clearly identifies homosexuality as the enemy. She seizes the publication of Green's study as an opportunity to revive debate about how parents can prevent their children from becoming homosexual. The bottom line in such discussions is always the need to discover a "cause" of homosexuality. Nobody is interested in the "cause" of heterosexuality because nobody is interested in stopping it. So, instead of teaching bullies to tolerate difference in young boys, a study of effeminacy in young males is used as an opportunity to teach such children how to modify their behavior to avoid ridicule. As Dr. Lawrence Mass has pointed out, this is akin to telling blacks that since we live in a racist society, they should straighten their hair to avoid offending bigots. Meanwhile, nowhere is society's real problem—its overwhelming discomfort with anything different—addressed.

The gay menace has probably never been identified so insultingly as when

Pauline Kael attacked George Cukor's *Rich and Famous* (1981) for having a covert gay sensibility. After describing Candice Bergen's character as a "big, goosey transvestite" (gays can't create real women), she moves on to the serious issue of gay versus straight sexuality but doesn't explore it seriously, preferring instead to take a cheap shot at George Cukor.

Rich and Famous was perhaps one of the first American films to treat males as sex objects without derision. Jacqueline Bisset's affairs with young men are shot from a point of view usually reserved for a heterosexual male vision of sex between men and women. After attacking a shot in which we see Matt Lattanzi's rear end encased in a pair of tight blue jeans, Kael characterizes the kind of casual sex Bisset has with various men in the film as homosexual in nature—"not something a woman would get into." George Cukor's homosexuality—which she couldn't overtly discuss while the director was still alive because it's such a disgusting thing to say about someone in print that you can be sued for it—is what Kael was really after. Her perceptions are correct. Jacqueline Bisset's sexuality in the film was gay insofar as it does not respect heterosexual hegemony. Cukor was portraying a kind of sexuality that people perceive as homosexual but that, in fact, doesn't belong to straights or gays. It's simply liberated from sexual orientation.

Kael subscribes implicitly to the notion that the straight world needs to be taken into account when an artist creates an idea. This is what the closet is all about—translating one's natural impulses into a heterosexual language. It appears that Kael is as much in favor of gays staying in the closet now as she was when she attacked *Victim* in 1961 for daring to treat homosexuals "with sympathy and respect—like Negroes and Jews."

The issues she raises are important ones. They are the issues of a gay artist tied to a straight sensibility and they were touched upon lightly by critic Myron Meisel in the *L.A. Reader*. "Perhaps the most fundamental element of Cukor's involvement in the film's ideas," he wrote of *Rich and Famous*, "relate to his homosexuality and unfortunately I must hesitate to make critical pronouncements in any detail on this important aspect of the film's viewpoint—suffice it to say that the film deals poignantly with the emotions associated with transient relationships, the role of friendships instead of family, sexual adventure, the privacy of intimate feelings and even the allure of young sex objects."

Although it is unclear why Meisel felt it impossible to explore such subjects further, he does identify the terrain of the gay world that may have been familiar to a man of Cukor's age and background. He at least attempted to point out an alternate sensibility at work in the film. Instead of exploring that sensibility, Pauline Kael simply calls George Cukor a faggot. It's as if the movies were a war between straights and gays and Kael had spotted the enemy hidden in a bush.

In 1981, *Christopher Street* magazine lampooned this mentality in a cartoon showing a brick wall on which is scrawled the graffiti LA CAGE AUX FOLLES II— HETEROSEXUALITY 0. Making a contest of gay versus straight perpetuates the folly that someone must lose if we permit a minority to openly exist. Whenever the idea surfaces, however briefly, that gay people may be acceptable, the battle lines are immediately drawn. The battle is real. If gays are given a measure of acceptance, heterosexuality does have to move over to make room for the truth. This is why each time gays make strides in social or civil rights, an opposing viewpoint is presented to keep their existence controversial. It is the same as if every time a Jew appeared on television, a Nazi guest were invited to create "balance." To be sure, there are anti-Semites available for such appearances, but they aren't asked because no sensible person in the media seriously questions the rights of Jews to exist.

The *New York Times* regularly publishes virulently homophobic op-ed columns. In one such column published on February 3, 1986, entitled "Defeat the Gay Rights Bill," Rabbi Yehuda Levin wrote, "Homosexuality, a moral wrong, cannot be the basis of a civil right. Society doesn't make allowances for alcoholics, murderers, or rapists even if they are biologically predisposed to do what they do. Why should we have lower standards for homosexuals?" The key phrase in this quote is clearly "to do what they do," pointing up that Levin and those who agree with him see homosexuality as something one "does" rather than as something one simply is—like Jewish, for instance.

In an op-ed piece published on March 18, 1986, entitled "Identify All the Carriers," William F. Buckley, ignoring the unfortunate analogy to Hitler's solution to the "Jewish problem," called for the tattooing of AIDS carriers. "Everyone detected with AIDS," wrote Buckley, "should be tattooed in the upper forearm to protect common needle users and on the buttocks to prevent the victimization of other homosexuals."

When asked by *Advocate* reporter George DeStefano why the *Times* would publish such commentaries, the response was that the op-ed page is a "platform for all views, even extreme and unpopular ones." Yet the *New York Times* does not publish anti-Semitic commentary or blatant appeals to racism. The very existence of gays, DeStefano points out, is open to debate in the *New York Times*.

A further example of this double standard is illustrated in the case of the firing of Al Campanis, vice-president of the Los Angeles Dodgers. Campanis appeared on Ted Koppel's *Nightline* on April 6, 1987, and let loose with what

New York Native reporter Ed Sikov termed "a wild string of racist statements about black people's stupidity." Responding to Koppel's question about the lack of black executives in baseball, Campanis announced that blacks didn't "have the necessities" to do the job. The following day, Campanis was fired by the Los Angeles Dodgers for his racist remarks. Campanis should have been fired. Yet editorial reporters like CBS' Andy Rooney regularly make sweeping homophobic statements with impunity. Racism is simply not tolerated. Expressions of homophobia, however, are routinely encouraged as "opinion" on an issue which remains controversial.

The closet mentality is largely responsible for relegating the simple fact of one's gayness to the realm of gossip and innuendo and encouraging the kinds of attacks quoted above. Not only is it impossible to openly discuss in print, with any specificity, the lives and experiences of gay actors, directors and screenwriters now working in Hollywood, but it is also impossible to have a conversation with such people about their sexuality. Fear of exposure is paralyzing. Scant historical evidence gives every indication that closeted gays have few heterosexual friends who support them on a political level. Indeed, most are unaware there is a political aspect to being gay.

A documentary film on the life of actor Montgomery Clift, made by the Italian television network RAI, is available on videotape. *The Rebels: Montgomery Clift* paints a portrait of the actor as tormented not only by his homosexuality but also by the fact that the people he loved most viewed his gayness as an aberration. The sheer stupidity of Clift's friends, as evidenced in on-camera interviews, is astonishing. Actor Kevin McCarthy blames Clift's psychiatrist for his homosexuality, saying that "Monty's latent homosexuality" was "allowed" to appear by a psychiatrist who was gay himself and therefore unable to help the actor. This assumes that Clift's problems stemmed from his homosexuality and that his homosexual behavior was self-destructive in and of itself and not because of society's disapproval. The suggestion that his psychiatrist was somehow unable to counsel him because he himself was homosexual would suggest also that heterosexual psychiatrists are not equipped to help men and women with marital problems. When Clift "behaved," everyone loved him. When he was "bad" and began being with men openly, his friends simply stopped seeing him.

That this reaction is not unusual is clear in Boze Hadleigh's book *Conversations with My Elders,* in which the author publishes six interviews with famous gay men who are now deceased, including Rock Hudson, Sal Mineo and George Cukor. The general consensus is that it is simply not possible to be openly gay in Hollywood and that a celebrity's closest friends will tolerate homosexuality only if the star is discreet. This is analogous to the situation of Jews in Hollywood in the 1940s. In *City of Nets*, Otto Friedrich writes, "In Hollywood, [Jewish] stars assumed neutral names like Fairbanks or Howard or Shaw; actresses underwent plastic surgery; some made a point of going to Christian churches or donating money to Christian charities. This was not so much a denial of Jewishness—although it was that—as an effort to make Jewishness appear insignificant, too unimportant to be criticized, or even noticed." If you substitute the word *gay* for *Jewish* and *straight* for *Christian* in that passage, you have the plight of gays today in Hollywood. The phrase "My private life is nobody's business," often used in answer to pointed questions about a celebrated person's sexuality, is another way of saying, "Don't call attention to this—it will cause trouble."

It does cause trouble. When *Making Love, Personal Best* and *Victor/Victoria* opened, television news shows like *20/20* and the CBS Nightly News presented major segments on the "meaning" of the new wave of gay films sweeping the country. The producers of *20/20* tried in vain to nail producer Daniel Melnick as a homosexual in order to characterize films like *Making Love* as gay propaganda. Darkly pointing out that most of the films were rated PG or R, a somber Hugh Downs noted that this was "not a lot of protection" for young people against such films. Richard Schickel, in *Time* magazine, termed homosexuality a "choice" that people make and announced that movies, like the rest of society, were just beginning to move beyond the notion that homosexuality is an illness. "Some people will never make that leap," he added. "Or abandon their understandable concern that gay love affairs depicted by role model movie stars may have a baneful influence on the impressionable young." This is like saying that seeing Paul Newman on the screen may influence young people to have blue eyes. When the concerned mother of one young man up for a role in Arthur J. Bressan's *Abuse* asked the director if playing the part would make her son gay, he replied, "No, and if he plays Hamlet he won't inherit Denmark, either."

Resistance to the legitimization of gays in society comes not only from conservatives. There was outrage as well when Alan Johnson remade Ernst Lubitsch's 1942 classic comedy *To Be or Not To Be* in 1983, starring Mel Brooks and Anne Bancroft as Polish actors during the Nazi occupation. Added to the new version was a gay character named Sasha (James Haake) who wore a pink triangle in the film, the symbol homosexuals were forced to wear by the Nazis during the Holocaust. Sasha was not only treated sympathetically but was made one of the heroes of the film, resourcefully saving a group of Jews in the end.

There were angry protests made against the character of Sasha by individuals and groups who bitterly resented the equation of Jews and homosexuals as equal victims of the Nazi purges. It was as though this equation somehow minimized the suffering of the Jews and worse, as though filmic references to the Holocaust were some sort of contest to determine who suffered most.

François Truffaut, who created lesbian and gay characters in a similar context in his film *The Last Metro* (1980), responded to the same kind of criticism by saying, "My film is not concerned merely with anti-Semitism but intolerance in general. I observed that the collaborationist extreme right-wing press in France condemned Jews and homosexuals in the same breath." The objections were not confined to the portrayal of gays in a historical context, which people often question. The underlying objection is to the legitimization of gays as an officially recognized minority group.

This situation is exacerbated by the fact that gays, as a group, have no natural allies. Gays are still a very low priority on the left's agenda. The problems of homosexuals aren't quite legitimate to people interested in the oppression of most other groups. One senses that the intellectual left simply wishes all those gays would just "stop that" and go away. In 1977, during the Anita Bryant campaign against homosexuals, writer Jeff Greenfield wrote in the *Village Voice* that homosexual activists who wanted the right to be openly gay were taking the left away from "the business of social justice." This attitude was illustrated dramatically by renowned cinematographer Nestor Almendros when he and Orlando Jimenez-Leal co-directed a documentary called *Improper Conduct* in 1984.

Improper Conduct is composed of interviews with Cuban refugees, from eminent writers to female impersonators, and footage shot by French television channel Antenne 2. It exposes the rounding up, in the 1960s, of an entire class of harmless people by the Castro government. Homosexuals, dissidents and Jehovah's Witnesses were swept into camps called UMAPs—Military Units to Aid Production. Though pro-Castro forces point out that such camps no longer exist, there is little evidence that attitudes toward gays in Cuba have changed significantly in the last twenty years. Homosexuality is still officially classed, with drug addiction and prostitution, as reformable vices, products of "a decadent capitalist society." The film is a political act directed principally at the leftist intelligentsia of Paris, London, Rome and Berlin.

"The film was greeted on the Left," said David Denby in *New York* magazine, "with the peculiar charge that Almendros and Leal are 'using' the issue of anti-homosexuality to discredit Castro in general. Well, of course that's what they're doing and the charge has weight only if you think institutionalized gay bashing is a trifle."

Improper Conduct enraged pro-Castro gays as well as heterosexual leftists.

"Never underestimate those Anglo Fidelistas whose dreams die hard," wrote Stephen Harvey in *Inquiry*. "Cultural reporters in the *Nation* and the *Village Voice* who are against anti-fag beastliness in principle but embrace Latin Marxism in practice really had to twist themselves into a pretzel over this one." The irony, of course, is that the film was most loudly applauded as an attack on Castro and communism by the very right-wing Reaganites who also despise homosexuals.

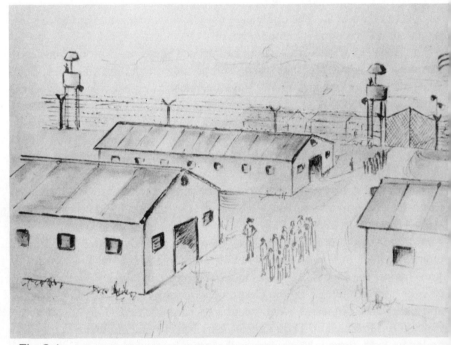

The Cuban concentration camps, subject of Improper Conduct *(1984), as remembered by painter Jaime Bellechasse.*

The truth is that gays are the football and nobody fights their battles willingly. Homosexuality continues to be seen as self-indulgent chosen behavior. Rarely are gays seen in life or onscreen as people born different. Refreshingly, the choice—not to be gay, but to be open about one's homosexuality—is drawn as a political act in Marek Kanievska's *Another Country* (1984), a film that also makes clear that there is a difference between seeing homosexuality as solely sexual and recognizing it as a natural state of being.

Based on the public school life of British spy Guy Burgess, *Another Country* displays a rare grasp of the issues surrounding the politics of homosexuality insofar as it champions the view that gayness is not something one chooses but something people simply discover in themselves at a certain point in their lives. The film also contains what is probably the single most romantic scene between two men ever put on the screen, the dinner sequence when Guy Bennett (Rupert Everett) and Harcourt (Cary Elwes) fall in love.

Rupert Everett and Colin Firth in Another Country *(1984).*

"I was desperate to avoid cliché gay images," says Kanievska. "The things I've felt for women in my life are similar to what my gay friends experience. The bond is the same. It's just a different way of expressing it physically."

The physical expression between Bennett and Harcourt is in fact almost nonexistent, consisting of a few brief caresses. "I wanted to emphasize the romance between Guy and Harcourt," said Kanievska to Stephen Harvey in the *Village Voice.* "The sight of two men kissing might have alienated the audience. I thought that by stressing the longing between them it would be much more poignant."

In a culminating political scene, the film achieves poignancy of another kind. Homosexuality is accepted in the British public school system with the understanding that it is transient and not discussed. Guy Bennett, however, makes the error of falling seriously in love with another boy and is made to pay the price. He tells his roommate Tommy Judd (Colin Firth), a committed Marxist, that he knows he "will never love a woman."

"That's ridiculous," replies Judd. "How could you possibly know something like that about yourself?"

"You didn't become a communist because you read Karl Marx," says Bennett evenly. "You read Karl Marx because you know you are a communist."

The real Guy Burgess was less serious-minded about gay politics than he was about his Marxism. In 1950 he was posted as Second Secretary of the British Embassy in Washington, D.C. On his first day, a superior warned him, "Guy, there are three basic 'don'ts' to bear in mind when you're dealing with Americans. The first is communism, the second is homosexuality and the third is the color bar."

"What you're trying to say in your nice long-winded way," replied Burgess, "is 'For God's sake, Guy, don't make a pass at Paul Robeson.' "

This is the Guy Burgess brilliantly captured in John Schlesinger's *An Englishman Abroad,* written for British television by Alan Bennett in 1984. Based on an actual encounter between Burgess and actress Coral Browne in Moscow in 1953, Schlesinger's telefilm is a model of sophistication and wit. Aside from being the best hour of television seen in a decade, *An Englishman Abroad* is an excellent example of how the sexuality of a celebrated figure is second nature to the project instead of the problem.

It is precisely this casual, seemingly unconscious integration of a character's gayness into a wider focus that is at the heart of gay films, whether they are made by gays or not. Recent gay independent films have differed from their predecessors in the sense that they are less likely to be pugnacious about issues or strictly didactic in tone. The fact that they are movies about self-defined gays often confuses people into thinking that they are films by gays about homosexuality. This confusion will end when gayness is no longer a controversial topic. As Quentin Crisp has said, "Homosexuality won't be accepted until it is completely seen as boring—a mundane, inconsequential part of everyday life." If Nagisa Oshima's extraordinary sexual odyssey *In the Realm of the Senses* is not about heterosexuality, then Donna Deitch's *Desert Hearts* is sure as hell not about lesbianism.

We take heterosexuality for granted. Lesbianism and gay male sexuality still give people a start. They become themes by their very presence. This will change with time. Films that are specifically gay in context are as valid and important as the unself-conscious appearance of gays in films in which the milieu is the dominant culture. Gay people have traditionally lived in both worlds, interacting with straight society as well as moving in a world filled with private signs and meanings that is exotic to straight society. We are now seeing gay films of both kinds that refuse to be defined by straight expectations.

There is a tendency on the part of politically committed lesbians and gay men to make allowances for the aesthetic shortcomings of films that offer a more accurate picture of gay life than has been previously seen. This is the temporary cultural reaction of people grateful for a refreshing change in the way their lives are reflected on the screen. This will also moderate with time. As critic Andrew Britton has pointed out, just because gays make films about gays does not mean that those films are going to be more radical or more advanced than any other. It certainly doesn't mean that they're going to be good films. The debate between politics and aesthetics will continue but in the end what most gay people want is interesting, challenging film experiences that do not make them feel insulted or invisible.

When *Desert Hearts, Parting Glances, My Beautiful Laundrette* and *Dona Herlinda and Her Son* opened in 1986, *Variety* announced, GAY-THEMED FEATURES HOT B.O. (BOX OFFICE) STUFF. MAINSTREAM AUDS MORE ACCEPTING. The story, by Richard Gold, said that the relative success of "gay-themed pix . . . demonstrates the ability of indie filmmakers and distributors to decisively address cinematic subject matter that's avoided or handled cautiously by the Hollywood majors." Independent features are beginning to routinely reflect what it traditionally takes Hollywood a decade to see, the writing on society's wall. There's an adult market for well-made films that aren't "safe."

Stephen Frears' *My Beautiful Laundrette* is a rich experience that explores illicit relationships of several kinds. Written by Anglo-Pakistani playwright Hanif Kureishi, it is set in London's Pakistani community and is about racism, assimilation and the rock Asians carry in Britain today. Johnny, an unem-

Daniel Day Lewis and Gordon Warnecke in My Beautiful Laundrette *(1986).*

ployed blond punker with a National Front past (Daniel Day Lewis) and Omar, (Gordon Warnecke), the son of an impoverished Pakistani writer, simply fall in love. Under the auspices of Omar's gaudy entrepreneur uncle, the two open a laundromat called Powders. A single scene in which Omar and Johnny make love behind a one-way mirror while Omar's uncle waltzes with his English mistress before the large picture windows of the laundrette is all the contrast needed to draw the proper degree of distance between two forms of socially illicit love.

"If you say to someone, 'Will you give me the money to make a film about a gay Pakistani laundry owner?' " says Stephen Frears, "they're going to look at you as if you're an idiot. I thought it had zero commercial potential so we made it in 16 millimeter for television." That *Laundrette* was commissioned by British television tells us all we need to know about American television.

The director defends the implicit gayness and explicit romance in the film as consistent with the ideas of a radical film. "I don't feel messianic or revolutionary," says Frears, "I just do it the way it seems right. This business of politics is confusing. I remember we ran *My Beautiful Laundrette* in Brixton and there was a lovely black gay man who came up to me and thanked me for showing gay people in a perfectly natural way and not as psychopaths or murderers. I told him that my next project was *Prick Up Your Ears,* the life story of Joe Orton in which Orton's lover Kenneth Halliwell murders him with a hammer. I asked him if he thought I should leave out the murder. He laughed and said, 'Oh, no, no, no. You must show life as it is. What we want is simply some balance.' England, like America, is filled with very nice private people and very unattractive public people who are beneath contempt. So every once in a while you make a film which celebrates private values and people come out to see it."

When writer Marcia Pally questioned playwright Kureishi in *Film Comment* about his impulse to put homosexual relations into a story already filled with controversial issues, he replied by defending the inclusion of the love affiar as natural. "When I started to write *Laundrette,"* he says, "Omar and Johnny weren't gay. But when I got all my characters together I had to decide who would drive the film and it was the boys. Now generally, the dynamics of a film is romance and *Laundrette* didn't have one. I could've made a buddy film like *Butch Cassidy.* I'm sure that Paul Newman and Robert Redford wanted to kiss. *Laundrette* is like *Cassidy,* only with kissing."

As Richard Goldstein has pointed out in the *Village Voice,* Frears' film is English before it's gay; it presents civility and charm as a resolution to conflict. Americans, on the other hand, wear their sexuality like a bloodstained banner. Bill Sherwood's remarkable first feature, *Parting Glances,* is particularly American. In fact, it's so specifically New York that it's a regional experience, not unlike the films of Woody Allen.

Set in contemporary gay Manhattan, *Parting Glances,* like Martin Scorsese's *After Hours,* takes place in a twenty-four-hour period during which nothing happens and everything happens, simply ending as abruptly as it begins. The gayness of the milieu is instantly taken for granted. Lovers for six years, Michael (Richard Ganoung) and Robert (John Bolger) move in the most realistic re-creation of the world in which New York gays actually live that has ever been put on the screen.

Robert works for a health organization and his imminent departure for Africa is more than a job transfer. His relationship is growing stale and Michael's ex-lover Nick (Steve Buscemi) has AIDS. Robert is fleeing a mess he doesn't want to handle. Stand-up comic Steve Buscemi's extraordinary performance as Nick illuminates that brief post–gay liberation nirvana when freedom was seized on the streets of Manhattan and in the dance palaces of Fire Island.

Through him, Michael is seeing a part of himself dying. Nick is the love of his life. In the center of the film is a long, brilliantly edited party sequence during which Nick and a young gay man offer each other visions of a gay past and a gay future neither will ever know.

The genius of *Parting Glances* is that none of it is about being gay or even about how gay people live. The film revealed that movies can explore gay life without being about gay life. It's a film about how people get along; in this case, most of them happen to be gays. Not one issue in the film is endemic to gay life, including Nick's AIDS diagnosis. The disease isn't milked for melodrama. It's there the way it is in New York City today; as a complex fact, dealt with differently by everyone. *Parting Glances* exposes audiences to a gripping array of feelings. Gays tend to forget that it's news to most Americans that gays have straight friends. *Parting Glances* doesn't show how gays react to AIDS; it shows how Nick's friends react.

Parting Glances was hailed in the mainstream press as the most promising feature film debut by a young American writer-director in several years. Critics compared Sherwood to Terence Malick, Steven Spielberg and Woody Allen. The Atlanta *Constitution* called it "virtually flawless" and the Cincinnati *Enquirer* said, "The day may come when movies like this one are part of the mainstream of American film—a time when people are regarded as people, no matter what their sexual preference."

Richard Ganoung as Michael embraces his ex-lover Nick, played by Steve Buscemi, in Parting Glances *(1986).*

When *American Film* magazine conducted a critics' forum on the new wave of so-called gay films from Hollywood in 1982, writer Doug Edwards said, "There are gay people in film schools who might have continued to make neutral films in the past but because of ten years or more of gay liberation they are perfectly willing now to make films that deal directly with their own experiences, desires and concerns." He might have been describing *Parting Glances* director Bill Sherwood, a onetime film student at Hunter College.

"I moved to New York when I was eighteen," says Sherwood, "and it was just six months after the Stonewall riots. Everywhere you turned it was gay rights. It was a great atmosphere and you felt sorry for anyone who'd grown up in the Forties and Fifties because they'd had such a dismal time. But you knew this wasn't going to be the case for you. I remember going to see *The Boys in the Band* and it was like watching people from Venus. I had no connection to it. I appreciated the wit but in terms of people getting drunk and bursting into tears because life was so hard, I thought, 'What? What life is hard?' I couldn't see the problem. The way I work as a filmmaker is that the gayness is assumed. Instead of starting out with some passionate cause or wanting to make a noble gay film, I just wanted to make a film. Period. I think it's just that I'm among the first people to emerge from that generation who turned out to be filmmakers."

Some heterosexual critics as well as straight-identified gays made a great show of preferring a film like *My Beautiful Laundrette* to *Parting Glances* simply because of the implicit gayness of Sherwood's milieu. They may say that they think *My Beautiful Laundrette* is a better film but there's an element of homophobia in the objections we hear. *New York* magazine's David Denby compared Donna Dietsch's *Desert Hearts* unfavorably to *My Beautiful Laundrette* because he felt that *Desert Hearts* was about "nothing but" lesbianism. This kind of criticism finds its way into the consciousness of filmmakers and alters future projects. Jill Godmilow's *Waiting for the Moon* (1987) is a fiction feature about Gertude Stein and Alice B. Toklas. It is a beautiful, literate and civilized film but strangely without emotional intimacy. This is largely because Godmilow made no secret of the fact that she wanted to avoid making a "lesbian film." If you don't want to make a lesbian film then don't make a film about two lesbians. Yet critics will appreciate this distancing on Godmilow's part because it makes them more comfortable with the material. One gets the feeling that Denby is saying *My Beautiful Laundrette* is a better film because the gayness recedes into its proper place.

"The most interesting thing you discover when the reviews come out," says Bill Sherwood, "is that your film becomes a litmus test for what various critics think about homosexuality. Critics who were not sympathetic to *Parting Glances* would cite *My Beautiful Laundrette,* saying that it wasn't a film completely about gay people but also about issues which they consider more real or more urgent or even more worthy. You get the opinion that it isn't entirely appropriate to have a film which is centered around gays. Spike Lee's *She's Gotta Have It,* which I like very much, is wholly supported by the *New York Times* and other papers, in part because black issues aren't something they would dare question or belittle. They also feel more comfortable with it. The *New York Times* discusses gays as if they were alien creatures. They'll say, 'We have been informed by various experts that it can be inferred that people of this type frequent certain establishments.' Are they kidding? All they have to do is ask someone in the office who's gay."

The insultingly homophobic debates created by book reviewers whenever gay novelists write from a gay perspective illustrate this regularly. A truly great writer like David Leavitt poses a serious problem for homophobes when he publishes a book like *Family Dancing* or *The Lost Language of Cranes,* in which homosexuality is a minor but strong theme. We are then treated to a discussion of whether or not such literature is "limited" in nature.

Reviewing *The Lost Language of Cranes* favorably in the *New York Times,* Christopher Lehmann-Haupt wrote, "Can we begin to discern a resolution to the old debate over whether or not homosexual art is inherently limited? Despite all its virtues, Mr. Leavitt's novel contains too many technical flaws to allow even a speculative answer. Its narrative voice is too unstable; it pretends to show everybody's point of view, but it is subtly biased in favor of Philip's outlook." Are other books "limited" because they are subtly biased in favor of their hero? We have black and Jewish writers who freely draw universal conclusions from their own particular experiences. Yet when gay people do the same it touches off a reaction that is fundamentally homophobic and intellectually facile.

Creating gays in a natural context does not and should not produce a fantasy world in which there is no oppression. Stuart Byron pointed out in *American Film* that when *The Boys in the Band* opened, some gays attacked the film as unrealistic. "I couldn't believe it," said Byron. "I finally said, 'If homosexuals weren't like that in the Sixties then why do we need gay liberation?' Nobody could answer me."

The portrayal of gay oppression onscreen should not be greeted as though it were a figment of someone's imagination. People are nasty to gays all the time, so why complain when that's shown onscreen? The problem is that historically mainstream films that have portrayed the oppression of gays have implicitly approved of such conditions, giving us oppressed characters without a cultural context. They have also failed to reflect any changes in the last two decades. Of course there are people who hate homosexuals and of course there are gays who hate themselves. There are also textured reasons for homophobia and reactions to it that go unnoticed in most films.

A concrete depiction of the daily oppression faced by gays and two casual responses to it, reflecting a transitional time, are shown in the cab ride in *Parting Glances*. Michael almost slugs a cab driver who calls him and his boyfriend "faggots." The scene is made truer because Robert abhors Michael's militant reaction and is embarrassed by it. The changes taking place in gay society are the subtext of this scene and it serves a higher purpose than a scene in a film where a cab driver takes a look at a flamboyant queen walking a poodle and yells "faggot" out the window.

What's different now is evident in a film like *Dona Herlinda and Her Son* (1986), in which Mexican director Jaime Humberto Hermosillo shows us a variety of institutionalized cultural oppressions linked to Latin American machismo and sexism. Instead of being pathetic, self-oppressed victims, the gay characters in *Dona Herlinda* are seen reacting to a concrete environment. Underneath the deliciously funny offbeat comedy of the film is a sense of sweet subversion mixed with a sly attack on machismo as well as social and religious conventions.

Mama knows best: one big happy family in Dona Herlinda and Her Son *(1986).*

Dona Herlinda (Guadalupe Del Torro) is an upper middle class Guadalajara widow whose handsome but decidedly dreary doctor son Rudolfo (Marco A Trevino) has an equally handsome young boyfriend named Ramon (Gustavo Meza). Mama is smart enough to see that if she breaks them up her son will hate her, so she engineers a plot that will make everyone happy. She marries off Rudolfo to a young woman, builds a big new house and invites Ramon to come live with them, creating one big happy family.

Dona Herlinda is a film about compromise and the subversion of machismo. Rudolfo is culturally and sexually a traditional Mexican male who expects his mother to do the cooking and both his wife and his lover to remain feminine. The twist is that his wife has plans to leave their new baby with Mama and spend a year getting involved in politics. Ramon, meanwhile, gives Mama's boy a jar of lubricant for his birthday, in a scene completely missed by most audiences. Rudolfo is about to become the smiling wife he always wanted. The oppression here is clear but it's subverted with crackpot humor instead of served by dreary polemics.

Hermosillo is out to challenge his audience in a way filmmakers have rarely attempted in Mexico. "A previous film I did, *Deceitful Appearances,*" says the director, "was a very shocking piece about a hermaphrodite who marries another man and takes the masculine role. It upset audiences but at the same time it was easy for them to rationalize it because they saw it as extraordinary —something which could never happen in their lives. With *Dona Herlinda* the audience is not safe from believing that this could actually happen to them. The only homosexuals portrayed on Mexican screens are flamboyant effeminate characters from whom the audience can be distanced because such portrayals cater to their prejudices. In my film it's just two handsome men who love each other. This doesn't happen in Mexican films. One of the actors I hired told me he couldn't do the role because his father hates homosexuals. 'He would understand if I were drunk and fucked with a boy,' he told me, 'but to be tender with another man . . . impossible.' "

Prejudice and oppression exist implicitly in *Dona Herlinda*. It is Mama, stretching the bounds of social convention to make room for her own happiness, who alters the terrain with money and sophistication. The subtext of the film is a bitter commentary on class and power. What about gay men in Mexico who don't have clever, wealthy, controlling mamas?

Oppression is also implicit in Donna Deitch's *Desert Hearts* (1986). Based loosely on Jane Rule's novel, Deitch's film is the story of a repressed schoolteacher named Vivian Bell (Helen Shaver) who falls in love with a free-spirited younger woman named Cay Rivvers (Patricia Charbonneau) while waiting for

Helen Shaver and Patricia Charbonneau in Desert Hearts *(1986).*

a divorce in Reno. *Desert Hearts* is a love story that recreates with perceptiveness and tenderness what it might have been like for two women of different generations and backgrounds to fall in love in the Fifties.

In November of 1985, Deitch told *Ms.* magazine that her intention was to make a traditional romantic fantasy. "At the time I bought the rights to the book," said Deitch, "there hadn't been a film about a relationship between two women that hadn't ended in suicide like *The Children's Hour* or in a bisexual triangle. I wanted to make just a love story, like any other love story between a man and a woman, handled in a frank and real way."

Deitch is a talented director, able to evoke the 1950s many of us remember while focusing on the conflicts that arise around the two women. Deitch's refusal to feature the straight world's reaction to lesbianism as the focus of her film made all the difference in the way the relationship between the women was perceived by audiences. "It was interesting," says Helen Shaver. "The fact that they were two women was totally important but at a certain point in the film it became truly unimportant. The story and the characters were seductive enough emotionally that they could keep the audience open to the relationship way past the point where the women became lovers. It cut through all the emotional bullshit so that the fact that they were both women didn't matter to the audience in the end."

It mattered to some critics. In the *New York Times,* Vincent Canby complained that we are not given enough information about the quality of Vivian's broken marriage, asking if perhaps her lesbianism was a hysterical reaction to her divorce. This is the point at which many heterosexual critics disqualify themselves from perceptively reviewing gay films. Richard Goldstein pointed this out succinctly in the *Village Voice*. "For me," he wrote, "her marriage was quite clearly the hysterical response. I'm more aware of what draws repressed homosexuals to marriage than Canby is. That doesn't make him a bigot . . . the problem is a more objective one: We don't live in the same world. I know their society but they still don't know mine."

Because her attitude toward gay life is relaxed, Deitch is free to proceed with a story not based on shocking revelations or contentious ideas. Like playwright Harvey Fierstein, who says he assumes everyone he meets is homosexual unless they tell him otherwise, so do gay films assume a lesbian and gay world in which heterosexuality exists as a natural extension of human behavior.

In such a world, the homophobia encountered is put into a more productive perspective. It isn't the mindless hatred we see in mainstream films nor is it the bogeyman responsible for all of life's disappointments we see in progaganda films. Bigots are real people. There's a reason why they hate what's different. They fear change; they don't understand losing control over a world they thought was theirs. In *Desert Hearts* we're able to see that even the adolescents who tortured us in our youth learned how to behave by watching the movies. When Charbonneau's surrogate mother, brilliantly played by Audra Lindley, lashes out at her daughter for being a lesbian, it's her own security and her own past that are at risk and we understand her.

One of the reasons this perspective has been missing until recently is that gay people have traditionally been disconnected from their past. It is uncanny how many lesbians and gay men have said that until they became adults, they literally thought they were the only gay people in the world. Documentaries made by lesbians and gay men have done the job that Hollywood and the history books have overlooked. Most of them have been aired on national PBS stations in addition to playing film festivals and theatrical runs, reaching even wider audiences than the most successful independent features.

In *Before Stonewall* (1985), Greta Schiller, Andrea Weiss and John Scagliotti unearthed a mass of unfamiliar material about gay life in America before the 1969 riots in Greenwich Village. Through newsreel footage, interviews and the home movies of ordinary lesbians and gay men, *Before Stonewall* recreates the days of the McCarthy witch-hunts and the secret gay political meetings of the Fifties at which blinds were drawn and doors were locked because the participants throught that it was illegal to talk about homosexuality. The rise of lesbian and gay clubs that functioned as community centers is traced from the turn of the century through World War II, when major port cities became points of contact for people discovering their own vast diversity.

Flyer for a gay event circa 1930, from Before Stonewall *(1985).*

THE GREENWICH VILLAGE BALL

15th Annual Edition

Friday, Jan. 15th
Webster Hall
119 East 11th St.
10 P. M. 'til dawn

Come all ye Revelers!—Dance the night unto dawn—come when you like, with whom you like—wear what you like—

Unconventional? Oh, to be sure—only do be discreet!

Tickets $2.00 in advance or $3.00 at the door
Boxes $15.00

Cynthia White, 11 Fifth Ave.   STuy. 9-4674

CONTINUOUS MUSIC
MIDNIGHT DIVERTISSEMENTS

Silent Pioneers (1985) continued the story on a more personal level by intimately delving into the lives of gay senior citizens. The series of mini-portraits created by filmmakers Lucy Winer, Harvey Marks, Pat Snyder and Paula DeKoenigsberg would have been fascinating no matter what the sexual orientation of the subjects. Yet their histories as lesbians and gay men are the most moving aspect of their stories.

A German Jew talks about life in the old country under the anti-gay Penal Code in which Paragraph 175 made homosexual acts illegal. "We must be grateful to the kids today," he says, "for continuing the battle." A Chicago waitress whose lover of five decades has recently died talks about reaching out to the lesbian community for the first time by calling a number listed in her telephone directory under "Counseling for Lesbians."

"Oh, boy!" she says, "I thought I'd hit the jackpot. I dialed the number but I keep getting the machine. Every once in a while I'd call just to hear that voice because I knew whose voice it was." A black grandmother says, "If the people in this building (a senior citizens residence) knew I was gay they'd probably go up in flames." Two Manhattan men reminisce about their relationship of fifty-four years, begun in a time when nobody talked about such things in public. Aside from the enormous emotional value of such history for people tradition-ally denied their own past, films like these function as historical references for future generations who will not have to know the pain of feeling that they are the only ones in the world who are gay.

Contemporary history is now told immediately by gay filmmakers. Robert Epstein's *The Times of Harvey Milk* (1985) is the story of an openly gay San Francisco city supervisor who was assassinated in 1976 along with Mayor George Moscone. It is also the story of San Francisco's brief golden age of gay freedom, coalition politics on an unprecedented scale and the emergence of an identifiable gay community.

Described in the mainstream press as a film about "American values in conflict," it represented much more to the gay community, already aware of the conflicts caused by their visibility. It was an affirmation that a community exists that stretches far beyond the boundaries of the San Francisco ghetto in which the murders took place. The fact that former fireman and city supervisor Dan White served only four years for manslaughter for the murder of two public officials brought home to millions of Americans that justice is something reserved for white, middle class heterosexuals. *The Times of Harvey Milk* won the Academy Award for Best Documentary Feature of 1985 as well as three Emmy Awards for its television broadcast the following year.

Lesbian and gay film festivals proliferate across America and have become

Gene Harwood and Bruhs Mero as they were in the 1940s and as they appear in The
Silent Pioneers *(1985).* (Photo by Patricia Giniger Snyder)

the venue for scores of films that would otherwise not find an audience. Yearly
festivals in San Francisco, New York, Chicago, Los Angeles and Key West
have now been supplemented by a fifty-city tour of the most popular films
from each event. In 1986, an international lesbian and gay film festival in
Amsterdam drew ten thousand participants from fifteen countries. Aside from

Harvey Milk, from the documentary The Times of Harvey Milk *(1985).* (Photo Daniel Nicoletta)

introducing exciting, sometimes radical films to an entire generation of gay people, such festivals also bring an awareness that gay visibility is global.

In 1985 alone, more than fifty new films from virtually every corner of the world were shown at American gay film festivals for specialized audiences of all persuasions. The films ranged from the virtually unwatchable to the sublime. In *Alexandria . . . Why?,* Youssef Chahine, undisputably the greatest Arab filmmaker, recalls his adolescence against the panoramic backdrop of wartime Alexandria. The film portrays two love affairs unprecedented in Arab cinema—one between a Jewish woman and a Muslim man, the other between an aristocratic Arab nationalist and a young English soldier. It was only at gay film festivals in 1985 that audiences had the opportunity to see Radu Gabrea's operatic film portrait of German director Rainer Werner Fassbinder, *A Man Like Eva.* In what one journalist called "a mistress stroke," German actress Eva Mattes embodied the late director by evoking his personality without imitating him. Significantly, the director's sexuality was integrated into a more fascinating look at his self-destructive use of sex as power.

Subjects unimagined by Hollywood are explored in gay cinema with increasing professionalism. Wieland Speck's *Westler—West of the Wall* (1986) is the story of two male lovers divided by the Berlin wall and their struggle to be together in neutral territory. The sequences in East Berlin were filmed in secret with a hidden camera. Koshi Shimada's *More and More Love* (1985) is a bizarre story about a young rock singer from a repressed, fanatical, almost

Eva Mattes as Rainer Werner Fassbinder in A Man Like Eva *(1985).*

insane Christian family who becomes obsessed with the fear that he has AIDS and commits ritual suicide. The depiction of gay life and sex is the most explicit yet seen in Japanese film.

Although some gay films, like Pedro Almovodar's *What Have I Done to Deserve This?,* Rosa von Praunheim's *Horror Vacuii* and *A Virus Has No Morals* and Derek Jarman's *Caravaggio* do receive limited runs in commercial cinemas in big cities, it is at gay film festivals that they are analyzed and discussed with the participation of the filmmakers. Outside of this context, such films are often curiosities. In truth, they are sometimes little more than curiosities within such contexts as well. Yet in the gay community they raise issues essential to the struggle of gay people against violence, prejudice and invisibility.

The subtleties of von Praunheim's *A Virus Has No Morals,* a comedy about AIDS, are contingent upon the viewer's knowledge of what an utter political sham AIDS research has actually been in the United States and Europe. His film contains observations on the AIDS crisis that mainstream cinema may get to in twenty years, if ever.

For mainstream audiences, Eloy de L'Iglesia's *Hidden Pleasures*, made in 1976 but brought to New York's gay festival in 1984, is the simple story of a powerful, closeted gay banker who falls in love with a straight youth. A festival audience watches the all-too-familiar spectacle of the contradictory forces of money, class, sex, intellect, convention and muscle resolving themselves in age-old violence. In Bruno Barreto's Brazilian film *The Kiss*, a man kisses a dying stranger on the street and a cynical, corrupt, homophobic press sets out to destroy his life.

Mainstream cinema is incapable of giving to members of any minority the kinds of films that truly touch their lives and experiences in such ways. Yet Hollywood is beginning to distribute such films as a sideline. In the last five years, independent companies have proved that it is possible to turn a healthy profit by making quality films aimed at a sophisticated audience. Because of the video market it is now viable to do low budget films that don't have to do tremendous business in theaters in order to make money.

Thanks to the extraordinary success of films like *A Room with a View*, *My Beautiful Laundrette* and *Blue Velvet*, Hollywood now has what may be termed an Off Broadway division. Major studios are jumping on the bandwagon by agreeing to distribute such films once they get made independently and, in some cases, even covertly financing them in order to strike lucrative distribution deals when they're finished. It was England's Merchant Ivory Productions which financed both *A Room with a View* and James Ivory's *Maurice*. It was the Samuel Goldwyn Company which produced Stephen Frear's *Prick Up Your Ears*. Hollywood can't help but take notice of the kinds of profits these films are making and they want a piece of the action. Films made for $3 or $4 million which often gross ten times those amounts can't be ignored.

Yet such small films will remain relegated to a ghettoized section of a larger industry which continues to turn out visual junk food for young audiences, the kinds of films which, as actress Debra Winger once said, "pick you up and shake you until six dollars falls out of your pocket." Hollywood, said someone once, is a place where people spend money they don't have on things they don't need to impress people they don't like. Hollywood doesn't like its audience. In fact, there is no Hollywood. As the movies were once created to give us a more acceptable illusion of ourselves, so is the place now mired in that illusion.

Hollywood is where a gay director makes anti-homosexual films so that he can continue to work with the big boys. Hollywood is where gay screenwriters churn out offensive teenage sex comedies and do it well because there isn't anything they don't know about pretending to be straight. Hollywood is where a lesbian rock singer arrives at the American Music Awards on the arm of a gay superstar. Hollywood is where Joan Rivers obligingly asks gay actors how many girlfriends they have and proceeds to tell fag jokes. Hollywood is where a timid rehash of *Some Like It Hot* called *Tootsie* can successfully pretend to have something to say about sex roles. Hollywood is too busy trying to make old formulas hit the jackpot again to see the future. Hollywood is yesterday, forever catching up tomorrow with what's happening today. This will change only when it becomes financially profitable, and reality will never be profitable until society overcomes its fear and hatred of difference and begins to see that we're all in this together.

Afterword

It has become clear since the first edition of this book was published that what we need is no more films about homosexuality. Mainstream commercial films and made-for-television movies that have as their subject the allegedly controversial issue of my existence may be necessary evils but they're not for me. They're for mothers in New Jersey, aunts in Kansas City and frightened fifteen-year-old gay kids in Mississippi who buy *Christopher Street* magazine from a blind newsdealer. I'm tired of trying to figure out whether the latest well-meaning soap opera has succeeded in convincing America that I don't have horns and a tail, that I am not interested in molesting their dreary children or that the Bible doesn't really say I'm headed for their world-famous but quite imaginary hell.

Mainstream films about homosexuality are not for gays. They address themselves exclusively to the majority. How should "we" (society) react to "them" (me)? In 1986, the *New York Times* published an editorial entitled "Don't Panic Yet, Over AIDS." It said that since the disease was still affecting only the high-risk groups (them), it was not yet time for the rest of "us" to panic. To whom is such an editorial addressed? It was as though I weren't the one holding the newspaper in my hands. Gays are not people in the popular media. If AIDS were happening to the straight, white, middle class, non-drug-using population, there would be global panic. Priorities? More media attention and federal funding ($22 million) were heaped upon the Tylenol murders in one week than on the AIDS crisis in the first three years of its existence. This attitude is pervasive.

The history of the portayal of lesbians and gay men in mainstream cinema is politically indefensible and aesthetically revolting. There may be an abundance of gay characters floating around on various screens these days but *plus ça change*. . . . Gay visibility has never really been an issue in the movies. Gays have always been visible. It's *how* they have been visible that has remained offensive for almost a century.

If virtually nothing has changed in Hollywood, there has been a significant shift in the way people perceive gay films. In the same way that Spike Lee's *She's Gotta Have It* is not about black people and *Chan Is Missing* is not about Chinese people, so *Desert Hearts* and *Parting Glances* and *Prick Up Your Ears* are not about lesbians and gay men. True, each of these films offers a unique cultural perspective defined by minority experience, but they are not about the issue of being different. They take difference for granted. The few times gay characters have worked well in mainstream film have been when filmmakers have had the courage to make no big deal out of them, when they have been implicitly gay in a film that was not about homosexuality.

So no more films about homosexuality. Instead, more films that explore people who happen to be gay in America and how their lives intersect with the dominant culture. Some years ago, New York's New Museum sponsored a forum called "Is There a Gay Sensibility and Does It Have an Impact on Our Culture?" After a lot of evasive huffing and puffing about everyone from Marcel Proust to Patti Page, journalist Jeff Weinstein said, "No, there is no such thing as a gay sensibility and yes, it has an enormous impact on our culture."

Gay sensibility is not something we have or share or use. It isn't even something that only gay people express. It's a blindness to sexual divisions, an inability to perceive that people are different simply because of sexuality, a natural conviction that difference exists but doesn't matter; that there's no such thing as normal even when a majority of people think so.

Such ideas are entering the collective consciousness of the mainstream because we are living in an age when independent lesbian and gay filmmakers are making interesting, exciting films that do not view the existence of gay people as controversial. But the hope that one day Hollywood will take a lesson from these filmmakers is best abandoned. So long as Hollywood has one eye on the box office and the other on the lowest common denominator in the audience, it will always be a chickenshit.

Once again, this book is meant to survey the portrayals of lesbians and gay men in mainstream, commercial American cinema. *The Celluloid Closet* deals with the past—where we came from. It is not meant to be the last word on this subject; it is meant to be a beginning—a starting point from which further, more specific analyses of where we're going may emerge. There are increasing numbers of openly lesbian and gay film critics who have consistently suggested a more radical analysis of the films discussed here to include readings that examine Marxist and/or feminist issues of class, race and power. It has been six years since the first edition of this book was published. Aside from a fascinating updated edition of Richard Dyer's brilliant collection of essays, *Gays and Film,* no other major works have emerged on the subject. An infantile leftist viewpoint has perpetuated a loser mentality with regard to such work. This viewpoint says, if it succeeds in reaching a large general public, it can't be any good. Let's all be hippies together and keep ourselves pure for the true struggle. Consequently, radical, revolutionary thought is shared among the same few people year after year. This is self-defeating nonsense. Further exploration of this subject for a mass audience is long overdue. Where is it?

Filmography

The filmography lists films in which obviously lesbian or gay characters appear and films in which reference is made to homosexuality. Where indicated, a film is included because homosexuality was deleted from it or from its original source material. Title, director and year of release are followed by a brief annotation.

ABUSE Arthur J. Bressan, Jr., 1983. A story about child abuse and an intergenerational love affair between a gay filmmaker and a young man.

ADAM'S RIB George Cukor, 1949. David Wayne as Kip, Katharine Hepburn's composer friend.

THE ADVERSARY Larry Klein, 1970. Howard Lawrence as Jimmy West.

ADVISE AND CONSENT Otto Preminger, 1962. Don Murray as Brig Anderson, the senator with a secret.

AFTER HOURS Martin Scorsese, 1985. Scorsese's least homophobic film thanks to the intervention of Robert Plunket, the actor who played Mark, the lonely homosexual picked up by Griffin Dunne.

ALEX AND THE GYPSY John Korty, 1976. A homosexual prisoner cut from the final print.

ALEXANDRIA . . . WHY? Youssef Chahine, 1978. Autobiographical film featuring a love affair between an aristocratic Arab nationalist and a young English soldier.

AMERICAN GIGOLO Paul Schrader, 1980. A gay killer, a lesbian pimp and a gay wife beater.

ANDERS ALS DIE ANDEREN Richard Oswald, 1919. Pioneer German gay liberation film.

ANDERS ALS DU UND ICH Veidt Harlan, 1957. Reactionary melodrama about a gay child molester.

THE ANDERSON TAPES Sidney Lumet, 1971. Martin Balsam as a cowardly gay thief.

ANGEL Robert Vincent O'Neil, 1984. Teenaged prostitute and, according to the *New York Times,* one of the top sleazemobiles of 1984. Throw in an alcoholic lesbian and a tacky drag queen.

THE ANNIVERSARY Roy Ward Baker, 1968. Bette Davis' transvestite son steals women's nylons from clotheslines.

ANOTHER COUNTRY Marek Kanievska, 1984. Sumptuously romanticized version of the Guy Burgess story, linking homosexuality with politics in a very tenuous manner.

ANY WEDNESDAY Robert Ellis Miller, 1966. An effeminate interior decorator.

ARMY OF LOVERS, OR REVOLT OF THE PERVERTS Rosa von Praunheim, 1978. A view of the American gay movement.

THE BAD NEWS BEARS Michael Ritchie, 1976. Nine-year-old Timmy Lupus can't play baseball but mixes a perfect martini.

THE BALCONY Joseph Strick, 1963. Shelley Winters as a madam who has a thing for her bookkeeper (Lee Grant).

BARBARELLA   Roger Vadim, 1968. Anita Pallenberg as the Black Queen and John Phillip Law as a gay angel.

BARRY LYNDON   Stanley Kubrick, 1975. A gratuitous and offensive scene, allegedly conceived by homophobe Ryan O'Neal, shows two gay soldiers bathing in a river.

BECKET   Peter Glenville, 1964. A gay love story.

BEDAZZLED   Stanley Donen, 1967. Two of the seven deadly sins, Vanity and Envy, are gay stereotypes.

BEFORE STONEWALL   Greta Schiller, 1985. Documentary history of pre-Stonewall gay liberation movement with rare film footage.

BELLE DE JOUR   Louis Buñuel, 1967. Genevieve Page as a lesbian madam.

BEN-HUR   Fred Niblo, 1926. An erotic scene of a naked slave chained to a ship's galley wall.

BEN-HUR   William Wyler, 1959. A submerged gay subtext between Messala and Ben-Hur.

THE BEST MAN   Franklin Schaffner, 1964. Cliff Robertson as the presidential candidate accused of homosexuality.

THE BEST WAY (LA MEILLEURE FAÇON DE MARCHER)   Claude Miller, 1976. *Tea and Sympathy* with a French accent and guts.

THE BETSY   Daniel Petrie, 1978. Paul Rudd as a gay who commits suicide.

BEVERLY HILLS COP   Martin Brest, 1984. Eddie Murphy's mindless fag routine is violently homophobic.

BEYOND THE VALLEY OF THE DOLLS   Russ Meyer, 1970. Middlebrow trash with a homophobic attitude.

LES BICHES   Claude Chabrol, 1968. A lesbian zipless fuck.

THE BIG SKY   Howard Hawks, 1952. Kirk Douglas and Dewey Martin rough it.

A BIGGER SPLASH   Jack Hazan, 1974. A documentary about the life and friends of a gay artist. Stultifying.

BILLY BUDD   Peter Ustinov, 1962. Terence Stamp drives the sailors wild.

BLACULA   William Crain, 1972. Weak, decadent white faggot gets bitten.

BLOOD AND ROSES   Roger Vadim, 1960. Lesbian vampires strike again.

BLOODBROTHERS   Robert Mulligan, 1978. A gay jeweler hates his father.

BLOOD MONEY   Rowland Brown, 1933. Sandra Shaw in a tuxedo.

BLOODY MAMA   Roger Corman, 1970. Dominant, aggressive mother, absent father.

BLUE VELVET   David Lynch, 1986. Dean Stockwell can easily be read as gay if you buy the idea that Lynch is recreating the Fifties here.

BONNIE AND CLYDE   Arthur Penn, 1967. Clyde's sexuality changed for the screen from bisexual to impotent.

BOOM!   Joseph Losey, 1968. Noel Coward as the Witch of Capri.

THE BOSTON STRANGLER   Richard Fleischer, 1968. Hurd Hatfield as a gay murder suspect.

THE BOYS IN THE BAND   William Friedkin, 1970. The first Hollywood film in which all the principal characters are homosexual

THE BOYS NEXT DOOR   Penelope Spheeris, 1986. Fascinating, violent splatter film about psychologically disturbed closet homosexual. A great performance by Kenneth Cortland in a small role.

THE BROADWAY MELODY   Harry Beaumont, 1929. A gay costume designer.

BUDDIES   Arthur J. Bressan, Jr., 1985. The first narrative feature about the AIDS crisis is personal and shattering. A story of love and politics.

BUMPING INTO BROADWAY   Hal Roach, 1919. Gus Leonard in drag as the land-lady of a theatrical boardinghouse.

BUS RILEY'S BACK IN TOWN   Harvey Hart, 1965. A lecherous gay mortician.

BUSTING   Peter Hyams, 1974. Sleazy gay bars, tearoom cruisers and hustlers versus the vice squad.

BUTLEY   Harold Pinter, 1974. Gay teacher (Alan Bates) makes everybody miserable.

BY DESIGN   Claude Jutra, 1981. Lesbian fashion designers contrive to have a baby by looking for a substitute father.

CABARET   Box Fosse, 1972. Michael York as a bisexual Brian.

LA CAGE AUX FOLLES   Edouard Molinaro, 1978. The first gay box office smash.

LA CAGE AUX FOLLES II   Edouard Molinaro, 1980. Dimwit sequel; featuring Albin jumping out of a cake looking like Ethel Merman.

LA CAGE AUX FOLLES III   Georges Lautner, 1985. Hideously boring crap that took five screenwriters to put together.

CAGED   John Cromwell, 1950. Lesbianism in a women's prison. "Who's the cute new trick?"

CAGED HEAT   Jonathan Demme, 1972. Lesbian subplot.

CALIFORNIA SPLIT   Robert Altman, 1974. A lesbian waitress doesn't fall for Elliot Gould and George Segal, so they belittle a transvestite.

CALIFORNIA SUITE   Herbert Ross, 1978. Michael Caine as the gay husband of movie star Maggie Smith.

CAMILLE   George Cukor, 1937. Rex O'Malley as Garbo's gay friend.

CAN'T STOP THE MUSIC   Nancy Walker, 1980. The Village People; not a gay film.

CAPRICE   Frank Tashlin, 1967. Ray Walston as a transvestite killer.

CARAVAGGIO   Derek Jarman, 1986. A highly personal, idiosyncratic meditation on the painter through his life and work.

CAR WASH   Michael Schultz, 1976. Antonio Fargas as Lindy the militant faggot transvestite.

CASANOVA   Federico Fellini, 1976. He tried men too.

CAT ON A HOT TIN ROOF   Richard Brooks, 1958. Why couldn't Paul Newman sleep with Elizabeth Taylor? A mystery movie.

CHANEL SOLITAIRE   George Kaczender, 1981. Frivolous romantic nonsense about Coco Chanel including brief reference to her lesbian affair with Misia Sert, played by Simone Signoret's daughter, Catherine Allegret.

UN CHANT D'AMOUR   Jean Genet, 1947. A revolutionary film about homo-eroticism and repression.

THE CHELSEA GIRLS   Andy Warhol, 1966. Faggots and dykes with messy apart-ments and boring opinions.

THE CHILDREN'S HOUR   William Wyler, 1962. Audrey Hepburn and Shirley MacLaine accused of having "sinful sexual knowledge of one another."

THE CHOIRBOYS   Robert Aldrich, 1977. Homophobic cops, and fags with pink poodles.

A CHORUS LINE   Richard Attenborough, 1985. Timid bowdlerization of the original musical with gay monologue cut to ribbons for a teen audience.

THE CHRISTINE JORGENSEN STORY   Irving Rapper, 1970. The famous sex change story played by John Hansen.

CHU HAI TANG   Japanese-Chinese co-production, 1943. A general and a female impersonator from the Peking opera.

CINDERELLA   Walt Disney, 1950. Jock and Gus-Gus aren't just good friends.

CLEOPATRA JONES   Jack Starrett, 1973. Shelley Winters as "Mommy," a lesbian gang leader.

CLEOPATRA JONES AND THE CASINO OF GOLD   Chuck Basil, 1975. Stella Stevens as a lesbian dragon-lady dope seller.

THE CLINIC   David Stevens, 1982. Australian farce set in a VD clinic wih several gay characters sprinkled throughout.

COLONEL REDL   Istvan Szabo, 1985. Head of Austrian imperial secret service exposed as homosexual and spy.

THE COLOR PURPLE   Steven Spielberg, 1985. Alice Walker's original concept that Celie finds love through intimacy with another woman completely thrown away by Spielberg.

COME BACK TO THE FIVE AND DIME, JIMMY DEAN, JIMMY DEAN   Robert Altman, 1983. Karen Black as the transsexual who comes back to haunt her childhood friends.

THE CONFORMIST   Bernardo Bertolucci, 1970. If you sleep with your family chauffeur as a child, it'll make you a fascist.

THE CONSEQUENCE   Wolfgang Petersen, 1977. Romantic melodrama; two gay lovers betrayed by the world around them.

COONSKIN   Ralph Bakshi, 1975. Snowflake the black drag queen as a sadomasochist.

CROSSFIRE   Edward Dmytryk, 1947. A story about homophobia changed to one about anti-Semitism.

CRUISING   William Friedkin, 1980. A policeman discovers his own homosexuality and becomes a killer.

THE DAMNED (LES MAUDITS)   René Clément, 1947. Michel Auclair plays a homosexual.

THE DAMNED   Luchino Visconti, 1969. Helmut Berger does Dietrich; the night of the long knives as an underwear party.

DANGEROUSLY THEY LIVE   Robert Florey, 1942. Connie Gilchrist as a Nazi lesbian.

DARLING   John Schlesinger, 1965. Julie Christie's gay photographer friend and a bisexual waiter who sleeps with them both.

DAY FOR NIGHT   François Truffaut, 1973. Jean-Pierre Aumont is given a handsome young lover but loses him in a car crash.

THE DAY OF THE JACKAL   Fred Zinnemann, 1973. Edward Fox kills a gay man he meets in a bathhouse.

THE DAY OF THE LOCUST   John Schlesinger, 1975. Stars former homosexual William Atherton and features Paul Jabara as an art deco transvestite.

THE DAY THE FISH CAME OUT   Michael Cacoyannis, 1967. Senseless confusion about homosexuals and the atom bomb; the film is an atom bomb.

DEATH IN VENICE   Luchino Visconti, 1971. Dirk Bogarde as Aschenbach.

DEATHTRAP   Sidney Lumet, 1982. Amorous relationship between Michael Caine and Christopher Reeve, lovers trying to do away with Caine's wife.
DELIVERANCE   John Boorman, 1972. Male rape spoils the fun on a buddy holiday.
THE DEPUTY   Eloy de la Iglesia, 1978. The socialist party is legalized in the wake of Franco's death and the fascists set a trap for a "faggot politico."
DESERT HEARTS   Donna Deitch, 1986. Adaptation of Jane Rule's novel about a divorcee who falls in love with a free-spirited woman in Reno in the 1950s.
DESIGNING WOMAN   Vincente Minnelli, 1957. Jack Cole as the choreographer.
THE DETECTIVE   Gordon Douglas, 1968. Homosexual murder on the New York waterfront. A film about the closet, covers the same ground as *Cruising* but more effectively and not offensively.
DIAMONDS ARE FOREVER   Guy Hamilton, 1971. Two gay lovers who kill people.
DIARY OF A MAD HOUSEWIFE   Frank Perry, 1970. The character played by Frank Langella, according to everyone who saw it.
A DIFFERENT STORY   Paul Aaron, 1978. Gays turn straight.
DR. STRANGELOVE   Stanley Kubrick, 1964. Homosexuality of Peter Seller's president of the United States reportedly removed.
DOCTORS' WIVES   George Schaefer, 1971. Rachel Roberts has an affair when a woman tries to take a cinder out of her eye and they suddenly see each other for the first time.
DOG DAY AFTERNOON   Sidney Lumet, 1975. The true story of a gay bank robber.
LA DOLCE VITA   Federico Fellini, 1960. Transvestite predicts that by the year 2000 everyone will be homosexual.
DOMESTIC BLISS   Joy Chamberlain, 1985. British made-for-television sitcom about lesbian lovers and their adventures with neighbors, children and ex-husbands.
DONA HERLINDA AND HER SON   Jaime Humberto Hermosillo, 1986. Lighthearted unusual film from Mexico about a mother, her son and his lover.
DOWN AND OUT IN BEVERLY HILLS   Paul Mazursky, 1986. Has the dubious distinction of containing the first tasteless AIDS joke in a major motion picture.
DRACULA'S DAUGHTER   Lambert Hillyer, 1936. Gloria Holden stalks Soho for young girls.
THE DRESSER   Peter Yates, 1983. Tom Courtenay as the prissy dresser who secretly loves the actor he serves.
DRUM   Steve Carver, 1976. A plantation owner (John Colicos) and his fey lover (Alain Patrick) who rape black men.
EASY LIVING   Mitchell Leisen, 1937. Franklin Pangborn as a man in ladies' hats.
THE EFFECT OF GAMMA RAYS ON MAN-IN-THE-MOON MARIGOLDS   Paul Newman, 1972. Joanne Woodward yells "Faggot!" at a guy she doesn't turn on.
THE EIGER SANCTION   Clint Eastwood, 1975. Jack Cassidy as Myles the gay killer, and his dog Faggot.
AN ENGLISHMAN ABROAD   John Schlesinger, 1984. The true story of Guy Burgess and his meeting with actress Coral Browne. One of the best hours of television ever produced.
ENTERTAINING MR. SLOANE   Douglas Hickox, 1970. Screen version of Joe Orton's play, seldom seen.

ENTER THE DRAGON   Robert Clouse, 1973. Bruce Lee chops a faggot.

ERIKA'S PASSIONS   Ula Stöckl, 1978. The second time around for a pair of lesbian lovers.

ERNESTO   Salvatore Samperi, 1979. Story of a man's homosexual awakening, based on an autobiographical novel by Italian poet Umberto Saba.

EVIL UNDER THE SUN   Guy Hamilton, 1982. Roddy McDowell as Rex Brewster, faggot gossip columnist.

EXODUS   Otto Preminger, 1960. "They used me—like a woman!" screamed Sal Mineo in some of the ads—and in the film.

FACE TO FACE   Ingmar Bergman, 1976. Liv Ullmann's doctor as a well-adjusted gay man.

FAME   Alan Parker, 1980. Paul McCrane as Montgomery, the only gay student at Performing Arts High School (if you can believe that one).

THE FAMILY WAY   Roy Boulting, 1966. Intelligent and quite moving homosexual panic film.

THE FAN   Edward Bianchi, 1981. Michael Biehn as yet another psychotic closet case.

FAREWELL, MY LOVELY   Dick Richards, 1975. Ambiguous underworld gay types; Mitchum plays with the possibilities as a no-nonsense dick.

THE FEARLESS VAMPIRE KILLERS   Roman Polanski, 1967. A gay vampire.

FIG LEAVES   Howard Hawks, 1926. A sexism primer.

FIREWORKS   Kenneth Anger, 1947. A homoerotic dream.

FIVE EASY PIECES   Bob Rafelson, 1970. Toni Basil and Helena Kallianiotes as lesbian hitchhikers.

FLAMING CREATURES   Jack Smith, 1963. An experiment with androgynous revels.

A FLORIDA ENCHANTMENT   Sydney Drew, 1914. A role reversal comedy from a Broadway play by a gay man.

FOR HEAVEN'S SAKE   Sam Taylor, 1926. Harold Lloyd as a sissy youth.

FORTUNE AND MEN'S EYES   Harvey Hart, 1971. An abortive attempt to film the John Herbert stage play.

FORTY DEUCE   Paul Morrissey, 1982. Inconsequential film version of Alan Bowne's brilliant play about Times Square street hustlers.

THE FOURTH MAN   Paul Verhoeven, 1983. Obsessive sexual desire and witchcraft. Fascinating in spite of its religious overtones.

THE FOX   Mark Rydell, 1968. Lesbians on a Canadian chicken farm.

FOX AND HIS FRIENDS (FAUSTRECHT DER FREIHEIT)   Rainer Werner Fassbinder, 1975. A film about class struggle often mistaken for a film about homosexuality.

FRÄULEIN DOKTOR   Alberto Lattuada, 1969. Lesbian spies and nerve gas.

FREEBIE AND THE BEAN   Richard Rush, 1974. Christopher Morley as a killer transvestite; lots of fag jokes.

FROM RUSSIA WITH LOVE   Terence Young, 1963. Lotte Lenya as Colonel Rosa Klebb, the dyke with the spike.

FUNNY LADY   Herbert Ross, 1975. Roddy McDowall plays a fag joke.

GARBO TALKS   Sidney Lumet, 1984. Harvey Fierstein as Bernie Whitlock, the lonely Fire Island homosexual.

GATOR   Burt Reynolds, 1976. Redneck faggot jokes.

THE GAY DECEIVERS Bruce Kessler, 1969. Larry Casey and Kevin Coughlin avoid the draft by pretending to be queer—but they can't hold a candle to Michael Greer's flaming portrait of Malcolm.

THE GAY DIVORCEE Mark Sandrich, 1934. Edward Everett Horton as "Pinky."

GEORGIA, GEORGIA Stig Bjorkman, 1972. Roger Furman as the gay road manager of a famous singer.

GETTING STRAIGHT Richard Rush, 1970. Homophobic radicalism.

GILDA Charles Vidor, 1946. Glenn Ford tells George Macready, "I was born the night you met me."

GIRLFRIENDS Claudia Weill, 1978. Lesbians as one of the hazards of feminist city living.

GIRLS IN PRISON Edward Cahn, 1956. Helen Gilbert stalks Joan Taylor.

THE GIRL WITH THE GOLDEN EYES Jean-Gabriel Albicocco, 1961. Françoise Prevost and Marie Laforet as teacher and student with eyes for each other.

GOLD Peter Hunt, 1974. Bradford Dillman as a gay villain.

GRANDMA'S BOY Fred Newmeyer, 1922. Harold Lloyd, sissy boy.

THE GRASSHOPPER Jerry Paris, 1970. Jacqueline Bisset's gay friends indicate how low she has sunk.

THE GROUP Sidney Lumet, 1966. Candice Bergen as Lakey.

GROUPIES Ron Dorfman and Peter Nevard, 1970. Gay groupies with dirty feet.

HAIR Milos Forman, 1979. Woof isn't queer, though he wouldn't throw Mick Jagger out of bed. The "White Boys" number is camp.

HAPPY BIRTHDAY GEMINI Richard Benner, 1980. An old-fashioned man accepts his gay son.

THE HAUNTING Robert Wise, 1963. Claire Bloom hugs Julie Harris—a lot.

HEAT Paul Morrissey, 1972. Sylvia Miles as a harpy with a lesbian child.

HIDDEN PLEASURES Eloy de la Iglesia, 1976. Powerful gay banker falls in love with straight boy and gets bashed.

HIGH INFIDELITY Franco Rossi, 1964. "The Scandal" episode, in which John Phillip Law flexes his muscle for Nino Manfredi.

THE HITLER GANG John Farrow, 1944. Hitler's homosexual leanings are darkly hinted.

HONKY TONK FREEWAY John Schlesinger, 1981. A jeep full of fags on the highway of life.

HORROR VACUII Rosa von Praunheim, 1984. Neo-expressionist film about gay man trying to save his lover from a religious cult.

THE HOSPITAL Arthur Hiller, 1971. A black homosexual welfare client.

THE HOTEL NEW HAMPSHIRE Tony Richardson, 1984. Paul McCrane as another shy, lonely gay who never has sex.

THE HOUSE ON 92ND STREET Henry Hathaway, 1945. Signe Hasso in drag.

THE HUNGER Tony Scott, 1983. Chic lesbian vampires Susan Sarandon and Catherine Deneuve.

I WANT WHAT I WANT John Dexter, 1972. Anne Heywood cuts off her penis with a piece of broken glass.

IF . . . Lindsay Anderson, 1968. Lyric gay puppy love among rebel students. Enchanting.

THE ILIAC PASSION   Gregory Markopoulos, 1967. Once-shocking homosexual passion.

IMPROPER CONDUCT   Nestor Almendros and Orlando Jimenez-Leal, 1984. Documentary about the fate of homosexuals in Castro's Cuba.

IN A LONELY PLACE   Nicholas Ray, 1950. Everyone but the screenwriter remembers a lesbian masseuse. Perhaps there should have been a lesbian masseuse.

IN COLD BLOOD   Richard Brooks, 1967. Capote's original references to gay relationship between two killers dropped.

INSIDE DAISY CLOVER   Robert Mulligan, 1966. Robert Redford as bisexual.

INTERNATIONAL HOUSE   Edward Sutherland, 1933. Franklin Pangborn as the hotel manager.

IRENE   Alfred E. Green, 1926. George K. Arthur as Madame Lucy.

THE IRON MAN   Tod Browning, 1931. Lew Ayres and Robert Armstrong.

IRRECONCILABLE DIFFERENCES   Charles Shyer, 1984. Another gratuitous faggot secretary.

IT IS NOT THE HOMOSEXUAL WHO IS PERVERSE BUT THE SOCIETY IN WHICH HE LIVES   Rosa von Praunheim, 1971. A Marxist harangue not without some political fascination.

IT'S LOVE I'M AFTER   Archie Mayo, 1937. Eric Blore at his best.

THE JACKPOT   Walter Lang, 1950. Alan Mowbray as an effeminate interior decorator.

JACQUELINE SUSANN'S ONCE IS NOT ENOUGH   Guy Green, 1975. A love affair between Melina Mercouri and Alexis Smith.

JOANNA   Michael Sarne, 1968. Donald Sutherland as Baby Huey and a black gay, tolerated in an offhand but hip way.

JOHNNY GUITAR   Nicholas Ray, 1954. Mercedes McCambridge and Joan Crawford square off.

JOHNNY MINOTAUR   Charles Henri Ford, 1971. The way some gay people were.

JUST IMAGINE   David Butler, 1930. Fantasy of a future society where kings are queens.

JUSTINE   George Cukor, 1969. Cliff Gorman as a vicious nellie faggot who dies with a hatpin in his neck.

KHARTOUM   Basil Dearden, 1966. Charlton Heston as a heterosexual version of General Charles Gordon.

THE KILLING OF SISTER GEORGE   Robert Aldrich, 1968. Beryl Reid and Susannah York are split by cobra-eyed Coral Browne.

KING OF HEARTS   Philippe de Broca, 1966. The gay barber.

KING RAT   Bryan Forbes, 1965. A sex change in the original became a transvestite on film.

THE KISS   Bruno Barreto, 1981. A man kisses a dying stranger on the street and a homophobic press sets out to destroy him.

KISS OF THE SPIDER WOMAN   Hector Babenco, 1985. William Hurt won an Oscar as Molina, the homosexual prisoner who survives through recreating old movie fantasies.

KNIGHTRIDERS   George Romero, 1981. Motorcyclist Pippin is a troubled homosexual who finds true love.

THE KREMLIN LETTER   John Huston, 1970. George Sanders in drag and a black lesbian spy for hire.

LADY OF THE PAVEMENTS   D. W. Griffith, 1929. Franklin Pangborn in an early sissy role.

LADY SCARFACE   Frank Woodruff, 1941. Judith Anderson is very butch as a gangster.

THE LAST MARRIED COUPLE IN AMERICA   Gilbert Cates, 1980. Steward Moss and Colby Chester as the happy homosexual couple down the street.

THE LAST METRO   François Truffaut, 1980. Truffaut's tale of a theater in occupied France points up homophobia as well as anti-Semitism.

THE LAST OF SHEILA   Herbert Ross, 1973. A gay film with a straight mentality.

THE LAUGHING POLICEMAN   Stuart Rosenberg, 1973. A gay killer on the loose in San Francisco.

LAWRENCE OF ARABIA   David Lean, 1962. Lawrence's homosexuality and the rape scene both cut—after initial release.

THE LEAGUE OF GENTLEMEN   Basil Dearden, 1960. Alan Bates as an effeminate dancer.

THE LEATHER BOYS   Sidney Furie, 1964. A homosexual buddy film.

THE LEGEND OF LYLAH CLARE   Robert Aldrich, 1968. Rosella Falk as a lesbian dope addict who has the hots for Kim Novak.

LENNY   Bob Fosse, 1974. Valerie Perrine has lesbian tendencies.

LIANNA   John Sayles, 1983. Simple coming-out film suffers from lack of humor and vitality.

LIBERTY   Hal Roach, 1929. A very gay Laurel and Hardy.

LILITH   Robert Rossen, 1964. Lesbianism in a mental hospital.

THE LINEUP   Don Siegel, 1958. A misogynist heterosexual killer who is often misidentified as homosexual.

THE LION IN WINTER   Anthony Harvey, 1968. Geoffrey (Richard the Lion-Hearted) and the king of France.

LISZTOMANIA   Ken Russell, 1975. The issue is the size of Franz Liszt's (Roger Daltry's) equipment; no proof is offered.

LITTLE BIG MAN   Arthur Penn, 1970. Robert Littlestar as Littlehorse, the gay Indian.

LIVE AND LET DIE   Guy Hamilton, 1973. The usual Bond cartoon dykes and faggots.

LOGAN'S RUN   Michael Anderson, 1976. A society in which homosexuality is accepted as normal.

THE LONELY KILLERS   Boris Szulzinger, 1972. Roland Maden and Dominique Rollin as gay mass murderers.

THE LONELY LADY   Peter Sasdy, 1983. Lesbian overtures to Pia Zadora in a Hollywood hot tub.

LONESOME COWBOYS   Paul Morrissey, Andy Warhol, 1968. Taylor Mead is unforgettable, Franklin Pangborn's only competition.

THE LONG GOOD FRIDAY   John Mackenzie, 1979. Paul Freeman as the homosexual underworld lieutenant whose murder triggers a bloodbath.

LOOKING FOR MR. GOODBAR   Richard Brooks, 1977. Heterosexual promiscuity, but gays get the rap when psychopathic pickup (Tom Berenger) kills Diane Keaton.

LOOT   Silvio Narizzano, 1971. From the play by Joe Orton.

LOSS OF INNOCENCE (THE GREENGAGE SUMMER)   Lewis Gilbert, 1961. Danielle Darrieux and Claude Nollier are lesbian lovers.

THE LOST WEEKEND   Billy Wilder, 1945. Homosexuality in the novel deleted on screen.

LOT IN SODOM   James Watson and Melville Webber, 1933. Stunning experimental film about a biblical city with glitter queens running the show.

LOVE AND DEATH   Woody Allen, 1975. "I wonder if Socrates and Plato took a house on Crete during the summer?"

THE LOVED ONE   Tony Richardson, 1965. Liberace plays a flaming homosexual casket salesman. Rod Steiger as Mr. Joyboy.

THE L-SHAPED ROOM   Bryan Forbes, 1962. Brock Peters as gay jazz musician and Cicely Courtneidge as lesbian song-and-dance woman.

LUDWIG   Luchino Visconti, 1972. Sleeping with a stable boy rots your teeth.

LUV   Clive Donner, 1967. Fag jokes.

MÄDCHEN IN UNIFORM   Leontine Sagan, 1931. Classic Christa Winsloe story of young girl in love with her teacher.

THE MAGIC CHRISTIAN   Joseph McGrath, 1970. Homophobia runs rampant as Yul Brynner dons drag.

MAGNUM FORCE   Ted Post, 1973. Clint Eastwood battles fascist policemen who seem sexually interested in each other.

MAHOGANY   Berry Gordy, 1975. Tony Perkins as a fashion photographer.

MAKING LOVE   Arthur Hiller, 1982. Hollywood's landmark film about a man who leaves his wife for another man was too blow-dried to please many people.

MALA NOCHE   Gus Van Sant, 1986. Gritty, authentic, low-budget film about a gay man in love with a Mexican migrant.

THE MALTESE FALCON   John Huston, 1941. Peter Lorre as Joel Cairo and Elisha Cook, Jr., as the gunsel.

MANHATTAN   Woody Allen, 1979. Meryl Streep leaves Woody for another woman.

A MAN LIKE EVA   Radu Gabrea, 1985. Brilliant, operatic evocation of German director Rainer Werner Fassbinder, with a sensational impersonation by Eva Mattes.

MANSLAUGHTER   Cecil B. De Mille, 1922. Two lesbians kissing in orgy scene.

THE MAN WHO FELL TO EARTH   Nicholas Roeg, 1976. Buck Henry as a gay lawyer.

MARA   Angela Linders, 1985. Cerebral hogwash about a woman soul-searching in Lisbon.

MARATHON MAN   John Schlesinger, 1976. Lover relationship between Roy Scheider and William Devane characters not retained in film version of William Goldman's novel.

MARJOE   Howard Smith and Sara Kernochan, 1971. Fundamentalist homophobia as theater from the preacher who wanted to be Mick Jagger.

M*A*S*H   Robert Altman, 1970. A good lay cures a sudden case of homosexuality.

MASS APPEAL   Glenn Jordan, 1984. Fraudulent claptrap posing as strong stuff about young priest admitting homosexual affair.

MAURICE   James Ivory, 1987. Merchant Ivory Production based on the Forster novel, projected for spring of 1987.

MEATBALLS PART II   Ken Wiederhorn, 1984. John Larroquette as a closeted gay assistant to military commandant.

THE MECHANIC   Michael Winner, 1972. A male love story is submerged in the relationship between characters played by Charles Bronson and Jan-Michael Vincent.

THE MEMBER OF THE WEDDING   Fred Zinnemann, 1953. Frankie Adams is a forerunner of Rita Mae Brown's Molly Bolt.

MERRY CHRISTMAS, MR. LAWRENCE   Nagisa Oshima, 1983. Homoeroticism in prisoner-of-war camp.

MIDNIGHT COWBOY   John Schlesinger, 1969. Dustin Hoffman and Jon Voight as Times Square lovers; assorted "real" homosexuals as losers and freaks.

MIDNIGHT EXPRESS   Alan Parker, 1978. A falsification of Billy Hayes' book about his experiences in a Turkish prison.

MIKE'S MURDER   James Bridges, 1982. Paul Winfield as sympathetic straightforward gay businessman.

MISHIMA   Paul Schrader, 1985. A tedious mess about the notorious Japanese sado-masochistic writer.

MISS FATTY'S SEASIDE LOVERS   Roscoe Arbuckle, 1915. Arbuckle in bathing beauty drag.

THE MISSOURI BREAKS   Arthur Penn, 1976. Brando in drag. He told the press, "Like many men, I too have had homosexual experiences and I am not ashamed."

MODESTY BLAISE   Joseph Losey, 1966. Unwatchable thriller with Dirk Bogarde as effeminate killer.

MONA LISA   Neil Jordan, 1986. Cathy Tyson as the prostitute in love with a young hooker.

MONSIEUR BEAUCAIRE   Sidney Alcott, 1924. Valentino, by acclamation.

MORE AND MORE LOVE   Koshi Shimada, 1984. Bizarre story of young Japanese rock star who becomes obsessed with fear of AIDS. Very daring for Japan.

MOROCCO   Josef von Sternberg, 1930. Marlene Dietrich in tails. Lesbian tease.

MOVIE CRAZY   Clyde Bruckman, 1932. Grady Sutton is a sissy.

LA MUERTE DE MIKEL   Imanol Uribe, 1984. Unusual film from Spain in which a man falls in love with a drag queen and is murdered by his own mother.

MURDER   Alfred Hitchcock, 1930. Esme Percy as a trapeze artist transvestite killer.

MURDER BY DEATH   Bob Moore, 1976. Peter Falk as a closet queen for laughs.

THE MUSIC LOVERS   Ken Russell, 1971. If you love your mother, you'll be a homosexual—but you won't like it.

MY BEAUTIFUL LAUNDRETTE   Stephen Frears, 1986. A movie about class, race and sexuality in Britain today. One of the few films to use incidentally homosexual characters. Has spawned a chain of laundromats named after the film.

MY BRILLIANT CAREER   Gillian Armstrong, 1979. Nobody could understand Sybylla's adamant refusal to marry handsome Harry Beecham and with good reason. This beautiful but fraudulent story omits the real-life lesbianism of the heroine.

MY HUSTLER   Andy Warhol, 1965. Fire Island and boring blond people.

MYRA BRECKINRIDGE   Michael Sarne, 1970. Rex Reed wakes up in a hospital bed and screams, "My tits! Where are my tits?"

NEW YORK AFTER MIDNIGHT   Jacques Scandalari, unreleased. A woman kills gay men when she discovers her husband is queer.

NEXT STOP, GREENWICH VILLAGE   Paul Mazursky, 1976. Antonio Fargas as Bernstein the depressed faggot.

NIGHT AND DAY   Michael Curtiz, 1946. The musical bio of a gay composer, but you'd never know it. And Monty Woolley too.

NIGHTHAWKS   Ron Peck and Paul Hallam, 1978. The gay bar syndrome from a gay perspective; insightful and moving.

THE NIGHT OF THE IGUANA   John Huston, 1964. Grayson Hall as Miss Fellowes.

NIGHT SHIFT   Ron Howard, 1982. Effeminate homosexual prison inmate.

NIJINSKY   Herbert Ross, 1980. A mess about a famous dancer. The homosexuality is "handled."

NO EXIT   Tad Danielewski, 1962. Rita Gam and Viveca Lindfors play tormented women involved in a sexually ambiguous relationship.

NORMAN, IS THAT YOU?   George Schlatter, 1976. The old folks find out Junior is a tinkerbelle.

NO SMALL AFFAIR   Jerry Schatzberg, 1985. Nerdy photography bug accused of homosexuality by his classmates.

NOVEMBERMOON   Alexandra von Grote, 1985. Lesbian love story set in occupied France.

NO WAY TO TREAT A LADY   Jack Smight, 1968. Rod Steiger as a "homo" hairdresser killer.

ODDS AGAINST TOMORROW   Robert Wise, 1959. Does a homosexual really try to pick up Harry Belafonte in a park?

ODE TO BILLY JOE   Max Baer, 1976. Now we know why Billy Joe jumped.

THE OLD DARK HOUSE   James Whale, 1932. A gay horror film.

OLIVIA (PIT OF LONELINESS)   Jacqueline Audry, 1951. Lace-curtain lesbos in a girls' school in Paris.

ONCE BITTEN   Howard Storm, 1985. Viciously offensive teen comedy of vampire Lauren Hutton and her faggot servant Cleavon Little.

ONCE UPON A TIME IN THE EAST   André Brassard, 1974. Superb film about gay life in the East End of Montreal. Has not had a commercial run in America.

ONE FLEW OVER THE CUCKOO'S NEST   Milos Forman, 1975. Two gay mental patients.

ONLY WHEN I LAUGH   Glenn Jordan, 1981. James Coco as the gay best friend of alcoholic actress Marsha Mason.

ONLY YESTERDAY   John Stahl, 1933. Franklin Pangborn with a boyfriend.

OPEN CITY   Roberto Rossellini, 1945. Maria Michi seduced by lesbian Giovanna Galletti.

OPERA DO MELANDRO   Ruy Guerra, 1987. Brazilian *Guys and Dolls* imitates old MGM musicals. Basically harmless singing and dancing gangsters—and the only character who really gets killed is the faggot.

OUTRAGEOUS!   Richard Benner, 1977. A gay *A Star Is Born* that works (unlike Streisand's).

THE PALM BEACH STORY   Preston Sturges, 1942. Franklin Pangborn.

PANDORA'S BOX   G. W. Pabst, 1929. Alice Roberts as the Countess Geschwitz.

PAPILLON   Franklin Schaffner, 1973. Gay predators in prison.

PARTING GLANCES   Bill Sherwood, 1986. Superbly written and directed independent film that captures gay life in New York in the 1980s.

PARTNERS   James Burrows, 1982. Mindless garbage about cops pretending to live
as a gay couple to catch a murderer.

THE PAWNBROKER   Sidney Lumet, 1965. Brock Peters as a homosexual pimp.

PEE WEE'S BIG ADVENTURE   Tim Burton, 1985. A classic example of an entirely
gay film in which there is no homosexuality whatever.

A PERFECT COUPLE   Robert Altman, 1979. A happy, well-adjusted lesbian couple
played by Meredith McRae and Tomi-Lee Bradley.

PERFORMANCE   Nicolas Roeg and Donald Cammell, 1970. Nonsense about androgynous Mick Jagger and gangster James Fox switching roles, misinterpreted
as significant by the hippie mentality.

PERSONA   Ingmar Bergman, 1966. Lesbian passion in slow motion.

PERSONAL BEST   Robert Towne, 1982. Mariel Hemingway and Patrice Donnelly
fall in love while training for the Olympics. Another in a long line of films that are
"not really about lesbians."

PETE 'N' TILLIE   Martin Ritt, 1972. René Auberjonois as one of the girls.

PETULIA   Richard Lester, 1968. Richard Chamberlain as a wife beater who likes little
boys.

PINK FLAMINGOS   John Waters, 1972. A truly gay film though it hasn't much to do
with homosexuality. A subplot has kidnapped children being sold to lesbian couples from the suburbs. And, of course, there is Divine.

PIXOTE   Hector Babenco, 1981. Devastating film about the cruelties of street life for
abandoned children in Brazil. Two of the kids are gay.

P.J.   John Guillermin, 1968. George Peppard fights the fairies.

PLAY IT AS IT LAYS   Frank Perry, 1972. Tony Perkins as a suicidal gay. Again.

POLICE ACADEMY   Hugh Wilson, 1984; POLICE ACADEMY 2   Jerry Paris, 1985.
Leather boys dancing the tango at the Blue Oyster gay bar. Also in the sequel.
The tango?

PORKY'S   Bob Clark, 1981. Plus endless sequels, all featuring dyke gym teacher and
fag jokes.

PORTRAIT OF JASON   Shirley Clarke, 1967. Two hours of Jason Holliday is like a
month in another country. An interview with a hustler.

POWER   Sidney Lumet, 1986. Reflects casual heterosexual interest in AIDS as potential gossip and nothing more.

PRICK UP YOUR EARS   Stephen Frears, 1987. Biography of Joe Orton based on
John Lahr's book.

THE PRIVATE FILES OF J. EDGAR HOOVER   Larry Cohen, 1978. Crude but fascinating look at Hoover; says his hangup was sex in general.

THE PRIVATE LIFE OF SHERLOCK HOLMES   Billy Wilder, 1970. Gay Sherlock.

PRIVATES ON PARADE   Michael Blakemore, 1982. Bitter satirical farce featuring
gays in wartime. Regional British humor, not for everyone.

THE PRODUCERS   Mel Brooks, 1968. Christopher Hewitt as a flaming fag—defended by Richard Schickel, who compared his condition to a withered arm and
called for compassion.

PROTOCOL   Herbert Ross, 1984. Herb Ross brings himself to treat Goldie Hawn's two gay roommates like human beings.

PUZZLE OF A DOWNFALL CHILD   Jerry Schatzberg, 1970. Viveca Lindfors plays a sophisticated, predatory lesbian fashion designer. Again.

THE QUEEN   Frank Simon, 1968. A drag contest at Town Hall; Miss Crystal rides again.

QUEEN CHRISTINA   Rouben Mamoulian, 1933. Garbo.

RACHEL, RACHEL   Paul Newman, 1968. Estelle Parsons as a psalm-singing lesbian spinster.

RADIO DAYS   Woody Allen, 1987. Robert Joy as the gay suitor of Dianne Wiest.

RAIDERS OF THE LOST ARK   Steven Spielberg, 1981. A gay student drops an apple on Harrison Ford's desk in opening sequence. Nice touch.

THE RAZOR'S EDGE   Edmund Goulding, 1946. Clifton Webb's death scene.

REBECCA   Alfred Hitchcock, 1940. Judith Anderson as Mrs. Danvers.

THE REBELS: MONTGOMERY CLIFT   1985. Documentary produced by RAI, Italian television, which deals extensively with Clift's homosexuality and the interesting homophobic reactions of his alleged best friends.

REBEL WITHOUT A CAUSE   Nicholas Ray, 1955. Sal Mineo as Plato.

RED RIVER   Howard Hawks, 1948. A cowboy love story.

REFLECTIONS IN A GOLDEN EYE   John Huston, 1967. Marlon Brando and Zorro David act equally homosexual.

REFORM SCHOOL GIRLS   Tom DeSimone, 1986. Wendy O. Williams as the leather-clad lesbian who rules the roost.

RICH AND FAMOUS   George Cukor, 1981. A film that is homosexual in ways that have little to do with its content. Elicited homophobic reaction from various bigoted critics.

RIOT   Buzz Kulik, 1969. James Brown faces a tough prison queen.

THE RITZ   Richard Lester, 1976. A Cleveland garbage man in a gay bathhouse.

THE ROAD WARRIOR   George Miller, 1981. Barbarian punk homosexuals threaten the survival of the family.

THE ROCKY HORROR PICTURE SHOW   Jim Sharman, 1976. Revolutionary film starring Tim Curry as a sweet transvestite from Transsexual, Translyvania.

ROPE   Alfred Hitchcock, 1948. John Dall and Farley Granger as a gay couple who murder a former classmate.

THE ROSE   Mark Rydell, 1978. Janis Joplin given lesbian panic.

RUSTLER'S RHAPSODY   Hugh Wilson, 1985. Comedy about heterosexual panic that backfires, becoming simplistic and offensive.

SAILOR'S LUCK   Raoul Walsh, 1933. Gay bathhouse attendant.

ST. ELMO'S FIRE   Joel Schumacher, 1985. Tired, cliché-ridden brat pack script in which homosexuals are less than human.

SAINT JACK   Peter Bogdanovich, 1979. George Lazenby as a gay senator.

SALO   Pier Paolo Pasolini, 1975. Fascist sexual degradation.

SALOME   Charles Bryant, 1923. Nazimova's tribute to Oscar Wilde.

SATURDAY NIGHT AT THE BATHS   David Buckley, 1975. Young man toys with bisexuality. Queen for a day. Condescending.

SATURDAY NIGHT FEVER   John Badlham, 1977. Travolta doesn't taunt the faggot.

SATYRICON   Federico Fellini, 1969. Fellini says he cast an American and an English-man in the leads because "there are no homosexuals in Italy."

SCARECROW   Jerry Schatzberg, 1973. Richard Lynch as the sadistic gay rapist.

SCORE   Radley Metzger, 1973. Bisexuality comes to town as the latest thing.

SCORPIO RISING   Kenneth Anger, 1963. Little Peggy March and a homosexual orgy. There has never been anything like it, before or since.

SCREAMING MIMI   Gerd Oswald, 1958. Anita Ekberg gets attention from a lesbian character.

SEBASTIANE   Derek Jarman and Paul Humfress, 1976. The martyrdom of St. Se-bastian according to nobody.

A SEPARATE PEACE   Larry Pierce, 1972. An Ivy League love story.

SERIAL   Bill Persky, 1980. Pea-brained homophobic twaddle about swinging singles in Marin County, California.

SERIOUS CHARGE   Terrence Young, 1959. British film about a priest charged by a young boy with homosexuality.

THE SERGEANT   John Flynn, 1968. Steiger kisses John Phillip Law and shoots himself.

THE SERVANT   Joseph Losey, 1963. James Fox and Dirk Bogarde as slave and master.

SEVEN SINNERS   Tay Garnett, 1940. Bruce in Bombay is the last straw.

SEVEN WOMEN   John Ford, 1966. Margaret Leighton as a lesbian spinster.

SHAMPOO   Hal Ashby, 1975. Not all hairdressers are gay.

SHE DONE HIM WRONG   Lowell Sherman, 1933. Two gay prisoners—the Cherry Sisters.

SHEILA LEVINE IS DEAD AND LIVING IN NEW YORK   Sidney Furie, 1975. A sex-starved lesbian proves that living in New York is dangerous for single women.

SIEGE (SELF DEFENSE)   Paul Donovan, 1981. A splatter film about anti-homosex-ual thugs who slaughter the patrons of a gay bar.

SILENT MOVIE   Mel Brooks, 1976. The usual Brooks sissy jokes.

SILENT PIONEERS   Lucy Winer, 1985. Moving documentary about gay senior citi-zens.

SILKWOOD   Mike Nichols, 1983. Virtually the only mainstream Hollywood film with an intelligently integrated lesbian character to appear in the last decade.

THE SINNERS (AU ROYAUME DES CIEUX)   Julien Duvivier, 1949. Nadine Basile as a dyke prisoner has "men" tattooed on one leg and "women" on the other.

SLEEPER   Woody Allen, 1973. A gay robot.

THE SOILERS   Hal Roach, 1923. Stan Laurel and a gay cowboy.

SOME KIND OF HERO   Michael Pressman, 1982. Homosexuality removed from James Kirkwood novel for the screen.

SOME LIKE IT HOT   Billy Wilder, 1959. Jack Lemmon has a good time in drag.

SOME OF MY BEST FRIENDS ARE . . .   Mervyn Nelson, 1971. Grand Hotel in a gay bar on Christmas Eve.

SOMETHING FOR EVERYONE   Hal Prince, 1970. Anthony Corlan and Michael York play star-crossed lovers.

SPARTACUS   Stanley Kubrick, 1960. Crassius (Laurence Olivier), Antoninus (Tony Curtis) and the oysters.

A SPECIAL DAY   Ettore Scola, 1977. Marcello Mastroianni; another Different Story.

SPIES LIKE US   John Landis, 1985. Moronic fag humor.

STAIRCASE   Stanley Donen, 1969. Rex Harrison and Richard Burton as depressing kvetches.

STAR!   Robert Wise, 1968. Daniel Massey as Noel Coward.

A STAR IS BORN   George Cukor, 1954. "It's the Downbeat club at two in the morning and you're singing for yourself and for the boys in the band."

STAR SPANGLED RHYTHM   George Marshall, 1942. "If Men Played Cards as Women Do."

STAYING ALIVE   Sylvester Stallone, 1983. John Travolta replaces gay dancer in Broadway show.

STRANGE CARGO   Frank Borzage, 1940. John Arledge and Albert Dekker (who was found dead in drag in 1968).

A STRANGE LOVE AFFAIR   Eric de Kuyper, 1985. Beautifully photographed but strangely unmoving meditation on lost love.

THE STRANGE ONE   Jack Garfein, 1957. Paul Richards as Cockroach and Ben Gazzara as Jocko DeParis.

STRANGERS ON A TRAIN   Alfred Hitchcock, 1951. Robert Walker as Bruno Anthony.

STREAMERS   Robert Altman, 1983. Metaphorical drama linking Vietnam-bound soldiers with their images of death, madness and homosexuality.

SUDDENLY LAST SUMMER   Joseph Mankiewicz, 1959. Tennessee Williams tale of madness, cannibalism and you know what.

SUMMER WISHES, WINTER DREAMS   Gilbert Cates, 1973. Ron Rickards.

SUNDAY, BLOODY SUNDAY   John Schlesinger, 1971. Peter Finch as Dr. Daniel Hirsch and Murray Head as his lover.

SWASHBUCKLER   James Goldstone, 1976. Peter Boyle as a pederast pirate.

SYLVIA   Gordon Douglas, 1965. Viveca Lindfors again. As the lesbian librarian.

THE TAKING OF PELHAM ONE-TWO-THREE   Joseph Sargent, 1974. A gay subway passenger.

THE TAMARIND SEED   Blake Edwards, 1974. Dan O'Herlihy as the gay British minister in Paris.

A TASTE OF HONEY   Tony Richardson, 1961. Murray Melvin as a shy gay guy.

TAXI ZUM KLO   Frank Ripploh, 1980. Refreshingly honest autobiographical comedy of promiscuity. The first post–gay liberation film.

TEA AND SYMPATHY   Vincente Minnelli, 1956. Be kind to shy heterosexuals.

TEEN WOLF   Rod Daniel, 1985. Unnecessary faggot references comparing gays unfavorably with werewolves.

TELL ME THAT YOU LOVE ME, JUNIE MOON   Otto Preminger, 1970. Bob Moore as Warren and Leonard Frey as his gay "father."

"10"   Blake Edwards, 1979. Dudley Moore's best friend loses his beach boy and ends up with the blues.

TENDERNESS OF THE WOLVES   Ulli Lommel, 1973. A true story about a gay vampire.

TENUE DE SOIRÉE (MÉNAGE)   Bertrand Blier, 1986. Droll sexual comedy with the most offensive ad campaign in memory.

TEOREMA Pier Paolo Pasolini, 1968. Terence Stamp as a pansexual angel.

THANK GOD IT'S FRIDAY Robert Klane, 1978. Disco is heterosexual music.

THANK YOU, MASKED MAN Lenny Bruce, 1967. Animated. The Lone Ranger and Tonto.

THAT CERTAIN SUMMER Lamont Johnson, 1973. Hal Holbrook and Martin Sheen in a pioneer television film.

THEATRE OF BLOOD Douglas Hickox, 1973. Robert Morley as an effete drama critic.

THERESE AND ISABELLE Radley Metzger, 1968. Softcore lesbianism.

THESE THREE William Wyler, 1936. Sanitized version of *The Children's Hour.*

THEY ONLY KILL THEIR MASTERS James Goldstone, 1972. June Allyson as a lesbian killer.

THE THIRD SEX Frank Winterstein, 1959. A young man is cured of homosexuality by his mother.

THIS SPECIAL FRIENDSHIP Jean Delannoy, 1964. Love story.

THUNDERBOLT AND LIGHTFOOT Michael Cimino, 1974. Clint Eastwood and Jeff Bridges play a preacher and a transvestite, crooks in love.

THE TIMES OF HARVEY MILK Robert Epstein, 1985. Academy Award–winning documentary about the slain San Francisco city supervisor.

TIMES SQUARE Allan Moyle, 1980. Rock and roll fable featuring unclear relationship between two young women. Many people see subtextual lesbianism here.

TO AN UNKNOWN GOD Jaime Chavarri, 1977. A gay magician is obsessed by García Lorca.

TO BE OR NOT TO BE Alan Johnson, 1983. Remake of 1942 Lubitsch classic about troupe of actors fighting Nazis in occupied Poland. Poignant gay character played by James Haake.

TO FORGET VENICE (DIMENTICARE VENEZIA) Franco Brusati, 1979. On growing up gay.

TO LIVE AND DIE IN L.A. William Friedkin, 1985. Muddled lesbian mini-plot is almost an afterthought.

TOMMY Ken Russell, 1975. Uncle Ernie reads *Gay News.*

TONY ROME Gordon Douglas, 1967. Lloyd Bockner as Rood, the gay junkie; a pathetic lesbian alcoholic and her stripper lover.

TOOTSIE Sydney Pollack, 1982. Overrated comedy with Dustin Hoffman in drag raising bogus lesbian panic in Jessica Lange during love scenes.

TOUCH OF EVIL Orson Welles, 1958. Mercedes McCambridge as a motorcycle tough.

TOUGH GUYS Jeff Kanew, 1986. Kirk Douglas gets out of jail to discover his favorite saloon is a gay bar.

TRASH Paul Morrissey, 1970. Michael Sklar and Holly Woodlawn fight over shoes.

TUNNELVISION Brad Swirnoff, 1976. Sophomoric fag jokes.

TURNABOUT Hal Roach, 1940. A role-reversal comedy with gay undertones.

THE TURNING POINT Herbert Ross, 1977. There are no homosexuals in ballet— especially not Baryshnikov.

2001: A SPACE ODYSSEY Stanley Kubrick, 1968. HAL says, "Happy Birthday, Hank."

AN UNMARRIED WOMAN   Paul Mazursky, 1978. The character of Jill Clayburgh's therapist was a lesbian in the original screenplay.

VALENTINO   Ken Russell, 1977. Well, was he or wasn't he?

VALLEY OF THE DOLLS   Mark Robson, 1967. Ted Casablanca the fag designer, played by Alex Davion.

A VERY NATURAL THING   Christopher Larkin, 1973. The first nonporno film about gay relationships.

A VERY SPECIAL FAVOR   Michael Gordon, 1965. Homosexuality as a curable neurosis.

VICTIM   Basil Dearden, 1961. Blackmail thriller about homosexuals.

THE VICTORS   Carl Foreman, 1963. Scenes deleted showing male prostitute.

VICTOR/VICTORIA   Blake Edwards, 1982. Occasionally funny farce with great performance by Robert Preston as Toddy but in the end timid and very straight.

A VIEW FROM THE BRIDGE   Sidney Lumet, 1962. Homosexuality as a false accusation.

VILLAIN   Michael Tuchner, 1971. Richard Burton as Vic Dakin.

VISION QUEST   Harold Becker, 1985. Hotel guest tries to put the make on room service waiter Matthew Modine.

WALK ON THE WILD SIDE   Edward Dmytryk, 1962. Barbara Stanwyck as Jo, Capucine as Hallie.

THE WARRIOR'S HUSBAND   Walter Lang, 1933. Ernest Truex.

THE WAR WIDOW   Harvey Perr, 1976. Television story of lesbian love affair.

WESTLER—WEST OF THE WALL   Wieland Speck, 1986. Two lovers divided by the Berlin Wall. Atmospheric personal vision.

WHAT HAVE I DONE TO DESERVE THIS?   Pedro Almodovar, 1984. Riotous black comedy from Spain about wacky family including gay teenager sold to local dentist by glue-sniffing mother.

THE WHEELER DEALERS   Arthur Hill, 1963. Assorted fairy decorators and queer art critics.

WHERE'S POPPA?   Carl Reiner, 1970. George Segal's brother rapes a cop in drag and the cop sends him flowers.

WHO KILLED TEDDY BEAR?   Joseph Cates, 1965. Elaine Stritch a lesbian victim.

WHY BRING THAT UP?   George Abbott, 1929. Two gay men in backstage sequence.

THE WILD PARTY   Dorothy Arzner, 1929. Intimations of sorority lesbianism.

THE WILD PARTY   James Ivory, 1975. Decadent Hollywood lesbians. Gay men play the piano at parties.

WINDOWS   Gordon Willis, 1980. A psychotic lesbian killer played by Elizabeth Ashley.

WITHOUT A TRACE   Stanley Jaffe, 1983. Keith McDermott as Philippe, the houseboy falsely suspected of kidnapping.

THE WIZARD OF OZ   Victor Fleming, 1939. Bert Lahr.

A WOMAN LIKE EVE   Nouchka von Brakel, 1982. A variation on John Sales' *Lianna* with a less politically correct but more believable outcome.

THE WOMAN NEXT DOOR   François Truffaut, 1981. A publisher and his young boyfriend are incidental characters, typical of Truffaut's ecumenism.

WOMAN OF THE YEAR   George Stevens, 1942. Hepburn's male secretary.

A WOMAN'S FACE George Cukor, 1941. Two lesbians dancing, but Cukor doesn't remember.

WOMEN IN LOVE Ken Russell, 1969. Nude wrestling between Alan Bates and Oliver Reed.

WONDER BAR Lloyd Bacon, 1934. Two gay men dance a waltz at a nightclub.

WON TON TON Michael Winner, 1976. Ron Leibman plays a gay Valentino.

WORD IS OUT Mariposa Film Group, 1977. Stunning documentary on gays in America.

THE WORLD ACCORDING TO GARP George Roy Hill, 1982. John Lithgow makes transsexual Roberta Muldoon a vibrant, three-dimensional character.

X, Y & ZEE Brian Hutton, 1971. Elizabeth Taylor does it with Susannah York.

YANKEE DOODLE IN BERLIN Richard F. Jones, 1918. An early drag comedy.

THE YEAR OF LIVING DANGEROUSLY Peter Weir, 1983. Noel Ferrier as Wally Sullivan, the Australian journalist with an Indonesian boyfriend.

YOUNG MAN WITH A HORN Michael Curtiz, 1950. Lauren Bacall as Amy North.

YOUNG TORLESS Volker Schlöndorff, 1966. Homosexuality and violence in prep school.

Z Constantin Costa-Gavras, 1969. A fascist killer who just happens to be gay.

ZACHARIAH George Englund, 1971. A rock buddy western epic.

ZÉRO DE CONDUITE Jean Vigo, 1933. The forerunner of *If . . .*

ZORRO, THE GAY BLADE Peter Medak, 1981. A swishbuckler. Not quite funny enough but inoffensive.

ZWEI WELTEN (TWO WORLDS) Gustaf Gründgens, 1940. Adventure story of two boys and two girls dubbed "a clever homosexual charade."

Necrology

Film	Character	Cause of Death
Advise and Consent (1962)	Brig Anderson (Don Murray)	Suicide (straight razor)
Anders als die Anderen (1919)	Paul Körner (Conrad Veidt)	Suicide (poison)
And Justice for All (1980)	Transvestite (Robert Christian)	Suicide (hanging)
The Betsy (1978)	Loren Hardeman, Jr. (Paul Rudd)	Suicide (poison)
The Boys Next Door (1986)	Chris (Richard C. Dancer)	Murder
Caged (1950)	Evelyn Harper (Hope Emerson)	Murder (stabbing)
Caprice (1967)	Dr. Clancy (Ray Walston)	Murder (pushed from balcony)
The Children's Hour (1962)	Martha Dobie (Shirley MacLaine)	Suicide (hanging)
The Choirboys	Gay high school student (Michael Wills)	Murder (shooting)
Cleopatra Jones (1973)	Mommy (Shelley Winters)	Murder (gunshot)
Cruising (1980)	Ted Bailey (Don Scardino)	Murder
	Loren Lucas (Arnaldo Santana)	Murder
	Joey (Keith Prentice)	Murder
The Damned (1969)	The entire SA	Mass murder
The Day of the Jackal (1973)	A nameless homosexual	Murder (gunshot)
The Detective (1968)	Teddy Lineman (James Inman)	Murder (bludgeoning)
	Colin MacIver (William Windom)	Suicide (leaping)
	Felix (Tony Musante)	Execution (electric chair)
Diamonds Are Forever (1971)	Wint (Bruce Glover) and Kidd (Putter Smith)	Murder (drowning)

Dracula's Daughter (1936)	Countess Alesca (Gloria Holden)	Murder (stake through the heart)
Drum (1976)	De Marigny (John Colicos)	Castration
The Eiger Sanction (1975)	Myles (Jack Cassidy)	Murder (exposure)
The Fan (1981)	Douglas (Michael Biehn)	Murder
Fortune and Men's Eyes (1971)	Rocky (Zooey Hall)	Suicide (straight razor)
The Fox (1968)	Jill (Sandy Dennis)	Suicide (falling tree)
Freebie and the Bean (1974)	A transvestite (Christopher Morley)	Murder
From Russia with Love (1963)	Rosa Klebb (Lotte Lenya)	Murder
Justine (1969)	The Homosexual (Cliff `Gorman)	Murder
The Long Good Friday (1979)	Colin (Paul Freeman)	Murder
Mädchen in Uniform (European version, 1931)	Manuela (Hertha Thiele)	Suicide (leaping)
Opera do Melandro	Geni (J.C. Violla)	Murder
Pandora's Box (1929)	Countess Geschwitz (Alice Roberts)	Murder (beating)
Play It as It Lays (1972)	B.Z. (Tony Perkins)	Suicide (pills)
The Private Files of J. Edgar Hoover (1978)	J. Edgar Hoover (Broderick Crawford)	Old age
The Road Warrior (1981)	The Golden Youth (Jimmy Brown)	Murder
The Sergeant (1968)	Sergeant Callan (Rod Steiger)	Suicide (shotgun)
Streamers (1983)	Richie (Mitchell Lichtenstein)	Murder
Suddenly Last Summer (1959)	Sebastian Venable	Murder (cannibalism)
Swashbuckler (1976)	Lord Durant (Peter Boyle)	Murder
Theatre of Blood (1973)	Meredith Merridew (Robert Morley)	Murder
This Special Friendship (1967)	Alexandre (Didier Haudepin)	Suicide

Victim (1961)	Barrett (Peter McEnery)	Suicide
Walk on the Wild Side (1962)	Hallie Gerard (Capucine)	Murder

Index